NEVER TRUST A CALM DOG
AND OTHER RULES OF THUMB

BY TOM PARKER

design by Michael Rider

illustrations by the author

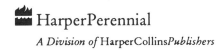
HarperPerennial

A Division of HarperCollinsPublishers

FIRST EDITION

Library of Congress Catalog Card Number 89-46484

ISBN 0-06-055265-4

ISBN 0-06-096520-7 (pbk.)

90 91 92 93 94 MPC 10 9 8 7 6 5 4 3 2 1

90 91 92 93 94 MPC 10 9 8 7 6 5 4 3 2 1 (pbk.)

FOR AMY, JOEY, JAMIE AND SUE

Never trust a calm dog.

Jessica Jellison

Don't run, swim or read after eating.

Elizabeth
Calderon

if you dont speak spanish dont go in my house.

Kelly Tigges

If you don't eat your dinner I'll crame it down your thost.

Jennifer Ann Tocatlian

Mrs. Cohen's 4th Grade Class, Placerville, California

A C K N O W L E D G E M E N T S

Quick: What's half a mile long, weighs less than a pickle, and is hard to understand if you're at the wrong end? Why, 2,688 rules of thumb in a row. That's why this book isn't printed on kite string. But we did want to try something different. Instead, we decided to design a new kind of reference book — one that reads in all directions — front to back, back to front, and top to bottom. That took lots of help. First, I'd like to thank my wife Sue for both her assistance and patience. I'd like to thank Michael Rider for collaborating on the design of this book. The brilliant idea of organizing it into stacks struck him while soaking in the bathtub. Thanks to Cheryl Russell and Rick Eckstrom for their editorial and production help. Thanks to John Parsons, Macintosh whiz, for patiently coming up with computing solutions to things that no one in their right mind would try on a Mac II. Thanks to Nancy Ten Kate for copy editing and to William "Kid" Kaupe, Ithaca, New York's only combo building inspector *and* master indexer. Once again, I'd like to thank my friend Gerard Van der Leun — Hey Gerard! — and John Michel of HarperCollins, Lou and Bob Badaracco of Typeline Inc., the staff of American Demographics magazine, The Gregory Paul Press, Triaxon of Ithaca, Jon Reis Photography, Dede Hatch, Shelly Droge, Steve Carver, Diana Souza, Jon Crispin, Amy Christian, Walter Pitkin, Henning Pape-Santos, Rebecca Wilson, Tom Exter and Peter Krakow. But most of all, I'd like to thank the Placerville, California 4th graders of Janet Cohen and Nora Winkler and the worldwide network of collectors who have been out there bagging rules of thumb. Without their help this book would not have been possible.

Try this: Count the number of times a cricket chirps in 15 seconds, and add 37. No, you didn't just calculate your age in cricket years — you measured the temperature outdoors in degrees Fahrenheit. You just used a rule of thumb.

A rule of thumb is a homemade recipe for making a guess, a mental tool that takes information you already have, and turns it into information you need. Where do rules of thumb come from? People just make them up. But rarely do they write them down.

That's my job. I've been collecting rules of thumb for nearly 10 years. Now I have enough to make a real reference book. Not a book with charts and tables and lots of numbers — this is home-brew stuff — this is the people's book of knowledge.

But that's not all. This book is in 3D! Take a look for yourself. Flip to any page and you'll

find some of the cleverest nuggets of human ingenuity assembled anywhere. Find something you like? How about a rule of thumb about romance? Ok, it's time to go 3D: Just turn the page and there, at the same spot on the next page is *another* rule of thumb about romance. There's even a special *romance icon* to mark the

spot. Now, by following the icon, you can zip through the book and read *all* the rules about romance.

Get it? Every rule of thumb in this book has been sorted into an invisible stack that runs through the book — just like a deck of cards. You can browse through the book and enjoy rules of thumb at random, like sampling a box of chocolates. Or you can read all the rules on a particular subject at once. The special ICONTENTS makes it easy: Just pick a subject, like DIETING or MONEY, flip to the starting page, match the icon — and go 3D! There's even an index to help you find a special rule of thumb when you need one. Never Trust a Calm Dog is — count them — three books in one: it's a book for browsers, a book for those who want to know everything about a subject, and a book for holy-cripes-here-comes-a-polar-bear-now-what-do-I-do? (Dodge to the left. As a rule of thumb, most polar bears are right pawed.)

So dive in and see what your friends and neighbors have been inventing. This is one book that's easy to read straight through!

Photo by Dede Hatch

CONTENTS

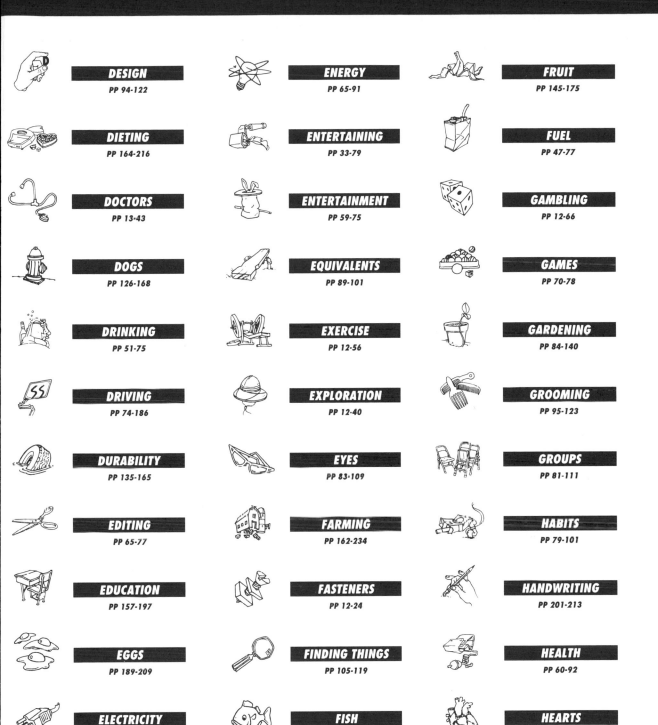

REAL ESTATE
PP 116-170

 RELATIONSHIPS
PP 156-204

 RELIGION
PP 135-157

 RESTAURANTS
PP 169-235

 ROMANCE
PP 98-120

 RUNNING
PP 181-209

 SAFETY
PP 213-235

 SALES
PP 174-212

 SCIENCE
PP 173-195

 SCUBA DIVING
PP 147-161

 SHELLFISH
PP 218-234

 SHOPPING
PP 216-234

 SLEEP
PP 161-183

 SPEAKING
PP 215-235

 SPORTS
PP 165-235

 STOCK
PP 174-234

 STORAGE
PP 187-209

 SURVIVAL
PP 102-128

 TELEPHONES
PP 199-235

 TEMPERATURE
PP 88-130

 TESTS
PP 217-235

 TEXTURE
PP 185-189

 THEATER
PP 191-203

 TIME
PP 210-234

 TOOLS
PP 213-235

 TRAINS
PP 227-235

 TRAVEL
PP 132-206

 TREES
PP 205-235

 VIDEO
PP 207-235

 WASTES
PP 203-221

 WATER
PP 225-235

 WEAPONS
PP 143-169

 WEATHER
PP 134-202

 WIND
PP 206-234

 WINE
PP 13-47

WRITING
PP 105-185

1 ... **MARKETING TO THE ELDERLY** For marketing purposes, elderly consumers think they are 15 years younger than they actually are. *Tracy Lux Frances, Bradenton, Florida*

2 ... **PLANNING A McDONALD'S** People are willing to walk for seven minutes to get to a McDonald's. That's why you'll find McDonald's restaurants a 14 minute walk apart in downtown areas. *Terry Moloney, applied geographer, Tydac Technologies Corporation, Arlington, Virginia*

3 ... **WINNING BLACKJACK** When you're playing blackjack, assume that any unseen card is an 8. *Norman Brenner, Fleetwood, New York*

4 ... **WORKING WITH RIVETS** You can figure that a properly riveted joint will have three-fourths of the strength of the pieces it joins together. *Mike Bauer, sheet metal worker*

5 ... **GETTING RID OF BACK PAIN** If your back hurts more when you climb stairs, walk up a hill, or get out of a chair, you need to do extension exercises. *Peggy Bodine-Reese, physical therapist, Gaithersburg, Maryland*

6 ... **CONTROLLING A CAT** If you don't want a cat to jump into your lap, don't make eye contact with it. *Kim Murphy, columnist, Portland, Maine*

7 ... **FORECASTING THE WEATHER** When ants travel in a straight line, expect rain. When they scatter, expect fair weather. *Steven M. Keisman, New York City high school resource coordinator*

8 ... **THE PREINDUSTRIAL RULE** The number of people occupying a house in a preindustrial culture can be estimated at one person for every ten square meters of enclosed dwelling space. *Thomas W. Neumann, anthropological archaeologist, wildlife ecologist, and field crew crisis manager*

9 ... **PAMPERING YOUR CAR** To get the most out of your car, treat it like a favorite cat or dog. *Walter Pitkin, literary agent, Weston, Connecticut*

10 ... **STARTING A MOTORBOAT** Don't pull the choke in a motor boat if the motor was running within the past 20 minutes. *Carolyn Lloyd, 15-year-old student, Montreal, Quebec*

11 ... **WATCHING BIRDS** When the bird and the bird book disagree, believe the bird. *Jack Barclay, biologist, pilot, flight instructor, Santa Cruz, California*

AS A RULE OF THUMB: YOU CAN UNDERSTAND WHAT PEOPLE THINK OR FEEL BY MIRRORING THEIR BEHAVIOR. MIMIC THEIR BODY LANGUAGE AND IMAGINE WHAT THEY SEE, AND YOU CAN OFTEN READ THEIR MINDS.
KELLY YEATON, TEACHER AND STAGE MANAGER, STATE COLLEGE, PENNSYLVANIA

ARCHITECTURE

12 ... **THE RUSSELL RULE OF PLEASING STREETS** A city street is most visually appealing if its width is the height of the buildings along it. *David and Penny Russell, Dilltown, Pennsylvania*

13 ... THE POLCE NEW TOP RULE If a one-drawer stand has more than two pieces of wood on the top, it's a new top. *Paul Polce, Ponzi's Antiques, Trumansburg, New York*

14 ... READING A GIFT BOOK Don't read a gift book unless it's one you would have bought yourself. Consider giving it to a friend who's interested in the topic. *Marilyn vos Savant, highest IQ ever recorded, in Bottom Line Personal*

15 ... THE RYAN RULE OF CHEST HAIR The year you start growing dark hair on your chest is the year that the loss rate of your head hair exceeds its growth rate. *Mark Ryan, Dallas, Texas*

16 ... BUYING DRY WINE The higher the alcohol level, the drier the wine. *Paul Grim, writer, wine sales (retail), N. Hollywood, California*

17 ... THE TOWNSEND PREMATURE BABY RULE A premature baby usually needs to be hospitalized until its due date. *Bickley Townsend, vice president, The Roper Organization, New York*

18 ... ADJUSTING YOUR BICYCLE On a bicycle with drop handlebars, the seat and handlebars are positioned properly if the handlebars block your view of the front axle. *R.A. Heindl, design engineer, Euclid, Ohio*

19 ... BUYING A TELESCOPE The price of a telescope increases by the cube of the lens diameter. *Tom Lucas, software artist, Berkeley, California*

20 ... WARMING YOUR FEET WITH YOUR HAT If your feet are cold, put on your hat. *Walter Pitkin, literary agent, Weston, Connecticut*

21 ... THE HEINDL MULTI-PURPOSE GADGET RULE Any gadget that does many things will do none of them as well as a single-purpose device. *R.A. Heindl, design engineer, Euclid, Ohio*

22 ... WINNING CHESS WITH AN ELDERLY OPPONENT Play the French Defense against an elderly opponent. You will baffle his cut-and-slash method of play. *Stephen Unsino, poet, Eastchester, New York*

23 ... TALKING TO AN AMERICAN If you are talking with an American whose legs are crossed and he wiggles his foot at what you say, he either disagrees with what you are saying, or he wants to add to it, or he wants to talk about something else. *The Blossoms, Fresno, California*

24 ... PREDICTING A MEDICAL STUDENT'S CAREER PATH The older the student upon starting medical school, the more likely it is that he or she will choose general practice rather than a specialty. *Gerry M. Flick, M.D., Ship's Surgeon, S.S. Constitution off Hawaii*

ADVERTISING

25 ... PLACING AN AD IN A MAGAZINE Unless you run your ad in a mail-order section, a position in the back of a magazine will produce a much lower response than the front. *Jim Kobs, Kobs and Brady Advertising, Chicago, Illinois.*

BUSINESS

26 ... ESTIMATING THE SOLVENCY OF CUSTOMERS Every consultant and small business person underestimates the client's ability to pay. *Steven Kropper, telecommunications consultant, Watertown, Massachusetts*

GAMBLING

27 ... WINNING BLACKJACK If the dealer has an upcard of 5, don't take any new cards because the dealer will probably bust. *Norman Brenner, Fleetwood, New York*

FASTENERS

28 ... SETTING UP STAGE LIGHTING If you can't hold it together with duct tape, replace it with something you can hold together with duct tape. *Liz Stone, SUNY College of Environmental Science & Forestry, Syracuse, New York*

EXERCISE

29 ... GETTING BACK IN SHAPE Recovering an unused physical skill takes one month for each year of layoff. *Norman Brenner, Fleetwood, New York*

CATS

30 ... WAKING UP WITH A CAT Generally speaking, if your cat nudges your feet in the morning, it wants to stay inside. If it nudges your face, it wants to go out. *Mark McMullen, accountant, Alexandria, Virginia*

PRECIPITATION

31 ... FORECASTING THE WEATHER Insects are more troublesome just before a rain. It's harder for them to fly in the high humidity, so they cling more. And when the atmospheric pressure is low, you give off more body odor, which attracts them. *Steven M. Keisman, New York City high school resource coordinator*

EXPLORATION

32 ... FINDING AN ARCHAEOLOGICAL SITE Prehistoric archaeological sites do not occur on slopes greater than 20 percent (9 degrees). *Thomas W. Neumann, anthropological archaeologist, wildlife ecologist, and field crew crisis manager*

AUTOMOBILES

33 ... THE KEISMAN RULE OF CLEAN CAR REPAIR Always wash your car before taking it in for service. Mechanics are more likely to take advantage of you if your car looks like it needs "everything." *Steven M. Keisman, New York City high school resource coordinator*

BOATS

34 ... NAVIGATING THE OCEAN Seagulls mean land ahead. *Joseph Liberkowski, ex-ocean lifeguard, Medford Lakes, New Jersey*

BIRDS

35 ... OBSERVING BIRDS Ten percent of the Sage Grouse males do 90 percent of the mating. *Scott Parker, data specialist, Beaumont, Texas*

ARCHITECTURE

36 ... WATCHING A BUILDING COLLAPSE The walls of an adobe structure going to ruin usually will fall outwards because the outside bases have been coved out by water rising through capillary action. *Chris Wilson, architectural historian, Albuquerque, New Mexico*

37 ... CHECKING AN ANTIQUE Never buy antique furniture without turning it over first. *Paul Polce, Ponzi's Antiques, Trumansburg, New York*

ANTIQUES

38 ... LOOKING FOR INTERESTING BOOKS To find the most interesting books in a library, look for the shelf where returned books are stored before they are reshelved. *Andy Steinberg, Louisville, Kentucky*

BOOKS

39 ... THE ROBERTS RULE OF BECOMING MORE SO People do not change as they get older. They just become more of what they are already. *Jean Roberts, Alton, New Hampshire*

AGES AND STAGES

40 ... BUYING BLENDED WINES The best wine value is in blends, not vintages. *Steven M. Keisman, New York City high school resource coordinator*

WINE

41 ... MONITORING YOUR UNBORN BABY If your unborn baby kicks less than 10 times in 12 hours, call your doctor immediately. You should also consult the doctor if the 10th movement is coming later each day. *Jay Butera, writer, American Health*

CHILDBIRTH

42 ... SELECTING BICYCLE TIRES On a lightweight bicycle, the tires should last 2,000 to 3,000 miles. If they last longer, they're too heavy. *R.A. Heindl, design engineer, Euclid, Ohio*

BICYCLES

43 ... PREDICTING AN ECLIPSE Eclipses often come in pairs. A lunar eclipse is followed frequently by a solar eclipse two weeks later, and vice versa. *Paul A. Delaney, meteorologist, Beltsville, Maryland*

ASTRONOMY

44 ... BUYING DRESS SLACKS The best dress slacks are hand stitched at the top of the waistband inside the slacks. *Steven M. Keisman, New York City high school resource coordinator*

CLOTHING

45 ... MICROWAVING A METAL CONTAINER You can use a metal container in a microwave if the ratio is at least 2/3 food to 1/3 metal. *Mary Ellen Parker, retired teacher, Cincinnati, Ohio*

APPLIANCES

46 ... WINNING CHESS Advance one or two pawns in the opening, one of which must be the king's or queen's pawn. *Norman Brenner, Fleetwood, New York*

CHESS

47 ... HEIBEL'S CURIOUS RULE OF FARTS A farting horse will never tire; a farting man is one to hire. *Louis G. Heibel, Alexandria, Virginia, from Walla Walla, Washington circa 1940*

BODY LANGUAGE

48 ... WAITING TO SEE THE DOCTOR Expect to wait at least half an hour when you go to the doctor or dentist unless you get the first appointment of the day or the one right after lunch. *Dean Sheridan, electronics technician and deaf actor, Torrance, California*

DOCTORS

ADVERTISING

49...BUDGETING ADVERTISING   Advertising costs should not drop below 10 percent of sales until a business has been around 20 years. *Captain Haggerty, animal trainer, actor, author, and philosopher, New York, New York*

BUSINESS

50...BUYING EQUIPMENT   Don't buy a new piece of equipment for your business unless it can pay for itself in three months. *Kevin Kelly, Athens, Georgia*

GAMBLING

51...SPOTTING A RIGGED GAME   If heads come up more than five times in a row, the game is rigged. *Norman Brenner, Fleetwood, New York*

FASTENERS

52...TOWLE'S RULE OF BUNDLED PAPER   It takes 7 feet of binder twine to tie a 6-inch stack of newspapers for recycling. A 60 yard ball of twine will tie 25 stacks. *John Towle, Salinas, California*

EXERCISE

53...THE TOO LATE RULE OF THIRSTY   If you're thirsty, you've waited too long. To avoid dehydration, drink water ahead of time. Put another way: If you're thirsty, drink water. If you're not thirsty, drink water anyway. *Dean Sheridan, electronics technician and deaf actor, Torrance, California*

CATS

54...FEEDING YOUR CATS   Feed your cat as much as it will eat in 30 minutes, twice a day. *Ronald Newberry, retired, Cayutaville, New York*

PRECIPITATION

55...THE NIGHT BLOOMING APPLE BLOSSOM RAIN RULE   When apple blossoms bloom at night, for 15 days no rain in sight. *Steven M. Keisman, New York City high school resource coordinator*

EXPLORATION

56...FINDING AN ARCHAEOLOGICAL SITE   If you're looking for a prehistoric archaeological site in North America, look within 90 meters of water. *Thomas W. Neumann, anthropological archaeologist, wildlife ecologist, and field crew crisis manager*

AUTOMOBILES

57...GETTING YOUR CAR SERVICED   The end of April is the best time to get your car serviced because it's the slowest time for auto mechanics. The mild weather makes people feel more confident about their cars, and many can't afford car repairs because they've just paid income taxes. *Steven M. Keisman, New York City high school resource coordinator*

BOATS

58...WINNING A SAILBOAT RACE   To be on the winning edge in sailing, you should cross the starting line early in one out of five starts. *Pete Lent, sailor*

BIRDS

59...APPROACHING A BIRD   The smaller the bird, the closer it will allow you to approach. *Thomas O. Marsh, writer and birdwatcher, Fairfield, Ohio*

AS A RULE OF THUMB: IF YOU'RE TRYING TO LOSE WEIGHT, A REASONABLE GOAL IS WHAT YOU WEIGHED AT HIGH SCHOOL GRADUATION. YOU'LL BE LUCKY IF YOU REACH YOUR GRADUATION WEIGHT PLUS HALF THE NUMBER OF YEARS SINCE GRADUATION IN POUNDS. DAVID KUMAKI, PHYSICIAN, SHELBURNE, NEW HAMPSHIRE

ARCHITECTURE

60...SIZING A SKYLIGHT   For kitchens, porches, and bathrooms, a skylight that takes up 15 percent of the ceiling will provide good illumination. Family rooms and bedrooms need 10 percent, while hallways and attics need as little as 5 percent. *Scott Parker, data specialist, Beaumont, Texas*

61 ... _POLCE'S RULE OF BLACK FURNITURE_ If antique furniture is painted black, don't buy it. _Paul Polce, Ponzi's Antiques, Trumansburg, New York_

ANTIQUES

62 ... _DISCOVERING YOUR INTERESTS_ If you're worried that you don't have any interests, browse in the nonfiction section of a library for five minutes. By then a book will catch your eye, whether it's about baking pie crusts or Icelandic crust formation. _Carolyn Lloyd, 15-year-old student, Montreal, Quebec_

BOOKS

63 ... _LEAVING THE NEST_ A child is most apt to leave home at age 17. _Anonymous_

AGES AND STAGES

64 ... _TESTING A WINE_ Taste a young white wine that has been opened and kept in the refrigerator for a week. This will give you some idea of how an unopened bottle of the same wine will age in your wine cellar. _Craig Goldwyn, publisher, International Wine Review_

WINE

65 ..._MEASURING THE PROGRESS OF A PREGNANCY_ Lay a cloth tape measure over the belly pressing one end on the pubic bone. The number of centimeters from the pubic bone to the top of the uterus is the number of weeks of pregnancy. _John McPhee in The New Yorker quoting Dr. Ann Dorney_

CHILDBIRTH

66 ... _RIDING A BIKE_ On a light bicycle traveling at 18 miles per hour, you use 80 percent of your energy overcoming air drag. _R.A. Heindl, design engineer, Euclid, Ohio_

BICYCLES

67 ... _CALCULATING DISTANCES_ A light-year (the distance light travels in a year) is to an Astronomical Unit (the distance from the Earth to the Sun) as a mile is to an inch. _Norman Brenner, Fleetwood, New York_

ASTRONOMY

68 ..._SPOTTING FOOT PROBLEMS_ A sneaker sole worn along the outer edge indicates flat feet. A sole worn along the inner edge indicates a high arch. _Steven M. Keisman, New York City high school resource coordinator_

CLOTHING

69 ... _SAVING ON COOLING_ For every one degree you raise the temperature setting on your air conditioner thermostat, you increase energy efficiency by three percent. _"Morning Edition," National Public Radio_

APPLIANCES

70 ... _WINNING CHESS_ A knight at the rim is grim. _Norman Brenner, Fleetwood, New York_

CHESS

71 ... _WATCHING A YACHT RACE_ Body English reveals a lot about a yacht racing tactician. When you see a tactician with his hands in his pockets, he's relaxed and comfortable with the way the race is going. When you see him with his hands folded across his chest, he's a little bit concerned. When his hands go on his hips, he's getting worried. _Gary Jobsen, yacht racing tactician and 12 meter specialist, ESPN America's Cup coverage_

BODY LANGUAGE

72 ... _THE LET'S AVOID THE HOSPITAL RULE_ Avoid going to the hospital in July. That's when all the new interns start work. _Norman Brenner, Fleetwood, New York_

DOCTORS

ADVERTISING

73 ... _RUNNING AN ADVERTISING AGENCY_   Expect 40 percent of your employees to quit each year. *Anonymous*

BUSINESS

74 ... _PLANNING TOILET FACILITIES_   One chemical toilet per 15 employees per week. *Steven M. Keisman, New York City high school resource coordinator*

GAMBLING

75 ... _PLAYING CARDS_   Don't bet more money than you have in your pocket on any card game. *Martin M. Bruce, Ph.D., psychologist, Larchmont, New York*

FASTENERS

76 ... _USING A ROPE_   If you are using a rope with a knot or a sharp bend, you should assume that its strength is reduced by 50 percent. *Frank Potts, Salem, Oregon*

EXERCISE

77 ... _CALCULATING THE VALUE OF EXERCISE_   For each hour that you're physically active, you can expect to live two hours longer. *Robert H. Thomas, writer, Northville, Michigan*

JOKER

78 ... _HEATING YOUR HOME_   If the cats aren't sleeping on the radiators, turn down the heat. *Rob Shapiro, flight instructor, Ithaca, New York*

PRECIPITATION

79 ... _FORECASTING RAIN WITH ANTS AND COWS_   If an ant covers its hole or if cows refuse to graze, it's going to rain. *Dean Sheridan, electronics technician and deaf actor, Torrance, California*

EXPLORATION

80 ... _THE ROSENSHINE THUMBNAIL COMPASS RULE_   To find your way on a cloudy day, place your knife point-down on your thumbnail. Turn the knife slowly and you'll see a faint shadow. When the shadow is thinnest, you've found east if it's early morning, north if it's midday, and west if it's dusk. *Barak Rosenshine, professor of education, Urbana, Illinois*

AUTOMOBILES

81 ... _BUYING A USED CAR_   Pick the type of car you want, choose the model that has the lowest resale value, then buy the best example you can find. *Steven M. Keisman, New York City high school resource coordinator*

BOATS

82 ... _THE WEEKEND SAILOR'S RULE_   The distance traveled in 3 minutes, measured in yards, divided by 100, equals your speed in knots. Conversely, your speed in knots, times 100, is how many yards you will travel in 3 minutes. Here's an example: 15 knots equals 1,500 yards every 3 minutes. *Robert Hastings, Master Chief Petty Officer, United States Coast Guard*

BIRDS

83 ... _SMITH'S RULE OF BIRD INTERPRETATION_   Bird calls are mostly adjectives with few verbs. They don't tell you what they are going to do — only how well they are going to do it. *Denis Smith, high school counselor, Camarillo, California*

ARCHITECTURE

84 ... _DEVELOPING REAL ESTATE_   Barring geographic barriers, cities will grow, and grow affluent, toward the northwest. *Michael Ridley, real estate developer, El Paso, Texas, quoted by Alan Weisman in La Frontera*

As a rule of thumb:
IF YOU FACE THE OCEAN ON
A BEACH WHERE THE BATHERS
WEAR SUITS, THE NUDE
BEACHES WILL BE TO YOUR
LEFT MORE OFTEN THAN
TO YOUR RIGHT.
GUSTAV LORENTZEN, PARADIS,
NORWAY

85 ... **BUYING ANTIQUES**   Don't buy antique wooden-wear that smells like vinegar. Chances are, it's a reproduction. *Paul Polce, Ponzi's Antiques, Trumansburg, New York*

86 ... **SPOTTING A GOOD BOOK**   You can tell a book by its cover. The nicer the cover, the better the publisher and the more experienced the author. *Carolyn Lloyd, 15-year-old student, Montreal, Quebec*

87 ... **GROWING TALLER**   A girl will reach her full height 18 months after she starts to menstruate. *Hilary Peterson, homemaker, West Chester, Pennsylvania*

88 ... **WATCHING A WINERY**   A winery's standards start to slip if it produces more than 50,000 cases of wine per year. *Richard Graff, chairman and chief operating officer, Chalone, Inc., Sonoma County, California*

89 ... **FOLLOWING LABOR**   If a woman can walk around during contractions, she is not fully dilated. *Dr. K. Emmott, Vancouver, British Columbia*

90 ... **BICYCLING SAFELY**   Bicyclists can expect to have one serious accident for every 10,000 miles they log. *Russell T. Johnson, Temple City, California*

91 ... **WATCHING THE SUNSET**   It takes two minutes for the sun to drop out of sight once it touches the horizon. *Emmon Bodfish, Oakland, California*

92 ... **DRESSING RIGHT**   If a person is poorly dressed, you notice the clothes. If impeccably dressed, you notice the person. *Steven M Keisman, New York City high school resource coordinator*

93 ... **USING A REFRIGERATOR FREEZER**   Don't even consider freezing a large mass of food in the freezer compartment of a conventional refrigerator. Add no more than three pounds of unfrozen food for each cubic foot of space in the box. *The Lobel Brothers, Madison Avenue butcher shop owners, New York City*

94 ... **WINNING CHESS**   Always check—it might be mate. *Norman Brenner, Fleetwood, New York*

95 ... **WATCHING PEOPLE'S SHOULDERS**   Genuine emotion is always expressed with the entire body. When uncertain of a person's sincerity, watch their shoulders. You should doubt anyone who is speaking with strong emotion and relaxed shoulders. *D. Klein, painter, Brooklyn, New York*

96 ... **FINDING A GOOD DOCTOR**   To find a good doctor, look for one with a long residency in a hospital affiliated with a medical school. The worst doctors are those with a short residency in a non-AMA approved program. *Steven M. Keisman, New York City high school resource coordinator*

ADVERTISING

97...SETTING YOUR ADVERTISING BUDGET   Your allowance for advertising should equal at least 2 percent of your company's gross income. Anything less will be ineffective.   *Marilyn Rider, Body & Soul, Ithaca, New York*

BUSINESS

98...THE CHELLBERG RULE OF SELLING A BUSINESS   The sale price of a small business is between seven and ten times the average profit of the last three years.   *Bill Chellberg, Elmhurst, Illinois*

GAMBLING

99...THE HAT RULE OF TICKET SALES   If you walk into a bar where a lot of people wear baseball caps, it's a good place to sell lottery tickets.   *Peter Leach, St. Paul, Minnesota*

FASTENERS

100...WORKING WITH RIVETS   Before it is hammered, the end of a rivet should stick out slightly more than its own diameter. This will give you enough metal to form a solid head.   *Mike Bauer, sheet metal worker*

EXERCISE

101...GETTING RID OF BACK PAIN   If your back hurts more when you walk down stairs, down a hill, or sit down in a chair, you need to do flexion exercises.   *Peggy Bodine-Reese, physical therapist, Gaithersburg, Maryland*

CATTLE

102...BUYING FENCE FOR CATTLE   One mile of regular cattle fencing costs 25 times as much as 1 mile of electric fence.   *Ken Scharabok, financial manager, Dayton, Ohio*

PRECIPITATION

103...FORECASTING THE WEATHER   If pimpernel flowers are folded, rain is approaching. If fully expanded, expect a fair day.   *Dean Sheridan, electronics technician and deaf actor, Torrance, California*

EXPLORATION

104...THE ICEBERG RULE   Arctic icebergs are tall and narrow. Antarctic icebergs are shaped like sheets.   *Paul A. Delaney, meteorologist, Beltsville, Maryland*

AUTOMOBILES

105...BUYING A CAR   Cars with four doors are cheaper to repair than cars with two doors, but two-door cars are stolen twice as often as four-door models.   *Steven M. Keisman, New York City high school resource coordinator*

BOATS

106...CLIMBING ABOARD A BOAT   If there are three or more inches of water in the bilge of a rowboat, don't get in it. Your weight will be enough to capsize the boat.   *Andrew Kuchinsky, boater, Boston, Massachusetts*

BIRDS

107...ED'S RULE OF HUNTING DUCKS   Wind in the East, ducks fly the least.   *Ed Timmerman, duck hunter, Burlington, Iowa*

ARCHITECTURE

108...PLANNING SPACE FOR A MUSEUM   A museum should have office, work, and storage space equal to its exhibit space.   *Dr. Gertrude Ward, Earlham College, Richmond, Indiana*

As A RULE OF THUMB: YOU CAN FIND THE TRAINED FLYING WEIGHT OF A WILD-CAUGHT FALCON, IF YOU SUBTRACT 10 PERCENT FROM THE BIRD'S WEIGHT AT CAPTURE.

DOUGLASS A. PINEO, BIOLOGIST AND FALCONER, SPOKANE, WASHINGTON

109... **BUYING ANTIQUES**   If you're buying an old car and the clock works, the rest of the car is probably good. *Paul Polce, Ponzi's Antiques, Trumansburg, New York*

110... **SIFTING THROUGH BOOK PROPOSALS**   Nearly half of all unsolicited proposals for novels will be about disasters. *Walter Pitkin, literary agent, Weston, Connecticut*

111... **FEELING YOUR AGE**   You are middle aged when your high school and college days are featured as nostalgia on TV. You are at old age when your wedding presents are sold as antiques. *Margaret M. Day, Locke, New York*

112... **PRODUCING CHAMPAGNE**   The amount of champagne a winery sells in three years is the amount it should have in its cellars to be properly stocked. *Barry Bassin, wine merchant, New York City*

113... **FOLLOWING LABOR**   If the waters do not break at the start of the labor, they will break at the start of the pushing stage. *Dr. K. Emmott, Vancouver, British Columbia*

114... **BICYCLING SAFELY**   Be especially cautious if you're bicycling near a hospital, movie theater, or nursing home. Visitors to those places are distracted and aren't paying attention. *Larry Gassan, Jolly Dino Art Direction, Los Angeles, California*

115... **MEASURING THE NIGHT SKY**   The moon covers half a degree of sky. *Tom Robinson, computer programmer, Berkeley, California*

116... **MAKING YOURSELF LOOK THIN**   Horizontal lines on clothes make you look fat, while vertical lines make you look taller and thinner. *Steven M. Keisman, New York City high school resource coordinator*

117... **TESTING MICROWAVE COOKWARE** If you are not sure if a piece of glassware is safe for use in a microwave oven pour 1/2 cup of water into a separate glass measure. Place both the dish you wish to test and the measure inside your oven and run it at full power for one minute. Check the temperature of the dish and of the water. If the water is warm but the dish is cool, it's safe for microwave cooking. *Better Homes and Gardens*

118... **WINNING CHESS**   For a child, an Elo rating of 300 plus 100 times the child's age is excellent. *Norman Brenner, Fleetwood, New York*

119... **READING BODY LANGUAGE**   Shuffling feet signify a restless listener. Feet flat on the floor show attention. Toe tapping indicates impatience. *Dean Sheridan, electronics technician and deaf actor, Torrance, California*

120... **FINDING A GOOD DOCTOR**   Don't go back to a doctor who prescribes medication for you without first asking about your diet and other drugs you're taking. He's either sloppy or ignorant. *Steven M. Keisman, New York City high school resource coordinator*

ADVERTISING

121... DESIGNING AN AD   If an ad is well designed, it will look just as good upside down. *Michele Rogers, advertising creative director, Warwick, Rhode Island*

BUSINESS

122... RUNNING A DIAPER SERVICE   The cost of diapers is about one-fifth the cost of doing business. *Clyde H. Farnsworth*

GAMBLING

123... ROLLING DICE   To calculate the odds of getting a certain roll from a pair of dice, take the difference between the number you want and 7, then subtract the result from 6. This will tell you how many chances in 12 you have of winning. *Paul A. Delaney, meteorologist, Beltsville, Maryland*

FASTENERS

124... WORKING WITH RIVETS   Install a rivet at least one and a half times its diameter from the edge of the piece it is in. *Mike Bauer, sheet metal worker*

EXERCISE

125... THE PAIN RULE OF EXERCISING AFTER AN INJURY   If your exercise is not pain-free after an injury, your injury will get worse. *Peggy Bodine-Reese, physical therapist, Gaithersburg, Maryland*

CATTLE

126... GETTING STARTED WITH CATTLE   When starting out, raise the same breed of cattle as your neighbors. Specialize later, when you have experience. *Ken Scharabok, financial manager, Dayton, Ohio*

PRECIPITATION

127... FORECASTING THE WEATHER   When a cow scratches its ear, a shower is very near. When it thumps its ribs with its tail, look out for thunder, lightning, and hail. *Dean Sheridan, electronics technician and deaf actor, Torrance, California*

EXPLORATION

128... PLANNING A TREK   Plan on 1 reindeer for every 75 pounds of supplies. *Brendon Rehm, military historian, Fairfax, Virginia*

AUTOMOBILES

129... GETTING YOUR CAR REPAIRED   If a mechanic tells you that you hit a pothole and need a new wheel or other part, check it out with another mechanic. *Martin M. Bruce, Ph.D., psychologist, Larchmont, New York*

BOATS

130... GAUGING THE SPEED OF ANOTHER BOAT   To gauge the speed of another boat, choose a point on the horizon that is behind the other boat and check how its bow moves relative to this point. If its bow appears to move ahead of the point, the other boat is moving faster than yours; if its bow appears to move backwards, your boat is going faster. If there is no relative movement, and your boats are on intersecting courses, you will collide. *Evan Gamblin, Carleton Place, Ontario*

BIRDS

131... WATCHING BIRDS   Study the bird, not the field guide. The bird will fly away. The guide won't. *Christine Jones, birdwatcher, San Francisco, California*

ARCHITECTURE

132... SUPERINSULATED HOUSES   A superinsulated house should have 12 square feet of windows for every 100 square feet of floor. At least two-thirds of the windows should be facing south. *Phillip Close, builder*

133 ... *THE GARAGE SALE RULE* One out of five items costing under $75 that you buy at a garage sale will end up in your garage sale within the next 1.5 years. *Steven M. Keisman, New York City high school resource coordinator*

ANTIQUES

134 ... *MEASURING BOOKS* Most books average 5 letters per word, 10 words per line, and 40 lines per page. *Norman Brenner, Fleetwood, New York*

BOOKS

135 ... *THE GAPPERT THINK AHEAD RULE* You can think ahead half your age. *Gary Gappert, social economist, Akron, Ohio*

AGES AND STAGES

136 ... *TASTING A CHAMPAGNE* You should not have to swallow a mouthful of good champagne twice in order to taste the wine around the bubbles—once should be enough. *Barry Bassin, wine merchant, New York City*

WINE

137 ... *MONITORING CONTRACTIONS* If a husband calls saying his wife (pregnant with their first child) is having really strong contractions, the birth is a long way off, but tell them to come to the hospital anyway. *Dr. K. Emmott, Vancouver, British Columbia*

CHILDBIRTH

138 ... *CHOOSING A BICYCLE FRAME* The crossbar on your bicycle frame should come just to your crotch when you straddle the bike barefoot with your feet flat on the ground. *Leslie Warren, music teacher, Kittery Point, Maine*

BICYCLES

139 ... *THE BUTLER RULE OF THE SUN AND THE MOON* For a given latitude, the path of the full moon across the sky at the summer solstice is approximately the path of the sun at the winter solstice, and vice versa. *Pierce Butler, Natchez, Mississippi*

ASTRONOMY

140 ... *BUYING A ROBE* If a robe needs any alteration other than shortening, don't buy it. *Steven M. Keisman, New York City high school resource coordinator*

CLOTHING

141 ... *BUYING A REFRIGERATOR-FREEZER* It will save you money if you buy the right size refrigerator-freezer for your family. You need a total of 8 cubic feet of space for two people, plus 1 foot for each additional family member. *Jill Phillips, home economist*

APPLIANCES

142 ... *WINNING CHESS* Bring out knights before bishops, preferably in front of the bishop's pawns. *Norman Brenner, Fleetwood, New York*

CHESS

143 ... *WAVING TO PEOPLE* If you're standing on an overpass, you can count on five out of ten drivers on the highway below returning a wave. *Carolyn Lloyd, 15-year-old student, Montreal, Quebec*

JOKER

144 ... *THE CAT SWING DOCTOR RULE* Never go back to an eye doctor whose examining room isn't large enough to swing a cat in. He's a frustrated doctor and will give up his practice soon. *Ann German, East Islip, New York*

DOCTORS

ADVERTISING

BUSINESS

GAMBLING

FASTENERS

EXERCISE

CATTLE

PRECIPITATION

EXPLORATION

AUTOMOBILES

BOATS

BIRDS

ARCHITECTURE

145... **PLANNING AN EFFECTIVE TELEVISION COMMERCIAL**
The visual part of a TV commercial accounts for 85 percent of the impact on the viewer; the sound track accounts for 15 percent. *John Koten, Staff Reporter, The Wall Street Journal*

146... **THE THOMPSON RULE OF BEAUTY SALONS** A beauty salon will sell for 0.25 to 0.75 times its gross income, plus equipment and inventory. *Terri Thompson, New York, New York*

147... **BETTING ON A HORSE** Bet on the horse with the highest butt. *Russell T. Johnson, Temple City, California*

148... **ESTIMATING MACHINE SCREW DIAMETERS** The diameter of a machine screw in inches is 13 times its gauge number divided by 1,000, plus 60 thousandths of an inch. *Ernst Luposchainsky, III ("Kahn"), philotechnic screw virtuoso, inter alia, Hollywood, California*

149... **EXERCISING** If you can't maintain a comfortable conversation while exercising, you are probably working beyond your aerobic target zone. *Kurt Ulrich, exercise specialist, Tompkins Community Hospital, Ithaca, New York*

150... **JUDGING THE AGE OF A CALF** A calf whose tail nearly reaches the ground is more than a year old. *Edward Dalrymple, dairy farmer*

151... **FORECASTING THE WEATHER** Drops of rain hanging on a wire clothesline mean another rain soon. *Marie Broyles, Pataskala, Ohio*

152... **EXPLORING A CAVE** You should have at least four people for any caving expedition. If someone is injured, two people can go for help while one stays with the injured spelunker. That way, no one is in the cave alone. *David R. McClurg, speleologist*

153... **THE GROSS INCOME CAR RULE** The highest price you should pay for a car you're buying with a car loan is one-half your annual gross income. *Augustin R. Anitart, Metairie, Louisiana*

154... **CHOOSING A FIN FOR A SAILBOARD** The higher the wind, the smaller the fin. *Jeremy Bishop, windsurfing expert, Hood River, Oregon*

155... **THE BIRD BILL RULE** The single best clue to a bird's identity is the shape of its bill. *Christine Jones, birdwatcher, San Francisco, California*

156... **PLANNING A HOSPITAL** A hospital should have four to four and a half beds for every thousand people in the community it serves. *Douglass A. Pineo, biologist and falconer, Spokane, Washington*

AS A RULE OF THUMB: FOR EVERY ONE-POINT INCREASE IN THE OCTANE RATING, YOU'LL GET 1 PERCENT BETTER MILEAGE. DON'T PAY MORE THAN 1 PERCENT PER POINT FOR PREMIUM, UNLESS YOUR ENGINE REQUIRES IT.

WILLIAM SALLACH, TELECOMMUNICATIONS MANAGER, CANAL WINCHESTER, OHIO

157...**DATING AN ARTIFACT**   The less complex or well executed, the more recent the object is. This is especially true for Thai brass.   *Thomas W. Neumann, anthropological archaeologist, wildlife ecologist, and field crew crisis manager*

ANTIQUES

158...**BUYING A GOOD BOOK**   If you're considering buying a book, open it at random and read a page. Do this three times. If you haven't stumbled onto a vital part of the story at least once, don't buy the book. *Gene Wolfe, Barrington, Illinois*

BOOKS

159...**THE ODD RULE OF AGE**   Odd-numbered ages seem older and more worldly wise than even-numbered ages. *Hamilton Pike, Richmond, Indiana*

AGES AND STAGES

160...**THE NOWICKI THREE CASE RULE**   Be methodical about accumulating wine in your cellar. If you can manage to get three cases ahead, you can stop worrying about having a good supply.   *David Nowicki, wine authority, Interlaken, New York*

WINE

161...**FOLLOWING LABOR**   If a woman is in labor and you want to know if there is time to get her to the hospital, check for the child's head during a contraction. If you can't see it and it is the woman's first child, you have at least an hour. If you can see a quarter's worth, you have 20 or 30 minutes. If you can see a quarter's worth and she has had a child before, you don't have time. *Dr. K. Emmott, Vancouver, British Columbia*

CHILDBIRTH

162...**TRAVELING BY BIKE**   On a good ten-speed bicycle you can travel 50 miles per day at a leisurely pace. Riding straight through with few rest stops can get you 70 to 80 miles per day with little effort. *Alwyn T. Perrin, editor, Explorers Ltd. Source Book*

BICYCLES

163...**WAITING FOR THE MOON**   The moon rises 50 minutes later than it did the day before. *Pierce Butler, Natchez, Mississippi*

ASTRONOMY

164...**THE LIMING RULE OF SMALL CLOTHING**   Clothes made outside the U.S. run small. *R. L. Liming, Indianapolis, Indiana*

CLOTHING

165...**HEATING A TRAVEL TRAILER**   To estimate the heater size for a travel trailer, figure 1,000 BTUs per foot of length. A 15-foot trailer will need a 15,000-BTU heater. *Ralph Young, camper*

APPLIANCES

166...**WINNING CHESS**   In the endgame, keep your rook between you and a passed pawn — either yours or your opponent's. *Norman Brenner, Fleetwood, New York*

CHESS

167...**ESTIMATING YOUR SURFACE AREA**   To estimate the surface area of your body, multiply the surface area of the palm of your hand by 100. *Gerry M. Flick, M.D., Ship's Surgeon, S.S. Constitution off Hawaii*

BODY RULES

168...**THE GERMAN RULE OF DECENT DOCTORS**   Don't go back to a doctor whose office staff has to stand all day. If he doesn't care about them, he won't care about you. *Ann German, East Islip, New York*

DOCTORS

ADVERTISING

169 ... SETTING AN ADVERTISING BUDGET   In the retail trade, budget 10 percent of sales for advertising and rent. *Dean Sheridan, electronics technician and deaf actor, Torrance, California*

BUSINESS

170 ... SELLING A CAR DEALERSHIP   A car dealership should sell for 1.25 to 2 times net, plus equipment and inventory. *Terri Thompson, New York, New York*

GAMBLING

171 ... PLAYING POKER   Out of ten opening poker hands, half will be no good, four will contain a pair, and one will beat a pair. *Anonymous*

JOKER

172 ... ESTIMATING THE COST OF A STEREO   The cost of the stereo system is inversely proportional to the cost of the house. *Bob Allen, morning show host, WRNJ, Hackettstown, New Jersey*

EXERCISE

173 ... SETTING THE WEIGHTS ON AN EXERCISE MACHINE   When you work out with an exercise machine, choose a weight setting that lets you do 8 to 12 repetitions comfortably. If you must struggle to get beyond 5 repititions, the setting is too heavy. If you complete 10 without feeling any fatigue at all, it is too light. *Bottom Line/Personal*

CATTLE

174 ... THE BULL RULE   You need 1 bull for every 25 cows. *Julian Silver, farm hand*

PRECIPITATION

175 ... FORECASTING THE WEATHER   If the cows are lying in the pasture, it will rain within three days. *Christine Tarbell, Greene, New York*

EXPLORATION

176 ... CAVING WITH BEGINNERS   There should be at least one experienced spelunker for every three beginners. However, never have less than two experienced spelunkers on any trip with beginners, so one can lead and one can bring up the rear. *David R. McClurg, speleologist*

AUTOMOBILES

177 ... CARING FOR YOUR CAR   If you want your car to make it to 100,000 miles, flush the cooling system every even-numbered year. This prevents engine damage from overheating. *Paul S. Amber, P.E., Royal Oak, Michigan*

BOATS

178 ... THE SAILBOARD CATAPULT RULE   If the least experienced windsurfers are getting catapulted over their sails, then it's time to sail your shortboard. *Jeremy Bishop, windsurfing expert, Hood River, Oregon*

BIRDS

179 ... LOOKING FOR BIRDS   Look for birds on the edges where two habitats meet—ocean beaches, stream banks, forest margins. Where two habitats meet, you can find organisms from both habitats, plus those adapted to the edge itself. *Christine Jones, birdwatcher, San Francisco, California*

ARCHITECTURE

180 ... DESIGNING AN OFFICE BUILDING   A well-planned office building should be able to accommodate one person for every 225 square feet of floor space. *William Payne, building supervisor*

181...PRICING ITEMS FOR A GARAGE SALE   Garage sale items should be priced at 10 percent of retail cost. *Jennifer Evans, writer, Austin, Texas*

182...MAKING A MOVIE   Only 1 in 50 published novels gets optioned as a movie, and only 1 in 200 gets made into a movie. *Anonymous*

183...ASSESSING YOUR AGE   You know you're old if all your baby pictures are in black-and-white. *Dean Sheridan, electronics technician and deaf actor, Torrance, California*

184...CHECKING A BOTTLE OF WINE   Be suspicious of any wine that does not have sediment or tannin crystals in it after 10 or 12 years of aging. *Cally Arthur, managing editor, American Demographics*

185...TRYING TO GET PREGNANT   It's time to consult a fertility specialist if you haven't gotten pregnant after 12 months of trying. *Dr. June Reinisch, syndicated columnist, United Feature Syndicate*

186...SHIFTING GEARS ON A BICYCLE   If the gear is too high, your legs will tire before your lungs. If the gear is too low, your lungs will tire first. *John S. Allen, author, The Complete Book of Bicycle Commuting*

187...THE BEAUMONT STAR TWINKLE RULE   Stars twinkle, planets don't. *Scott Parker, data specialist, Beaumont, Texas*

188...BEING REMEMBERED   People are more likely to remember you if you always wear the same outfit. *Paul A. Delaney, meteorologist, Beltsville, Maryland*

189...USING A BRICK BAKE OVEN   First, the bricks must all look red. If the black spots are not all burned off, it is not hot enough. Next, sprinkle flour on the oven hearth; if it burns black right away, the oven is too hot. Finally, insert the tender part of your wrist toward the inside front corners of the oven and count. If you cannot hold your hand in longer than the count of twenty, it is hot enough. If you can count to thirty, it is not hot enough for bread. *Richard Bacon, writer and historian*

190...THE CHESS OPENING RULE OF TWO   Move no piece in the opening twice. *Norman Brenner, Fleetwood, New York*

191...COUNTING THE DAYS IN A MONTH   Put your hands together, thumb to thumb. Name the months from left to right across the backs of your hands. The months falling on a knuckle have 31 days, while those falling in hollows have 30 or fewer. *Norman Brenner, Fleetwood, New York*

192...GETTING PAID   Patients who ask for expensive medical tests or surgical procedures saying they don't care how much it costs aren't footing the bill. The doctor will be paid by some sort of insurance, by the government, or no one at all. *Gerry M. Flick, M.D., Ship's Surgeon, S.S. Constitution off Hawaii*

AS A RULE OF THUMB:
THE INTERMEDIATE STAGE BETWEEN SOCIALISM AND CAPITALISM IS ALCOHOLISM.
NORMAN BRENNER, FLEETWOOD, NEW YORK

ANTIQUES

BOOKS

AGES AND STAGES

WINE

CHILDBIRTH

BICYCLES

ASTRONOMY

CLOTHING

APPLIANCES

CHESS

BODY RULES

DOCTORS

ADVERTISING

193... ***PROFITING FROM ADVERTISING***   A going company will usually profit from advertising an amount equal to its advertising expenses.   *Peter Reimuller, Point Arena, California*

BUSINESS

194... ***SELLING A BUSINESS***   A gas station will sell for $1.25 to $2 per gallon pumped per month.   *Terri Thompson, New York, New York*

GAMBLING

195... ***FINDING A GOOD SLOT MACHINE***   Slot machines closest to the doors are the most generous. Bar slots pay better than the machines that show apples, oranges, and cherries. Machines with several slots requiring more than one coin per pull pay better.   *Scott Parker, data specialist, Beaumont, Texas*

HOUSE AND HOME

196... ***FEELING YOUR CEILING***   If you can touch your ceiling with the palm of your hand, your ceiling is too low.   *Bob Horton, consultant and writer, Largo, Florida*

EXERCISE

197... ***SWEATING***   You lose about 2 to 3 percent of your body weight as sweat for every hour of heavy exercise, but don't confuse temporary dehydration for real weight loss. Losing more than 4 percent of your body weight as sweat can hurt your athletic performance.   *Ned Frederick, writer, Exeter, New Hampshire*

CATTLE

198... ***WEANING A CALF***   Wean a calf when it has gained 15 pounds over its birth weight.   *Edward Dalrymple, dairy farmer*

PRECIPITATION

199... ***FORECASTING THE WEATHER***   If it's raining hard enough to make bubbles in a puddle, it will rain all day.   *Delores Biggie, Tonawanda, New York*

EXPLORATION

200... ***FEEDING PEOPLE***   For long trips and expeditions, plan on taking at least two pounds of food per person per day.   *G. Brooks, Flagstaff, Arizona*

AUTOMOBILES

201... ***BUYING THE RIGHT CAR***   Try to buy a car made on a Wednesday. Assembly-line workers are off-rhythm on Mondays and Tuesdays because of the weekend. They're tired and bored on Thursdays and Fridays because of the week. This makes cars built on Wednesdays the best.   *Chic Volturno, storehouse of worthless information, Hollywood, Florida*

BOATS

202... ***THE WINDSURFING RULE***   In a 35 knot wind, you need a 35-square-foot sail for windsurfing. For every 5 knots of wind less, add 5 square feet of sail. For flat water, add an extra 5 square feet.   *Jeremy Bishop, windsurfing expert, Hood River, Oregon*

BIRDS

203... ***BIRDWATCHING***   You will hear one-third to one-half again as many chickadees and juncos as you will actually see, and there are one-third again as many out there that you neither hear nor see.   *Ellen Klaver, musician, Boulder, Colorado*

ARCHITECTURE

204... ***PLANNING A HIGHWAY***   A divided highway will occupy about 40 acres of land per mile. Other roads occupy between 6 and 12 acres per mile.   *William S. Stevens, highway engineer*

AS A RULE OF THUMB: IF YOU WANT TO MAKE X PER HOUR AS A FREELANCE ILLUSTRATOR, BILL YOUR CLIENTS 3X PER HOUR. YOU WILL SPEND 2X ON OVERHEAD, HUSTLING, DAYDREAMING, AND OTHER NONBILLABLES.
JON BULLER, LYME, CONNECTICUT

205... COLLECTING COINS There have to be 1,500 to 2,000 coins minted with an error to make a market for collectors. *Robert E. Wilhite, editor, Numismatic News, Iola, Wisconsin*

ANTIQUES

206... CONSULTING FOR SMALL PUBLISHERS If small publishers contact you, they're usually short on time, money, or knowledge. If they call you more than once, they have boxes of unsold books in their garage. If they insist on hiring you, even if you decline, their partner is on their back about wasting money on the publishing venture. *Cliff Martin, Eugene, Oregon*

BOOKS

207... SHELTERING YOUR CHILDREN Never tell a child how a used-car dealer prices automobiles, how a butcher makes sausage, or how a Texas politician makes money. *Richard Malone, Vancouver, Washington*

JOKER

208... CHOOSING A BORDEAUX Presidential election-year Bordeauxs generally are bad. *Mark Matthews quoting Richard M. Nixon, in the Washington Journalism Review*

WINE

209... DOUBLING A BABY The average newborn baby takes six months to double its weight. *L.M. Boyd, The San Francisco Chronicle*

CHILDBIRTH

210... ADJUSTING BICYCLE HANDLEBARS The distance from the front of your seat to the handlebar cross member should equal the length of your forearm from elbow to fingertip. *Peter van Berkum, Kittery Point, Maine*

BICYCLES

211... MAKING A TELESCOPE For a first-time telescope maker, it is faster to make a four-inch mirror, and then a six-inch mirror, than it is to make a six-inch mirror first. *Bill McKeeman, Wang Institute, Communications of the ACM*

ASTRONOMY

212... BUYING CLOTHES THAT FIT A suit coat fits well if you can stick four fingers in the sleeve in front of your shoulder. *Rick Eckstrom, plan review officer, Ithaca, New York*

CLOTHING

213... USING A MICROWAVE OVEN With your microwave oven at its most powerful setting, figure one and a half to two minutes per cup of casserole. *Irma Dalton, artist, Westminster, California*

APPLIANCES

214... WINNING CHESS Move your knight to square K5, well supported, and your game will play itself. *Norman Brenner, Fleetwood, New York*

CHESS

215... ESTIMATING DISTANCES Hold your thumb at arm's length against a distant background. Estimate how far your thumb jumps on the background when you look at it with one eye and then the other. The background is ten times that distance from you. *Norman Brenner, Fleetwood, New York*

BODY RULES

216... SIZING UP A PATIENT If a patient is proud of claiming that no physician has been able to diagnose what is wrong with him, don't plan on being the first doctor to break his record. *Gerry M. Flick, M.D., Ship's Surgeon, S.S. Constitution off Hawaii*

DOCTORS

ADVERTISING

BUSINESS

GAMBLING

HOUSE AND HOME

EXERCISE

CATTLE

PRECIPITATION

EXPLORATION

AUTOMOBILES

BOATS

BIRDS

ARCHITECTURE

217...***DONATING SPACE FOR ANNOUNCEMENTS***   People looking for free newspaper space for announcements typically want them to run more than once. The old newspaper rule: one announcement is news, two announcements is advertising.   *Ben Hansen, editor, The Beaumont Enterprise, Beaumont, Texas*

218...***SELLING A BUSINESS***   A grocery store will sell for 0.25 to 0.33 times its gross income, plus inventory.   *Terri Thompson, New York, New York*

219...***BETTING ON A HORSE***   If you don't know any of the horses in a race, bet on the one with the thinnest waist.   *Thomas O. Marsh, writer and coroner's investigator, Fairfield, Ohio*

220...***ESTIMATING YOUR MORTGAGE RATE***   Your mortgage rate drops by 1/4 to 1/6 of a percent for every additional 1 percent you pay at the closing.   *Norman Brenner, Fleetwood, New York*

221...***MAINTAINING YOUR BODY FLUIDS***   You can maintain your fluid levels by drinking at least 4 gulps of water every 20 minutes during prolonged exercise.   *Ned Frederick, writer, Exeter, New Hampshire*

222...***WEANING A CALF***   Wean a calf when it consumes more than a pound of grain a day on a regular basis.   *John C. Porter, Cooperative Extension agent*

223...***FORECASTING THE WEATHER***   If leaves are turned and birds are on the ground, it will rain.   *Marie Shetler, Hamburg, New York*

224...***FINDING CAVES***   In the colder parts of the country, you will often find caves in areas where the soil is red.   *David R. McClurg, speleologist*

225...***MAKING A FUSE IN A PINCH***   If your car blows a wierd-looking fuse and you don't have a spare—one wrap of cigarette-pack foil around the old fuse will give you a 20 amp emergency fuse; two wraps will give you about 35 amps.   *Douglass A. Pineo, biologist and falconer, Spokane, Washington*

226...***CHOOSING A SAILBOARD***   Beginning windsurfers should use a sailboard that is from 20 to 40 liters of volume greater than their body weight. A 150-pound person should sail a board that has 170 to 190 liters of volume.   *Jeremy Bishop, windsurfing expert, Hood River, Oregon*

227...***WATCHING CANADA GEESE***   The farther north, the smaller the Canada geese; the farther west, the darker the color.   *Mary Ellen Parker, retired teacher, Cincinnati, Ohio*

228...***DESIGNING A ROOF***   When you are planning a house, make the angle of the roof noticeably more or noticeably less than a right angle; otherwise, the appearance is depressing.   *Susan Pitkin, librarian*

AS A RULE OF THUMB:
THE MORE PEOPLE AN
ORGANIZATION INVITES TO A
NEWS CONFERENCE, THE
LESS IMPORTANT THE NEWS.
TRUDIE MASON, ASSIGNMENT ⤵
EDITOR/REPORTER, CJAD RADIO
NEWS, MONTREAL, QUEBEC

229 ... **THE BIG SPENDER RULE OF ANTIQUES** The big spenders never come before noon. *Anonymous*

230 ... **SELLING POETRY** A book of poetry sells no more than 800 copies, on average. *Scott Parker, data specialist, Beaumont, Texas*

231 ... **THE LIBRARY CARD RULE** Children should get library cards when they are able to write their full names. *Norman Brenner, Fleetwood, New York*

232 ... **TASTING A CHAMPAGNE** A yeasty taste means a young champagne that could use more time in the bottle. *Rick Eckstrom, plan review officer, Ithaca, New York*

233 ... **TODD'S CLOWN AND CHIMPANZEE RULE** Never walk past a chimpanzee while wearing a clown suit. *Todd Strong, circus school student, Chalons-sur-Marne, France*

234 ... **WEARING GOGGLES** Wear goggles on a bike when the temperature is below 40 degrees F. *Tanya Kucak, Palo Alto, California*

235 ... **MEASURING SOMETHING IN THE SKY** Hold your hand in front of you at arm's length. With your palm facing in and your pinkie on the horizon, the width of your hand covers 15 degrees of arc above the horizon. *Hugh Crowell, Columbus, Ohio*

236 ... **BUYING CLOTHES THAT FIT** A sleeve is the right length if there are four to five inches between the end of the sleeve and the tip of your thumb. *Rick Eckstrom, plan review officer, Ithaca, New York*

237 ... **COOLING WITH GRASS** Eight average front lawns have the cooling effect of about 20 central air conditioners. *Curt Suplee, writer and editor, in The Washington Post magazine*

238 ... **WINNING CHESS** Never take the opponent's queen's knight's pawn with your queen. *Norman Brenner, Fleetwood, New York*

239 ... **ESTIMATING DISTANCES** If you hold your thumb at arm's length against a distant background, it is 2 degrees wide (four times the width of the full moon). *Norman Brenner, Fleetwood, New York*

240 ... **DIAGNOSING A PATIENT** Seventy percent of medical diagnoses can be made by taking a good medical history. Another 20 percent can be made by doing a good physical exam. Only 10 percent require laboratory procedures and X-rays. *Gerry M. Flick, M.D., Ship's Surgeon, S.S. Constitution off Hawaii*

ADVERTISING

241 ... *RUNNING ADS ON TV* You should run a TV commercial at least four times a day, four days a week, three weeks a month. If you run it less than that, your ad money would be better spent elsewhere. *Scott Parker, data specialist, Beaumont, Texas*

BUSINESS

242 ... *SELLING A BUSINESS* An insurance agency will sell for one to two times its annual renewal commissions. *Terri Thompson, New York, New York*

GAMBLING

243 ... *PICKING A WINNER AT THE HARNESS TRACK* When you're at the harness track, bet on a horse that runs a fast first half-mile and has final quarter times under 31 seconds. *Don Valliere, track manager and author, Fort Erie, Ontario*

HOUSE AND HOME

244 ... *THE SACCO RULE OF FURNITURE MOVING* If friends ask you to help them move, remember that the work will begin an hour after you get there, you'll finish an hour later than expected, the pizza will be colder than the beer, and the beer will be in lesser quantities than promised. *Tom Sacco, West Des Moines, Iowa*

EXERCISE

245 ... *ADJUSTING TO HEAT AND ALTITUDE* It takes one week to get used to exercising in the heat, but about three weeks to adjust to altitude. *Ned Frederick, writer, Exeter, New Hampshire*

CATTLE

246 ... *FATTENING A BEEF COW* To fatten a beef cow for slaughter, feed it 1 pound of grain per day per 100 pounds of weight. *George Bernius, Cincinnati, Ohio*

PRECIPITATION

247 ... *FORECASTING THE WEATHER* If birds sing after a rain, it won't rain for at least one hour. *Annie Hunger, grandmother*

EXPLORATION

248 ... *THE CAVE ROPE RULE OF 100* A caving rope should be retired after 100 days of use. *The British Mountaineering Council*

AUTOMOBILES

249 ... *THE SCHRODT RULE OF CATASTROPHIC FAILURES* If a car that was working stops or won't start, the problem probably is simple to fix. Catastrophic failures of major parts are rare. The apparent frequency of major breakdowns is due to unscrupulous or lazy repair shops that don't look for the simple solutions, and the publicity surrounding auto racing, where catastrophic failure is more common. *Phil A. Schrodt, Associate Professor, Northwestern University, Evanston, Illinois*

BOATS

250 ... *THE SAILBOARD UPHAUL BODY WEIGHT RULE* You can uphaul a sailboard that is up to 30 liters less than your body weight in pounds. *Jeremy Bishop, windsurfing expert, Hood River, Oregon*

BIRDS

251 ... *THE GOOSE RULE* If a flock of geese is in a close V formation, it is almost certainly Canada geese. If it is a looser V, rippling and waving, or if it is a long line like one leg of a V, it is more likely the less common snow geese. *Hal Borland, Book of Days*

ARCHITECTURE

252 ... *HEATING WITH PEOPLE* Ten people will raise the temperature of a medium-size room one degree per hour. *John Brink, building superintendent, Masonic Temple*

AS A RULE OF THUMB: YOU SHOULD STILL HAVE HALF YOUR HAY AND HALF YOUR FIREWOOD ON THE FIRST DAY OF FEBRUARY. SUSAN WATERSTRIPE, TOWN SUPERVISOR, SHEDS, NEW YORK

253...**SELLING ANTIQUES**   People who are eating when they enter an antique shop won't buy anything. *Anonymous*

253...**ANTIQUES**

254...**BUYING A USED BOOK**   If a used book store has more than one copy of a book written before 1975, it will be worth your while to check each one. The cover prices will probably differ. *Bruce Reznick, associate professor of mathematics, Urbana, Illinois*

BOOKS

255...**CARING FOR TEETH**   If you hear a pop when you pull the thumb out of your four-year-old child's mouth, he is at risk of tooth deformity. Try to break him of the thumb-sucking habit. *Dean Sheridan, electronics technician and deaf actor, Torrance, California*

CHILDREN

256...**MAKING CHAMPAGNE**   It takes 3.25 tons of grapes to make 1 case of champagne. *Rick Eckstrom, plan review officer, Ithaca, New York*

WINE

257...**PLANNING A PARTY**   Only half of those you invite to a large gathering, such as a wedding or retirement party, will come. But expect a 90 percent turnout if you're inviting a small, select group of friends or family. If it's a child's party, plan on at least one uninvited brother or sister tagging along. *Dean Sheridan, electronics technician and deaf actor, Torrance, California*

ENTERTAINING

258...**BICYCLING UPHILL**   Change gears on hills so that your legs pump at a constant rate. *Norman Brenner, Fleetwood, New York*

BICYCLES

259...**LOOKING FOR EXTRATERRESTRIAL DUST**   Hoping to find samples of cosmic dust, NASA scientists carefully inspect tiny particles captured by high-flying planes. They have a rule of thumb: If a particle is large enough to see without a microscope, it is probably contamination of their sample and not extraterrestrial debris. *Dr. Uel Clanton, associate curator for cosmic dust, Johnson Space Center*

ASTRONOMY

260...**DECIDING WHAT CLOTHES TO WEAR**   Wear a shirt whose color is the one that appears least in your skirt or slacks. *Sarah Innerarity and A. Hill, Midland, Texas*

CLOTHING

261...**USING A MICROWAVE**   You can cook more dishes in a microwave oven that's deep and low than in one that's shallow and tall. *Steven M. Keisman, New York City high school resource coordinator*

APPLIANCES

262...**THE SACRIFICE RULE OF WINNING CHESS**   The sacrifice of one pawn is worth three free moves. *Norman Brenner, Fleetwood, New York*

CHESS

263...**CATCHING A BALL**   To catch a ball, the ends of your pinkie fingers should touch if the ball is coming at you below the waist. The ends of your thumbs should touch if the ball is coming in above your waist. *Steven M. Keisman, New York City high school resource coordinator*

BODY RULES

264...**CHOOSING A SURGICAL ASSISTANT**   If you are a surgeon, choose an assistant surgeon whose height is within five inches of yours. Otherwise, you will disagree on the height of the surgery table and if an operation is long, one of you will end up with back pain. *Gerry M. Flick, M.D., Ship's Surgeon, S.S. Constitution off Hawaii*

DOCTORS

ADVERTISING

265... **THE RETAIL MARKETING RULE**   You should figure it will take three months for an effective retail marketing campaign to take hold.   *Scott Parker, data specialist, Beaumont, Texas*

BUSINESS

266... **SELLING A BUSINESS**   A manufacturing company will sell for 1.5 to 2.5 times its net income, including equipment, plus inventory.   *Terri Thompson, New York, New York*

GAMBLING

267... **PICKING A WINNER AT THE HARNESS TRACK**   You should bet on a horse with good early speed; the winning horse is usually among the first four horses at the half-mile.   *Don Valliere, track manager and author, Fort Erie, Ontario*

HOUSE AND HOME

268... **DECORATING YOUR HOME**   In interior decorating, a fashion cycle lasts from 7 to 15 years.   *Linnea Lannon, reporter, Detroit Free Press, Michigan*

EXERCISE

269... **EXERCISING IN THE HEAT**   When exercising in the heat, drop your performance expectations by about 2 percent for every 10 degrees above 55 degrees F. The same 2 percent adjustment works for every 1,000 feet above 5,000 feet altitude.   *Ned Frederick, writer, Exeter, New Hampshire*

CATTLE

270... **BUTCHERING BEEF**   You are doing O.K. if you get half a beef cow's live weight in usable meat.   *Ken Leach, meat cutter*

PRECIPITATION

271... **FORECASTING THE WEATHER**   If birds are taking dirt baths, it's going to rain.   *Annie Hunger, grandmother*

EXPLORATION

272... **TRAVELING IN THE WILDERNESS**   For best speed in unmarked wilderness, always aim for the heaviest timber.   *Peggy Kerber, editor, Mountaineering*

AUTOMOBILES

273... **CHECKING YOUR SHOCKS**   To check your shock absorbers, bounce your car up and down with your foot. If the car keeps on bouncing after you stop, you need new shocks.   *Tom Robinson, computer programmer, Berkeley, California*

BOATS

274... **THE ECKSTROM RULE OF SHIP COLLISIONS**   To avoid being run down by other ships on the ocean, check the horizon every 15 minutes. A fast ship can get dangerously close within 15 minutes.   *Rick Eckstrom, plan review officer, Ithaca, New York*

BIRDS

275... **IMPORTING PARROTS**   Only 1 in 50 parrots taken from the wild survives to live in a private home.   *Scott Parker, data specialist, Beaumont, Texas*

ARCHITECTURE

276... **HEATING WITH PEOPLE**   According to my roommate in a Swiss boarding school, architects and engineers figure that, as far as heat is concerned, three people equal one radiator.   *Helen D. Haller, Ithaca, New York*

AS A RULE OF THUMB:
IF IT HAS TO DO
WITH ROMANCE, AND
YOU NEED TO TALK
ABOUT IT, YOU PROBABLY
SHOULDN'T DO IT.
ROBBIE ACETO, MUSICIAN

277 ... *TIMING A GARAGE SALE* Hold a garage sale the first weekend of the month because people who get paid monthly have more money to spend then. *Ann Kimbrough, Blaine, Tennessee*

ANTIQUES

278 ... *SETTING THE PRICE OF A BOOK* When setting the price of a nonfiction book, estimate the cost of producing the first printing (including royalties). Then set a tentative list price that will allow you to make a 20 percent pretax profit if the first printing sells. *Richard A. Balkin, Coda: Poets and Writers Newsletter*

BOOKS

279 ... *WEANING YOUR BABY* Wean your baby from breast-feeding when it gets its first tooth. *Anonymous*

CHILDREN

280 ... *SQUEEZING GRAPES* One ton of grapes makes 120 gallons of wine. *Peter Reimuller, Point Arena, California*

WINE

281 ... *PLANNING A PARTY* You need one toilet per keg of beer. *Steven M. Keisman, New York City high school resource coordinator*

ENTERTAINING

282 ... *ADJUSTING YOUR BICYCLE SEAT* Position the seat so that your legs must almost fully stretch out to reach the pedals. *Norman Brenner, Fleetwood, New York*

BICYCLES

283 ... *THE OFT FORGOTTEN RULE* A stitch in time saves nine. *V. G. Walkendifer, Churchton, Maryland*

JOKER

284 ... *GOING TO A LAUNDROMAT* Plan on spending 90 minutes at the laundromat. If you go on a weekend after 8 a.m., or on a weekday after 5:30 p.m., add 15 minutes per load to your time estimate. *Joe Rappaport, straphangers campaign coordinator and long-time laundromat user*

CLOTHING

285 ... *THE REPAIR RULE* If the cost of repairing an item is more than half the price of a new one, buy a new one. *Dennis Palaganas, Gainesville, Florida*

APPLIANCES

286 ... *WINNING CHESS* To win an endgame, you need at least one extra pawn. Without pawns, you need at least one extra rook or its equivalent. *Norman Brenner, Fleetwood, New York*

CHESS

287 ... *PREDICTING INTELLIGENCE* The heavier the brain compared to the weight of the spinal cord, the more intelligent the animal. *Liz Stone, SUNY College of Environmental Science & Forestry, Syracuse, New York*

BODY RULES

288 ... *KEEPING UP WITH MEDICAL SCIENCE* The half-life of knowledge in medical school is four years. Fifty percent of what you learn as a freshman is obsolete when you graduate. *Dr. Lawrence Senterfit, microbiologist, Cornell Medical School*

DOCTORS

ADVERTISING

BUSINESS

GAMBLING

HOUSE AND HOME

EXERCISE

CATTLE

PRECIPITATION

EXPLORATION

AUTOMOBILES

BOATS

BIRDS

ARCHITECTURE

289...**PLACING AN AD IN A MAGAZINE**   The first right-hand page and the back cover are usually the best places for advertisements. These are followed by the other cover positions and the front section of the magazine.   *Jim Kobs, Kobs and Brady Advertising, Chicago, Illinois.*

290...**SELLING A BUSINESS**   A newspaper will sell for 0.75 to 1.25 times its gross income, including equipment.   *Terri Thompson, New York, New York*

291...**PICKING A WINNER AT THE HARNESS TRACK**   It's usually safe to bet on a horse that has just been assigned a leading full-time driver. The trainer probably believes the horse is ready to win.   *Don Valliere, track manager and author, Fort Erie, Ontario*

292...**MOVING TO A NEW PLACE**   The urge to fix up a house you've just moved into is strongest during the first 30 days. To save money, wait for a month before you do any repairs.   *John H. Beauvais, Cambridge, Massachusetts*

293...**COMPARING SWIMMING TO RUNNING TO CYCLING**   Swimming 1 mile is equivalent to running 5 miles or cycling 12 miles.   *Ned Frederick, writer, Exeter, New Hampshire*

294...**FEEDING LIVESTOCK**   Two heifers eat as much as one cow; one cow eats as much as seven sheep.   *Monica Crispin, Cooperative Extension agent*

295...**FORECASTING THE WEATHER**   If a crescent moon is tipped so that water could not run out of it, it won't rain.   *Bob, Davenport, Iowa*

296...**PACKING WITH HORSES**   You need at least three variations of each meal for pack trips lasting more than a week. Anything less gets monotonous.   *Francis Davis Long Eddy, packer*

297...**COOLING YOUR CAR**   A car's air conditioner should produce air that is 28 to 30 degrees below the outside temperature.   *Scott Parker, data specialist, Beaumont, Texas*

298...**MAKING TIME IN A KAYAK**   In moderate whitewater, expect to average about four to five miles per hour if you paddle straight down river and don't stop to play.   *Martha Betcher, medical technician, Incline Village, Nevada*

299...**HOUSING PIGEONS**   The inside of a pigeon loft should be low enough so that a pigeon can't fly over your head and small enough so that you can touch all four walls while standing in the middle.   *Dr. Herbert R. Axelrod, retired pigeon racer*

300...**GIVING OFF HEAT**   People normally produce about 500 BTUs per hour. People who are exercising produce three or four times that much heat.   *Brenda Poole, biologist*

AS A RULE OF THUMB:
IF A WORD IS MISSPELLED MORE THAN ONCE, READERS WILL NO LONGER ASSUME IT IS A TYPOGRAPHICAL ERROR.
RONALD ARTURI, TEACHER, SANTA BARBARA, CALIFORNIA.

301... **CLEANING ANTIQUE WEAPONS**   Anything a novice does to improve the looks of an antique weapon probably will lower its value or destroy it as a collector's piece. *Jim Barber, historian and collector, Springfield, Missouri*

ANTIQUES

302... **CATALOGING A LIBRARY**   For a single subject library, a medical library for example, use the Library of Congress cataloging system. For a general interest library, use the Dewey Decimal System. *Denis Smith, high school counselor, Camarillo, California*

BOOKS

303... **CARING FOR CHILDREN**   The more children cry, the less they urinate. *Anonymous*

304... **DRINKING WINE**   Wine before meals increases hunger. Wine during a meal quells the appetite. Wine at the end of a meal can drown the desire for dessert. *Maria Simonson, Johns Hopkins Medical Institutions, Baltimore, Maryland*

CHILDREN

WINE

305... **KNOWING WHEN YOU'RE BUSY**   When you're booked ten days of the month, you're booked solid. *D. J., WPCX-106*

306... **BUYING A BICYCLE**   An imported bicycle is always a better value than the comparable bicyclc made in the United States. *Steven M. Keisman, New York City high school resource coordinator*

ENTERTAINING

307... **ESTIMATING THE LIFE OF A LIGHT BULB**   If you increase the voltage of an incandescent light bulb by 10 percent, its light output increases by 40 percent, but its life expectancy falls by a factor of three. Decreasing the voltage has the opposite effect. *R.A. Heindl, design engineer, Euclid, Ohio*

BICYCLES

308... **SEWING WITH PIGS**   It takes two pigs to make a pair of pigskin pants. *Mary Ellen Parker, retired teacher, Cincinnati, Ohio*

ELECTRICITY

309... **USING A MICROWAVE**   To determine whether cookware can be used in a microwave, put it in the microwave empty and turn on the high setting for 15 seconds. If the cookware is cool to the touch, it's safe to use in the microwave. *Dean Sheridan, electronics technician and deaf actor, Torrance, California*

CLOTHING

310... **WINNING CHESS**   There are three principles for winning a chess game. The Principle of Force—the player who is ahead in pieces should win. The Principle of Mobility—the player who has more room for moving his pieces has an advantage. The Principle of Safety—the safety of the king is most important. *Walter Pitkin, literary agent, Weston, Connecticut*

APPLIANCES

311... **ESTIMATING YOUR RING SIZE**   At least for men, ring size equals glove size equals shoe size. *R. L. Liming, Indianapolis, Indiana*

CHESS

312... **WAITING FOR A DOCTOR**   To be safe, plan on sitting around for at least half an hour on any visit to a doctor or dentist. You can save yourself time by taking the first appointment of the day or the first appointment after lunch. *Peter F. Ayer, professor of music, West Bend, Wisconsin*

BODY RULES

DOCTORS

ADVERTISING

BUSINESS

GAMBLING

HOUSE AND HOME

EXERCISE

CATTLE

PRECIPITATION

EXPLORATION

AUTOMOBILES

BOATS

BIRDS

ARCHITECTURE

313...**SPONSORING LARGE SPORTS EVENTS**   There aren't any precise studies showing what sponsorship is worth, but the rule of thumb is that putting $1,000 behind a sports event will generate the same exposure as $10,000 in advertising. *The Wall Street Journal*

314...**SELLING A BUSINESS**   A restaurant will sell for 0.25 to 0.5 times its gross income. *Terri Thompson, New York, New York*

315...**PLAYING POKER**   It is time to quit playing poker when you get so sleepy that you can't remember your hole card and you have to keep checking it. *Bill Spivey, San Francisco, California*

316...**BUYING A HOUSE**   You can afford to buy house that costs twice your annual income. *Blayne Cutler, editor, American Demographics*

317...**PREDICTING YOUR COLLAPSE POINT**   Your collapse point is about three times the average distance you swim, cycle, or run each day. For example, if you run an average of three miles a day, you should be able to run nine miles without stopping.   *Ned Frederick, writer, quoting statistician Ken Young, Exeter, New Hampshire*

318...**MAKING MILK**   A cow needs about three pounds of water to make a pound a pound of milk. *Monica Crispin, Cooperative Extension agent*

319...**FORECASTING RAIN**   If the temperature rises rapidly while it's raining, it will rain harder soon. *Walter Pitkin, literary agent, Weston, Connecticut*

320...**SQUEEZING THROUGH A HOLE**   If a spelunker can get his head through a tight spot, the rest of his body will go through, too. However, this assumes that the passage is at least a yard wide and is really tight for eight inches or less. *David R. McClurg, speleologist*

321...**THE LAMPE RED CAR RULE**   You'll get more money at resale time if you buy a red car. *Paul Lampe, writer and poet, St. Louis, Missouri*

322...**LEANING A KAYAK**   In a kayak, when in doubt, lean downstream. *Martha Betcher, medical technician, Incline Village, Nevada*

323...**SHOOTING AT DUCKS**   It is usually safe to assume that if you are missing shots at crossing birds you are shooting behind them. *Nelson Bryant, The New York Times*

324...**THE BODY HEAT RULE**   A resting human gives off as much heat as a 150-watt light bulb. You can use this fact to keep the temperature in a greenhouse constant, even as you come and go. Just turn the light out whenever you go in. *John Schubert, senior editor, Bicycling magazine*

ANTIQUES

325 ... **TESTING YOUR SCRIMSHAW**   Test your scrimshaw by touching the surface of the tooth with a red hot needle. If it smokes, it's plastic. If it doesn't smoke, make sure the tooth is hollow from the base to the tip; fake scrimshaw is hollow only partway up.   *Susan J. Macovsky, writer, Money magazine*

BOOKS

326 ... **STOCKING A BOOKSTORE**   A bookstore needs to stock a minimum of 10,000 books to have any hope of having what people ask for.   *Dave Ewan, Wind Chimes Book Exchange, Millville, New Jersey*

CHILDREN

327 ... **THE HAIR RULE**   Thick hair and thick skulls go together.   *Anonymous*

WINE

328 ... **MAKING WINE FROM GRAPES**   One ton of grapes will make 170 gallons of wine.   *L. Wagner, vintner*

329 ... **THE PARTY RULE FOR KIDS**   Have a party on even numbered years.   *Suzanne Leddy, director, Purdue Child Care Program, Lafayette, Indiana*

ENTERTAINING

330 ... **CRASHING AN AIRPLANE**   Three acts of poor judgment equal one airplane accident.   *Jim Corcy, airport administrator*

JOKER

331 ... **ESTIMATING THE COST OF ELECTRICAL WORK**   To increase your electrical service entrance capacity, figure on $5 per amp.   *Greg from Cincinnati Gas & Electric*

ELECTRICITY

332 ... **BUYING CLOTHES**   If you have to convince yourself that you want a particular article of clothing, don't buy it — you'll be adding another dust collector to your closet.   *Andrea Frankel, computer scientist, engineer, holistic health practitioner, San Diego, California*

CLOTHING

333 ... **ESTIMATING THE LIFE OF AN APPLIANCE**   Dehumidifiers have the longest life expectancy of any home appliance, about 15 years. Humidifiers have the shortest life expectancy, just half that of dehumidifiers. Humidifiers burn out because they often are left running after the water has evaporated.   *Steven M. Keisman, New York City high school resource coordinator*

APPLIANCES

334 ... **WINNING CHESS**   Your primary goal is to be equally proficient in the opening, the middle-game, and the endgame.   *Stephen Unsino, poet, Eastchester, New York*

CHESS

335 ... **MEASURING AN INFANT**   The circumference of a normal infant's head should equal the distance from the crown of the head to the rump.   *Thomas O. Marsh, writer and coroner's investigator, Fairfield, Ohio*

BODY RULES

336 ... **GOING INTO DERMATOLOGY**   You need one dermatologist for every 40,000 people.   *Dr. Robert Horn, dermatologist*

DOCTORS

AS A RULE OF THUMB:
A BOXER SHOULD STAB, JAB, MOVE, AND KEEP HIS FANNY OFF THE FLOOR.
CHARLIE ROSS, DIRECTOR, VETERAN BOXERS ASSOCIATION, SO. BOSTON, MASSACHUSETTS

ADVERTISING

337 ... *WRITING AN AD* When writing an ad, use sentences of less than 12 words. *David Ogilvy, advertising expert, The Ogilvy and Mather Agency*

BUSINESS

338 ... *SELLING A BUSINESS* A retail business will sell for 0.75 to 1.5 times its net, plus equipment and inventory. *Terri Thompson, New York, New York*

GAMBLING

339 ... *CHOOSING YOUR GAME* Never make a bet when the house advantage is more than 1.5 percent. In U.S. casinos, this means you can play blackjack, baccarat, and craps, but nothing else. *Marvin Karlins, Ph.D, author and gambling authority, Psyching Out Vegas*

HOUSE AND HOME

340 ... *CARPETING A FLOOR* You need 10 percent less pad than carpet. *Anonymous carpet layer, Decatur, Georgia*

EXERCISE

341 ... *RESTING AFTER EXERCISE* Allow 24 hours of recovery for every hour of highly stressful workout. *Ned Frederick, writer, Exeter, New Hampshire*

CATTLE

342 ... *THE PFAFF RULE OF DAIRY WATER* A dairy operation uses a lot of water. You should plan on using 50 gallons of water per day for every cow in your herd. *Gary Pfaff, dairy farmer*

PRECIPITATION

343 ... *FORECASTING THE WEATHER* A southeast wind brings rain. *Joseph Liberkowski, ex-ocean lifeguard, Medford Lakes, New Jersey*

344 ... *THE CROOKED RIVER RULE* Under normal conditions, the distance that a river will run straight is never greater than ten times its width. *Doug Knowles, guitar maker*

EXPLORATION

345 ... *KEEPING A CAR* For every dollar of gas you put into your car each year, you'll need to put in a dollar's worth of repair or maintenance. *Rev. Dan Orine, Athens, Georgia*

AUTOMOBILES

346 ... *FINDING DEEP WATER* To find the deepest water in a river, look for the middle of the inverted V of glossy water where the main current flows. At a bend in a river, the water's deepest on the outside of the turn. *Martha Betcher, medical technician, Incline Village, Nevada*

BOATS

347 ... *SHOOTING AT DUCKS* For every 1,000 ducks shot at with lead shot, 155 will be bagged and 46 wounded. For every 1,000 shot at with steel shot, 114 will be bagged and 51 wounded. At ranges greater than 35 yards, lead shot cripples more ducks than steel shot. *Jack Mosher, wildlife biologist, South Berne, New York, in The New York State Conservationist*

BIRDS

348 ... *SETTING UP AN OFFICE* Provide 250 square feet of floor space for each vice president, 200 for middle managers and 175 for clerks. *Underhill T. Powell, architect*

ARCHITECTURE

AS A RULE OF THUMB: AT AGE 43 YOU CAN STILL SEE HOW A MAN LOOKED AS AN ADOLESCENT, YET YOU CAN ALSO SEE — FOR THE FIRST TIME — HOW HE'LL LOOK AS AN OLD MAN. ROBERT KANIGEL, WRITER AND EDITOR, BALTIMORE, MARYLAND

349 ... FIXING UP OLD CARS As a rule, the average old-car enthusiast can fix up a car to rate about 75 on a scale of 100 points for perfection. Restoring a car as an investment is another matter. A high-dollar car needs to rate a 99 or 100. *LeRoi Smith, writer and car builder*

ANTIQUES

350 ... SELLING BOOKS Ten percent of bookstore customers buy 90 percent of the books. Ten percent never buy anything. *Dave Ewan, Wind Chimes Book Exchange, Millville, New Jersey*

BOOKS

351 ... RAISING CHILDREN Start to teach children right from wrong when they first put a comb to their hair. *Anonymous*

CHILDREN

352 ... SERVING WINE Red wines should "breathe" two minutes for every year between the vintage and the present date. *Janet Blumer, math grad student, Denver, Colorado*

WINE

353 ... PLANNING A PARTY FOR CHILDREN Plan on one hour of party for every three years of age. *Anonymous*

ENTERTAINING

354 ... ESTIMATING ATMOSPHERIC PRESSURE For every 18,000 feet (or 3 1/2 miles) in elevation, atmospheric pressure falls by half. *Ernst Luposchainsky, III ("Kahn"), collector of obscure technical data, inter alia, Hollywood, California*

FLYING

355 ... TAPING WIRES It takes four layers of electrical tape to waterproof an electrical connection properly. *Dennis Pollack, builder, Danby, New York*

ELECTRICITY

356 ... THE TIE COLLECTION RULE A 3 1/2" wide tie will never go out of style. *John Green, Ann Arbor, Michigan*

CLOTHING

357 ... THE UNIVERSAL RULE OF TOAST Toast it until it smokes, and then 20 seconds less. *Paul Goldschmidt, disc jockey, Johnson City, New York*

JOKER

358 ... UNSINO'S SALIENT POSITION RULE In chess, a piece in a salient position should be defended more often than it is attacked. *Stephen Unsino, poet, Eastchester, New York*

CHESS

359 ... DROPSHO'S OFT SUBMITTED RULE OF TWICE Twice around the thumb is once around the wrist; twice around the wrist is once around the neck; twice around the neck is once around the waist. *D. Dropsho, Madison, Wisconsin and countless others*

BODY RULES

360 ... SETTING OBSTETRICS FEES To set your fee for obstetric care, start with the local fee for embalming — about $500 to $800. Two or three times that amount is appropriate for the care of a pregnant woman and the delivery of a baby. *A professor of obstetrics and gynecology, quoted in OBGYN News*

DOCTORS

ADVERTISING

361 ... DESIGNING A BILLBOARD   People are exposed to outdoor advertisements for only a few seconds. A good billboard should have no more than seven words and two things to look at. *Glen Lane, Massillon, Ohio*

BUSINESS

362 ... SELLING A BUSINESS   A travel agency will sell for 0.04 to 0.1 times its gross income. *Terri Thompson, New York, New York*

GAMBLING

363 ... THE KARLINS RULE OF GAMBLING PARTNERS   You will almost always gamble better if you gamble alone. *Marvin Karlins, Ph.D, author and gambling authority, Psyching Out Vegas*

HOUSE AND HOME

364 ... PAINTING A ROOM   It takes as much time to paint the trim in a room as it does to paint the walls and ceiling. *R. A. Heindl, design engineer, Euclid, Ohio*

EXERCISE

365 ... PLANNING YOUR TRAINING   Never increase your training by more than 10 percent a week. Increases of 10 to 15 percent every three weeks make more sense. *Ned Frederick, writer, Exeter, New Hampshire*

CATTLE

366 ... THE DAIRY RULE   A dairy farm needs about three acres of land per cow for buildings, crops, and pasture. *William Menzi, Cooperative Extension agent*

PRECIPITATION

367 ... FORECASTING THE WEATHER   If the children are wild, it's going to rain or snow within 24 hours. This is a better barometer than the weather man. *Alice Chadwick, teacher, Bronx, New York*

JOKER

368 ... THE CAMPING TRIP CONDOMS RULE   My daddy told me to always take condoms on camping trips. They are great for protecting wrist watches, safeguarding money and other things. One time he didn't. *Denis Smith, high school counselor, Camarillo, California*

AUTOMOBILES

369 ... BREATHING THROUGH YOUR HEATER COIL   Check your car's heater coil for obstructions after you backflush it. If you can blow through it as easily as you can breathe, it's free of debris. *Steve Overback, radio announcer*

BOATS

370 ... THE BOAT PLANKING SCARF JOINT RULE OF 12   Two pieces of wood can be attached end to end by tapering each piece and overlapping the tapers. The splice that is formed is called a scarf joint. For planking a boat, the length of the tapers should be 12 times the thickness of the boards being joined. *Larry Beck, joiner, Ludlowville, New York*

BIRDS

371 ... SETTING UP A CHICKEN COOP   Provide at least three square feet of floor space for each chicken. *Terry Hayward, medical technician*

JOKER

372 ... SCULPTING WITH PAPER   You can sculpt a full-size likeness of two five-year-old kids from one copy of the Sunday New York Times, if you save the Book Review for yourself. *David Finn, printmaker, New York City*

373 ... SELLING ANTIQUES   As a rule, people don't buy antiques at Christmas time. *Dean Miller, antique dealer*

ANTIQUES

374 ... LIGHTING A BOOKSTORE   One continuous strip of fluorescent tube eight feet high above the center of the aisle is enough light for a bookstore. *Dave Ewan, Wind Chimes Book Exchange, Millville, New Jersey*

BOOKS

375 ... RAISING CHILDREN   Never fill a child's glass more than half full. *L. Musselman, office manager and mother of young children*

CHILDREN

376 ... OPENING WINE   When deciding when to open a bottle of wine, remember most wine is as good when it's a year old as it will ever be and will go downhill after its third birthday. *The Joy of Cooking*

WINE

377 ... PLANNING A PARTY FOR CHILDREN   A child's birthday party is just like a play. There's a beginning and an end, and every minute is accounted for. *Meredith Brokaw, author*

ENTERTAINING

378 ... BUYING A USED JETLINER   Never expect to pay less for a used jet than it cost new. *Walter Pitkin, literary agent, Weston, Connecticut*

FLYING

379 ... WORKING WITH ELECTRICAL ENGINEERS   The finished product will usually draw 50 percent more power than the electrical engineer estimated when he or she designed the circuit. *Michael D. Miles, Aloha, Oregon*

ELECTRICITY

380 ... DEALING WITH LAUNDRY   An average adult will generate one load of laundry per week. Athletes, children, and people who work outside will generate twice that much. *Gail Smith, parts unknown*

CLOTHING

381 ... MAKING DECISIONS   If you're trying to make a decision, say to yourself, "I will choose ____." Note whether you feel a pang of regret. Then try the other option by saying, "I will choose ____." Again, take note of your feelings. This allows you to weigh your feelings rather than your choices. *Carolyn Lloyd, 15-year-old student, Montreal, Quebec*

EMOTIONS

382 ... SPOTTING AN INSIDE JOB   All large-scale crimes are inside jobs. *Slim Pickens, in Rancho Deluxe*

JOKER

383 ... MIKE'S TEST FOR SILICONE   A woman has had silicone implants in her breasts if her nipples turn down. *Mike Garside, corrections officer, Ithaca, New York*

BODY RULES

384 ... THE PHYSICAL THERAPY RULE   If a physical therapist offers you a hot pack, he's running behind schedule. *Richard Farnham, physical therapist, Ithaca, New York*

DOCTORS

AS A RULE OF THUMB:
IF APPLYING PRESSURE WITH YOUR FINGERS CAUSES A CHANGE IN A CHEST PAIN, IT IS PROBABLY A MUSCULAR PAIN.
MARILYN RIDER, BODY & SOUL, ITHACA, NEW YORK

ADVERTISING

BUSINESS

GAMBLING

HOUSE AND HOME

EXERCISE

CATTLE

PRECIPITATION

HIKING

AUTOMOBILES

BOATS

BIRDS

ART

385 ... **MAGAZINE ADVERTISEMENTS**   The average woman reads four ads in an average issue of an average magazine. *David Ogilvy, advertising expert, The Ogilvy and Mather Agency*

386 ... **RUNNING AN AMUSEMENT PARK**   It takes an investment in new attractions of $5 million to $15 million to increase attendance 10 to 20 percent. *Michael Demetria, president, Marine World-Africa USA, Vallejo, California*

387 ... **KNOWING WHEN TO QUIT GAMBLING**   End any gambling session after winning half of your session's stake. If you start a session with $2,000, quit when you reach $3,000. You may ride out a hot streak; but as soon as you lose one bet, it's time to quit, convert your profits to traveler's checks, and mail them home. *Marvin Karlins, Ph.D, author and gambling authority, Psyching Out Vegas*

388 ... **PERUSING YOUR ROOF**   The more bends, gables, and troughs in your roof, the more likely it will leak.   *Russell T. Johnson, Temple City, California*

389 ... **THE FREDERICK RULES OF THREE**   You have to exercise at least three times a week. If you leave more than three days between exercise sessions, gains will be cancelled out; and three weeks is about how long it takes your body to adjust to a new level of exercise. *Ned Frederick, writer, Exeter, New Hampshire*

390 ... **RUNNING A DAIRY**   A good Holstein cow should produce about 5 gallons of milk a day for 305 days a year. *Carol Gallagher, Lexington, Kentucky*

391 ... **FORECASTING THE WEATHER**   When seagulls fly in imperfect circles, with several turns going in opposite directions, it will rain within 72 hours. *L. Geer, San Diego, California*

392 ... **ESTIMATING WALKING SPEED**   With a 3-foot stride, count the number of steps you take in 2 minutes and divide it by 30. That will give you the speed you're walking in miles per hour. *James V. Vaughter, Carmichael, California*

393 ... **WARMING UP YOUR CAR**   The time it takes to clean off the windshield is the time it takes to warm up your engine. *Rob Shapiro, flight instructor, Ithaca, New York*

394 ... **DROPPING ANCHOR**   Under normal conditions use 7 feet of anchor line for each foot of water. If the water is 10 feet deep, you'll need 70 feet of anchor line. *Peter Kim, San Diego, California*

395 ... **WATCHING BIRDS**   Among birds of prey, females are about one-third larger than males. *Scott Parker, data specialist, Beaumont, Texas*

396 ... **FRAGA'S RULE OF JUDGING MODERN ART**   If you like it, it's probably good. *Mack Fraga, Alameda, California*

As A RULE OF THUMB:
YOU SHOULD CHECK
THE CORNERS TO CHECK
THE JOB. AND THAT APPLIES
TO ANY KIND OF JOB.
W.G. MOSS, JR., USN (RET.),
LAKE ZURICH, ILLINOIS

397 ... SELLING COLLECTIBLES   To cover costs and show a profit, try to triple your money on things that sell for less than $5 and double your money on things that sell for more than $5. *Sam Gaben, Indianapolis, Indiana*

398 ... STOCKING A BOOKSTORE   If you stock six of any bookstore item, you'll sell three in one week, two more in one month, and still have the last one when you retire. *Dave Ewan, Wind Chimes Book Exchange, Millville, New Jersey*

399 ... FEEDING CHILDREN   Finicky eaters will eat only half the amount of food they ask for. *L. Musselman, office manager and mother of young children*

400 ... THE WINE BOTTLE RULE   There are six glasses of wine in a bottle. *Tom Werner, Athens, Georgia*

401 ... PLANNING A PARTY FOR CHILDREN   One adult for every five children under age five. One adult for every eight older children. *Meredith Brokaw, author*

402 ... FLYING AN AIRPLANE   Start your descent three miles from your destination for every thousand feet of altitude. Subtract ten miles if you're flying in a headwind. Add ten miles if you're in a tailwind. *P. Douglas Combs, professional airline pilot, aviator & aircraft mechanic, flight instructor, Tempe, Arizona*

403 ... AVOIDING LIGHTNING   During a lightning storm, if the hair on your arms and head starts to stand on end, lightning is going to strike in your immediate vicinity. Drop to your knees and bend forward, putting your hands on your knees. Don't place your hands on the ground, or you will be vulnerable to ground current if a lightning bolt hits within 50 yards. *Scott Parker, Beaumont, Texas, quoting the National Fire Protection Association*

404 ... THROWING OUT CLOTHING   Sometimes when cleaning out your closet you'll come across a garment that you don't wear because nothing goes with it. If you aren't ready to spend any money to make the item work for you, you probably are ready to give it to Goodwill. *Dalma Heyn, McCall's*

405 ... THE FEET AND FEELINGS RULE   If your feet have very high arches, you're likely to be thin and tense. *Steven M. Keisman, New York City high school resource coordinator*

406 ... MAKING YOUR HOME SECURE   Making your home appear to be occupied when it isn't can be more effective in preventing burglary than $1,000 invested in special security equipment. *Walter Pitkin, literary agent, Weston, Connecticut*

407 ... DRINKING MILK   According to the Masai, one should be able to consume a gourd of milk the size of one's thigh at a single sitting. *Anonymous quoting W. Phillip Keller*

408 ... ESTIMATING THE COST OF A DOCTOR VISIT   The fee for a routine office visit is the same price as a first-class postage stamp multiplied by 100. *Gerry M. Flick, M.D., Ship's Surgeon, S.S. Constitution off Hawaii*

ADVERTISING

409 ... **WRITING ADVERTISEMENTS**   A good ad will have at least 14 references to people for every 100 words of copy. *David Ogilvy, advertising expert, The Ogilvy and Mather Agency*

BUSINESS

410 ... **MAKING YOUR IDEAS CLEAR**   A clear idea is one that fits on the back of a business card. *Morris Cooper, St. Johns, Michigan*

GAMBLING

411 ... **BETTING ON A BALL GAME**   Bet on any pitcher who starts on his birthday. Bet on any starter who is pitching on the road but happens to be in his own home town. *George Ignatin, professor of economics, University of Alabama*

HOUSE AND HOME

412 ... **PAINTING A ROOM**   Allow at least half a day to prepare and paint the walls and ceiling of a 9-by-12 foot room with a latex fast dry primer and a finish coat of paint. *John Towle, Salinas, California*

EXERCISE

413 ... **CARRYING EXTRA WEIGHT**   Carrying a one-pound weight in each hand while walking boosts your energy expenditure by about 1 percent. Carrying the same weights on your feet boosts your energy expenditure by 2 percent. *Ned Frederick, writer, Exeter, New Hampshire*

CATTLE

414 ... **FEEDING A COW**   One dairy cow eats one acre's worth of corn silage per year. *Monica Crispin, Cooperative Extension agent*

PRECIPITATION

415 ... **THE DUTCH RULE FOR RAIN**   If the birds are out in the rain, the rain will continue for the rest of the day. *Dirck Z. Meengs, management consultant, Canoga Park, California*

HIKING

416 ... **BUYING A TENT**   Figure on 18 square feet of surface area for each adult camper. *Alan R. Reno, Watertown, New York*

AUTOMOBILES

417 ... **CHOOSING A CAR COLOR**   When buying a new car, choose a color that matches the ads for your particular model. That's the color most likely to grab a used-car buyer's eye as well. *Rich and Jean Taylor Constantine, Parade magazine*

BOATS

418 ... **SAILING A CANOE**   On an extended voyage along the coast of Alaska and British Columbia, three-quarters of your time will be spent paddling, but half your distance will be covered in the one-quarter of the time spent under sail. *George B. Dyson, boatbuilder, British Columbia, Canada*

BIRDS

419 ... **FLYING FALCONS**   When approaching your bird to take her hawking, she's ready to fly if she flies toward you. If she flies away from you, don't take her hunting that day. *Jack Barclay, biologist, pilot, flight instructor, Santa Cruz, California*

ART

420 ... **VISUAL COMMUNICATION**   Only 25 percent of people are good at coming up with visual images. *Dr. Barbara Brown, author*

As a rule of thumb: IF YOU HAVE THE ADVANTAGE, YOUR OPPONENT IS MORE LIKELY TO GIVE UP AFTER YOU MAKE A DEFENSIVE MOVE RATHER THAN AFTER YOU MAKE AN OFFENSIVE MOVE. STEPHEN UNSINO, POET, EASTCHESTER, NEW YORK

421 ... SHOPPING AT GARAGE SALES   Garage sales are good places to shop. As a rule, half the things for sale are underpriced. However, keep in mind that a quarter of the things for sale will be overpriced. *George Perfect, antique dealer*

ANTIQUES

422 ... LOOKING AT BOOKS IN BOULDER   In any batch of fiction books, there will be more books by authors whose last names begin with "M" than any other letter. "S" will be second. *Ellen Klaver, musician, Boulder, Colorado*

BOOKS

423 ... GETTING YOUNG CHILDREN TO EAT   When feeding young children, put only one item on their plate at a time. Give them more than that and they will have to make a choice. Nothing will get eaten. *L. Musselman, office manager and mother of young children*

CHILDREN

424 ... CELLARING WINE   When cellaring a wine, add about 1 year of aging time for every 2 degrees the cellar averages below 65 degrees Fahrenheit. *Craig Goldwyn, publisher, International Wine Review*

WINE

425 ... PLANNING A PARTY   The worst parties are those with the most carefully chosen mix of guests. *Russell T. Johnson, Temple City, California*

ENTERTAINING

426 ... FLYING AN AIRPLANE   The maximum horsepower for reciprocating aircraft engines is approximately half of the cubic-inch displacement. *P. Douglas Combs, professional airline pilot, aviator & aircraft mechanic, flight instructor, Tempe, Arizona*

FLYING

427 ... DESIGNING AN ELECTRIC MOTOR   The higher the frequency, the smaller the size of the motor. A motor designed to run on 400Hz alternating current is about one-fourth the size of a motor designed for 60 Hz. *Scott Parker, data specialist, Beaumont, Texas*

ELECTRICITY

428 ... THE BUTTON MEASURE OF IQ   Intelligence can be measured by the number of buttons fastened on a person's shirt. The more buttons fastened, the higher the IQ. *Curtis Cloaninger, agriculture teacher, Asheville, North Carolina*

CLOTHING

429 ... THE HAPPINESS RULE   People who can't kill time are unhappy with themselves. *Dean Sheridan, electronics technician and deaf actor, Torrance, California*

EMOTIONS

430 ... CHECKING YOUR DOORS FOR SECURITY   A door is as strong as its lock, its frame, or its hinges — whichever is weakest. *Walter Pitkin, literary agent, Weston, Connecticut*

CRIME

431 ... WEIGHING YOUR SKIN   To estimate the weight of your skin, divide your weight by 16. *Scott M. Kruse, biogeographer, Fresno, California*

BODY RULES

432 ... MAKING ETHANOL   One ton of corn will make about 50 gallons of ethanol. *Bob Horton, consultant and writer, Largo, Florida*

FUEL

ADVERTISING

433 ... _DESIGNING ADVERTISEMENTS_   Five times as many people read the headline as read the rest of an ad. *David Ogilvy, advertising expert, The Ogilvy and Mather Agency*

BUSINESS

434 ... _BUYING BUSINESS EQUIPMENT_   To get turn-key quality business equipment instead of a do-it-yourself job, count on paying 14 percent more. *Steven Kropper, telecommunications consultant, Watertown, Massachusetts*

GAMBLING

435 ... _DECIDING WHEN TO BLUFF_   There are three factors involved in successful bluffing. (1) Your opponent: It is easier to bluff a strong player than a weak one. (2) Your position in the game: It is easier to bluff a big loser than a big winner. (3) Money: The bigger the stakes, the easier it is to bluff. Don't bluff unless you have at least two of these factors on your side. *Edwin Silberstang, games expert*

HOUSE AND HOME

436 ... _LUNCHING WITH YOUR HELP_   You have to have lunch with your cleaning lady once a month in order to keep her caring about your possessions. *Laura H. Holmberg, attorney, Ithaca, New York*

EXERCISE

437 ... _FALLING OUT OF SHAPE_   It takes twice as long to fall out of shape as it took to get into shape. *Ned Frederick, writer, Exeter, New Hampshire*

CATTLE

438 ... _DAHL'S RULE OF MONEY MAKING COWS_   A cow starts milking when it is two years old. It won't start making you any money until its second lactation, when it is three and a half years old. *Chris Dahl, dairy farmer*

PRECIPITATION

439 ... _PREDICTING RAIN_   If three pregnant women in a row check into the hospital with ruptured membranes, but not in labor, it is going to rain within 24 hours. *Elizabeth Kasehagen, R.N., delivery room head nurse, Santa Barbara, California*

HIKING

440 ... _THE RENO SLANTED TENT DOOR RULE_   A tent with a slanted door means rain on the floor. *Alan R. Reno, Watertown, New York*

AUTOMOBILES

441 ... _BUYING A NEW CAR_   The best time to but a new car is the last day of the month because the sales staff want their monthly reports to look good and are more likely to bargain. You can increase your chances of getting a good deal by choosing the youngest salesperson on the floor. *Scott Parker, data specialist, Beaumont, Texas*

BOATS

442 ... _CHOOSING A CANOE PADDLE_   To check a canoe paddle for size, stand it on the ground in front of you. The handle should come to the height of your chin if you plan to paddle from the bow of the canoe; it should come to the height of your eye if you plan to paddle from the stern. *Peter van Berkum, Kittery Point, Maine*

JOKER

443 ... _RAISING CHICKENS_   On average, one in ten chickens runs around with its head cut off. It depends on the heat of the blade. *Brad Edmondson, editor, American Demographics*

ART

444 ... _OLGA'S RULE OF SELF PORTRAITS_   An artist's self portrait is usually his best portrait. *Olga K. Pitkin, Northampton, Massachusetts*

AS A RULE OF THUMB:
YOU SHOULDN'T MOURN A
FAILED ROMANCE FOR
LONGER THAN IT LASTED.
DAVID GLUCK, CINEMATOGRAPHER,
PHOTOSYNTHESIS PRODUCTIONS,
ITHACA, NEW YORK

445...**ADAM PERL'S RULE**   Don't buy a piece of antique furniture if you can find three things wrong with it.   *Adam Perl, antique dealer*

ANTIQUES

446...**WRITING A BLURB**   It takes 4 times as long to write an effective book jacket blurb that is 5 words long as it does to write one 30 words long. But the shorter copy is 7 times better.   *Walter Pitkin, literary agent, Weston, Connecticut*

BOOKS

447...**THE SNOWSUIT RULE**   Up to age 6, double a child's age to determine the size.   *L. Musselman, office manager and mother of young children*

CHILDREN

448...**DROPPING A GLASS**   If a cafeteria glass bounces more than twice, it will break.   *Sharon K. Yntema, writer, Ithaca, New York*

JOKER

449...**PLANNING A CHEESE PLATE**   When planning a cheese plate for a party, figure one-half ounce of cheese per guest.   *Liz Biss, caterer, Ithaca, New York*

ENTERTAINING

450...**FINDING YOUR MINIMUM SINK SPEED**   The minimum sink speed for a forced landing is 130 percent of stall speed, gear up and flaps up.   *P. Douglas Combs, professional airline pilot, aviator & aircraft mechanic, flight instructor, Tempe, Arizona*

FLYING

451...**MAKING A SPARK**   A spark needs 25,000 volts for every inch of air it has to jump.   *Scott Parker, Beaumont, Texas, quoting Mr. Wizard*

ELECTRICITY

452...**CHOOSING FABRIC FOR CLOTHING**   Texture and sheen look bigger; smooth and dull look smaller. This is why most of us should never appear in public in tight pink satin jeans.   *Donna Salyers, The Cincinnati Enquirer*

CLOTHING

453...**PREDICTING YOUR MOOD**   If you had a good weekend, you'll feel bad on Monday.   *Glenn Kornblum, St. Louis, Missouri*

EMOTIONS

454...**THWARTING A BURGLAR**   The average burglar will spend only five or six minutes trying to break into a house. If you make your place look formidable, he'll go to your neighbor's instead.   *Walter Pitkin, literary agent, Weston, Connecticut*

CRIME

455...**GROWING FINGERNAILS**   The longer your fingers, the faster your nails grow.   *Scott Parker, data specialist, Beaumont, Texas*

BODY RULES

456...**SAVING MONEY ON GASOLINE**   If you need to get gas while driving on an interstate, look for exits with at least two gas stations. The competition will mean a lower price per gallon.   *Bob Horton, consultant and writer, Largo, Florida*

FUEL

ADVERTISING

457...AIMING YOUR ADVERTISEMENTS To attract women, show babies and women. To attract men, show men. *David Ogilvy, advertising expert, The Ogilvy and Mather Agency*

BUSINESS

458...GETTING WORK DONE People do best when they're working at 80 percent of their capacity. At 50 percent, they get bored. At 100 percent, stress gets them. *Anonymous*

GAMBLING

459...DECIDING WHEN TO BLUFF One or two bluffs per poker game are enough. Overindulgence can produce a bluffaholic. *Dale Armstrong, card player*

HOUSE AND HOME

460...CHOOSING A CHANDELIER The diagonal dimension of a chandelier in inches should equal the diagonal dimension of the dining room in feet. Also, the diameter of the chandelier should be at least 12 inches less than the diameter of the dining room table. *American Home Lighting Institute*

EXERCISE

461...INCREASING YOUR PERFORMANCE Every hour, up to ten hours, you add to your weekly training can increase your athletic performance by 5 percent. *Ned Frederick, writer, Exeter, New Hampshire*

CATTLE

462...RUNNING A DAIRY You need half a ton of hay per cow per month or six tons a year per cow. *Monica Crispin, Cooperative Extension agent*

PRECIPITATION

463...THE HASTINGS RULE OF HASTY RAIN When the rain or snow starts light and slow, it will last a long time; when it starts quick and is heavy, it won't last long. *Robert Hastings, Master Chief Petty Officer, United States Coast Guard*

HIKING

464...RESCUING LOST PEOPLE Half of all those who get lost and die in remote areas do so within 24 hours. *Gurney Williams III, author*

AUTOMOBILES

465...BUILDING A CAR Painting accounts for nearly half the cost of automobile assembly. *Scott Parker, data specialist, Beaumont, Texas*

BOATS

466...DESIGNING A SUBMARINE A submarine will move through the water most efficiently if it has a length-to-beam ratio of between 10 to 1 and 13 to 1. *Brent Wiggans, artist, computer scientist, and military buff*

ANIMALS

467...IDENTIFYING ELEPHANTS The African elephant has an ear shaped like Africa. The Indian elephant has an ear shaped like India. *Norman Brenner, Fleetwood, New York*

ART

468...HANGING A PICTURE Hang pictures no more than ten inches above your furniture. *Penny Russell, artist, Dilltown, Pennsylvania*

As A RULE OF THUMB:
IF YOU CAN SEE THE SLIGHTEST PART OF THE OPENING AT THE END OF SOMEONE ELSE'S GUN BARREL, THEY ARE NOT HANDLING THEIR GUN SAFELY. PETER F. AYER, PROFESSOR OF MUSIC, WEST BEND, WISCONSIN

469 ... SPOTTING A GOOD GARAGE SALE The brighter the colors, the worse the garage sale. *David T. Russell, retired high school teacher, Dilltown, Pennsylvania*

470 ... TALKING TO YOUR PUBLISHER If you ask a publisher if a new book is selling well, and she replies, "It's too soon to tell," — it isn't — and it isn't. *Walter Pitkin, literary agent, Weston, Connecticut*

471 ... HELPING CHILDREN CLIMB Don't help children climb. Left to themselves, they will climb only as high as they can manage. Even so, be ready to catch them. *John H. Beauvais, Cambridge, Massachusetts*

472 ... MAKING PUNCH To make an alcoholic punch, figure one of sour, two of sweet, three of strong, 4 weak. *Gordon Stewart, Niagara Falls, New York*

473 ... HIRING HELP FOR A PARTY You need 1 waiter per 10 guests for a buffet supper or 3 waiters per 20 guests for seated dinner service. For receptions or cocktail parties, you will need 1 bartender, 1 kitchen helper (a waiter may double in this function), and 1 waiter per 50 guests. For more than 50 guests, you will need a supervisor as well. *Food and Wine magazine*

474 ... FLYING FAST The mach number times 10 on jets is the number of miles traveled by the jet each minute. So, mach .80 = 8.0 miles per minute. *P. Douglas Combs, professional airline pilot, aviator & aircraft mechanic, flight instructor, Tempe, Arizona*

475 ... WIRING A HOUSE To quickly estimate the amp load of a circuit, figure one amp per fixture or bulb. *Ray Barbkcnccht, counsclor*

476 ... DRESSING YOURSELF Wearing dark colors on the bottom and light colors on the top is usually more visually appealing than the reverse. *Donna Salyers, The Cincinnati Enquirer*

477 ... FIGURING SOMEONE OUT If you want to know how people really feel about something, watch what they do. *Juanita Peterson, Sheridan, Colorado*

478 ... SPOTTING EMBEZZLEMENT In good times, the rate of embezzlement rises and the chance of getting caught declines because people are more relaxed and trusting. *Walter Pitkin, literary agent, Weston, Connecticut*

479 ... DETERMINING YOUR FRAME SIZE To determine the size of your frame, wrap a dollar bill around your wrist. If the ends of the bill touch, you have a small frame. If there's a finger's width or less between them, you have a medium frame. Anything more than a finger's width and you have a large frame. *Scott Parker, data specialist, Beaumont, Texas*

480 ... ESTIMATING FUEL USE Aircraft carriers get six inches to the gallon. *Phillip Williams, Jr., University of Michigan, Ann Arbor, Michigan*

ADVERTISING

481 ... *MAKING A TV COMMERCIAL* Limit yourself to one sales point per television commercial. *Jennifer Johnson, Knoxville, Tennessee*

BUSINESS

482 ... *RUNNING A HOTEL* Here's a formula for breaking even in the hotel business. Build a hotel by borrowing 80 percent of the construction cost at a 10 percent interest rate. Make sure the hotel averages a 60 percent occupancy rate. And charge $1 per room for every $1,000 per room in construction costs. *Scott Parker, data specialist, Beaumont, Texas*

GAMBLING

483 ... *PLAYING POKER* Don't enter a poker game unless you have 40 times the betting limit in your pocket. If you plan to play poker for a living, start with a bankroll at least 200 times the maximum bet. *Edwin Silberstang, games expert*

HOUSE AND HOME

484 ... *PICKING A NEW PLACE TO LIVE* You can live happily in a new house or apartment if, on your first visit, you immediately can visualize yourself and your family engaged in your normal activities among your current possessions. If you have to stop and think about how you'd use each area or how your furniture would fit in the place, forget it. *Andrea Frankel, computer scientist, engineer, holistic health practitioner, San Diego, California*

485 ... *STICKING WITH A FITNESS PROGRAM* If you can follow a fitness program for 21 consecutive days, you can follow it for life. *Kenneth Blanchard, author, quoted in Boardroom Reports*

EXERCISE

486 ... *FEEDING A COW* A cow should have 3 pounds of hay per day for every 100 pounds of weight. *Roger Seeley, Albany, New York*

CATTLE

487 ... *WAITING FOR RAIN* If there's dew on the spiderwebs in the grass in the morning, it won't rain. *Pete Stewart, auctioneer, Armagh, Pennsylvania*

PRECIPITATION

488 ... *GETTING SOMEWHERE* If it takes you a half hour to walk somewhere, it will take you one minute to drive there. *Anonymous*

HIKING

489 ... *CHECKING EXHAUST* Blue smoke from your exhaust may mean your car needs a complete engine overhaul. Black smoke usually means a maladjusted carburetor. White smoke: Ignore it if the engine is cold, but if it keeps up after the engine has warmed, you may have a leaking head gasket. *Reader's Digest, reported in Bottom Line Personal*

AUTOMOBILES

490 ... *THE AMERICAN TALKING RULE* Americans stand just far enough apart when talking that, arms extended, they could insert their thumbs in each other's ears. *Roger Axtell, Janesville, Wisconsin, author of "Do's and Taboos Around the World," in The New Yorker*

JOKER

491 ... *FINDING ELEPHANTS* To find an elephant, look within 300 meters of water. *Thomas W. Neumann, anthropological archaeologist, wildlife ecologist, and field crew crisis manager*

ANIMALS

492 ... *INKING A RUBBER STAMP* The finer the detail on a rubber stamp, the less ink it takes and the easier it is to get a good impression. *Alan T. Whittemore, YMCA Physical Director, South Deerfield, Massachusetts*

ART

AS A RULE OF THUMB: PEOPLE WHO SAY, "IN TERMS OF," DON'T KNOW WHAT THEY'RE TALKING ABOUT.
Elizabeth Kasehagen, R.N., Delivery Room Head Nurse, Santa Barbara, California

493...*REVIVING A COMPUTER AFTER A FIRE* If a computer's plastic casing has not been deformed by the heat, which begins to happen at 250 degrees F, then the computer will work. *Dean Sheridan, electronics technician and deaf actor, Torrance, California*

COMPUTERS

494...*REMEMBERING A BOOK* For every worthwhile book you read, there will be one statement or story you'll remember for at least a decade. *Scott Parker, data specialist, Beaumont, Texas*

BOOKS

495...*CHECKING DIAPERS* If babies thoroughly wet their diapers at least six times a day, they are getting enough milk. *Cheryl A. Russell, demographer, mother, editor-in-chief, American Demographics*

CHILDREN

496...*DEALING WITH A DRUNK* The Bouncer's Rule of Six: If you're explaining something to an intoxicated person that a sober person would understand after being told once, expect to repeat yourself five times. *Rick Rosner, bouncer and stripper, New York City*

DRINKING

497...*BUYING CHEESE FOR A PARTY* For a wine and cheese party, count on having one pound of cheese for every five guests. *Maria Martin, art history student and former cheese shop employee, Kingston, Ontario*

ENTERTAINING

498...*FLYING AN AIRPLANE* On a jet, the fuel flow on approach with gear and flaps extended will be about one-third of the fuel flow when cruising at altitude. *P. Douglas Combs, professional airline pilot, aviator & aircraft mechanic, flight instructor, Tempe, Arizona*

FLYING

499...*AVOIDING HIGH VOLTAGES* When you are working in the vicinity of high voltage, keep 1 foot of distance between you and the power source for each 1,000 volts. For instance, stay 13 feet away from a 13,000 volt power source. *Bob Crews, design scientist, Chicago, Illinois*

ELECTRICITY

500...*BUYING FURS* As a rule, short-haired furs like Persian lamb and mink look best on short people; long haired furs like skunk and fox look best on tall people. *Frank G. Ashbrook, biologist and fur-trade expert*

CLOTHING

501...*MANAGING FEAR* In skiing and body-boarding, the Fear Scale (FS) ranges from fun (1) to pure terror (10). If you're approaching a slope or wave and the FS is in the middle, do it. Like the Richter Scale, the Fear Scale is open-ended. *Larry Gassan, Jolly Dino Art Direction, Los Angeles, California*

EMOTIONS

502...*THE HARD TIMES EMBEZZLEMENT RULE* In bad times, commercial morality is enormously improved. Money is watched with a narrow, suspicious eye. *Walter Pitkin, literary agent, Weston, Connecticut*

CRIME

503...*FITTING A SHOE* You should have a thumb's width of space between the longest toe and the tip of your shoe. *Charles J. Gudas, DPM, associate professor, department of surgery, University of Chicago Medical Center*

BODY RULES

504...*GENERATING STEAM POWER* For creating steam, one ton of coal is equivalent to two cords of wood. *John Fischer, volunteer fireman, Joliet, Montana*

FUEL

ADVERTISING

BUSINESS

GAMBLING

HOUSE AND HOME

EXERCISE

CATTLE

PRECIPITATION

HIKING

AUTOMOBILES

CONVERSATIONS

ANIMALS

ART

505... **DESIGNING SIGNS AND BILLBOARDS**   The letters on a sign or billboard are designed to be readable at a certain distance. Take half the letter height in inches and multiply by 100 to find the readable distance in feet.   *Thos. Hodgson, Hodgson Signs, Martha's Vineyard, Massachusetts*

506... **SELLING CARS**   A well-run car dealership will make from 1 to 2 percent on sales.   *Scott Parker, data specialist, Beaumont, Texas*

507... **SCARNE'S POKER RULE OF 60**   Don't enter a poker game unless you have 60 times the betting limit in your pocket. When you have doubled this amount, it is time to quit for the day.   *John Scarne, gambling authority*

508... **PAPERING A WALL**   When papering an average wall with a print or striped wallpaper, expect to lose at least one foot of paper per strip to make them match.   *Johnnie Putnam, WIND radio, Chicago, Illinois*

509... **SWIMMING FOR EXERCISE**   A swimmer needs to exert less energy than a runner to get the same aerobic benefit because his body is in a horizontal position and his heart pumps more blood per beat than it does when his body is upright. To calculate your ideal heart rate while swimming, subtract your age from 205 and multiply by .70. If your rate is higher than 205 minus your age times .85, you're working harder than you have to.   *William McArdle, exercise physiologist, in American Health*

510... **USING UP A COW**   The useful life of a dairy cow is five to seven years.   *Chris Dahl, dairy farmer*

511... **THE FLY BITING RAIN RULE**   If flies bite, it will rain.   *Johnnie Putnam, WIND radio, Chicago, Illinois*

512... **FINDING A PLACE TO PITCH YOUR TENT**   Farmers are three times more likely than rural nonfarmers and 10 times more likely than suburban people to let you pitch your tent on their land. And you should know better than to ask city people.   *Geanne Toma, massage therapist, Lebanon, New Hampshire*

513... **HAVING YOUR CAR FIXED**   Any time a mechanic starts a conversation by telling you how lucky you are that you brought your car in when you did, plan on spending at least $100.   *Carl Frandsen, Trumansburg, New York*

514... **INTERVIEWING SOMEONE**   If someone you're interviewing makes the same point more than twice, it's the most important thing to him, and a crucial clue to his personality.   *Robert Kanigel, writer and editor, Baltimore, Maryland*

515... **SLAUGHTERING AN ANIMAL**   To kill an animal with a hammer, draw an imaginary line from its left ear to its right eye and another from its right ear to its left eye. Strike where the lines cross.   *Jeff Brown, astronomer, Bloomington, Indiana*

516... **ALEX'S ALL-ENCOMPASSING RULE OF PORTRAITURE**   Your portraits won't look so gimpy if the eyes are on a line half-way between the top of the head and the chin, the inside corners of the eyes are one eye-width apart, the nose is almost halfway between the eyes and chin, the nose is as wide as the distance between the eyes, the corners of the mouth fall directly below the pupils of the eyes, the top of the ears are on eye level, and the bottom of the ears come between the bottom of the nose and the mouth.   *Alex Stewart, Atlanta, Georgia*

COMPUTERS

517 ... **USING SOFTWARE** The average memory requirement of computer software doubles every 2.5 years. *Norman Brenner, Fleetwood, New York*

BOOKS

518 ... **FINDING TYPOGRAPHICAL ERRORS** Cheap paperback novels average one typographical error for every ten pages. *Joe Applegate, typo hunter, Los Angeles, as reported by Fred T. Shuster, Associated Press*

CHILDREN

519 ... **RAISING CRABBY BABIES** Crabby babies get more attention than quiet babies, and babies who get more attention have higher IQs. *Millie Denmark, Meridian, Mississippi*

DRINKING

520 ... **SOBERING UP** Sippers sober up faster than gulpers. *Anonymous*

521 ... **SERVING POTATOES AND ROLLS** For the average dinner, plan on one medium potato per person and one and a half dinner rolls. *Myrtle F. Synquist, Burlington, Iowa*

ENTERTAINING

522 ... **WORKING FOR AN AIRLINE** For each hour of paid flight time, airline schedules require pilots to be away from home four hours. *P. Douglas Combs, professional airline pilot, aviator & aircraft mechanic, flight instructor, Tempe, Arizona*

FLYING

523 ... **CAUSING A SPARK** Electricity will arc, or jump, a gap of about 1/4 inch for each 10,000 volts. This rule is often used by TV repairmen and electronic technicians to quickly check a high-voltage power supply, a practice that is not recommended for the novice. *Renard Braun, physicist*

ELECTRICITY

524 ... **RENTING A TUXEDO** Tuxedos last a long time and rarely go out of style. If you need to wear one even once a year, it pays to buy one and avoid the ordeal of renting. *Doug Weaver, accountant*

CLOTHING

525 ... **TRUSTING YOUR TICKLER** People don't laugh when they're tickled unless they trust the tickler. *Scott Parker, data specialist, Beaumont, Texas*

EMOTIONS

526 ... **PREVENTING A RADIO RIP OFF** Hiding or disguising the speakers of your car radio is as important as hiding or disguising the stereo. *Steven M. Keisman, New York City high school resource coordinator*

CRIME

527 ... **COOKING SPAGHETTI** Your thumb and index finger will encircle four modest servings of uncooked spaghetti. *James Colby, civil engineer*

BODY RULES

528 ... **BUYING GASOLINE** Since ten gallons of gasoline will expand by nearly a quart with a temperature increase of 30 degrees F, it is most economical to fill a gas tank early in the morning. *Paul A. Delaney, meteorologist, Beltsville, Maryland*

FUEL

ADVERTISING

BUSINESS

GAMBLING

HOUSE AND HOME

EXERCISE

CATTLE

PRECIPITATION

HIKING

AUTOMOBILES

CONVERSATIONS

ANIMALS

ART

529 ... **NEGOTIATING FOR RADIO ADVERTISING**   Subtract 30 percent from the rate on the rate card. Then negotiate downward. *Eliot Schein, president, Schein/ Blattstein Advertising, Inc., New York*

530 ... **SELLING CARS**   In good times, a car dealer should get a return on investment equal to the 90-day Treasury bill rate plus 20 percent. *Scott Parker, data specialist, Beaumont, Texas*

531 ... **THE SILVERSTANG DOUBLE YOUR MONEY RULE**   It is time to quit for the day if you have doubled your money. However, if the cards are still going your way, reinvest 20 percent of your till. If you lose that, leave the game at once. *Edwin Silverstang, games expert*

532 ... **INSTALLING A KITCHEN SINK**   Install a kitchen sink so that its bottom is at the same height as the hip bone of the tallest person using it. Everybody else can stand on little kick-away platforms. *Fred Pape, Union City, California*

533 ... **SWIMMING**   Swimming a quarter of a mile is roughly equal to running one mile. *Cynthia Gaines, photographer*

534 ... **MENZI'S RULE OF DAIRY DOLLARS**   Getting started in the dairy business will cost you $5,000 per cow in animals, land, buildings, and equipment. *William Menzi, Cooperative Extension agent*

535 ... **WAITING FOR SNOW**   T'won't snow 'till the brooks flow. *Clem Braczyk, quoting George, an old woodcutter, Webster, Massachusetts*

536 ... **THE CAMP RULE**   A camping trip is in jeopardy whenever early risers or night owls exceed 50 percent of the party. If either is a majority, the other campers should reassess their plans. *Denis Smith, high school counselor, Camarillo, California*

537 ... **BUYING CAR PARTS**   A used car part should cost no more than 60 percent of the new part list price. A used mechanical or electrical part should go for half the rebuilt and one-quarter the new price. *LeRoi Smith, writer and car builder*

538 ... **MAKING CONVERSATION**   You can break an awkward pause in a conversation by commenting on a person's name. The person will tell you how he was named, an odd spelling of his name, or how rare his name is—a solid ten minutes of conversation. *Carolyn Lloyd, 15-year-old student, Montreal, Quebec*

539 ... **COUNTING CHIPMUNKS**   The year after a season of heavy acorn production there will be one more chipmunk living on each quarter-acre plot. *Stephen Unsino, poet, Eastchester, New York*

540 ... **SELLING A PAINTING**   Paintings in galleries sell for twice the price they sell for at art auctions. *Richard Merkin, painter*

AS A RULE OF THUMB: EXPENSIVE RESTAURANTS DON'T POST THEIR MENUS OR PRICES NEAR THEIR FRONT DOORS. PETER AND LARRY WONG, SAN FRANCISCO, CALIFORNIA

541 ... **DEBUGGING SOFTWARE**   If a glitch occurs twice, it's a reproducible bug. If a glitch occurs only once, it's transient and much harder to find.   *Norman Brenner, Fleetwood, New York*

COMPUTERS

542 ... **HYPING A BOOK**   You can hype a book by a famous author to 250,000 copies. After that, success or failure depends upon word of mouth.   *John Gill, publisher*

BOOKS

543 ... **LISTENING TO KIDS AT PLAY**   Your kids are behaving themselves if all you hear is soft vowel sounds, but there's trouble brewing if you hear hard vowels.   *Sally Wilcox, Michigan*

CHILDREN

544 ... **SPOTTING A REFORMED ALCOHOLIC**   Reformed alcoholics usually will have a non alcoholic drink in their hands or sitting in front of them.   *Mark Bills, former drinker, Mystic, Iowa*

DRINKING

545 ... **PLANNING A CLASS PARTY**   If you teach in an elementary school and you are going to have a class party, you should a) have it on a day when there is no school the next day, b) have it during the last period of the day, and c) NEVER have it last more than one hour.   *Leonard F. Ferretti, elementary school teacher, Miami, Florida*

ENTERTAINING

546 ... **FLYING AN AIRPLANE**   For fuel efficiency when flying, if your pitch angle in level flight exceeds 3 1/2 degrees nose up, add power. If the pitch angle is less than 1 degree nose up, reduce power.   *P. Douglas Combs, professional airline pilot, aviator & aircraft mechanic, flight instructor, Tempe, Arizona*

FLYING

547 ... **LEARNING HOW TO JUGGLE**   If you can do 20 consecutive throws of a new juggling act without dropping anything, you've learned the trick.   *Todd Strong, circus school student, Chalons-sur-Marne, France*

JOKER

548 ... **THROWING AWAY CLOTHING**   Wait one year before throwing out a piece of clothing. If you haven't worn it in a year, you will never miss it.   *Betsy Wackernagel, Ithaca, New York*

CLOTHING

549 ... **PREDICTING VIOLENT BEHAVIOR**   A patient who suddenly can't sit still is about to become violent.   *Gerry M. Flick, M.D., Ship's Surgeon, S.S. Constitution off Hawaii*

EMOTIONS

550 ... **THE OBVIOUS RULE**   The higher the price of a car, bike, or motorcycle, the higher the theft rate.   *Steven M. Keisman, New York City high school resource coordinator*

CRIME

551 ... **BUYING SOCKS THAT FIT**   Wrap the bottom part of a sock around your fist. If the sock is the right size, the heel will just meet the toe.   *Nelson Smith, physical education teacher, Cincinnati, Ohio*

BODY RULES

552 ... **REACHING A GAS STATION**   If your tank is on empty and you're trying to make it to the next gas station, cut your speed to 35 miles per hour.   *R. C. Woods, teacher, Miranda, California*

FUEL

ADVERTISING

553...RUNNING AN AD CAMPAIGN   If you get a good - or even lukewarm - response to an ad, it's always better to stick with the same copy than to change it.   *Steven M. Keisman, New York City high school resource coordinator*

BUSINESS

554...CHOOSING A BIDDER   Throw out the highest and lowest bids. Average the rest and choose the one closest to the average.   *Chic Volturno, storehouse of worthless information, Hollywood, Florida*

GAMBLING

555...BLUFFING AT POKER   Don't bluff during the first hour of play or when your strong hands are being called. A good time to bluff is after you have won two or three pots in a row.   *Dale Armstrong, card player*

HOUSE AND HOME

556...MOWING A WET LAWN   The lawn is too wet to mow until all the puddles evaporate from the asphalt driveway.   *Brad Edmondson, editor, American Demographics*

JOKER

557...GASPING WHILE YOU EXERCISE   Never exercise so hard that you are gasping for breath. In fact, never do anything so hard that you are gasping for breath.   *Byron Roth, biochemist*

CATTLE

558...TAKING CARE OF CATTLE   One person can take care of up to 200 cattle.   *Pat Woodruff, television repairman*

PRECIPITATION

559...WATCHING WIND AND RAIN   Wind before rain; you'll be sailing again. Rain before wind; take your sails in.   *Tim Slack, Chief Mate, S.S. Constitution, off Hawaii*

HIKING

560...ESTIMATING YOUR STRIDE   Your leg length is equal to the length of your stride when you walk.   *Ned Frederick, writer, Exeter, New Hampshire*

AUTOMOBILES

561...TURNING OFF YOUR ENGINE   It pays to turn off your engine if it will be idling for more than one minute.   *Owen Chambers, petroleum distributor*

CONVERSATIONS

562...MAKING CONVERSATION   It takes eight seconds, on average, for someone you know to say something once you've entered a room. The time is less if you're staring at your watch counting the seconds.   *Carolyn Lloyd, 15-year-old student, Montreal, Quebec*

ANIMALS

563...MEASURING AN ELEPHANT   The circumference of an elephant's front foot is equal to the height of its shoulder from the ground.   *David Kumaki, physician, Shelburne, New Hampshire*

ART

564...THE SILK-SCREEN PRINTING RULE   Some serigraphs or silk-screen prints are smudged or damaged during production. You can plan on losing 10 percent of an edition each time you add a color.   *David Finn, printmaker, New York City*

As A RULE OF THUMB: TO MAKE AN AUDIT WORTHWHILE, THE IRS MUST FIND $300 WORTH OF ADDITIONAL INCOME OR ERRONEOUS DEDUCTIONS PER HOUR OF INVESTIGATION.

P. Douglas Combs, Professional Airline Pilot, Aviator and Aircraft Mechanic, Flight Instructor, Tempe, Arizona

565...BRENNER'S RULE OF PAUSING PROGRAMMERS   If an expert pauses while testing a new program, that's where a beginner will fail. *Norman Brenner, Fleetwood, New York*

COMPUTERS

566...SELLING SCIENCE FICTION   Science fiction books with green covers don't sell as well as those with blue covers. *Anonymous publisher*

BOOKS

567...RATIONING DIAPERS   Figure on one good-quality diaper every two hours. *L. Musselman, office manager and mother of young children*

CHILDREN

568...WATCHING YOUR DRINKING   You may be on the brink of a drinking problem if you're drinking four alcoholic drinks a day, three times a week. *J. R. Malone, Fairbanks, Alaska*

DRINKING

569...THE CATERER'S RULE   When planning a party, figure three pieces per person (of whatever you're serving). *Shelby Herman, economist*

ENTERTAINING

570...AVOIDING BIRDS IN FLIGHT   Birds dive to avoid oncoming airplanes. To avoid them, climb and reduce your speed to give them more time to get out of the way. *Seth B. Golbey, author*

FLYING

571...BETTING ON A ROCK BAND   Rock bands with far-out names almost never make it to the top because they usually play music that's equally far-out. *Dean Sheridan, electronics technician and deaf actor, Torrance, California*

ENTERTAINMENT

572...ANN LANDERS' PENCIL TEST   To determine whether you need to wear a bra, place a pencil under you breast. If the pencil falls to the floor, you don't need to wear a bra; if it stays, you need one. *Ann Landers, advice columnist*

CLOTHING

573...CHECKING YOURSELF FOR STRESS   Warm hands indicate relaxation. Cool hands indicate tension. Place your hands on your neck, which is always warm; if they feel cool, concentrate on relaxing. *Jan Lowenstein, writer*

EMOTIONS

574...GETTING AWAY WITH TICKETS   You're more likely to get away with a parking violation if you argue your case in person rather than by mail. *Steven M. Keisman, New York City high school resource coordinator*

CRIME

575...HANDLING TEST EQUIPMENT   Don't tap the face of a sticky gauge any harder than you would tap the bridge of your nose. *Steve Parker, aerospace engineer, Princeton, New Jersey*

BODY RULES

576...STARTING A FIRE   One stick can't burn, two sticks won't burn, three sticks might burn, four sticks will burn, and five sticks make a nice fire. *Gail Smith, parts unknown*

FUEL

ADVERTISING

577 ... *JUDGING THE EFFECTIVENESS OF AN AD* The more often you see an ad, the more effective it is, regardless of how dull or uncreative. *Steven M. Keisman, New York City high school resource coordinator*

BUSINESS

578 ... *THE HOTEL RULE OF THREE* The third owner of a hotel will make a profit. The cost of the building now reflects its true market value. *Dirck Z. Meengs, management consultant, Canoga Park, California*

GAMBLING

579 ... *THE PROFESSOR'S RULE OF POKER* In a poker game, call a bet when you have better than two out of five chances of winning the pot, and do not risk more than you stand to gain if you do win. *Professor Horace C. Levinson, mathematician*

HOUSE AND HOME

580 ... *REBUILDING YOUR FAUCETS* When you first think about how hard it is to turn a faucet, it's time to rebuild it. *Mitch Doll, builder, draftsman, Ithaca, New York*

HEALTH

581 ... *DECIDING WHICH HOSPITALS ARE BEST* The best hospitals have more than 500 beds. *Steven M. Keisman, New York City high school resource coordinator*

CATTLE

582 ... *RUNNING A DAIRY* You need 1 person for every 30 cows to run a self-sufficient dairy farm. *Chris Dahl, dairy farmer*

PRECIPITATION

583 ... *THE RAIN OR SNOW RULE* If it is snowing and the tree trunks appear to darken in mid-day, the snow will change to rain. *Walter Pitkin, literary agent, Weston, Connecticut*

HIKING

584 ... *WALKING AND BACKPACKING* You can walk three miles per hour at a normal walk and one mile per hour all day with a backpack. *Peter Reimuller, Point Arena, California*

AUTOMOBILES

585 ... *CHECKING YOUR TIRES* Your tire tread should come to the top of Lincoln's head on a penny held on edge upside down. *Barbara Gilbert, bank teller*

CONVERSATIONS

586 ... *BELIEVING THINGS* People are most credulous when they are most happy. *Walter Pitkin, literary agent, Weston, Connecticut*

ANIMALS

587 ... *HUNTING FOR FOOD* If a turtle covers the bottom of a five-gallon bucket, then it will make a decent meal. *Wayne Jennings, maintenance mechanic, Cayutaville, New York*

ART

588 ... *THE ASHLEY MILLER RULE OF CALLIGRAPHY* The most pleasing height for lower-case italic letters is five times the width of the penpoint, or nib. *Ashley Miller, calligrapher*

AS A RULE OF THUMB:
THE WORSE THE MEN'S ROOM SMELLS, THE EASIER IT WILL BE TO SELL LOTTERY TICKETS AT THE BAR.
PETER LEACH, ST. PAUL, MINNESOTA

589... LEARNING HOW TO USE SOFTWARE   If you can't figure out how to do it after ten minutes of reading the manual and trying, ask someone for help. *Norman Brenner, Fleetwood, New York*

590... PLANNING AN INDEX   Allowing space for an index in a book is no problem once the type has been set and the indexing has been done. But with a new manuscript, you can only guess. As a rule of thumb, allow 1 page of index to every 40 pages of manuscript with average copy, 1 to 30 for a manuscript with a lot of names or technical terms, 1 to 50 for a book with comparatively few. Check your guess with the editor and use his figure if it differs from yours. *Marshall Lee, bookmaker*

591... LISTENING TO BABIES   When babies start grunting, wait 20 minutes before changing them. That way you will change only one messy diaper, not two. *L. Musselman, office manager and mother of young children*

592... STORING BEER   You lose one day of shelf life for every degree you let your beer get above 20 degrees Centigrade. *Dave Graham, engineer and authority on beer*

593... HIRING A BARTENDER   You need 1 bartender for every 100 guests at a party. *Joel Blumberg, student, Austin, Texas*

594... FLYING INTO HEADWINDS AND TAILWINDS   For fuel efficiency in a tailwind, reduce your speed by a quarter of the tailwind component. In a headwind, increase your speed by a sixth of it. *Peter Garrison, writer and pilot*

595... FOLLOWING ENTERTAINERS   Performers are washed up if they frequently make headlines in Las Vegas. *Dean Sheridan, electronics technician and deaf actor, Torrance, California*

596... FITTING A MAN'S JACKET   You can check the length of a dress jacket with your arms relaxed at your sides. The hem of the jacket should reach the tip of your thumbs. *Danny Speer, composer*

597... TRACKING EMOTIONAL PROBLEMS   If someone has an emotional problem, look for the person who aggravates him or her the most. If it's another person with an emotional problem — bingo! *Cookie Ohlson, teacher, Prospect Park Middle School, Pennsylvania*

598... BEATING A TICKET   If you're trying to beat a parking ticket, you have a better chance of winning if you wear a jacket and tie or dress. *Steven M. Keisman, New York City high school resource coordinator*

599... ESTIMATING THE SIZE OF YOUR FOOT   The distance from your elbow to your wrist equals the length of your foot. *Carla Corin, biologist, Eagles River, Alaska*

600... DRILLING FOR OIL AND GAS   Seven of every 10 exploratory oil wells are dry holes. Of those that hit oil or gas, only 1 in 40 is commercially successful. *Scott Parker, data specialist, Beaumont, Texas*

ADVERTISING

601 ... WRITING AD COPY   To find out which words sparkle and which are duds, read the copy backwards.   *Timothy Wenk, magician, West Stockbridge, Massachusetts*

BUSINESS

602 ... STARTING A NEW BUSINESS   Do not start a new business unless you can wait at least one year before realizing a profit.   *Thomas O. Marsh, writer and coroner's investigator, Fairfield, Ohio*

GAMBLING

603 ... PLAYING POKER   After the deal, a player who stays in the game and plays out more than one hand in five is overstraining the law of averages and is on his way to the poorhouse.   *Dale Armstrong, card player*

HOUSE AND HOME

604 ... INSTALLING A FAN IN A SUN ROOM   To move hot air out of an overheated sun room, you need a thermostatically controlled fan with a flow rate of four to six cubic feet per minute per square foot of glass in the sun room.   *Jan F. Kreider, consulting engineer, Popular Science*

HEALTH

605 ... PROTECTING YOUR SKIN   To protect your skin from the sun, use sunscreen when your shadow is shorter than you are.   *Anonymous*

CATTLE

606 ... THE BEEF CARCASS RULE OF ONE-QUARTER   A properly butchered beef carcass is one-quarter steaks, one-quarter ground beef and stew meat, one-quarter roasts, and one-quarter waste.   *Harry Pound, Pound's Meat Cutting*

PRECIPITATION

607 ... THE SECOND RAIN OR SNOW RULE   If snow or rain is likely and the air appears gray, it will snow. If it has a bluish haze, expect rain.   *Walter Pitkin, literary agent, Weston, Connecticut*

HIKING

608 ... TRAVELING ON FOOT   Without a pack, you should be able to walk 25 miles a day without serious strain. With a pack one-fourth your weight or less, 15 miles a day is reasonable on a decent trail.   *J. Baldwin, designer and writer*

AUTOMOBILES

609 ... THE MONEY FOR CARS RULE   By the time you finish paying for them, most cars will be worth about $1,000 and will constantly need minor repairs. So anyone who can do minor repairs on a car should only spend $1,000 to buy one in the first place.   *Bill Marsh, printer*

CONVERSATIONS

610 ... INTERVIEWING SOMEONE   Ask the rude and unpleasant questions next to last, then finish with something polite, if they're still talking to you.   *Jennifer Evans, writer, Austin, Texas*

ANIMALS

611 ... ESTIMATING METHANE PRODUCTION   The average cow belches twice a minute, producing ten gallons of methane a day.   *Paul A. Delaney, meteorologist, Beltsville, Maryland*

JOKER

612 ... THE JOKE RULE OF AIRPORTS   Airport designers should keep walking distances shorter than 2,000 feet from gates to baggage.   *L. K. Bolef, St. Louis, Missouri*

COMPUTERS

613 ... **PRICING COMPUTERS AND BOOKS** Computers and books sell for six times their manufacturing costs. *Norman Brenner, Fleetwood, New York*

JOKER

614 ... **WRITING A SPORTS BOOK** The sales success of a sports book is inversely proportional to the size of the ball used in the sport. *Frank Deford, senior editor, Sports Illustrated, quoting George Plimpton on "Morning Edition," National Public Radio*

CHILDREN

615 ... **TRAVELING WITH CHILDREN** When going out with young children, count on one-half hour of preparation per child in the summer, and one hour per child in the winter. *L. Musselman, office manager and mother of young children*

DRINKING

616 ... **SPOTTING A DRUNK** If someone wipes his mouth right after taking a drink, he has probably been overindulging. *Scott Parker, data specialist, Beaumont, Texas*

ENTERTAINING

617 ... **PLANNING A WEDDING** You need 2 ushers for every 50 wedding guests. *Rose Rollins, Greenville, South Carolina*

FLYING

618 ... **CORRECTING FOR WIND IN A PLANE** To correct for wind on the outbound leg, double the correction you used on the inbound leg. *Robert B. Davis, Holister, California*

ENTERTAINMENT

619 ... **SPOTTING THE FAMOUS** A person is only famous if you can remember his last name. *Christine Tarbell, Greene, New York*

CLOTHING

620 ... **DRESSING FOR AN EVENT** When in doubt, overdress. It is easier to dress down than up. *Steven M. Keisman, New York City high school resource coordinator*

JOKER

621 ... **RECOGNIZING A PESSIMIST** A pessimist is someone who lives with an optimist. *Alan R. Brown, New York, New York*

CRIME

622 ... **SPOTTING A HIGH-CRIME AREA** The fewer the residents, the more shoppers and workers and the higher the crime rate. *Steven M. Keisman, New York City high school resource coordinator*

BODY RULES

623 ... **PRODUCING HUMAN HORSEPOWER** Working hard, the average person can generate about one-quarter horsepower. *Kevin Kelly, Athens, Georgia*

FUEL

624 ... **THE BIG TRUCK FUEL RULE** The average tractor-trailer gets four to five miles per gallon on the highway. *L. M. Boyd, The San Francisco Chronicle*

ADVERTISING

625... GENERATING PUBLICITY   One personal call to a newspaper reporter is worth 20 news releases to newspapers. *Terry Larimore, writer and therapist, Houston, Texas*

BUSINESS

626... THE TAX FORM RULE   For every 150 W-2 forms you mail to employees at the end of the year, you should expect four or five returns. They'll need new addresses, corrections, or better carbon copies. *Jackie Creble, secretary, Burlington, Iowa*

GAMBLING

627... LOSING YOUR MONEY   You should drop out of a poker game when you have lost more than 20 times the maximum bet allowed in the game. *Edwin Silberstang, games expert*

HOUSE AND HOME

628... FLOOD'S ATTIC INSULATION RULE   If the coldest temperature in your attic is within one or two degrees Fahrenheit of the coldest temperature outdoors, your ceiling is fairly well insulated. *Steven Flood, Saginaw, Michigan*

HEALTH

629... SAVING YOUR LUNGS   Every hour you spend in a smoky bar is equal to smoking one or two cigarettes. *Rick Rosner, bouncer and stripper, New York City*

CATTLE

630... CASTRATING CALVES   Castrate a calf when his testicles are the size of a squirrel's head. *Jim Crissman, veterinary pathologist, Midland, Michigan*

PRECIPITATION

631... PREDICTING RAIN   The number of stars visible inside the ring around the moon is the number of days before rain. *Glenn Saha, builder*

HIKING

632... PLANNING A HIKE   To estimate your hiking time, figure half an hour for each mile plus half an hour for each 1,000-foot increase in altitude. *Pierre Gremaud, Waitsfield, Vermont*

AUTOMOBILES

633... CHANGING YOUR OIL   If your car holds 5 quarts of engine oil or more, change the oil every 3,000 miles. For every half quart less than 5 that your engine holds, decrease your between-change mileage by 500. For example, a car that has an oil capacity of 3 and a half quarts should have its oil changed every 1,500 miles. *Will Parker, Georgian music authority*

CONVERSATIONS

634... REMEMBERING NAMES   If a person whose name you should know but can't remember is approaching you, relax. When the person has come within three feet of you, you will remember the name. *Eleanor Benelisha, library and information services, Richmond, California*

ANIMALS

635... IDENTIFYING SEA MAMMALS   Fish have vertical tails. Mammals have horizontal tails. *Paul A. Delaney, meteorologist, Beltsville, Maryland*

BUILDING

636... DESIGNING A HOME   Architects design homes to last about 50 years. Technological advances and social change make houses obsolete after that length of time. *Dean Sheridan, electronics technician and deaf actor, Torrance, California*

637 ... **PROTECTING YOUR EYES**　To protect your eyes from strain, make sure the screen is just beyond arm's length when you work on a computer. *Dean Sheridan, electronics technician and deaf actor, Torrance, California*

638 ... **EDITING A NEWSPAPER**　Kill everything that you don't understand. *Joel Garreau, editor, The Washington Post*

639 ... **RAISING CHILDREN**　An umbilical hernia that has not closed spontaneously by the time a child is 4 will require surgery. *Dean Sheridan, electronics technician and deaf actor, Torrance, California*

As A RULE OF THUMB:
WHEN DEEP FRYING
CHICKEN IN A
COMMERCIAL DEEP
FRYER, THE CHICKEN IS
COOKED WHEN A LEG
FLOATS TO THE TOP.
TONY CAMPO JR., SALES
REPRESENTATIVE FOR FOOD
SERVICE EQUIPMENT,
COUNTRYSIDE, ILLINOIS

640 ... **REASONER'S RULE OF DRINKING**　The farther north you go, the more drinking is a problem. *Harry Reasoner, CBS News report on alcohol use in Greenland*

641 ... **PLANNING A DINNER**　Inviting more than 25 percent of the guests for a university dinner party from the economics department ruins the conversation. *Martha Farnsworth Riche, editor, The Numbers News*

642 ... **ENTERING A HOLDING PATTERN**　If your holding radial is opposite the direction of flight, your entry will be direct. If your holding radial is about the same as your heading, your entry will be either teardrop or parallel. *Robert B. Davis, Holister, California*

643 ... **THE ENTERTAINER'S RULE**　Look good, sound good, and do something good. To make a steady living, you need all three. To be on television, you can get away with only two. *Timothy Wenk, magician, West Stockbridge, Massachusetts*

644 ... **KEISMAN'S RULE OF POWER ACCESSORIES**　A man's watch and shoes are his most important power accessories. *Steven M. Keisman, New York City high school resource coordinator*

645 ... **NORMAN BRENNER'S JOULE OF A RULE**　It takes one Joule of energy to print a square centimeter, no matter what the electronic technology. *Norman Brenner, Fleetwood, New York*

646 ... **FINDING A SECURE APARTMENT**　Avoid apartments on the top floor, especially those accessible from the roof by a fire escape. They are most likely to be burglarized. *Steven M. Keisman, New York City high school resource coordinator*

647 ... **MEASURING THINGS**　The first joint of your thumb measures about one inch, your foot measures about one foot, and your pace measures about one yard. *Stephen Gibian, architect and stonemason, Ithaca, New York*

648 ... **BUYING BATTERIES**　In most cases, a lithium battery will last as long as four alkaline batteries, and an alkaline battery will last as long as ten carbon-zinc batteries. *W. Price, transistor radio lover*

NEVER TRUST A CALM DOG　**65**

JOKER

649 ... **MARKETING A NEW PRODUCT**   Americans will not buy something they cannot pronounce.   *Robert M. McMath, new products guru, Canandaigua, New York*

BUSINESS

650 ... **WORKING WITH MASS TRANSIT**   When a mass transit system hikes fares by 10 percent, ridership usually declines permanently by 3 percent.   *Joseph Schofer, transportation authority, In These Times*

GAMBLING

651 ... **PLAYING POKER**   An old rule of thumb says that when your turn comes to call, don't do it — raise or fold. Not always, of course, but amateurs will call a lot more often than professionals.   *Dale Armstrong, card player*

HOUSE AND HOME

652 ... **THE WOODSTOVE RULE**   If you are trying to decide what size woodstove you need, you can start by figuring 2.5 cubic feet of firebox per 1,000 square feet of living space.   *Dan Hoffman, city council alderman*

HEALTH

653 ... **TRACKING SKIN CANCER**   For every 1 percent drop in the ozone level in the upper atmosphere, there is a 4 percent increase in the incidence of skin cancer.   *Paul A. Delaney, meteorologist, Beltsville, Maryland*

CATTLE

654 ... **RAISING BEEF**   A properly fed beef cow should gain two or three pounds a day.   *Pat Woodruff, television repairman*

PRECIPITATION

655 ... **PREDICTING RAIN**   If the barometric pressure is falling rapidly, a ring around the moon means rain in 18 to 24 hours, about 75 percent of the time.   *Paul E. Lehr, meteorologist*

HIKING

656 ... **PLANNING A HIKE**   To estimate your hiking time, figure one hour for every three miles plus one hour for every 2,000-foot increase in elevation.   *Kevin Kelly, Athens, Georgia*

AUTOMOBILES

657 ... **INCREASING YOUR GAS MILEAGE**   Radial tires get two to three miles per gallon more than bias-belted or bias-ply tires.   *Steven M. Keisman, New York City high school resource coordinator*

CONVERSATIONS

658 ... **SAYING SOMETHING**   If you find yourself thinking that something goes without saying, it is probably in the best interest of everyone involved to say it.   *William Krieger, English Department chairman, Gig Harbor, Washington*

ANIMALS

659 ... **THE CROCODILE RULE**   Zigzag to outrun a crocodile.   *Anonymous*

BUILDING

660 ... **PLANNING FLOOR JOISTS**   Divide the span (in feet) by two. The result plus one (in inches) is the depth of the joist.   *R.W. Ramage, Cheshire, Great Britain*

AS A RULE OF THUMB: IF A CAR FOLLOWING YOU AT NIGHT DOESN'T HAVE PERFECTLY ALIGNED HEADLIGHTS, IT IS NOT A POLICE CAR.
ERIC KIMPLE, MOTORCYCLE RACER, COLUMBUS, OHIO

661...*ESTIMATING THE COST OF ELECTRONICS* The price of electronics declines by 30 percent a year. *Dave Chapman, computer consultant, Forestville, California*

662...*PROOFREADING* Two rounds of proofreading catch 98 percent of the errors in a book. *Bill Kaupe, consultant, Philadelphia, Pennsylvania*

663...*RAISING CHILDREN* Young children who say "I'm not tired" are very tired. *Cliff Martin, Eugene, Oregon*

664...*DRINKING LIQUOR* As far as getting drunk is concerned, 1 jigger of liquor is equal to a 12-ounce beer. *Robert Morley, unemployed*

665...*INVITING GUESTS* If you invite 100 people to a cocktail party, plan on 75 coming; 25 will send regrets. *Alan Amsler, graphic designer*

666...*FLYING AN AIRPLANE* If you're low on fuel, two actions are essential: One, throttle back; two, mixture back until the engine barely continues to run smoothly. These actions will double, maybe even triple, the amount of time you can stay airborne. *Kevin Garrison*

667...*THE ENTERTAINER'S RULE OF CLOTHING* You should spend about four times your fee for a single gig on a suit or dress for your performance and one night's fee on the shoes. *Timothy Wenk, magician, West Stockbridge, Massachusetts*

668...*CHOOSING A TIE* It is more important for the color of a man's necktie to agree with the color of his shirt and trousers than with his jacket. *Steven M. Keisman, New York City high school resource coordinator*

669...*SOLAR ENERGY* The maximum amount of solar energy available is one horsepower per square yard, or one kilowatt per square meter. *Norman Brenner, Fleetwood, New York*

670...*SPOTTING A BAD CHECK* Ninety percent of bad checks carry numbers below 150, indicating a new account. *Francine Green, Cherry Hill, New Jersey*

671...*FOLLOWING LOS ANGELES* According to an authority at the University of California, the continental drift is such that Los Angeles is moving north toward San Francisco at about the rate your fingernails grow. *J. Eichelberger, Alameda, California*

672...*COOKING OUTDOORS* Cooking outside a tent requires twice as much fuel as cooking inside a tent. *Peggy Kerber, editor, Mountaineering*

COLOR

BUSINESS

JOKER

HOUSE AND HOME

HEALTH

CATTLE

PRECIPITATION

HIKING

AUTOMOBILES

CONVERSATIONS

ANIMALS

BUILDING

673 ... **USING UP MARKERS**   Black is always the first color to wear out in a marker set. Green or red is next. *Carolyn Lloyd, 15-year-old student, Montreal, Quebec*

674 ... **THE 80/20/30 RULE**   If you get rid of the 20 percent of your customers who cause 80 percent of your headaches, your profit will increase by 30 percent. *Alex Stewart, Atlanta, Georgia*

675 ... **PLAYING THE MIDWAY**   At an amusement park, ask the person at the game booth to demonstrate the game. If he refuses, it's because he can't win a prize. This means your chances of losing are too high. *Carolyn Lloyd, 15-year-old student, Montreal, Quebec*

676 ... **MOVING TO A NEW HOUSE**   Each time you move, things are lost, broken, or discarded. For the average family, six moves equal one house fire. *Carl Mitcham, philosophy teacher, Brooklyn, New York*

677 ... **THE INFECTION RULE**   Bacterial infections are localized — a patient will complain of a sore throat, or a runny nose, or an upset stomach. Viral infections are more generalized — a patient will complain of a sore throat, and a runny nose, and an upset stomach. *Russell T. Johnson, Temple City, California*

678 ... **THE STILLMAN DAIRY RULE**   The average dairy farmer spends half his time milking or doing chores related to milking. *William Stillman, dairy farmer*

679 ... **WATCHING LEAVES**   When trees start showing the whitish undersides of their leaves, it's getting ready to rain. *A. Bardsley, Mt. Kisco, New York*

680 ... **TRAVELING ON FOOT**   There is a simple test for checking your pace: If you can't keep it up, hour after hour, it is too fast. *Peggy Kerber, editor, Mountaineering*

681 ... **CHOOSING A SAFE CAR**   An automobile's size is more important than its weight in determining its safety. *Steven M. Keisman, New York City high school resource coordinator*

682 ... **WATCHING YOUR STEP**   The feller that agrees with everything you say is either a fool or he is getting ready to skin you. *Kin Hubbard, Brown County, Indiana, ca. 1920, via Phil A. Schrodt*

683 ... **DODGING A CHARGING POLAR BEAR**   If a polar bear charges you, dodge to the right. Eskimos say most polar bears are left-pawed. *L.M. Boyd, The San Francisco Chronicle*

684 ... **HANGING CABLE**   Wires or cables strung from point to point or pole to pole assume a catenary curve with a sag 1/20 of the span. A lesser sag signals excessive tension in the wire or cable. A greater sag calls for more poles, closer together. *George H. Amber, p.e., Royal Oak, Michigan*

AS A RULE OF THUMB: NEW VIDEO EQUIPMENT LOSES MORE THAN HALF ITS VALUE AFTER ONE USE. Brad Lowry, Freelance Producer of International Video, Philadelphia,

685...*SIZING UP A SOFTWARE JOB* Finding out what kind of computer a person is using is 80 percent of a software job. Those who use odd or obsolete computers probably did everything else wrong, too. *Dave Chapman, computer consultant, Forestville, California*

686...*EDITING A MAGAZINE* You should plan on reading through at least 200 unsolicited manuscripts to find one that is usable. *M. Lafavore, editor, Organic Gardening magazine*

687...*ADOPTING A CHILD* Traditional adoption agencies work best with average couples. *Cheryl A. Russell, demographer, mother, editor-in-chief, American Demographics*

688...*DRINKING AND DRIVING* If you are going to drive home from a party, don't have more than one drink per hour. *Betsy Green, painter*

689...*PROTECTING YOUR PARTY GUESTS* Do not invite a determined raconteur to a party to be held in a space of less than 600 square feet, not counting the piano. Otherwise, it will be hard for people to escape him or her, as the case may be, without walking out on you. *John Boyd, florist*

690...*DESIGNING AN AIRPLANE* In a conventionally configured airplane with a tail surface one-sixth the size of the wing and located three wing chord lengths aft of it, the aerodynamic center of the ensemble would be at about 68 percent of chord. *Peter Garrison, writer and pilot*

691...*ADDING A HARP TO YOUR ACT* A vaudeville act with a harp in it will get $5 more than one without a harp. *Minnie Marx, mother of Harpo Marx, cited by Bill Marx, Harpo's son*

692...*DRESSING YOURSELF* You can wear anything below the waist as long as you have a tie on. *Jon Crispin, photographer, Swampscott, Massachusetts*

693...*POWERING YOUR BODY* Your body runs on about the same energy as a 100-watt bulb. About a quarter of the energy goes to your muscles including your heart. Another quarter goes to the liver and spleen. Only about one-fifth is consumed by the brain. *Scott Parker, data specialist, Beaumont, Texas*

694...*PROTECTING YOUR HOME FROM BURGLARS* The next time you come home, pretend you don't have your keys. The way you get in your house is the way a burglar will too. *Scott Parker, data specialist, Beaumont, Texas*

695...*PREDICTING JUMPING ABILITY* The distance from the heel to the articulation of the calf muscle is an indication of jumping ability. For high-jumping dancers and athletes, the distance should be equal to or greater than the length of the foot. *Stephanie Judy, writer, British Columbia, Canada*

696...*WATCHING THE PRICE OF OIL* A change of $1 per barrel in the price of crude oil means a change of 2.5¢ per gallon in the price of gasoline. *Michael Rider, art director, American Demographics*

COLOR

697 ... **KEEPING UP WITH FASHIONS**   Color cycles in fashion usually last 18 months to 2 years. *Linnea Lannon, reporter, Detroit Free Press*

BUSINESS

698 ... **CONSULTING**   A consultant should spend two-thirds of his or her time consulting with clients and one-third lining up new work and doing PR. *Peter K. Francese, President, American Demographics, Ithaca, New York*

GAMES

699 ... **WINNING MONOPOLY**   The person who makes the most deals wins. *Jennifer Evans, writer, Austin, Texas*

HOUSE AND HOME

700 ... **GETTING RID OF THINGS**   If you are simply trying to get rid of some unwanted household "stuff," three moves equal one house fire. *Peter Leach, St. Paul, Minnesota*

HEALTH

701 ... **TRACKING A DIABETIC**   If you find ants around a toilet, suspect that a diabetic is using it. *Gerry M. Flick, M.D., Ship's Surgeon, S.S. Constitution off Hawaii*

CATTLE

702 ... **BUILDING A POND FOR LIVESTOCK**   A pond supplied entirely by surface water should be built to hold at least six times the amount of water you need for your livestock. *Carl S. Winkelblech, New York State Cooperative Extension agent*

PRECIPITATION

703 ... **WAITING FOR GOOD WEATHER**   The rain is over when dry spots appear on the blacktop. *Dorinda Ryan, Manuchula, Florida*

HIKING

704 ... **THE AVERAGE WALKING SPEED RULE**   At a pace of 120 steps per minute, the average man will walk about four miles an hour, and the average woman will walk about three miles an hour. *Craig Evans, walking expert, in Bottom Line/Personal*

AUTOMOBILES

705 ... **PRESERVING YOUR CAR**   Diligently caring for your car with frequent washings, including the underbody, can add two years to its life. *Kenn Marash, writer*

CONVERSATIONS

706 ... **YEATON'S MEETING PEOPLE AT PARTIES RULE**   At a party or public event, the person who laughs spontaneously at the same time you do probably is worth cultivating as a friend. *Kelly Yeaton, teacher and stage manager, State College, Pennsylvania*

ANIMALS

707 ... **THE CIRCUS RULE**   Don't stand within five meters of the lion tunnel when the lions are entering or exiting the ring. The lions will pee on you. *Todd Strong, circus school student, Chalons-sur-Marne, France*

BUILDING

708 ... **BUILDING WITH STEEL**   The depth of a steel beam should be about 11 percent of its span. *King Royer, structural engineer*

AS A RULE OF THUMB:
A DESIGN IS WHAT THE DESIGNER HAS WHEN TIME AND MONEY HAVE RUN OUT.
JAMES POOLE, CHIEF ARCHITECT FOR DISNEYLAND, TOPANGA, CALIFORNIA

709... ESTIMATING PROGRAMMING TIME   It takes those who program in assembly language five to ten times as long to write a program as those who write in C or PASCAL. *Dave Chapman, computer consultant, Forestville, California*

COMPUTERS

710... EDITING AN ARTICLE   When editing an article, you rarely go wrong crossing out the first page and a half. *Bryant Robey, founding editor, American Demographics*

EDITING

711... SCREENING YOUR BABY FOR CYSTIC FIBROSIS   Kiss your baby. If he or she tastes extremely salty, check with your doctor about getting the baby tested for cystic fibrosis. *Tom Ferguson, M.D., editor, Medical Self-Care, Inverness, California*

CHILDREN

712... MIXING A DRINK   Keep the quantity of the basic ingredient — gin, whiskey, etc. — up to 60 percent of the total drink, never below half. *The Joy of Cooking*

DRINKING

713... INVITING GUESTS   If you are giving a party and you live in the suburbs, invite two times the number of people you want to attend. If you live within range of public transportation, invite one and a half times the number of people you want. If you are in the heart of the city, invite one and a quarter times the number of people you want. *Janet Blum, Denver, Colorado*

ENTERTAINING

714... THE HOVERING HELICOPTER ROTORWASH RULE   The dangerous gale-force rotorwash of a hovering helicopter extends outward to a distance three times the diameter of the main rotor. *David A. Shugarts, editor, Aviation Safety*

FLYING

715... TIMING A BULLFIGHT   The average bull lasts 20 minutes in a bullfight. *L. M. Boyd, The San Francisco Chronicle*

ENTERTAINING

716... TAKING PHOTOGRAPHS AT NIGHT   To compensate for reciprocity failure in night-time photography, open the aperture one additional f-stop if exposure time is more than 1 second, 2 f-stops if the exposure is over 10 seconds, and 3 f-stops if the exposure is more than 100 seconds. *Ernst Luposchainsky, III ("Kahn"), celestial photographer, inter alia, Hollywood, California*

PHOTOGRAPHY

717... AIMING A SOLAR WATER HEATER   For year-round use, the slope of home hot-water solar collectors should be equal to the latitude at which they are installed. *Stephen Gibian, architect and stonemason, Ithaca, New York*

ENERGY

718... SPOTTING A CRIMINAL   Violent criminals are likely to have been abused as children, had problems wetting the bed, and have tattoos. *Scott Parker, data specialist, Beaumont, Texas*

CRIME

719... SIZING A HAT OR A RING   Your wedding ring size is the same as your hat size. *Doris Jennings, printer's assistant*

BODY RULES

720... BURNING COAL   A pound of coal will provide slightly more than twice as much heat as a pound of wood. *A. Alvarez, Johnstown, Pennsylvania*

FUEL

COLOR

721 ... *BUYING A FIRE TRUCK* Yellow fire trucks are twice as safe as red ones. *Scott Parker, data specialist, Beaumont, Texas*

BUSINESS

722 ... *SIZING UP A BUSINESS* If the clerical staff is pleasant, you can bet that their bosses are pleasant to work for. *Gerald Gutlipp, mathematician, Chicago, Illinois*

GAMES

723 ... *PLAYING SCRABBLE* As a rule, I can beat anyone at Scrabble who does crossword puzzles better than me. *Sharon Yntema, author, Vegetarian Baby*

HOUSE AND HOME

724 ... *A MOUSE IN YOUR HOUSE* If you see one mouse in your house, you probably have a dozen. *C. A. Lacey, town historian, Richford, New York*

HEALTH

725 ... *PLANNING A FULL BODY MASSAGE* It takes 90 minutes to give a full body massage, plus an additional 5 minutes for each bad joke the client makes before the session. The number of bad jokes is directly proportional to the thickness of a person's body armor. *Geanne Toma, massage therapist, Lebanon, New Hampshire*

CATTLE

726 ... *KEEPING A FAMILY COW* The average family cow needs two acres of good pasture. *Phyllis Wood, press operator, Meriden, Connecticut*

PRECIPITATION

727 ... *LISTENING TO TRAINS* Loud train, plan on rain. *Lewis Ramsey, historical restorations contractor*

HIKING

728 ... *KEEPING WARM WHILE CAMPING* For warmth and comfort when you're camping, put as much under you as over you. *Steven M. Keisman, New York City high school resource coordinator*

JOKER

729 ... *BUYING A CAR* Don't buy a car with a horsepower greater than your IQ. *Scott Parker, data specialist, Beaumont, Texas*

730 ... *CATCHING A LIAR* A good liar will look his victim in the eyes in an attempt to be convincing. Two tip-offs are an increase in his rate of blinking and overly complicated explanations. *Dr. Joyce Brothers, The Syracuse Post Standard*

CONVERSATIONS

731 ... *COUNTING BACTERIA* There are about a million bacteria per milliliter in the middle of an average lake or ocean. *David Glaser, Ph.D, microbial ecologist, Boston, Massachusetts*

ANIMALS

732 ... *SUPPORTING A BEAM* A beam supported by two columns will carry the greatest even distribution load if each column is positioned 22 percent of the length of the beam away from each end. The columns are then separated by 56 percent of the length of the beam. These figures also apply to two people carrying a flexible pipe. *King Royer, structural engineer*

BUILDING

As A RULE OF THUMB: IT'S BETTER TO SHOW UP FOR AN APPOINTMENT TEN MINUTES EARLY BUT A DAY LATE THAN AN HOUR LATE ON THE RIGHT DAY. ALEX FRASER, WASHINGTON, D.C.

733 ... SPOTTING A GOOD PROGRAMMER   Programmers who know assembly language are better than those who don't, even at jobs that don't require assembly language.   *Dave Chapman, computer consultant, Forestville, California*

COMPUTERS

734 ... EDITING A MAGAZINE   Three double-spaced typewritten pages of manuscript can be edited into one magazine column without anyone, not even the author, noticing that 20 percent of the words are gone.   *John Kelsey, editor, Fine Woodworking magazine*

EDITING

735 ... BUYING SHOES FOR KIDS   Four-year-olds will wear out the tops of their shoes before wearing out the soles, but they usually will outgrow them before either happens.   *Denis Smith, high school counselor, Camarillo, California*

CHILDREN

736 ... DRINKING VODKA   You need four cans of tomato juice for one bottle of vodka. You need four bottles of vodka and one package of lemons per bottle of hot sauce.   *David A. Lloyd-Jones, Tokyo, Japan*

DRINKING

737 ... PLANNING DRINKS FOR A PARTY   When you are planning drinks for a party, figure two drinks per guest for the first half hour and one drink per hour after that.   *Lisa Dahl, conference manager, Aurora, New York*

ENTERTAINING

738 ... MAINTAINING A USED AIRPLANE   During the first five years of ownership, the cost of maintenance will nearly equal the purchase price of a used airplane.   *Sarah Padula, teacher and pilot, Freeville, New York*

FLYING

739 ... PLANNING A PUBLIC-ADDRESS SYSTEM   Professional sound crews plan on using one watt of amplification per person for an indoor audience, a watt and a half per person for an outdoor audience.   *James Arthur, sound engineer*

ENTERTAINING

740 ... TAKING A PICTURE   The background of a photograph is as important as the subject.   *Walter Pitkin, literary agent, Weston, Connecticut*

PHOTOGRAPHY

741 ... BOILING WATER AWAY   Changing boiling water to vapor takes about six times the energy needed to raise the same amount of water from freezing to boiling.   *John Hollowell, cook*

ENERGY

742 ... TIMING A CRIME   Find out when the police change shifts in the neighborhood where you plan to commit a crime. You can count on 25 minutes with no patrols starting with the last 15 minutes of the shift that's ending. During this time, policemen are usually writing up reports and talking to the incoming officers.   *Sheridan Chaney, Cindy Latham, & Dale West, former street painters, Hereford, Texas*

CRIME

743 ... BUYING NEW PANTS   You can check the fit of new pants without trying them on. With the top of the pants closed and the button snapped, the waistband should just wrap around your neck.   *Harvey Ferdschneider, photographer*

BODY RULES

744 ... SPLITTING KINDLING RULE OF TWO   When you think your kindling is split small enough, split it two more times.   *Diane Gerhart, accountant*

FUEL

COLOR

745... **THE ECKSTROM GREY COFFEE RULE** If the cream swirls up brown, you have a cup of freshly brewed coffee. If it swirls up grey, the coffee has been sitting on the burner too long. *Rick Eckstrom, plan review officer, Ithaca, New York*

BUSINESS

746... **WATCHING A TAKEOVER** When a company is taken over by another firm in the same field, and it was doing well before the takeover, it will do less well afterwards. If it was not doing well before the takeover, its future will be about as murky as before—or a little more so. *Walter Pitkin, literary agent, Weston, Connecticut*

GAMES

747... **PLAYING POOL** In a game of eight ball, let your opponent sink half his balls before you sink your first. That way, your balls will interfere with his shooting, but his balls won't be there to interfere with your shooting. *John Lilly, mechanical engineer and cliff diver*

HOUSE AND HOME

748... **MAKING A PATH** If, when removing dirt to make a path of stepping stones, you are vexed by buried rocks, more your path a few feet; somebody else had the same idea 50 or 100 years before you. *James McConkey, writer, Trumansburg, New York*

HEALTH

749... **THE HOT-AIR HAND DRYER HEALTH RULE** If you are too busy to use hot-air hand dryers in public restrooms, your lifestyle is too busy for your own health. *Gerald Gutlipp, mathematician, Chicago, Illinois*

CATTLE

750... **KEEPING A GUERNSEY COW** A good Guernsey cow will produce more than 1,000 gallons of whole milk and cream a year. This is enough to feed a family of two adults and three children, with ample skimmed milk left over to feed a veal calf, a pig, and a flock of chickens. An additional bonus: You get 14 tons of manure. *Richard Bacon, writer and historian*

PRECIPITATION

751... **PREDICTING SNOW** You should expect deep snow when hornets build their nests higher than usual. *Robert B. Thomas, The Old Farmer's Almanac*

JOKER

752... **MAKING A MODEL VOLCANO** One-quarter cup of potassium permanganate and one eyedropper of glycerine will do the job. But it is best to use only enough chemicals to create a two-foot flame. *Christopher Cook, Oxnard, California*

DRIVING

753... **RUNNING A YELLOW LIGHT** Three cars can squeeze a left-hand turn out of a yellow light. *Bob Horton, consultant and writer, Largo, Florida*

CONVERSATIONS

754... **DOING SOMETHING FOR MONEY** If someone says, "It's not the money, it's the principle," it's the money. *Dr. Angelo Valenti, consulting psychologist, Nashville, Tennessee*

ANIMALS

755... **SHOWING OFF YOUR TARANTULAS** When stuffed tarantulas are displayed in a glass case, two out of four people will find them interesting. One person will refuse to look and one will want to inspect them closely. All will recoil at the idea of the glass top being removed. *Alan T. Whittemore, YMCA Physical Director, South Deerfield, Massachusetts*

BUILDING

756... **THE POLCE GOOD ROOFER RULE** A good roofer can finish 100 square feet an hour. *Paul Polce, Ponzi's Antiques, Trumansburg, New York*

757 ... AVOIDING MISTAKES When writing a software program, your chances of making a mistake double with each telephone interruption. *R. L. Liming, Indianapolis, Indiana*

758 ... THE RUSSELL PROOFREADING RULE If you find one error while proofreading, there are likely to be several more in the same contiguous paragraphs. *Cheryl A. Russell, demographer, mother, editor-in-chief, American Demographics*

759 ... AVOIDING DANGEROUS TOYS If a toy is smaller than a child's fist, don't buy it; if it can fit in the mouth, it can also get caught in the throat. *Elaine Tyrrell, Children's and Recreational Products Program, Consumer Product Safety Commission*

760 ... PREDICTING THE EFFECTS OF ALCOHOL One drink for a woman is the same as two for a man. *Dr. Charles S. Lieber, Mount Sinai School of Medicine, in The New York Times*

761 ... MAKING COFFEE FOR LARGE GROUPS A one-pound can of regular grind tossed into a commercial urn will brew 50 cups of decent coffee or 60 cups of weak coffee. A pound and a half of regular grind will make 90 cups of decent coffee. *John Brink, building superintendent, Masonic Temple*

762 ... HANDLING AN IN-FLIGHT EMERGENCY When in doubt, fly low and slow; when in extreme doubt, kick top rudder. *Ray Pineo, fly fisherman and pilot, retired, Newville, Pennsylvania*

763 ... PREDICTING THE FATE OF A HIT SONG Songs that hit #1 in December, January, or February are most likely to be ranked #1 for the year on Billboard's charts. *Dennis Palaganas, Gainesville, Florida*

764 ... TAKING A PHOTOGRAPH To determine the average light, measure the light reflected from grass or from a newspaper. The light reflected from Caucasian skin is about twice as bright as average. *Norman Brenner, Fleetwood, New York*

765 ... MAKING ELECTRICITY FROM COAL It takes about a pound of coal to produce a kilowatt hour of electricity. Your electric bill will list the number of kilowatt hours you use every month. You can use this figure to find how much coal was burned to meet your demand for electricity. *John Kellog, electrical engineer*

766 ... COPPING A PLEA If you get arrested, and you did it, and it's your first offense, skip the lawyer, plead guilty, and take your fine and/or probation. It will save you time and money, and it's the best "deal" most attorneys can arrange. *Carl Reddick, probation officer, Newport, Oregon*

767 ... CARRYING THINGS You can lift, for a short time, twice your weight. You can carry and move your own weight. For a long distance you can carry, uncomfortably, half your weight, or comfortably, one-fourth your weight. *J. Baldwin, designer and writer*

768 ... BURNING SOLID FUELS When you are burning solid fuels, a 40 degree Fahrenheit rise in stack temperature indicates a 1 percent reduction in combustion efficiency. *Scott Adams, central heating plant operator, Cornell University*

COLOR

769 ... ***BRUCE'S SOUTHERN CALIFORNIA RULE*** During the 1970s in Southern California, the lighter the blond, the darker the blouse. *Bruce Reznick, associate professor of mathematics, Urbana, Illinois*

BUSINESS

770 ... ***KEEPING YOUR CUSTOMERS*** For every complaint a company receives, there are 26 other customers with problems, and 6 are serious. *Technical Assistance Research Programs, in Microservice Management*

GAMES

771 ... ***PLAYING VIDEO GAMES*** To avoid looking like a beginner, plan on spending $5 the first time you play a video game. If you don't have $5, watch someone else play $5 worth. *Trevor Poole, video game hotshot*

HOUSE AND HOME

772 ... ***PAINTING A HOUSE*** It takes the average person 1 hour to paint 1,000 square feet, plus 1 hour for each window or door. *Rebecca Crowell, artist, Tempe, Arizona*

HEALTH

773 ... ***LOOKING AT URINE*** As a rough estimate of how well hydrated a person is, or as one indicator of high sugar level in a diabetic, look at his or her urine. The darker the color, the higher the specific gravity, the greater the concentration of solutes, and the less hydrated the person is. *Scott M. Kruse, biogeographer and Martha Betcher, medical technologist, Fresno, California*

CATTLE

774 ... ***KEEPING A FAMILY COW*** A family cow won't pay its keep unless your family needs well over a dollar's worth of butter and milk per day. *Phyllis Wood, press operator, Meriden, Connecticut*

PRECIPITATION

775 ... ***RAINING EARLY*** Rain before 7:00, done by 11:00. *Steve Ramsey, antiquarian*

CLIMBING

776 ... ***ESTIMATING HEIGHT*** The rate at which an object falls is independent of how fast it is traveling laterally. To determine the height in feet of a slope, throw a rock out level and time its fall. Square the number of seconds it takes the object to land, then multiply by 16. This will be your height in feet above the landing site. *Thomas W. Neumann, anthropological archaeologist, wildlife ecologist, and field crew crisis manager*

DRIVING

777 ... ***MERGING WITH TRAFFIC*** When merging into a line of traffic, the chances that someone will let you into line increase the more common you look. Expensive cars and junkers get ignored. *Bob Horton, consultant and writer, Largo, Florida*

CONVERSATIONS

778 ... ***ASKING QUESTIONS*** If you ask a negative question, you will get a negative answer. *Denis Smith, high school counselor, Camarillo, California*

ANIMALS

779 ... ***BREEDING BUFFALOES*** You need at least 1 bull buffalo for every 15 cows. *The National Buffalo Association*

BUILDING

780 ... ***ESTIMATING YOUR CONSTRUCTION COSTS*** In construction, you'll spend one dollar on labor for every one dollar you spend on materials. *Captain Haggerty, animal trainer, actor, author, and philosopher, New York, New York*

As a rule of thumb:
IF NO ONE IN THE SCREENING
ROOM NOTICES A PROBLEM IN
A SHOOT THE FIRST THREE
TIMES IT'S PROJECTED, IT CAN
GO INTO THE MOVIE.
Percy Angress, Special Effects
Producer, Santa Monica,
California

781... **THE FINANCIAL CONDITION RULE** The financial strength of a Silicon Valley company is inversely proportional to the glitz in its reception area. *Ben Cota, technology marketing guy, Oakland, California*

782... **PROOFREADING STATISTICS** Always expect to find at least one error when you proofread your own statistics. If you don't, you are probably making the same mistake twice. *Cheryl A. Russell, demographer, mother, editor-in-chief, American Demographics*

783... **RAISING YOUR CHILDREN** Parents teach more by example than by words. Reading parents have reading children; achieving parents have achieving children. *Denis Smith, high school counselor, Camarillo, California*

784... **DEALING WITH A DRUNK** The easiest way to quiet a drunk is to whisper to him. *Scott Parker, data specialist, Beaumont, Texas*

785... **COOKING BEANS** Eight quarts of dried beans will feed 100 people. *The Lansing Methodist Church Women's Society*

786... **FINDING HALF THE ATMOSPHERE** At 18,000 feet, half of the earth's atmosphere is below you. *W. R. C. Shedenhelm, wind salesman, Encino, California*

787... **JUDGING YOUR STATUS** If you have to tell someone what you are, you aren't. *R.A. Heindl, design engineer, Euclid, Ohio*

788... **HOLDING A CAMERA STEADY** If you're older than 40, don't take pictures at less than 1/125th of a second unless you use a tripod. *Martin M. Bruce, Ph.D., psychologist, Larchmont, New York*

789... **MAKING ELECTRICITY FROM COAL** How much coal do you use each year? An electric water heater uses 2 tons of coal for an average-size family. Electric ranges and clothes dryers use another half ton of coal each. A color television uses about 500 pounds of coal each year, and an electric frying pan uses 200. *John Kellog, electrical engineer*

790... **THE BURGLARY RULE OF THREE** To determine the true value of items stolen in a burglary, take the reported value and divide by three. *Thomas O. Marsh, writer and former police chief, Fairfield, Ohio*

791... **ESTIMATING YOUR ADULT HEIGHT** Your adult height will be twice your height at the age of 22 months. *Steve Parker, aerospace engineer, Princeton, New Jersey*

792... **MELTING METAL** A pound of coke will melt 20 pounds of bronze or 9 pounds of iron. *C. W. Ammens, founder*

COLOR

793...**ATTRACTING HONEYBEES**   Red flowers usually are ignored by honeybees; blue flowers usually attract them. *Pierce Butler, Natchez, Mississippi*

BUSINESS

794...**KEEPING YOUR CUSTOMERS**   Complainers are more likely than dissatisfied noncomplainers to do business again with the company that upset them, even if the problem is not satisfactorily resolved. *Technical Assistance Research Programs, in Microservice Management*

GAMES

795...**WINNING AT WHEEL OF FORTUNE**   Doing crosswords will improve your ability at Wheel of Fortune, and vice versa. *Dennis Palaganas, Gainesville, Florida*

HOUSE AND HOME

796...**THE SAG RULE**   There is cause for concern if the ridge of a house sags more than 1/2 inch per year. *Albert Snyder, Albuquerque, New Mexico*

HEALTH

797...**CHOOSING MARGARINE**   Regarding cholesterol content, the margarine sold in tubs is better for you than that sold in sticks. *Dr. Stephen S. Scheidt, Professor of Clinical Medicine, Cornell University Medical College, New York City*

CATTLE

798...**DIGGING A POST HOLE**   A hole for a cattle-fence post should be an arm's length deep, plus the length of your fingers. *Adrienne Garreau, farmer*

PRECIPITATION

799...**FAIRLEIGH'S WET WORKSITE RULE**   If you need a four-wheel drive vehicle to get to and maneuver about a worksite, it is probably too wet to work anyway. *Fairleigh Brooks, landscaper, Louisville, Kentucky*

CLIMBING

800...**THE ALTITUDE AND INFORMATION RULE**   The higher you go, the more information you can get about altitude sickness. *Jon Yawn, mechanic, Ithaca, New York*

DRIVING

801...**MERGING WITH TRAFFIC**   Your chances of merging into a line of traffic increase if you make eye contact with a driver in the line. *Bob Horton, consultant and writer, Largo, Florida*

CONVERSATIONS

802...**OFFERING HELP**   Some people aren't really looking for help. If someone responds to three valid suggestions with a "yes, but..." he or she is more interested in playing games than solving problems. *Andrea Frankel, computer scientist, engineer, holistic health practitioner, San Diego, California*

ANIMALS

803...**WEIGHING WHALES**   To estimate the weight of a gray whale, figure one ton per foot of length. *Anonymous Whale Watcher, Marna Del Rey, California*

AS A RULE OF THUMB:
SUBDIVISIONS ARE NAMED
FOR WHAT THEY DESTROYED.
GREG KOOS,
MCLEAN CO. HISTORICAL SOCIETY,
BLOOMINGTON, ILLINOIS

BUILDING

804...**MANAGING A CONSTRUCTION PROJECT**   In supervising construction work, your logic is better than a craftsman's explanation. *Captain Haggerty, animal trainer, actor, author, and philosopher, New York, New York*

805... **PREDICTING A LAYOFF**   When the lights are on after six in the personnel department of a Silicon Valley company, look for layoffs within two weeks. *Ben Cota, technology marketing guy, Oakland, California*

806... **THE TIME RULE**   When a popular phenomenon reaches the cover of TIME, it is already out of fashion. *Richard L. Holloway, Associate Professor, University of Minnesota*

807... **CARING FOR A SICK CHILD**   If your child is four months old or younger and is running a rectal temperature greater than 100 degrees F, get medical help. *Scott M. Kruse, biogeographer and Martha Betcher, medical technologist, Fresno, California*

808... **KEEPING YOUR COFFEE WARM**   If you like hot coffee, add the cream immediately after you pour yourself a cup. Don't wait until you're ready to drink it. *Gerry M. Flick, M.D., Ship's Surgeon, S.S. Constitution off Hawaii*

809... **TELLING A JOKE**   Choosing the right inflection and tone of voice is important when telling a joke. It's also important to eliminate all unnecessary conjunctions. When in doubt, do Tonto. *Esquire magazine, "how to tell a joke"*

810... **STAYING PROFICIENT AS A PILOT**   You should fly at least 100 hours a year to stay proficient as a fair-weather pilot. If you're flying on instruments, or IFR, make that 200 hours a year. *Jack Barclay, biologist, pilot, flight instructor, Santa Cruz, California*

811... **EDITING A MOVIE**   If you can't direct-cut a film, your story's in trouble. *Dean Sheridan, electronics technician and deaf actor, Torrance, California*

812... **SHOOTING PHOTOGRAPHS**   A professional photographer should plan on exposing one roll of film per hour on the job. *Jon Reis, photographer, Ithaca, New York*

813... **GENERATING POWER**   When generating power on a large scale, no more than 15 percent should come from any one source. Things get screwed up when more than 15 percent of a system is out of service. *Joel Garreau, author*

814... **AGREEING TO TAKE A LIE DETECTOR TEST**   If you are innocent, do not take a lie detector test. If you're guilty, take it, because it may exonerate you. *Kevin Kelly quoting Discover*

815... **DETERMINING YOUR FRAME SIZE**   You can determine your body frame size by wrapping your thumb and index finger around your wrist. If the thumb extends past the index finger, you have a small frame; if the thumb and index finger just meet, you have an average frame; and if the thumb and index finger do not meet, you have a large frame. *Terry Hayward, medical technician*

816... **PICTURING AN OIL WELL**   A deep oil well has the same proportions as a human hair ten feet long. *Harold E. Haynes, addicted to statistical curiosities, Cherry Hill, New Jersey*

COLOR

BUSINESS

JOKER

HOUSE AND HOME

HEALTH

CATTLE

PRECIPITATION

CLIMBING

DRIVING

CONVERSATIONS

ANIMALS

BUILDING

817...**GLAZING A BUTCHER SHOP**   If you have a butcher shop with raw meat on display, the greener the glass in the window, the more the flies will stay away. Unfortunately, it has the same effect on customers. *Diana Souza, illustrator, Ithaca, New York*

818...**KEEPING YOUR CUSTOMERS**   Between 54 percent and 70 percent of customers who complain to a company will do business again with the company if their complaint is resolved. That figure increases to 95 percent if the customer feels the complaint was resolved quickly. *Technical Assistance Research Programs, in Microservice Management*

819...**ENTERING A CONTEST**   If a contest calls for "25 words or less," try to use as close to 25 words as possible. Never use less than 15 words. *Allen Glasser, contest expert*

820...**MANUFACTURING OXYGEN**   A lawn 50 by 50 feet in size supplies the complete oxygen needs of a family of four. *Curt Suplee, writer and editor, in The Washington Post Magazine*

821...**COMPARING SHRIMP TO EGGS**   It takes two dozen jumbo shrimp to match the cholesterol contained in one egg yolk. *Dr. Stephen S. Scheidt, Professor of Clinical Medicine, Cornell University Medical College, New York City*

822...**BUYING BEEF**   Beef fat tinged with yellow means an animal was grass fed; white fat means grain fed. *Dennis Palaganas, Gainesville, Florida*

823...**THE RULE OF OUTDOOR CONSTRUCTION**   When raindrops hit your windshield faster than you can count them, it's time to knock off work for the day. *Gene Beitel, contractor*

824...**AVOIDING ALTITUDE SICKNESS**   To avoid altitude sickness, don't sleep more than 1,000 feet higher than you did the night before. You can ascend higher during the day to establish routes, but you should descend to the 1,000-foot interval before settling down for the night. *David Kumaki, physician, Shelburne, New Hampshire*

825...**MERGING WITH TRAFFIC**   If you want to merge into a line of traffic quickly, do it in front of big trucks or buses. They take longer to catch up with traffic and often leave just enough space for a car to squeeze in. *Bob Horton, consultant and writer, Largo, Florida*

826...**CARTMILL'S PUNK RULE OF CULTURAL VALUES**   You are unlikely to have a productive discussion about cultural values with anyone who thinks the terms "new wave" and "punk" are synonymous and will not believe that any distinction between the two exists. *Rusty Cartmill, Athens, Georgia*

827...**FOLLOWING A DEER**   If deer droppings are black, moist, and glossy, the deer left them within 15 or 20 minutes and is in the immediate vicinity. If the droppings are no longer glossy, they have been on the ground for an hour or more and the deer is probably bedded down on a southern slope. *Sigmund Sameth, Irvington, New Jersey*

828...**SIZING A PIPE**   Doubling the diameter of a pipe increases its capacity by four. *John Fischer, volunteer fireman, Joliet, Montana*

829 ... INVESTING IN SILICON VALLEY In boom times, 30 percent of Silicon Valley venture capitalists will be funding identical projects. As with everybody else, they take creative risks only when they need to — like in a downturn. *Ben Cota, technology marketing guy, Oakland, California*

COMPUTERS

830 ... THE MAGAZINE RULE If you find one interesting thing in a magazine, then it's worth getting a subscription. *Cally Arthur, managing editor, American Demographics*

MAGAZINES

831 ... PUNISHING A CHILD When you use the time-out method to discipline a child, use one minute for each year of the child's age. *John Fischer, volunteer fireman, Joliet, Montana*

CHILDREN

832 ... MAKING A GOOD CUP OF COFFEE If your coffee is too strong, the grind is too fine. If your coffee is too weak, the grind is too coarse. The faster the brewing method, the finer the grind. *Dean Sheridan, electronics technician and deaf actor, Torrance, California*

HABITS

833 ... FEEDING LARGE GROUPS Three tofu buckets of chopped vegetables will feed 100 people. *Christiann Dean, sociologist*

JOKER

834 ... PAYING FOR AN AIRPLANE On all airplanes, from little ones to 747s, the price of the engine, or engines, is from 20 to 25 percent of the retail price of the airplane. *Richard L. Collins, aviation writer*

FLYING

835 ... MAKING MONEY FROM A MOVIE Movies must make three times their cost of production to cover distribution costs. *Norman Brenner, Fleetwood, New York*

MOVIES AND FILM

836 ... RUNNING A PHOTOGRAPHY STUDIO For every hour photographers are on the job shooting film, they spend four hours working in the studio. *Jon Reis, photographer, Ithaca, New York*

PHOTOGRAPHY

837 ... THE SOUTH-FACING WINDOW RULE One square foot of a south-facing window that is insulated at night will provide about 100,000 BTUs of heat per winter. *Robert Mendenhall, Boulder, Colorado*

ENERGY

838 ... CATCHING A PYROMANIAC A pyromaniac is proud of his work, and may be found in the crowd watching the fire. The professional will be somewhere else, establishing an alibi. *Anonymous*

CRIME

839 ... THE OUTSTRETCHED ARMS TO HEIGHT RULE As a rule, the distance between your fingertips, with your arms outstretched at shoulder height, is equal to your height. *C. Dees, Stockton, California*

BODY RULES

840 ... RUNNING A PRODUCTIVE MEETING At a meeting, productivity is inversely proportional to the number of people attending above four. *Steven M. Keisman, New York City high school resource coordinator*

GROUPS

COLOR

841 ... PAINTING A CAR   When you're choosing paint for a car, navy blue, burgundy, or black cherry connote "luxury." Bright yellow and red are "sporty." Black and white are classics, while grays and silvers seem "European." Greens are hard to sell. *Rich and Jean Taylor Constantine, quoting Debbie Weber, manager of Color Development Design at the Ford Motor Co., Parade magazine*

BUSINESS

842 ... KEEPING YOUR CUSTOMERS   The average customer who has had a problem with a company tells nine or ten people about it. *Technical Assistance Research Programs, in Microservice Management*

INSURANCE

843 ... BUYING LIFE INSURANCE   Parents with young children should have five or six times their salaries in life insurance. People without children should have enough to pay off their debts. *Sharon Yntema, writer, Ithaca, New York*

JOKER

844 ... SPOTTING A SCHIZOPHRENIC   Schizophrenics almost never yawn. *Scott Parker, data specialist, Beaumont, Texas*

HEALTH

845 ... CHECKING OUT A NURSING HOME   If you smell urine when you enter a nursing home, it is not a place to put someone you care about. *Edward J. Garrison, nursing home administrator, Watsonville, California*

JOKER

846 ... GROWING CHRYSANTHEMUMS   If you cultivate mums, don't leave home for more than three days. *Walter Pitkin, literary agent, Weston, Connecticut*

PRECIPITATION

847 ... WATCHING YOUR CHICKENS   If your chickens run for cover when it starts to rain, the shower will be brief. If they stay outside, it is going to rain all day. *Lewis and Paulette Ramsey, Howardsville, Virginia*

CLIMBING

848 ... THE MOUNTAINEER'S WIND RULE   A plume of snow blowing from a peak higher than 7,000 meters means a wind of at least 100 miles per hour on the summit. *David Kumaki, physician, Shelburne, New Hampshire*

DRIVING

849 ... LLOYD'S RULE OF COUNTING LICENSE PLATES   On a highway, 1 in 22 cars will have a license plate from a foreign province or state. *Carolyn Lloyd, 15-year-old student, Montreal, Quebec*

CONVERSATIONS

850 ... WAITING FOR A CHANCE TO SAY SOMETHING   People will lapse into silence after every 20 minutes of conversation. *Margie Halpin, unemployed sprinkler fitter's apprentice, Cincinnati, Ohio*

ANIMALS

851 ... RAISING WILD ANIMALS   Keep baby animals in something that is 90 to 95 degrees Fahrenheit until their eyes open, then lower the temperature 5 degrees a week to room temperature. *Carl Grummich, veterinarian*

BUILDING

852 ... LAUNCHING AN ARCHITECTURE PROJECT   It takes nine months to launch an architecture project. *Ted Hatch*

AS A RULE OF THUMB: YOU'RE DONE WHIPPING WHEN YOU CAN TURN THE BOWL UPSIDE DOWN AND THE CREAM DOESN'T FALL OUT. CAROLYN DEDRICK, ENDWELL, NEW YORK

853...SELLING SOFTWARE A new hardware product will start to sell two to three months sooner than a new software product. That's because hardware is built to solve obvious needs, like lack of memory. Software is designed to solve less obvious needs. No one believes software will work until they read a product review. *Ben Cota, technology marketing guy, Oakland, California*

COMPUTERS

854...SELLING MAGAZINES If your magazine has a car on the cover, you'll sell more copies at the newsstand if the car is red. *Paul A. Delaney, meteorologist, Beltsville, Maryland*

MAGAZINES

855...KEEPING YOUR KIDS IN SHOES Children aged 6 to 10 outgrow their shoes every 84 days. *Mason Speed, WTKO radio, Ithaca, New York*

CHILDREN

856...SPOTTING AN ADDICT The more abused as a child, the more addictions as an adult. *Patrick Carnes, creator of the first inpatient program for sex addicts*

HABITS

857...APPROXIMATING YOUR FIELD OF VIEW The hook of a coat hanger equals the binocular field of view (7 to 8 degrees) of a standard pair of binoculars when held 15 to 18 inches from the eyes. *Dean Sheridan, electronics technician and deaf actor, Torrance, California*

EYES

858...THE GROUND CUSHION RULE The ground cushion is an invisible area near the runway where the interaction between the airplane's wing and the ground cause changes in an airplane's flight characteristics. Measured scientifically, the height of the ground cushion is about equal to the wingspan of the airplane. A pilot, however, will notice the effects at an altitude half the wingspan of the airplane. *Richard L. Collins, aviation writer*

FLYING

859...SPOTTING A HIT MOVIE Any war movie with the word "force" in the title is a bomb. *Liz Stone, SUNY College of Environmental Science & Forestry, Syracuse, New York*

MOVIES AND FILM

860...LISSECK'S RULE OF PHOTOGRAPHIC FILTERS Any filter will lighten objects of its own color and darken those of a complementary hue. *Paul Lisseck, health food broker, North Hampton, Massachusetts*

PHOTOGRAPHY

861...SAVING OIL RESOURCES One square foot of a south-facing window that is insulated at night saves 1 gallon of oil per year. *Tom Wilson, energy consultant*

ENERGY

862...HIJACKING AN AIRPLANE Only hijack an airplane as part of a team. If there's a long standoff, someone has to stand guard while you go to the bathroom. *Gordon Hard, assistant editor, Consumer Reports, Mount Vernon, New York*

CRIME

863...USING A PENCIL If the painted area of a pencil is smaller than the width of your four fingers, the pencil is too small to use comfortably. Throw it out. *Steven F. Scharff, cartoonist, Union, New Jersey*

BODY RULES

864...CHOOSING A TREASURER In a small organization that does not pay its officers, the treasurer's position is likely to be held by the one member who will accept it. *Alan R. Brown, New York, New York*

GROUPS

COLOR

BUSINESS

INSURANCE

ILLNESS

HEALTH

GARDENING

PRECIPITATION

CLIMBING

DRIVING

CONVERSATIONS

ANIMALS

BUILDING

865... **WALKING ON THIN ICE**   Blue ice is safer than black ice.   *Cally Arthur, managing editor, American Demographics*

866... **KEEPING YOUR CUSTOMERS**   Customers who have complained to a company and who had their complaint satisfactorily resolved tell an average of five people about it.   *Technical Assistance Research Programs, in Microservice Management*

867... **THE THUMB-VALUE RULE**   A thumb is worth 40 percent of the whole hand in worker's compensation cases.   *Scott Parker, data specialist, Beaumont, Texas*

868... **APPRAISING HALLUCINATIONS**   If someone is experiencing auditory hallucinations, the diagnosis usually is mental illness. If someone is experiencing hallucinations involving sight, smell, or touch, the diagnosis usually is a physical illness.   *Gerry M. Flick, M.D., Ship's Surgeon, S.S. Constitution off Hawaii*

869... **DECIDING WHAT KINDS OF FOOD TO EAT**   Food that ants like to eat is food that people should avoid (ants in our kitchen go for sweets and deep-fried tortilla chips).   *David Leventer, psychotherapist, Santa Cruz, California*

870... **GROWING PLANTS INDOORS**   Most indoor plants do best in 1,000 to 1,200 foot-candles of light. You can determine whether you have enough light in a room by taking a camera with a built-in light meter, setting the ASA to 200, the f stop to 1/16, and the shutter speed to 1/60th of a second. If there is enough light for a picture, then there are 1,000 to 1,200 foot-candles of light.   *Thomas W. Neumann, anthropological archaeologist, wildlife ecologist, and field crew crisis manager*

871... **FORECASTING THE WEATHER**   Big flakes mean little snow. Little flakes mean a lot of snow.   *Stanley G. Laite, St. John's, Newfoundland, Canada*

872... **CLIMBING IN THE SMOKIES**   Climbing 1,000 feet in altitude in the Great Smoky Mountains in North Carolina results in a change in vegetation equal to traveling 100 miles north—the Smoky Mountains at 6,000 feet look like northern New England or southern Canada.   *Doug Rugh, agricultural economist, Sevierville, Tennessee*

873... **AVOIDING DEER ON THE ROAD**   Half of all the deer hit by cars are struck in May or November.   *Walter Pitkin, literary agent, Weston, Connecticut*

874... **LISTENING TO PEOPLE**   When someone speaks in a passive voice, he is trying to conceal something.   *Alfred Kahn, economist*

875... **DOUBLING YOUR POPULATION**   You can quickly calculate the number of years it will take for a population to double by dividing the number 72 by the population's growth rate.   *David T. Russell, retired high school teacher, Dilltown, Pennsylvania*

876... **ESTIMATING THE STRENGTH OF A BEAM**   The strength of a beam is proportional to the square of the dimension parallel to the direction of the load.   *Paul A. Delaney, meteorologist, Beltsville, Maryland*

877 ... **BUYING A COMPUTER**   A computer will be out of date three years after it first became available. *Marc Pelath, student and programmer, Michigan City, Indiana*

COMPUTERS

878 ... **SELLING MAGAZINES**   On a magazine cover, young sells better than old. Television sells better than movies. Politics should be avoided. And when in doubt run, Princess Di. *Scott Parker, data specialist, Beaumont, Texas*

MAGAZINES

879 ... **SETTING A CHILD'S ALLOWANCE**   A child's allowance should be large enough to cover some basics with a little left over, yet small enough to require choices. Too little or too much of an allowance will not teach a child how to deal with money. *Dian Nafis, New York State Cooperative Extension*

CHILDREN

880 ... **QUITTING SMOKING**   To quit smoking, it takes the average smoker three or four serious attempts over seven to ten years. *Janice M. Prochaska, professor, University of Rhode Island*

HABITS

881 ... **SPOTTING A FARSIGHTED PERSON**   A farsighted man always knows where his glasses are. *Thomas W. Neumann, anthropological archaeologist, wildlife ecologist, and field crew crisis manager*

EYES

882 ... **LANDING AN AIRPLANE**   To make every landing as much the same as possible, enter the ground cushion with the airplane trimmed to 1.2 to 1.3 times its stalling speed. *Richard L. Collins, aviation writer*

FLYING

883 ... **SPOTTING A GOOD MOVIE**   Never waste your money on any movie that has a simian for a co-star. *Dan Wagner, San Jose, California*

MOVIES AND FILM

884 ... **SELLING PHOTOGRAPHS**   Photographs on file with a stock agency will bring you 50 cents per image per year. *Jon Reis, photographer, Ithaca, New York*

PHOTOGRAPHY

885 ... **STORING HEAT IN A GREENHOUSE**   Containers of water are excellent for storing heat in a solar greenhouse. Start with 1 cubic foot of water for each square foot of greenhouse glass. *Janet Hopper, New York City*

ENERGY

886 ... **SOLVING A CRIME**   To solve a crime, remember two things: The most obvious solution is probably the correct one; and if you've eliminated all the other possibilities, whatever is left, however improbable, is what happened. *Stephen G. Michaud quoting F.B.I. agent Howard D. Teten quoting Sherlock Holmes in The New York Times*

CRIME

887 ... **APPROXIMATING THE SIZE OF YOUR BRAIN**   You can approximate the size of your brain by putting your fists together so that your wrists touch and your thumbnails face you side by side. *Dennis Palaganas, Gainesville, Florida*

BODY RULES

888 ... **SPOTTING A COMPLAINER**   The more complaining a person does about an organization, the less that person participates in the organization. *Alberta D. Phillips, Little Meadows, Pennsylvania*

GROUPS

COLOR

889 ... GERMAN'S RULE OF GIFTS FOR MEN   When buying a gift for a man, anything packaged in yellow will probably please him.   *Ann German, East Islip, New York*

BUSINESS

890 ... MARKETING A FAD   You have 90 days to make and ship a novelty item and 90 days to sell it out. After that, inventory costs swallow up the profits.   *Ellis E. Conklin, UPI feature writer, quoting Fred Reinstein, fad merchant*

INSURANCE

891 ... CLAIMING YOUR MEDICAL INSURANCE   If you're fully insured, you will spend two full days doing insurance paperwork to cover seven days in the hospital.   *John E. Harney, Concord, New Hampshire*

ILLNESS

892 ... MINIMIZING THE SIDE EFFECTS OF MEDICATIONS   Prescribe the smallest dose that will produce the desired result.   *Walter Pitkin, literary agent, Weston, Connecticut*

HEALTH

893 ... ANALYZING YOUR DIET   If your turds float, there's too much fat in your diet.   *Michael Rider, art director, American Demographics*

GARDENING

894 ... PLANTING PEPPERS   When the crocuses bloom, plant peppers and eggplant indoors.   *Vivian Brubaker, Bettendorf, Iowa*

JOKER

895 ... SHIVERING   Shivering produces as much heat as running at a slow pace or roughly the amount of heat generated from eating two medium-sized chocolate bars per hour.   *Peggy Kerber, editor, Mountaineering*

CLIMBING

896 ... AVOIDING AVALANCHES   A snowfall of one inch or more per hour indicates a very high avalanche potential.   *Scott M. Kruse, biogeographer, Fresno, California*

DRIVING

897 ... THE DEBATABLE RULE OF SLOW DRIVERS   The speed of a vehicle drops by 10 percent for each gray-haired person in a car.   *Bob Horton, consultant and writer, Largo, Florida*

CONVERSATIONS

898 ... TALKING TO REPORTERS   Don't tell a reporter anything you don't want printed. Not that they can't be trusted, but what you tell reporters off the record can lead them to another source who may not be so discreet.   *Lester R. Bittel, management consultant*

ANIMALS

899 ... THE PAPER PLATE RULE OF HUNTING   The vital area on a whitetail deer is about the size of a paper plate. Never shoot from farther away than you can consistently hit a paper plate.   *Dr. Timothy Haywood, physicist, Wilmington, North Carolina*

BUILDING

900 ... DESIGNING A BUILDING   Only 20 percent of buildings are designed by architects.   *Scott Parker, data specialist, Beaumont, Texas*

AS A RULE OF THUMB: YOU CAN ESTIMATE DISTANCE IF YOU CLOSE ONE EYE AND LOOK AT A DISTANT OBJECT OVER THE THUMB OF YOUR OUTSTRETCHED ARM. NOW CLOSE THE EYE AND OPEN THE OTHER ONE. YOUR THUMB WILL BE FIXED ON ANOTHER POINT NEAR THE OBJECT. ESTIMATE THE DISTANCE BETWEEN THESE TWO POINTS AND MULTIPLY BY SEVEN. THIS WILL GIVE YOU THE APPROXIMATE DISTANCE FROM YOU TO THE OBJECT.   WOLF JUCKOFF, FORMER GERMAN BOY SCOUT, REXVILLE, NEW YORK

901...WRITING A COMPUTER PROGRAM   To write a good program, write and debug the entire program, get it documented and working perfectly, then start over again from scratch based on what you learned the first time through. This process can be repeated as many as four times and still be cost effective, but you should always do it at least once.   *Phil A. Schrodt, Associate Professor, Northwestern University, Evanston, Illinois*

902...SAVING MONEY IN MAGAZINE PUBLISHING   Every 1/8-inch reduction in a magazine's trim size, will save you about 2 percent of your paper.   *Cally Arthur, managing editor, American Demographics*

903...SUPPORTING A CHILD   Child-support payments for one child will usually equal 20 percent of the gross income of the parent who doesn't have custody.   *Carol Benjamin, Scottsdale, Arizona*

904...STARTING TO SMOKE   If you don't start smoking or drinking before age 25, you're unlikely to start after that age.   *Scott Parker, data specialist, Beaumont, Texas*

905...HIDING THINGS   Never hide an object at eye level. If you're hiding something from children, never hide it below your eye level.   *Jeff Brown, astronomer, Bloomington, Indiana*

906...SPEEDING UP AN AIRPLANE   If you put a larger engine in your airplane, you can expect the cruise speed to increase by one-third the percent you've increased the power. For example, pump up the power by 30 percent and you'll see a 10 percent increase in your cruise speed.   *Bill Cox, Plane and Pilot*

907...SPOTTING A GOOD MOVIE   Never waste your money on any movie that is called "zany" or a "laff riot."   *Dan Wagner, San Jose, California*

908...PHOTOGRAPHING A CAR   A three-quarter front view makes the most effective photograph for selling a car.   *Paul Douglas, photographer*

909...TURNING OFF YOUR LIGHTS   If you have to leave a room for more than a minute, turn off the lights. Otherwise, leave them on. For fluorescent lights, use one hour as the rule.   *Bob Horton, statistics consultant, West Lafayette, Indiana*

910...FOLLOWING CRIME   Bad weather is a cop's best friend. When it's raining and cold, nobody is outside committing crimes.   *Eric Hanson, Houston Chronicle, quoting Houston Police spokesman Sgt. J.C. Mosier.*

911...AUTHENTICATING A HUMAN SCALP   To tell a real human scalp from a fake, look for a tiny bald spot in back of the crown from which the hair radiates.   *Kate Gladstone, Brooklyn, New York*

912...GOING TO THE BATHROOM   It takes four teenage girls to accompany one to the bathroom. Young adults go in threes, and older women go in pairs.   *Phillip Williams, Jr., University of Michigan, Ann Arbor, Michigan*

COLOR

913...**AVOIDING POISONOUS SNAKES**   Red next to yellow can kill a fellow, but red next to black is a friend of Jack.   *Dennis Palaganas, Gainesville, Florida*

BUSINESS

914...**LOOKING AT BUSINESS LETTERS**   One out of every three business letters does nothing more than seek clarification of earlier correspondence.   *Scott Parker, data specialist, Beaumont, Texas,*

INSURANCE

915...**BUYING CAR INSURANCE**   If your car is worth $1,500 or more, you should carry collision insurance. However, you can save money by choosing a policy with a higher deductible. As a rule, your collision deductible should equal one week's take-home pay.   *Paul Majka, author, You Can Save a Bundle on Your Car Insurance*

ILLNESS

916...**TRANSFUSING BLOOD**   The transfusion of one unit of packed red blood cells should raise a patient's hemoglobin by about one gram per deciliter and raise the hematocrit by approximately 3 percent.   *John H. Bloor, M.D., Ph.D., Buffalo, New York*

HEALTH

917...**MACMILLAN'S RULE OF EXHALING**   A healthy adult should be able to completely exhale a deep breath in three seconds.   *James Macmillan, M.D.*

GARDENING

918...**PLANTING BY DAFFODILS**   When daffodils bloom, sow tomatoes, cabbage, and lettuce indoors.   *Vivian Brubaker, Bettendorf, Iowa*

TEMPERATURE

919...**BOILING WATER TO DETERMINE YOUR ELEVATION**   For every 550 feet in elevation, the boiling point of water falls by 1 degree Fahrenheit. To determine your elevation, measure the boiling point of water, subtract the temperature from 212 degrees, and divide the difference by 1.8. This will give you your approximate elevation in thousands of feet.   *Ernst Luposchainsky, III ("Kahn"), adventurer, mage, philogynist, inter alia, Hollywood, California*

CLIMBING

920...**CHOOSING AN ICE AX**   An ice ax, standard equipment for climbing snow or ice, should reach from your wrist to the ground with your arms at your sides.   *R. Maynard, Fullerton, California*

DRIVING

921...**SAFE DRIVING SPEEDS**   It's safe to drive ten miles per hour faster than that the highway caution signs.   *Norman Brenner, Fleetwood, New York*

CONVERSATIONS

922...**CONTROLLING OFFICE RUMORS**   If you don't want to start an office rumor, don't say anything you wouldn't write in a memo.   *Nancy Humphries, personnel consultant, Ithaca, New York*

ANIMALS

923...**THE RAT HOLE RULE**   A grown rat can pass through a hole the size of a quarter.   *Whetstone, Lafayette, Louisiana*

BUILDING

924...**BUILDING AN IGLOO**   An igloo should be built in an area where the snow is packed just loose enough to make a footprint, but not so loose that a footprint blows away in a high wind.   *Dennis Eskow, science editor, Popular Mechanics*

AS A RULE OF THUMB: IF YOU HAVE TO WORK NEAR A DOWNED ELECTRIC LINE, KEEP THE DISTANCE BETWEEN YOU AND THE LINE EQUAL TO YOUR HEIGHT.
JOHN FISCHER, VOLUNTEER FIREMAN, JOLIET, MONTANA

925...SPENDING MONEY ON COMPUTERS Average users of personal computers will spend as much on software as they did on the original machine. Sophisticated users will spend as much on additional hardware as they spent on the original machine, and twice as much on software. *Phil A. Schrodt, Associate Professor, Northwestern University, Evanston, Illinois*

COMPUTERS

926...SAVING MONEY IN MAGAZINE PUBLISHING If your print order is below 1.25 million, you should use offset. Above that, look at gravure. *Cally Arthur, managing editor, American Demographics*

MAGAZINES

927...CORRELATING BRAIN DAMAGE WITH IQ Among brain-damaged children who were 5 years old or older when their brain damage occurred, each 1 percent of brain destroyed means a 4-point drop in IQ. *Laurence Miller, Psychology Today*

CHILDREN

928...SHORTENING YOUR LIFE WITH CIGARETTES Each cigarette you smoke shortens your life by the amount of time you took to smoke it, plus ten minutes. *Gerry M. Flick, M.D., Ship's Surgeon, S.S. Constitution off Hawaii*

HABITS

929...SPOTTING A BAD COP Cops who wear sunglasses on dark days or at night are either alcoholics or don't like their jobs. *John H. Beauvais, Cambridge, Massachusetts*

EYES

930...TAKING OFF IN A PLANE A good minimum runway length for a light airplane is double the manufacturer's recommended distance to climb to 50 feet. *J. Mac McClellan, senior editor, Flying*

FLYING

931...SPOTTING A GOOD MOVIE Never waste your money on any movie for which the names of the technical crew only all end in vowels. *Dan Wagner, San Jose, California*

MOVIES AND FILM

932...USING A TELEPHOTO LENS The longer the focal length of a lens, the more important it is to hold it steady, especially at slow shutter speeds. You can generally hand hold a camera with a shutter speed that is equal to the reciprocal of the focal length of the lens. Slower speeds require a tripod. *Jim Crissman, veterinary pathologist, Midland, Michigan*

PHOTOGRAPHY

933...MOVING ENERGY THROUGH THE FOOD CHAIN Different levels in the food chain are called trophic levels. As organisms eat and get eaten, food energy is passed along the food chain. From one trophic level to the next, there is a 90 percent loss of energy. *M. N., Enterprise, Oregon*

ENERGY

934...LOOKING FOR SHOPLIFTERS Shoplifters are most active on Fridays and Sundays between 3 p.m. and 6 p.m. *Roger Griffin, retail security agency official, Van Nuys, California, in Parade magazine*

CRIME

935...ESTIMATING WEIGHT A "Newton" is equivalent to the weight of a small apple. *Scott Parker, data specialist, Beaumont, Texas*

EQUIVALENTS

936...GETTING WORK DONE When working unsupervised, two people get more done than three. *Captain Haggerty, animal trainer, actor, author, and philosopher, New York, New York*

GROUPS

COLOR

937 ... ATTRACTING ATTENTION   Red is the color most likely to attract attention. This includes the attention of the police if you drive a red car. *Dennis Palaganas, Gainesville, Florida*

BUSINESS

938 ... DESIGNING A SUPERMARKET   Supermarket efficiency increases with store size to a maximum of 22,000 square feet. After that, economies of scale are offset by communication problems. *Retail Management Letter*

INSURANCE

939 ... BUYING LIFE INSURANCE   The average family should have life insurance coverage worth at least six times its annual income. *Stephanie Betz, accountant*

ILLNESS

940 ... MEASURING BLOOD GLUCOSE   In patients with high blood glucose, the true value of their serum sodium is approximated by subtracting 100 from the measured glucose, multiplying the result by 1.6, and adding this result to the measured serum sodium in mg per deciliter. *John H. Bloor, M.D., Ph.D., Buffalo, New York*

HEALTH

941 ... WATCHING YOUR BLOOD PRESSURE   Blood pressure levels vary with age and sex. A rule of thumb for estimating the normal systolic pressure in a male is to add 100 to the age of the patient, up to the level of 100 mm Hg. *John Fischer, volunteer fireman, Joliet, Montana*

GARDENING

942 ... PLANTING TOMATOES   When lilies of the valley bloom, plant tomatoes outside. *Vivian Brubaker, Bettendorf, Iowa*

TEMPERATURE

943 ... ESTIMATING A COUNTRY'S GNP   A change of 1 degree C in the average annual temperature will result in a 2 percent change in the country's GNP. *Thomas W. Neumann, anthropological archaeologist, wildlife ecologist, and field crew crisis manager*

CLIMBING

944 ... CHECKING A ROPE   Get a new rope when 50 percent of the surface strands are worn to fuzz. *Peggy Kerber, editor, Mountaineering*

DRIVING

945 ... PARALLEL PARKING   To parallel park, start beside the car in front of the space. Back into the space in a tight arc until the headlights of the car behind disappear from your rearview mirror. *Norman Brenner, Fleetwood, New York*

CONVERSATIONS

946 ... SPOTTING A TROUBLEMAKER   Beware those who preface a suggestion with, "I don't see why you can't..." *Leonard Morgenstern, pathologist, Moraga, California*

ANIMALS

947 ... INVESTIGATING THE DIET OF A DEAD DEER   Check the bone marrow of a deer's thighbone. If it resembles red or yellow jelly, the deer starved to death. If the marrow is solid fat flecked with a little red, or even red but still solid, the deer was well fed. *Paul Kelsey, biologist*

BUILDING

948 ... VENTILATING YOUR ATTIC   You need 1 square foot of attic vent for every 150 square feet of attic ceiling area. *Rick Eckstrom, plan review officer, Ithaca, New York*

As A RULE OF THUMB: CHOOSE A GOLF CLUB THAT SHOULD LAND THE BALL ON THE BACK FRINGE. MORE OFTEN THAN NOT, IT WILL LAND IN THE CENTER OF THE GREEN, ESPECIALLY IF THE SHOT IS LONGER THAN 130 YARDS. JUD TOWN, AUTHOR, SAINT ALBERT, CANADA

949...WRITING A COMPUTER PROGRAM   In most computer programs, 10 percent of the program accounts for 90 percent of the processing time. Finding and rewriting this part of the program so that it runs fast is always cost effective. *Phil A. Schrodt, Associate Professor, Northwestern University, Evanston, Illinois*

950...GETTING QUOTES FOR A MAGAZINE PRINT JOB   If a job is more than 10 percent of the year's printing budget, get six quotes. Smaller jobs, get three. *Camilla Walter, Hood River, Oregon*

951...TALKING TO BABIES   Too much talking can overstimulate your baby, while too little can leave your child quiet and unresponsive. The optimum amount of time for baby talk is 25 percent to 30 percent of the time your infant is alert and responsive. If your baby is alert for half an hour, limit talk to seven to ten minutes. *Marilyn Elias, quoting UCLA child psychologist Kiki V. Roe in American Health*

952...SMOKING IN THE DARK   If you enjoy smoking in the dark, it will be harder for you to give up cigarettes than someone who only smokes in daylight or well-lit situations. *Gerry M. Flick, M.D., Ship's Surgeon, S.S. Constitution off Hawaii*

953...SPOTTING A CARNIVORE   Mammals with eyes looking straight ahead are carnivorous. Mammals with eyes looking to the side are vegetarian. This is also true for most fish and birds. *Gerry M. Flick, M.D., Ship's Surgeon, S.S. Constitution off Hawaii*

954...LANDING A LEAR JET   A Lear jet 25G will float about 100 extra feet down the runway for each knot over its proper landing speed. *Richard Collins, pilot and writer*

955...THE CONFUSING RULE OF CHOOSING MOVIES   If a movie looks good and the critics love it, you'll like it. If a movie looks good and the critics hate it, you'll love it. If it looks bad and the critics love it, try it. Otherwise, don't bother. *Marc Pelath, student and programmer, Michigan City, Indiana*

956...SHOOTING A FILM   A professional photographer feels pleased if he or she gets one good shot on a roll of film. *Jeff Furman, Ben & Jerry's Ice Cream, business consultant*

957...GENERATING STEAM   Managing flue gases is an important part of generating steam on a large scale. You should plan on one pound of flue gas for every three pounds of steam you generate. *John H. Parker, mechanical engineer*

958...RAISING CRIMINALS   Children of criminals are three times as likely to become criminals as children of non-criminals. *Scott Parker, data specialist, Beaumont, Texas*

959...EATING AN ELEPHANT   One elephant will provide as much meat as 100 antelopes. *Pygmy hunters in the Ituri forest of Zaire, from NOVA*

960...PREDICTING WORK EFFORT   People work 5 to 10 percent harder by themselves than when they're in a group. *Scott Parker, data specialist, Beaumont, Texas*

JOKER

961 ... *THE JAPANESE RULE OF FLOWER ARRANGING* Put into the vase one-third as many flowers as you think you need, then take half of them out. *Lewy Olfson, contemplative, Stonington, Connecticut*

BUSINESS

962 ... *WATCHING A BUSINESS START* If a recently opened store spreads its inventory thin by devoting a large amount of shelf space to each product, the owner is showing a healthy caution by not investing heavily before he has developed a clientele and a knowledge of his customers. *Walter Pitkin, literary agent, Weston, Connecticut*

INSURANCE

963 ... *SNYDER'S RULE OF FINANCIAL SECURITY* For a minimum level of financial security, your net worth (the cash value of all of your assets) minus all your debts should equal one year's income. *J. Snyder, credit manager*

ILLNESS

964 ... *MEASURING SERUM CALCIUM* In patients with low serum albumin, the true value for total serum calcium is approximated by subtracting the measured albumin from 4.0, multiplying the result by 0.8, and adding this result to the measured total serum calcium in mg per deciliter. *John H. Bloor, M.D., Ph.D., Buffalo, New York*

HEALTH

965 ... *AVOIDING CARCINOGENS* Any substance with "chloro" or "fluoro" in its name should be considered a probable carcinogen or mutagen. *Steven M. Keisman, New York City high school resource coordinator*

GARDENING

966 ... *PLANTING OUTDOORS* When irises bloom, put peppers, cucumbers, and eggplant outdoors. *Vivian Brubaker, Bettendorf, Iowa*

TEMPERATURE

967 ... *ESTIMATING TEMPERATURE* The average annual temperature of an area is the same as the temperature of water just emerging from a spring. *Thomas W. Neumann, anthropological archaeologist, wildlife ecologist, and field crew crisis manager*

CLIMBING

968 ... *CHECKING A ROPE* A climbing rope is overdue for retirement when you can no longer feel the separate strands as your hand slides along it. *Peggy Kerber, editor, Mountaineering*

DRIVING

969 ... *DRIVING IN TRAFFIC* The heavier the traffic, the less you gain by changing lanes. *Steven M. Keisman, New York City high school resource coordinator*

CONVERSATIONS

970 ... *SPOTTING THE SMARTER BROTHER* The smarter brother will talk faster. *Kelly Yeaton, teacher and stage manager, State College, Pennsylvania, quoting a Navy doctor*

ANIMALS

971 ... *TELLING SHEEP FROM GOATS* Some breeds of sheep look like goats and some breeds of goats look like sheep. In general, sheep's tails hang down and goats' tails stand up. *Mary Ellen Parker, retired teacher, Cincinnati, Ohio*

BUILDING

972 ... *BUILDING STAIRS* Any combination of riser height plus tread width that adds up to 17 1/2 inches will be comfortable to use and will not cause people to stumble. *Don Naish, Dryden, Michigan*

973 ... **WRITING A COMPUTER PROGRAM**   No good computer program can be written by more than ten people; the best programs are written by one or two people.   *Phil A. Schrodt, Associate Professor, Northwestern University, Evanston, Illinois*

COMPUTERS

974 ... **FINDING DIRTY MAGAZINES**   Two out of every three magazines tossed along the roadsides will be pornographic.   *Rusty Cartmill, Athens, Georgia*

MAGAZINES

975 ... **PETERSON'S RULE OF SERVINGS**   Children don't need huge servings of food. Start with one tablespoon of each item per year of age.   *Gayle Peterson, mother, Columbus, Ohio*

CHILDREN

976 ... **RECOVERING FROM LSD**   It takes ten years to recover from serious use of LSD.   *Leonard Cohen, poet and songwriter, quoted in USA Today*

HABITS

977 ... **BUYING FISH**   To determine whether fish is fresh, check the eyes. They should be clean, bulging, shiny, and bright.   *Jeff Smith, The Frugal Gourmet*

EYES

978 ... **SOARING CROSS-COUNTRY**   When flying a sailplane on a cross-country flight, expect thermals to be five times as far apart as they are high.   *John Campbell, glider pilot, Ann Arbor, Michigan*

FLYING

979 ... **SPOTTING A BAD MOVIE**   Never see a movie whose title ends in a number.   *Paul Lisseck, health food broker, North Hampton, Massachusetts*

980 ... **TAKING PICTURES UNDER WATER**   Most leaks in an underwater camera housing show up at very shallow depths. If no leaks appear within 15 feet of the surface, there is a 95 percent chance that none will appear at greater depths.   *Flip Schulke, underwater photographer*

MOVIES AND FILM

981 ... **CRACKING YOUR KNUCKLES**   After cracking your knuckles, it takes 30 minutes for the vaporized joint fluid to go back into solution, which it must do before you can crack them again.   *Jim Crissman, veterinary pathologist, Midland, Michigan*

PHOTOGRAPHY

982 ... **MAKING CRIME PAY**   Steal from large numbers of people as indirectly as possible. Individuals are afraid of crimes directed specifically at them. The threat disappears when the crime is impersonal, the loss indirect — the more impersonal and indirect, the better.   *Stephen Gillers, journalist*

JOKER

983 ... **COMPARING THE PRICE OF GOLD TO OIL**   Under ideal conditions, the price of an ounce of gold should equal the price of 13 barrels of oil.   *Anonymous expert*

CRIME

984 ... **MANAGING PEOPLE**   No matter how many public announcements are made, 10 percent of the troops won't get the word.   *Rubinsol, New York*

EQUIVALENTS

AS A RULE OF THUMB:
YOU CAN SUBSTITUTE A
COUGH FOR A SNEEZE BY
FORCING YOUR EYES
OPEN WITH BOTH HANDS.
CAROLYN LLOYD, 15-YEAR-OLD
STUDENT, MONTREAL, QUEBEC

GROUPS

DESIGN

985 ... *JUDGING DESIGN* When simple things need instructions, it is a sign of poor design. *Dean Sheridan, electronics technician and deaf actor, Torrance, California*

BUSINESS

986 ... *WATCHING A BUSINESS FAIL* If an older store begins to spread its stock thin, and especially if it seems to feature old inventory, it is in serious distress and is likely to fail. *Walter Pitkin, literary agent, Weston, Connecticut*

INSURANCE

987 ... *ASSURING SUCCESS* To succeed against all possible odds, count on at least 1 in 4 things going wrong. In other words, you need a 33 percent margin of safety. If you have to have 30 of something, plan to make 40. *Stanley J. Goodman, How to Manage a Turnaround*

ILLNESS

988 ... *INVESTIGATING KIDNEY FAILURE* If the ratio of BUN (blood urea nitrogen) to serum creatinine is greater than 25, the cause of kidney failure is probably pre-renal (i.e., dehydration). If the ratio is less than 20, the cause is probably intrinsic renal disease. Ratios between 20 and 25 are ambiguous. *John H. Bloor, M.D., Ph.D., Buffalo, New York*

JOKER

989 ... *CRISPIN'S RULE OF PHYSICAL WELL-BEING* If you piss white, you're all right. *Jon Crispin, photographer, Swampscott, Massachusetts*

GARDENING

990 ... *THE MELON RULE* When peonies bloom, plant melons. *V. Brubaker, Bettendorf, Iowa*

991 ... *THE FROZEN NOSE RULE* Take a deep breath through your nose. If the moisture in your nose momentarily freezes, it is 0 degrees F or below. *Seamus O'Connolly, New Mexico*

TEMPERATURE

992 ... *CLIMBING MOUNT EVEREST* The death rate for climbers on Mount Everest is one for every seven to make it to the top. The rate is lower for Sherpas and women, higher for military people. *David A. Lloyd-Jones, Tokyo, Japan*

CLIMBING

993 ... *DRIVING IN RUSH HOUR* Ignore reports of traffic jams on the radio during rush hour. By the time you hear about them, the traffic usually has cleared up — except for jackknifed tractor trailers. *Steven M. Keisman, New York City high school resource coordinator*

DRIVING

994 ... *REGAINING YOUR TRAIN OF THOUGHT* If you lose your train of thought while on the phone, hang up on yourself. As soon as you hang up, your thoughts will return and you can redial. The other person will assume it's a disconnect. *Terry Larimore, writer and therapist, Houston, Texas*

CONVERSATIONS

995 ... *TAKING A PET TO THE VET* If it's not a life-threatening illness, wait three days after a pet seems sick before seeing a vet. In most cases the illness will pass. *Steven M. Keisman, New York City high school resource coordinator*

ANIMALS

996 ... *SIZING LUMBER* Standard framing lumber spaced on 16" centers will span a distance, in feet, that is twice its wider dimension, in inches. For example, a 2 x 8 will span 16 feet. *Larry Beck, joiner, Ludlowville, New York*

BUILDING

Aₛ A RULE OF THUMB:
IN COMPLETE KIDNEY FAILURE,
THE SERUM CREATININE SHOULD
NOT RISE BY MORE THAN 1 MG
PER DECILITER PER DAY.
John H. Bloor, M.D., Ph.D.,
Buffalo, New York

997 ... **DEALING WITH A COMPUTER**   When dealing with a computer, a good rule to remember is to treat it as you would a small, retarded (but very obedient) child. *Bob Horton, consultant and writer, St. Petersburg, Florida*

COMPUTERS

998 ... **PUBLISHING A MAGAZINE**   A magazine or newspaper needs to be about 50 percent advertising to survive financially. *John Schubert, senior editor, Bicycling magazine*

MAGAZINES

999 ... **TALKING ABOUT YOUR CHILD**   A child will become as you describe him to others. *attributed to Danny Kaye*

CHILDREN

1000 ... **CALLY'S COFFEE RULE**   It takes four hours to come down from your last cup of coffee. *Cally Arthur, managing editor, American Demographics*

HABITS

1001 ... **APPRAISING ALLIGATORS**   The distance between an alligator's eyes in inches is its length in feet. *Joan Isbell, horticulturist, Phoenix, Arizona*

EYES

1002 ... **TAKING OFF IN AN AIRPLANE**   If you haven't left the ground in the first half of the runway, abort the takeoff. *John Stickle, chief pilot and flight instructor*

FLYING

1003 ... **FILMING A MOVIE**   If you don't get it in three takes, you're never going to get it. *Captain Haggerty, animal trainer, actor, author, and philosopher, New York, New York*

MOVIES AND FILM

1004 ... **TAKING A PICTURE**   A good guide for exposing film on a clear day with the sun at your back is to set the aperture at f16 and the shutter speed to the ASA of the film. *Jon Reis, photographer, Ithaca, New York*

PHOTOGRAPHY

1005 ... **CLEANING YOUR HANDS**   If you want to sterilize the dirt on your hands, use the warm-air hand dryer. If you want to get the dirt off your hands, find a towel. *Alan R. Brown, New York, New York*

GROOMING

1006 ... **MAKING CRIME PAY**   Commit a federal crime rather than a state crime. Federal judges are worldly and less likely to send you to jail, or give you as long a sentence. Also, federal prisons are nicer places to stay. *Stephen Gillers, journalist*

CRIME

1007 ... **THE LIPPMANN RULE OF SNOW**   One inch of rain would make ten inches of snow. *Amy Lippmann, Haifa, Israel*

EQUIVALENTS

1008 ... **PLANNING A CO-OP**   Unless you are forming some sort of intentional or spiritual community, four people is the best number for an adult cooperative household. It provides good levels of intimacy and manageability. *Geanne Toma, massage therapist, Lebanon, New Hampshire*

GROUPS

DESIGN

1009 ... ***JUDGING DESIGN*** If you wonder how you're going to remember the explanation, the design has failed. *Dean Sheridan, electronics technician and deaf actor, Torrance, California*

BUSINESS

1010 ... ***BRUMAN'S RULE OF FINISHED PRODUCTS*** The materials for a mass-produced electronic device should cost about 10 percent of the retail price of the finished product. *Ray Bruman, Berkeley, California*

INSURANCE

1011 ... ***BUYING INSURANCE FOR YOUR SON*** The monthly cost of car insurance for a teenage boy is roughly five times the amount they could earn by doing every conceivable chore around the house. *Warren Harris, Sacramento, California*

ILLNESS

1012 ... ***CATCHING A COLD*** You will catch a cold within two weeks of starting a new job. *Beth Blinick, sales promotion and marketing, Skokie, Illinois*

HEARTS

1013 ... ***AVOIDING A FATAL SHOCK*** A current of 0.1 amps through the heart kills. *Norman Brenner, Fleetwood, New York*

GARDENING

1014 ... ***IDENTIFYING A SEDGE*** Sedges have edges (round rushes have none). *Scott M. Kruse, biogeographer, Fresno, California*

TEMPERATURE

1015 ... ***USING A HEAT GUN*** If you place your palm in front of a heat gun and it feels like a hairdryer, it's about 200 degrees F. If it's so hot you have to yank your hand away, then it's about 300 degree F. *Dean Sheridan, electronics technician and deaf actor, Torrance, California*

CLIMBING

1016 ... ***CLIMBING WITHOUT SUPPLEMENTARY OXYGEN*** I need one week to acclimate my body for climbing a 5,000-meter mountain without oxygen, two weeks for a 6,000-meter mountain, three for 7,000 meters, and at least four weeks for an 8,000-meter mountain. *Reinhold Messner, mountaineer, via Henning Pape, West Berlin, Germany*

DRIVING

1017 ... ***AVOIDING A SPEEDING TICKET*** You can safely exceed the posted speed limit on stretches of road without shoulders. *Steven M. Keisman, New York City high school resource coordinator*

JOKER

1018 ... ***CALLING SOMEONE UP*** If you are a single woman, never call a person with whom you have a sexually ambiguous relationship when you are drunk. *Ruth Anne Schultz, rain check coordinator, Kingston, Massachusetts*

ANIMALS

1019 ... ***FLEEING A BEAR*** Bears can outrun, outclimb, and outswim a human. Your only hope is to run downhill. A bear's center of gravity makes it difficult for them to run downhill. *Steven M. Keisman, New York City high school resource coordinator*

BUILDING

1020 ... ***BUILDING A HOUSE*** Sixty percent of the construction costs for a frame house are labor, 40 percent are materials. *J. Johnson, Fort Collins, Colorado*

1021 ... **PICKING A PROGRAMMER**   Never hire a computer programmer who knows only one programming language. *Andrea Frankel, computer scientist, engineer, holistic health practitioner, San Diego, California*

1022 ... **SELLING SUBSCRIPTIONS**   Increase the price of your magazine by 10 percent and you can expect to receive 10 percent fewer subscription orders. *Cathy Elton, San Francisco, California*

1023 ... **THE BIRTHDAY RULE OF PARTY GUESTS**   The number of guests at a child's birthday party should be limited to the age of the child. Invite three for a three-year-old, five for a five-year-old. *Diane Gerhart, accountant*

1024 ... **SMOKING CIGARETTES**   You need three books of matches for every two packs of cigarettes you smoke. *Bob Horton, statistics consultant, West Lafayette, Indiana*

1025 ... **CHECKING YOUR SUNGLASSES**   For high-altitude skiing, you need sunglasses that are dark. With your sunglasses on, look in a bathroom mirror. If you can see your eyes, the glasses aren't dark enough. *Rick Eckstrom, plan review officer, Ithaca, New York*

As a rule of thumb: blueberries are white when they're green.
S\tanley G. L\aite, S\t. J\ohn's, N\ewfoundland, C\anada

1026 ... **AVOIDING OTHER AIRPLANES**   If you spot another airplane and it is above the horizon, it is above you. If it is below the horizon, it is below you. If the other airplane is at the same level as the horizon, it is at your altitude. If an approaching airplane appears motionless, it is on a collision course with you. *John Stickle, chief pilot and flight instructor*

1027 ... **SPOTTING A BAD MOVIE**   If a TV movie starts out badly and has not improved by the first commercial, it won't. *Eleanor Benelisha, library and information services, Richmond, California*

1028 ... **TAKING PICTURES INTO THE SUN**   When you are shooting subjects into the sun, open the aperture an extra one and a half f-stops. *Jon Reis, photographer, Ithaca, New York*

1029 ... **MAKING YOUR HAIR SHINE**   To add shine to your hair, rinse it with cold water. *Carolyn Lloyd, 15-year-old student, Montreal, Quebec*

1030 ... **MAKING CRIME PAY**   Commit a crime that a judge can relate to. *Stephen Gillers, journalist*

1031 ... **FEEDING DAIRY COWS**   For feeding dairy cows, three tons of corn silage equal one ton of hay. *Monica Crispin, Cooperative Extension agent*

1032 ... **PLANNING SPACE FOR A BUSINESS MEETING**   For a business meeting, find a room large enough to provide at least 30 square feet of space per person. *Cally Arthur, managing editor, American Demographics*

DESIGN

1033 ... JUDGING DESIGN   The right design minimizes the need for labels. Wherever labels seem necessary, consider another design. *Dean Sheridan, electronics technician and deaf actor, Torrance, California*

BUSINESS

1034 ... WORKING WITH A NEW CLIENT   A job with a new client will take about 25 percent longer than the same job with an established client. *Michael Rider, art director, American Demographics*

JOKER

1035 ... GUESSING A MAN'S AGE   To guess a man's age, take his height and multiply it by the number of times a day he goes to the bathroom. *Henning Pape-Santos, linguist, Ithaca, New York*

ILLNESS

1036 ... RECUPERATING   For every day you spend in the hospital, plan on one week to recuperate. *Jon Crispin, photographer, Swampscott, Massachusetts*

HEARTS

1037 ... AVOIDING HEART DISEASE   Eat fish once a week to lower your chances of developing heart disease. Eating fish more than once a week does not significantly affect your chances of developing the disease. *Norman Brenner, Fleetwood, New York*

GARDENING

1038 ... STORING SEEDS AT ROOM TEMPERATURE   If you are storing seeds at room temperature, each percentage point you reduce their moisture content will approximately double their longevity. *J. L. Hudson, seedsman, Redwood City, California*

TEMPERATURE

1039 ... SQUEAKING SNOW   If snow squeaks when you walk on it, the temperature is 10 degrees F or less. *R.A. Heindl, design engineer, Euclid, Ohio*

CLIMBING

1040 ... CLIMBING MOUNTAINS   According to the 1952 Everest Expedition, one pound added to your boots equals five pounds added to your back. Buy the lightest boots that are safe. *David A. Lloyd-James, Tokyo, Japan*

DRIVING

1041 ... DRIVING SAFELY   A safe car with unsafe tires is an unsafe car. *Steven M. Keisman, New York City high school resource coordinator*

ROMANCE

1042 ... COMMUNICATING WITH YOUR LOVER   If your companion asks "why?" after you've said "I love you," it's a bad sign. *Dean Sheridan, electronics technician and deaf actor, Torrance, California*

ANIMALS

1043 ... PLANNING A CAGE FOR A SNAKE   A snake needs a cage whose perimeter is equal to or greater than its body length. *Terry Larimore, writer and therapist, Houston, Texas*

BUILDING

1044 ... CHOOSING FLOOR JOISTS   When you are building a floor, use floor joists hefty enough to limit deflection at the center of the floor to 1/360th of the span. *Albert G. H. Dietz, Dwelling House Construction*

1045 ... *LOOKING OVER A COMPUTER MANUAL* If a manual's table of contents lists names of programs or components instead of tasks, the manual isn't "user friendly." *Bruce Nevin, editor and technical writer, Gloucester, Massachusetts*

1046 ... *FINANCING A MAGAZINE* The price of ads in a commercial magazine should be 12 times the printing costs per unit area, including film, separation, and production charges. *David A. Lloyd-Jones, Tokyo, Japan*

1047 ... *FINDING BOOKS FOR KIDS* You can teach your children how to find books at their own reading level. Tell your child to open a book near the middle and read from the top of any full page. If there are five words the child doesn't know before getting to the end of the page, the book is too hard. *Eliza Brownrigg Graue, Is Your Child Gifted?*

1048 ... *SMOKING HASHISH* Good hashish should make you cough on the first hit. *Anonymous hashish smoker, Poplar Ridge, New York*

1049 ... *STARING AT SOMEONE* Two people who stare each other in the eye for 60 seconds straight will soon either be fighting or making love. *Pierce Butler, Natchez, Mississippi*

1050 ... *PLANNING A FLIGHT* Add half a gallon of fuel per cylinder to normal fuel consumption to determine the climb fuel for a normally aspirated light airplane. Also add a couple of gallons for taxi and takeoff. *Bruce Landsberg, pilot and writer*

1051 ... *SPOTTING A BAD MOVIE* No good movie has ever included a hot-air balloon. *Paul A. Delaney, meteorologist, Beltsville, Maryland*

1052 ... *CAPTURING SOMETHING ON FILM* If you want to capture something on film but you can't take several exposures, overexpose the metered value by one-half to one f-stop. The information has a better chance of being recorded. *Carl Ebeling, engineer, Pittsburgh, Pennsylvania*

1053 ... *ADJUSTING YOUR BATH* Use both faucets when you're adjusting the temperature of a bath or shower. *Stephen Unsino, poet, Eastchester, New York*

1054 ... *DEBUGGING AN OFFICE* Checking an office for phone taps and electronic bugging devices takes at least four hours for each 5,000 square feet of office space (two hours for a sweep using instruments and two hours for a physical search). *Boardroom Reports*

1055 ... *STORING CORN* Two bushels of ear corn equal one bushel of shell corn. *Martin Stilwell, farmer*

1056 ... *THE VOLUNTEER RULE* Any volunteer organization is alive and well if at least 35 percent of its members volunteer consistently. *John Towle, Salinas, California*

DESIGN

1057 ... **CREATING A WORK SPACE**   No matter how big a draftsman's table, there will be a 12" x 18" uncluttered area upon which to work.   *Richard Malone, Vancouver, Washington*

BUSINESS

1058 ... **CHARGING FOR CONSULTING**   A consultant should never charge for less than half a day of work. *Daniel Corbitt, consultant*

MEASURING

1059 ... **MEASURING SOMETHING**   To measure something with a 100-foot steel tape held only at the ends, the stretch of the tape will cancel the sag in the middle. The ends of the tape will be 100 feet apart, no matter how much the tape weighs.   *King Royer, surveyor, author of one surveying text*

ILLNESS

1060 ... **CREATING YOUR OWN PROBLEMS**   A creative person is 35 times more likely than the average person to need treatment for a mental problem.   *Scott Parker, Beaumont, Texas, quoting Omni*

HEARTS

1061 ... **THE ONE DRINK RULE**   To lower your chances of developing heart disease, have one—and only one—alcoholic drink a day. *Norman Brenner, Fleetwood, New York*

GARDENING

1062 ... **STORING SEEDS AT LOW TEMPERATURE**   If you are keeping seeds in cold storage, each 10 degrees Fahrenheit you lower their temperature will double their longevity. *J. L. Hudson, seedsman, Redwood City, California*

TEMPERATURE

1063 ... **ESTIMATING TEMPERATURE VARIATION**   The greater the distance from a large body of water, the greater the difference between high and low temperatures on a daily and an annual basis. *Paul A. Delaney, meteorologist, Beltsville, Maryland*

JOKER

1064 ... **THE HOPELESSLY LOST SOLITAIRE RESCUE RULE**   If you're ever lost in the woods, pull out a deck of cards and play solitaire. Before long, someone will come along and tell you to put the red jack on the black queen. *Captain Haggerty, animal trainer, actor, author, and philosopher, New York, New York*

DRIVING

1065 ... **AVOIDING A SPEEDING TICKET**   To avoid a speeding ticket, drive at the speed everyone else is driving. When in doubt, drive 62.5 mph, which is the de facto national speed limit.   *Thomas W. Neumann, anthropological archaeologist, wildlife ecologist, and field crew crisis manager*

ROMANCE

1066 ... **THE PHONE NUMBER RULE**   If a woman answering your personal ad does not give you her phone number, you'll never meet her.   *John H. Beauvais, Cambridge, Massachusetts*

JOKER

1067 ... **SPOTTING A MOUSE**   If you think you saw a mouse, you did.   *Cheryl A. Russell, demographer, mother, editor-in-chief, American Demographics*

BUILDING

1068 ... **LOOKING AT HOUSES**   In house building, the lighter the framing, the more recent the construction. *Greg Koos, McLean Co. Historical Society, Bloomington, Illinois*

1069 ... BUYING A NEW COMPUTER   If you are unsure of yourself when buying a new computer, ask the same questions you would ask a new car salesperson.   *Paul Hoffman, writer, Berkeley, California*

1070 ... STACKING MAGAZINES   To prevent a stack of magazines from falling over, change the direction of the binding every sixth issue.   *Dennis Palaganas, Gainesville, Florida*

1071 ... MEASURING CHILDREN   The height of a child on its second birthday will be about half its adult height, though girls will be a little shorter when grown.   *J. Eichelberger, Alameda, California*

1072 ... GRINDING COFFEE BEANS   Grind coffee beans three seconds for each coffee measure of beans.   *Warren Harris, Sacramento, California*

1073 ... INSPECTING SPECTACLES   When trying on glasses, put them on and look at your feet. If they start to slip off your face, they are too loose.   *Paul Lampe, writer and poet, St. Louis, Missouri*

As a rule of thumb:
CLEAR WATER IS TWICE
AS DEEP AS IT LOOKS.
Rev. Fred Puttere,
Tour Boat Captain, Wicki
Wachie River, Florida

1074 ... PLANNING A FLIGHT   A fuel stop will add 45 minutes to the total trip time. The average fuel stop includes personal refreshment, at least one phone call, paying the fuel bill, and a walk around to check fuel caps and sumps. Add 10 minutes if a squall line is approaching and you are hoping to depart before the weather arrives.   *Bruce Landsberg, pilot and writer*

1075 ... FIGURING OUT A MOVIE   In a thriller, you can be certain that any road detour is just a trick to kidnap the occupants of the car.   *Paul A. Delaney, meteorologist, Beltsville, Maryland*

1076 ... MAKING CONTACT PRINTS   You should expose your contact prints just long enough to get a solid black print through the clear edge of the film. This will make your good negatives look good and your bad negatives look bad, which saves time later when you are searching for a photo to print.   *Mike Rambo, photographer, Ithaca, New York*

1077 ... USING A PUBLIC TOILET   In a public restroom, the middle toilet stalls are used the most.   *Scott Parker, data specialist, Beaumont, Texas*

1078 ... SHOPLIFTING   You can figure that 1 out of every 40 to 60 people in a store is a shoplifter. Only 1 in every 200 shoplifters gets caught.   *Eugene A. Sloane, security expert*

1079 ... THICKENING THINGS   For thickening soups and sauces, you can use cornstarch instead of flour. One tablespoon of cornstarch equals two tablespoons of flour.   *Kay Parker, artist and quilt designer*

1080 ... PLANNING A MEETING   A meeting without an agenda will take twice as long and accomplish half as much as a meeting with an agenda.   *Andrea Frankel, computer scientist, engineer, holistic health practitioner, San Diego, California*

DESIGN

1081 ... **THE LUNCHBOX RULE** A popular lunchbox design will have three or four good years before fading into oblivion. *Anonymous*

BUSINESS

1082 ... **STARTING A BUSINESS VENTURE** The idea for a new venture is likely to be strategically unsound if it can't be put into one coherent sentence. *Kenichi Ohmae, The Mind of the Strategist*

MEASURING

1083 ... **THE SPEED RULE** Speed in feet per second is about 1.5 times speed in miles per hour. *R.A. Heindl, design engineer, Euclid, Ohio*

ILLNESS

1084 ... **CONSIDERING GALL BLADDERS** White women with blond hair, light skin, and light eyes are the most likely victims of gall bladder problems. *Scott Parker, data specialist, Beaumont, Texas*

HEARTS

1085 ... **CHECKING YOUR HANDS** Look at the tendons on the back of your hand as you wiggle your fingers. If you see lumps of fat on those tendons, you probably have high cholesterol. *Anonymous*

GARDENING

1086 ... **PLANTING SHRUBBERY** Never plant more than three of the same shrub in a row. Always offset. *Steven M. Keisman, New York City high school resource coordinator*

TEMPERATURE

1087 ... **FORECASTING THE WEATHER** If the temperature is warmer than normal, the weather is likely to change — perhaps violently. *Anonymous*

SURVIVAL

1088 ... **HIDING SOMETHING** To hide outdoors at night, pick a place that's darker than the immediate surroundings of your pursuers. Also, pick as noisy an area as possible. *Jeff Brown, astronomer, Bloomington, Indiana*

DRIVING

1089 ... **DRIVING SAFELY** The more transient the population, the more dangerous the driving. *Thomas W. Neumann, anthropological archaeologist, wildlife ecologist, and field crew crisis manager*

ROMANCE

1090 ... **THE TWO OUT OF THREE RULE** You can have a hot job, a hot lover, or a hot apartment. But you can't have all three at the same time. *Armistead Maupin*

INSECTS

1091 ... **HARVESTING HONEY** A skilled beekeeper can get as much as 100 pounds of honey per hive per year. *Dave Peyton, Gannett News Service*

BUILDING

1092 ... **WORKING WITH WATER PRESSURE** Ten feet of elevation gives four pounds of pressure in a water pipe. *Peter Reimuller, Point Arena, California*

AS A RULE OF THUMB: SUSPECTS FLEEING THE SCENE OF A CRIME IN A CAR WILL MAKE RIGHT TURNS MORE OFTEN THAN LEFT BECAUSE THEY DON'T WANT TO WASTE VALUABLE TIME WAITING FOR CROSS TRAFFIC TO CLEAR. IF YOU DIDN'T SEE WHICH WAY THEY WENT, TRY TURNING RIGHT.

JOHN HOWSDEN, POLICE SERGEANT, FREMONT, CALIFORNIA

1093 ... *THE SILICON VALLEY RULE*   To be considered a success in Silicon Valley, you must make more than twice your age in thousands and your spouse must be less than half your age plus seven. *Roy A. Berg, Los Altos, California*

COMPUTERS

1094 ... *LEARNING NEW THINGS*   Humans cannot learn more than seven new concepts at a time. *David Kumaki, physician, Shelburne, New Hampshire*

JOKER

1095 ... *HIRING BOYS*   One boy's a boy; two boys are half a boy; three boys are no boy at all. *Margaret "Granny" Cochron, 102 years old*

CHILDREN

1096 ... *GETTING GOOD ADVICE*   Avoid career counselors. If they knew how to get a good job, they'd have one. *Pierre F. Angier, Jersey City, New Jersey*

JOKER

1097 ... *FINDING YOUR DOMINANT EYE*   To find your dominant eye, make a circle of your thumb and forefinger about 6 inches in front of your face. Look through the circle with both eyes at an object across the room. Now close one eye; if the object stays in the circle, the open eye is the dominant one. *Donald H. Dunn, in Business Week*

EYES

1098 ... *PLANNING A FLIGHT IN A HOT AIR BALLOON*   You get about half an hour of flight in a hot air balloon per 20-pound tank of propane gas. *Barbara Frederking, balloonist*

FLYING

1099 ... *FIGURING OUT A MOVIE*   In a murder mystery, if there's a close-up scene of a character for no apparent reason, that character is most likely the killer. *Paul A. Delaney, meteorologist, Beltsville, Maryland*

MOVIES AND FILM

1100 ... *MAKING PRINTS FROM SLIDES*   If there's some light on a subject's face in an underexposed slide, chances are you can get a satisfactory print if you order special-order highlighting. *Dean Sheridan, electronics technician and deaf actor, Torrance, California*

PHOTOGRAPHY

1101 ... *CUTTING YOUR HAIR*   People who wear their hair short will generally need a haircut within a week after their hair looks perfect. *Ann Kimbrough, Blaine, Tennessee*

GROOMING

1102 ... *SELLING STOLEN PAINTINGS*   A stolen painting will sell for one-tenth of what it would sell for on the open market. *Kat Dalton, artist, Ithaca, New York*

CRIME

1103 ... *BRITISH THERMAL UNITS*   One BTU is roughly equal to the amount of heat energy given off by burning a wooden kitchen match. *Robert G. Flower, engineer*

JOKER

1104 ... *WORKING WITH GROUPS*   Twenty percent of any group will be critical of the rest. *Marilyn Rider, Body & Soul, Ithaca, New York*

GROUPS

DESIGN

1105 ... _LOOKING AT SPECKS_   If your eyes can see it, you need to worry about it. That's the rule for any faint mark or strange speck on artwork headed for the printer. Otherwise, if you want something to show up, it won't and if you don't want something to show up, it will.   *Michael Rider, art director, American Demographics*

BUSINESS

1106 ... _THE MARKETING RULE OF THREE_   Any new product should have at least three easily recognizable advantages over its competition.   *Lloyd Barringer, sales representative*

MEASURING

1107 ... _USING A MICROSCOPE_   If you can see an object with a light microscope, its dimensions can be conveniently expressed in millionths of a meter (micrometers).   *Derek D. Cardy, zoologist, University of British Columbia, Vancouver, British Columbia, Canada*

ILLNESS

1108 ... _TAKING TONSILS OUT_   A conservative doctor will recommend a tonsillectomy if a child has seven attacks of tonsillitis within a year, or five in each of the preceding two years. A less conservative doctor will recommend the operation if a child has three to five attacks in each of two consecutive years.   *William A. Nolen, M.D.*

HEARTS

1109 ... _THE HEART RULE_   A healthy person's heart is about the size of his or her fist.   *Thomas O. Marsh, writer and coroner's investigator, Fairfield, Ohio*

GARDENING

1110 ... _GROWING BONSAI_   If it takes more than one minute for the water to drain from your bonsai pot, it's time to repot.   *Rick Eckstrom, plan review officer, Ithaca, New York*

TEMPERATURE

1111 ... _THE MEENGS RULE OF INLAND WATER BODIES_   As you move inland from a large body of water during the summer, the temperature will increase 1 degree F per mile for the first 10 miles. During the winter, the temperature will decrease accordingly.   *Dirck Z. Meengs, management consultant, Canoga Park, California*

SURVIVAL

1112 ... _THE LONG RULE OF EDIBILITY_   If you are foraging for food but are not sure about the edibility of a plant, take a small amount in your mouth, chew it, and hold it there without swallowing for five minutes. If you feel no ill effects — such as stinging, burning or numbness — swallow, and then wait for eight hours. If by that time you have not experienced any cramps, pain, numbing, vomiting, or diarrhea, eat another handful of the plant and wait another eight hours. If there are still no problems, consider the plant safe to eat.   *Michael Rozek, reporting on the Air Force Survival School, in National Wildlife*

DRIVING

1113 ... _AVOIDING A SPEEDING TICKET_   If the tractor trailers on the freeway around you slow for no obvious reason, there's probably a cop, a wreck, or a traffic jam ahead. If the cars with local license plates slow, a speed trap may be ahead.   *Jeff Brown, astronomer, Bloomington, Indiana*

ROMANCE

1114 ... _THE BELSITO ODIOUS BEDROOM RULE_   The honeymoon's over when, if you fart, you pull the cover over your spouse's head.   *Sam Belsito, broadcast engineer, Lansing, Michigan*

INSECTS

1115 ... _PRODUCING SILK_   It takes 110 cocoons to make a tie, 630 to make a blouse. A heavy silk kimono might equal the work of 3,000 silkworms, and they will have eaten 135 pounds of mulberry leaves.   *Nina Hyde, writer, National Geographic magazine*

BUILDING

1116 ... _PICKING STEEL CABLE_   The safe working load of steel cable, in tons, is the diameter in inches squared times eight. For example: 1/2" squared times 8 = 2 tons; 5/8" squared times 8 = 3.125 tons.   *Paul Carter, stage hand, New York City*

1117 ... **GETTING USED TO COMPUTING**   It will take you about a year to feel comfortable using a home computer if you've never used one before.   *Mark McMullen, accountant, Alexandria, Virginia*

1118 ... **KNOWING WHEN TO QUIT RESEARCHING**   You're done with your research when those you interview urge you to interview people you've already interviewed.   *Robert Kanigel, writer and editor, Baltimore, Maryland*

1119 ... **THE FUSSY KIDS RULE**   A child will start fussing ten minutes before the end of a trip, no matter how long the trip.   *Lynn Smith, accountant, Tustin, Califonia*

1120 ... **GETTING A JOB**   Never send a resume longer than one page unless you're in the entertainment field, or think you are.   *Gerry M. Flick, M.D., Ship's Surgeon, S.S. Constitution off Hawaii*

1121 ... **THE OPTOMETRIST OPTIMISM RULE**   Eighty-five percent of people will wear prescription eyeglasses by age 45.   *Peter Potenza, optician, Ithaca, New York*

1122 ... **FLYING A SAILPLANE**   If your tow rope breaks below 200 feet, land straight ahead.   *Tom Knauff, glider pilot*

1123 ... **THE MOVIE KID RULE**   Little girls wearing glasses always tell the truth. Little boys wearing glasses always lie.   *Paul A. Delaney, meteorologist, Beltsville, Maryland*

1124 ... **THE UNSINO ULTRA-SPECIFIC DAFFODIL RULE**   In the New York City area, the Peruvian daffodil (Ismene calathina) blooms around St. Anthony's Day, June 13.   *Stephen Unsino, poet, Eastchester, New York*

1125 ... **USING A PUBLIC WASHROOM**   In a public washroom, always use the toilet farthest away from the door. It is normally the cleanest and least used.   *Tony Campo Jr., sales representative for food service equipment, Countryside, Illinois*

1126 ... **ROBBING SUBWAY PASSENGERS**   The seats next to the doors on a subway car are the easiest targets for a purse snatcher or robber.   *Steven M. Keisman, New York City high school resource coordinator*

1127 ... **FINDING AN ADDRESS**   When you think you've gone too far, go for at least another mile or two. Ninety percent of the time the address you're looking for will be just a little bit further.   *Greg Fletcher, Jr., veteran of the Los Angeles Freeway System, Northridge, California*

1128 ... **REPORTING A DEMONSTRATION**   The police will report that only one-third to one-half as many people are at a demonstration as were actually there. Newspapers will do the same, but television will reduce it even more.   *Ellen Klaver, musician, Boulder, Colorado*

A~S A RULE OF THUMB:~
IF THE FACE IS RED,
RAISE THE HEAD.
IF THE FACE IS PALE,
RAISE THE TAIL.
K~ATE~ G~LADSTONE,~
B~ROOKLYN,~ N~EW~ Y~ORK~

DESIGN

1129 ... *ILLUSTRATING YOUR DATA* If your data include fewer than 20 pieces of information, a graphic presentation is unnecessary. *Edward R. Tufte, author, The Visual Display of Quantitative Information*

BUSINESS

1130 ... *PREDICTING YOUR PROFITS* No matter what you do, no matter how large or small the project, no matter how much or how little time you spend on it, no matter what the profit margin, everything STILL equals $5.00 per hour. *Timothy Wenk, magician, West Stockbridge, Massachusetts*

MEASURING

1131 ... *ESTIMATING SIZE WITH MATCHES* At arm's length, the width of a paper matchstick covers a space 5 yards wide 1,000 yards away. The narrow width of a carpenter's pencil spans 10 yards. Conversely, if you know the size of the object you're sighting, you can work backwards to figure out how far away it is. *Bob Chaney, Carlsbad, California*

ILLNESS

1132 ... *CALLING IN SICK* In half of all cases, when an employee calls in sick, he's actually sick. *Walter Pitkin, literary agent, Weston, Connecticut*

HEARTS

1133 ... *WORRYING ABOUT BLOOD PRESSURE* The systolic (top) pressure for an adult female under 40 should be her age plus 90. *Dennis Pollack, builder, Danby, New York*

GARDENING

1134 ... *PLANTING BY THE MOON* Plant root crops at the full moon. Above-ground crops should be planted at the new moon. *Larry Beck, joiner, Ludlowville, New York*

TEMPERATURE

1135 ... *CHECKING YOUR CHARCOAL* Your fire is ready when the charcoal is light gray. Test the heat by holding your hand, palm side down, over the coals at grid level and counting the seconds you can hold it there. Five seconds indicates a low temperature fire, four seconds — medium temperature, three seconds — medium-high, two seconds — hot, and one second indicates a fire that is too hot. *Carolyn Flournoy, Gannett News Service*

SURVIVAL

1136 ... *FINDING DIRECTIONS* The bark on a dead tree holds moisture on the northern side. For this reason, the tree is usually wet under the bark on the north side, while the other side is dry. This damp side is the first to rot. The center of the damp or rotten area is usually slightly east of north. *Alwyn T. Perrin, editor, Explorers Ltd. Source Book*

DRIVING

1137 ... *FOLLOWING ANOTHER CAR* When you're following a car on the highway, stay one yard behind it for each mile per hour of speed. *Jud Town, author, St. Albert, Canada*

ROMANCE

1138 ... *THE LIBERKOWSKI TOO LATE NO DATE RULE* No date by 2:30 means a lonely night. *Joseph Liberkowski, ex-ocean lifeguard, Medford Lakes, New Jersey*

INSECTS

1139 ... *COUNTING ROACHES* Set a roach trap and check it after 24 hours. For every roach you've caught in your trap, you've got 800 more in your kitchen. If you find more than 1 or 2 in your trap, you have a serious roach problem. *Richard S. Patterson, entomologist, The Washington Post Weekly*

BUILDING

1140 ... *POURING A SLAB* Expansion control joints in a concrete slab should be cut to a depth of one-fourth of the slab's thickness. *William C. Panarese, Manager, Building Technology Department, Portland Cement Association, Popular Science magazine*

1141 ... **WRITING SOFTWARE** Adding manpower to a late software project will make it even later more times than not. *Joan Howe, Arlington, Massachusetts, quoting Frederick P. Brooks Jr., The Mythical Man-Month*

COMPUTERS

1142 ... **KNOWING WHEN TO QUIT RESEARCHING** You've done almost enough research when those you interview tell you what you already know. You've done too much when you know what your interview subject is going to say before he says it. *Robert Kanigel, writer and editor, Baltimore, Maryland*

WRITING

AS A RULE OF THUMB:
ADVENTURE IS NOT FUN
WHILE IT'S HAPPENING.
PETER REIMULLER,
POINT ARENA, CALIFORNIA

1143 ... **WATCHING A KID FOR TROUBLE** A child who constantly mutters under his breath is a time bomb. *Cookie Ohlson, teacher, Prospect Park Middle School, Pennsylvania*

CHILDREN

1144 ... **LOOKING FOR A JOB** If they don't call you back in a week, they won't. *Norman Brenner, Fleetwood, New York*

JOBS

1145 ... **THE SUNKEN EYEBALLS RULE** Sunken eyeballs in a sick infant indicate at least 10 percent dehydration. So does a sunken soft spot, or fontanelle, on the top of the head. *James Macmillan, M.D.*

EYES

1146 ... **FLYING A SAILPLANE** To determine the best speed to fly in wind, add half the wind speed to what you calculate otherwise. *John Campbell, glider pilot, Ann Arbor, Michigan*

FLYING

1147 ... **WRITING A TELEPLAY** One minute of teleplay is 40 seconds of air time. *Russell T. Johnson, Temple City, California*

MOVIES AND FILM

1148 ... **LEARNING GEOGRAPHY** If you know where Malta is, you're either good at maps or your Aunt Sally lives there. *Carolyn Lloyd, 15-year-old student, Montreal, Quebec*

CERTAIN PLACES

1149 ... **CHOOSING A WIG** A long face needs a full wig; a round face needs height at the crown; but a woman with an oval face can wear anything. *Eva Gabor, Eva Gabor International, the world's largest wig company*

GROOMING

1150 ... **CHOOSING A CAR COLOR** Black or red cars are most likely to be stolen. *Steven M. Keisman, New York City high school resource coordinator*

CRIME

1151 ... **SPOTTING FRAUD IN SCIENCE** For every case of fraud uncovered in scientific research, 100 others go unreported. *Scott Parker, data specialist, Beaumont, Texas*

FINDING THINGS

1152 ... **ORGANIZING A BUNCH OF PEOPLE** A cooperative effort loses effectiveness when it includes more than 12 to 15 people. *Peter Reimuller, Point Arena, California*

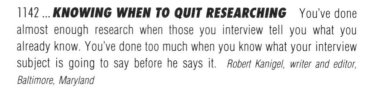
GROUPS

DESIGN

1153 ... *THE CARVER RULE OF MODERN CHAIR DESIGN* If you're designing a chair and want to know how well your design will stand the test of time, imagine 30 of them lined up in a laundromat. *Steve Carver, illustrator, Ithaca, New York*

JOKER

1154 ... *KEEPING UP WITH NEWSPAPERS* If you buy a newspaper, read it as soon as you can and in one sitting if possible. If you postpone reading the paper or interrupt yourself halfway through, you probably won't get back to it. *D. Branner, New York City*

MEASURING

1155 ... *REACHING THE HORIZON* The distance to the horizon, in miles, is the square root of half again your height, in feet. If you're 6 feet tall, you can see 3 miles. From 600 feet, you can see 30 miles (sq. rt. of 900). Conversely, you can see a 150-foot building from 15 miles away (sq. rt. of 225). *Dani Zweig, Pittsburg, Pennsylvania*

ILLNESS

1156 ... *PASSING A KIDNEY STONE* A urinary calculus, or kidney stone, that is less than ten millimeters in diameter will generally pass out of the body on its own. *James Macmillan, M.D.*

HEARTS

1157 ... *WATCHING YOUR HEART RATE* Your maximum safe heart rate is equal to 220 minus your age. For example, a 40 year old would have a maximum heart rate of 220-40 = 180 beats per minute. Your target heart rate for aerobic exercise is equal to 160 minus your age. That's the number of beats per minute you need to maintain or exceed during aerobic workouts. *Ned Frederick, writer, Exeter, New Hampshire*

GARDENING

1158 ... *WATERING YOUR PLANTS* For watering houseplants, when in doubt, don't. But for plants on your patio or windowsill, when in doubt, do. *Andrea Frankel, computer scientist, engineer, holistic health practitioner, San Diego, California*

TEMPERATURE

1159 ... *THE QUICK RULE OF TEMPERATURE CONVERSION* To quickly convert Centigrade to Fahrenheit, double the temperature and add 30. Thus 10C is 50F and 20C is 70F. To convert from F to C, you subtract 30 from the F value and divide by 2. The exact formula is F= 9/5 C + 32. *Stephen J. Lambrechts-Forester, Green Oaks, Illinois*

SURVIVAL

1160 ... *THE WIND CHILL RULE OF THIRTY* At 30 degrees below zero Fahrenheit, in a 30-mile-per-hour wind, exposed flesh freezes in 30 seconds. *Lory Peck, social worker, Alpine, New York*

DRIVING

1161 ... *FINDING A PARKING SPACE* The best parking places are in the side rows because more people look for parking in the center rows. *Jennifer Evans, writer, Austin, Texas*

ROMANCE

1162 ... *COOKIE'S CAR ROMANCE RULE* If he doesn't have a car, don't let him get too comfortable in yours, or you'll have a steady boyfriend whether you want one or not. *Cookie Ohlson, blonde, Upland, Pennsylvania*

INSECTS

1163 ... *FEEDING COCKROACHES* Twelve cockroaches can live on the glue of a postage stamp for a week. *Austin Friedman, entomologist*

BUILDING

1164 ... *MAKING ICEBERGS* Arctic engineers make their own icebergs to use as runways. It takes 26 inches of manmade ice to support a Caterpillar grader, 5 feet to support a 737 jet. Homemade ice forms faster and harder when the water is sprayed rather than flooded, but if the stream is aimed too high, the water falls as snow. *John Urquhart, staff reporter, The Wall Street Journal quoting Larry Sagriff, ice engineer, Panarctic Oils Ltd., of Calgary*

1165 ... BUDGETING YOUR TIME When you budget your time for a software job, figure one-third planning, one-sixth coding, one-fourth component and early system tests, and one-fourth final system tests. *Frederick P. Brooks Jr., The Mythical Man-Month*

COMPUTERS

1166 ... KNOWING WHEN TO START WRITING You're ready to stop reviewing your research material and start writing on the day after your first strong urge to write. *Robert Kanigel, writer and editor, Baltimore, Maryland*

WRITING

1167 ... PUNISHING CHILDREN The well-adjusted child may complain, but will accept fair punishment as due. If the child balks, there's a problem with the child or the punishment. *Cookie Ohlson, teacher, Prospect Park Middle School, Pennsylvania*

CHILDREN

1168 ... FINDING A JOB It will take an executive who has been laid off more than four months to find a new job. But nine out of ten will find a job that is at least as good or better paying than their old job. *James Challenger, Challenger, Gray & Christmas*

JOBS

1169 ... WEARING CONTACT LENSES It takes your eyes a number of weeks to adjust to wearing contact lenses. In most cases, it will take about one week for each year you have been wearing glasses. *Irene Fudge, lab technician*

EYES

1170 ... SOARING When flying a sailplane on a cross-country flight, fly toward the next thermal showing as much sink as you did lift in the previous thermal. *Dick Schreder, glider pilot*

FLYING

1171 ... THE STAR RULE If you've heard of the stars of a movie but you haven't heard about the movie itself, it's probably a stinker. *Bruce Reznick, associate professor of mathematics, Urbana, Illinois*

MOVIES AND FILM

1172 ... ASKING DIRECTIONS IN NEW YORK CITY When asking directions from a pedestrian in New York City, get another opinion before proceeding. *Martin M. Bruce, Ph.D., psychologist, Larchmont, New York*

CERTAIN PLACES

1173 ... THE TEENAGER JEWELRY RULE Teenage girls should lay out the jewelry they want to wear, then put away one-third of the items. For make-up, they should lay out everything they'd like to use, then put away all but two items. *Tim Hoff, 20th century bureaucrat, APO New York*

GROOMING

1174 ... STEALING FROM YOUR EMPLOYER Never steal anything from your employer that has a market value of less than one year's salary. This includes stamps and pencils. *Steven M. Keisman, New York City high school resource coordinator*

CRIME

1175 ... FINDING A MISSING PERSON The elderly head for low ground. Suicides head for the highest elevation. Hunters wander uphill within a three-mile radius or downhill within a six-mile radius of where they were last seen. *Scott Parker, data specialist, Beaumont, Texas*

FINDING THINGS

1176 ... RUNNING A CLUB Don't expect more than one-third of any professional-club members to attend a meeting. Build up a large membership so there are enough members around to make up for those who are away or otherwise engaged. *Dr. Barbara Pletcher, National Association of Professional Saleswomen, Sacramento, California*

GROUPS

DESIGN

1177 ... **SETTING TYPE**   Avoid setting type in lines more than 65 characters long. Longer lines cause readers to read the same line twice. *Peter Smith, Peter Smith Associates*

MANAGEMENT

1178 ... **HIRING SECRETARIES**   You need one secretary for every four junior executives. *Dean Sheridan, electronics technician and deaf actor, Torrance, California*

MEASURING

1179 ... **WATCHING A THUNDERSTORM**   You can tell how many miles you are from a thunderstorm by counting the seconds between the lightning and thunder and dividing by five. *Millie Stoerdeur, Cincinnati, Ohio*

ILLNESS

1180 ... **THE COLD RULE OF THREE**   It takes three days to get a cold, three days to have a cold, and three days to get over a cold. *Veronica Cunningham, chemist, Plattsburg, New York*

HEARTS

1181 ... **INCREASING YOUR AEROBIC FITNESS**   To increase your aerobic fitness, get your heart rate above your target rate for at least 90 minutes a week. *Ned Frederick, writer, Exeter, New Hampshire*

GARDENING

1182 ... **THE BAFFLING RULE OF PLANTING OATS**   Plant your oats when the shad is in the blow. *Steve Sierigk, artist, Ithaca, New York*

TEMPERATURE

1183 ... **WATCHING YOUR BREATH**   When you see your breath, it is below 45 F. *Thomas Lack, somewhere on the east shore of Lake Michigan*

SURVIVAL

1184 ... **FINDING A MISSING PERSON**   One trained dog equals 60 search-and-rescue workers. *Charles Stoehr, robotics technician, Cincinnati, Ohio*

DRIVING

1185 ... **DRIVING SAFELY**   To determine which way a car is about to swerve, watch the wheels. *Jennifer Evans, writer, Austin, Texas*

ROMANCE

1186 ... **THE GOOD LOOKS RULE**   Good cooking is almost as important as good looking. *Scott Parker, data specialist, Beaumont, Texas*

INSECTS

1187 ... **STALKING A HOUSEFLY**   If you're more than three feet away from a housefly, it can't see you. *L. M. Boyd, The San Francisco Chronicle*

BUILDING

1188 ... **THE ONE IN FIVE RULE OF BUILDERS**   One in 5 building companies survives for 15 years; 1 in 5 fails within 5 years. *Rick Eckstrom, plan review officer, Ithaca, New York*

AS A RULE OF THUMB: THE RETURNS FROM A BOTTLE OF WINE DIMINISH AS THE PRICE INCREASES. A $20 WINE IS USUALLY BETTER THAN A $10 WINE, BUT NEVER TWICE AS GOOD. CRAIG GOLDWYN, PUBLISHER, INTERNATIONAL WINE REVIEW

1189 ... *USING A SUPER-COMPUTER* A super-computer operating at the highest frontier speeds will fail every month or so. *Kevin Kelly quoting Seymour Cray, computer wizard*

COMPUTERS

1190 ... *WRITING SOMETHING INTERESTING* If you're bored with your writing, others will be too. *Robert Kanigel, writer and editor, Baltimore, Maryland*

WRITING

1191 ... *DRESSING A BUNCH OF KIDS* Dress the best-behaved child first. They are less likely to undo your preparations by the time you're ready to leave. *L. Musselman, office manager and mother of young children*

CHILDREN

1192 ... *WORKING WITH A HEADHUNTER* If a headhunter mentions the names of other people he's placing, drop him immediately. The next time it could be your name he drops in a conversation — perhaps to your boss. *Thomas E. Burdick and Charlene A. Mitchell, authors*

JOBS

1193 ... *THE UNIVERSAL NERD RULE* A nerd never knows he's a nerd. *Paul Carter, ex-nerd, New York City*

JOKER

1194 ... *FLYING A SAILPLANE* If you are above 3,000 feet, stay on course. If you are between 2,000 and 3,000 feet, head for a good landing area. If you are between 1,000 and 2,000 feet, pick a landing field. If you are below 1,000 feet, stick to the field you've picked. *Ed Byars, glider pilot*

FLYING

1195 ... *CHOOSING A MOVIE* If a new movie is on TV or cable and you haven't heard of it, it's probably a stinker. *Bruce Reznick, associate professor of mathematics, Urbana, Illinois*

MOVIES AND FILM

1196 ... *FORECASTING THE WEATHER* In Seattle, for every rainy day in the winter you'll get a sunny day in the summer. *Christa Childsen, Bellevue, Washington*

CERTAIN PLACES

1197 ... *BRUSHING YOUR TEETH* Get a new toothbrush as soon as your old one gets frayed. If you're not going through four toothbrushes a year, you're not brushing your teeth enough. *Gerald Gutlipp, mathematician, Chicago, Illinois*

GROOMING

1198 ... *DIGGING A GRAVE* When digging a grave by hand, haul away 17 wheelbarrow loads of dirt and pile the rest by the hole. You will have just the right amount to backfill. *Randall Lacey, wind-power engineer*

JOKER

1199 ... *FINDING A BALL IN THE ROUGH* To find a golf ball, first look ten yards past where you think you hit it out, then look ten yards short, and finally look five yards further into the rough. *Michael D. Miles, Aloha, Oregon*

FINDING THINGS

1200 ... *ORGANIZING PEOPLE* The people who stay at a demonstration when it starts to rain are the ones you can count on. *Anonymous, dedicated to a University of California at Davis draft demonstration*

GROUPS

DESIGN

1201 ... SETTING TYPE   Avoid setting type in lines less than 35 characters long. Shorter lines cause sentences to be so broken they are hard to understand. *Peter Smith, Peter Smith Associates*

MANAGEMENT

1202 ... WATCHING SOMEONE BEING CREATIVE   Insights flourish best when the thinker is apparently wasting time. *Walter Pitkin, literary agent, Weston, Connecticut*

MEASURING

1203 ... APPROACHING THE HORIZON   The distance to the horizon is equal to the square root of your altitude multiplied by 1.22. *Doug Combs, aviator and nice person, Incline Village, Nevada*

JOKER

1204 ... MAKING BEAR GREASE   One black bear yields 12 gallons of bear grease. *Anonymous*

HEARTS

1205 ... CHECKING YOUR HEART WHEN YOU WAKE   Keep tabs on your resting heart beat first thing in the morning. An increase of seven beats per minute or more is a sign of overtraining. *Ned Frederick, writer, quoting track coach Dick Brown, Exeter, New Hampshire*

GARDENING

1206 ... PLANTING PEAS   When you see coots in the pond in the park, you know it's warm enough to plant peas. *Peggy Macneale, writer, Flower and Garden*

TEMPERATURE

1207 ... THE TEMPERATURE RULE   If you add 18 to the temperature at 6:00 a.m., you'll find the high temperature for the day. *John Schaedler, Schaedler Quinzel Lehnert Green, Inc., New York City*

SURVIVAL

1208 ... WEARING NO PANTS   On a cold day, soaking wet blue jeans will draw heat from your lower body twice as fast as wearing no pants at all. *Rob Weinberg, Tassajara Zen Mountain Center, Carmel Valley, California*

DRIVING

1209 ... DRIVING SAFELY   If the driver of one car causes the driver of another car to slam on his brakes, the driver of the first car is not a good driver. *W. G. Moss, Jr., USN (ret.), Lake Zurich, Illinois*

ROMANCE

1210 ... HAVING AN OFFICE ROMANCE   Women are twice as likely as men to be fired after an office affair. *Scott Parker, data specialist, Beaumont, Texas*

INSECTS

1211 ... DISTRIBUTING PRAYING MANTISES   It takes 16 praying mantis egg cases per acre to keep other insects under control. *Ronald Newberry, retired, Cayutaville, New York*

BUILDING

1212 ... ESTIMATING A CONSTRUCTION JOB   If a construction estimator wins a bid and it is within 10 percent of the next lowest bid, it means he probably will make money on the job and he didn't underestimate the costs. *Harvey Mitchell, construction estimator, Beaumont, Texas*

AS A RULE OF THUMB: YOU WILL REMEMBER ONLY 10 PERCENT OF WHAT YOU THINK YOU LEARNED IN COLLEGE. IsABEL T. COBURN, AUTHORITY AT LARGE, PEMAQUID BEACH, MAINE

1213 ... **EXPLAINING COMPUTERS**   When explaining a computer command, a computer language feature, or a piece of computer hardware, first describe the problem it is designed to solve. *David Martin, Norristown, Pennsylvania, Communications of the ACM*

COMPUTERS

1214 ... **READING WHAT YOU WROTE**   Read your work out loud to locate problems. If you run out of breath, the sentence is too long. *Robert Kanigel, writer and editor, Baltimore, Maryland*

WRITING

1215 ... **WATCHING KIDS FOR DRUG ABUSE**   Inappropriate seasonal dress is one of the first signs of a youngster abusing drugs. *Steven M. Keisman, New York City high school resource coordinator*

CHILDREN

1216 ... **GETTING A JOB**   If the interviewer talked more than you did, then the interview went well. *David Shinn, graduate student, Ziegler, Illinois*

JOBS

1217 ... **TRANSLATING GERMAN**   To guess the English word for an unknown German word, replace German T with D; Z or SS with T; D with TH; EI with O or I; AU with EE or EA; CH with CK or CH; B with F or V; PF with P; and SCH as the first letters of a word with S. The German word PFLANZ becomes plant; ZWEI becomes two. *Norman Brenner, Fleetwood, New York*

LANGUAGE

1218 ... **STUNT FLYING**   If the top of your head feels hot at the bottom of an outside loop, you should relax a little of the forward pressure on the control stick. Negative G forces are pushing too much blood into your brain, a condition that can cause a loss of consciousness, or "red out," if left unchecked. *Steve Poleskie, artist and stunt pilot*

FLYING

1219 ... **WORRYING ABOUT THE BOMB**   When the movies stop mentioning the bomb, you know it's on everybody's mind. *Tom Shales, movie critic, National Public Radio*

MOVIES AND FILM

1220 ... **PARKING AT L.L. BEAN**   If you're trying to park at L.L.Bean, drive through the small lot in front of the store. Chances are, someone parked there will be leaving. If you don't find a space the first time through, try a second time. After that, give up and park with the hordes. *Kim Murphy, columnist, Portland, Maine*

CERTAIN PLACES

1221 ... **THE RULE OF HEAD EXFOLIATION**   Normal daily hair loss is 100 to 200 hairs per day. *Dr. Jonathan Zizmor, hair expert*

GROOMING

1222 ... **ADJUSTING TO A RECENT DEATH**   After you attend a funeral, expect to go into a cleaning and organizational frenzy when you get home. *Lois Haywood Jimenez, Merced, California*

DEATH

1223 ... **THE TRASH RULE OF THREE**   You have to look through a wastebasket three times to find a missing piece of paper. *Anne Herbert, writer*

FINDING THINGS

1224 ... **THE CAVALRY DRINKING RULE**   Cider on beer, no fear. Beer on cider, no rider. *The Very Rev. Emmet C. Smith, Largo, Florida*

JOKER

DESIGN

1225 ... SETTING TYPE   Avoid setting type using all capital letters. They slow reading speed and take 30 percent more space than lower-case letters. *Peter Smith, Peter Smith Associates*

MANAGEMENT

1226 ... MAKING DECISIONS   you're not sure whether to do it or not—do it. *Bob Hale, construction worker, Sacramento, California*

JOKER

1227 ... THE ALL-TERRAIN VEHICLE OWNERSHIP RULE   Ownership of all-terrain vehicles is inversely proportional to the acreage owned. *David T. Russell, retired high school teacher, Dilltown, Pennsylvania*

COOKING

1228 ... GRILLING MEAT   Think of a grill as a target. Put food that requires quick searing heat in the middle and food that needs slow, steady grilling further out. *Dean Sheridan, electronics technician and deaf actor, Torrance, California*

HEARTS

1229 ... ESTIMATING YOUR BLOOD   You can estimate the volume of blood in your body if you know your weight. Your weight in kilograms multiplied by 0.08 equals your blood volume in liters. *Ned Frederick, writer, Exeter, New Hampshire*

GARDENING

1230 ... STARTING SWEET POTATOES   Sweet potatoes are started from slips, or cuttings. Eight potatoes will provide enough slips for a 100-foot row of potatoes. *Gary Nelson, home gardener, Oakland, Arkansas, in Flower and Garden*

TEMPERATURE

1231 ... ESTIMATING THE TEMPERATURE   To estimate the temperature outdoors in degrees Fahrenheit, count the number of times a lone cricket chirps in 15 seconds and add 37. *Steven Harper, Big Sur, California*

SURVIVAL

1232 ... FINDING YOUR WAY USING TREES   Tall, pointed trees such as spruce usually have their tips leaning slightly to the north of east. *Alwyn T. Perrin, editor, Explorers Ltd. Source Book*

DRIVING

1233 ... DRIVING IN HEAVY TRAFFIC   When stopped at a red light with a long line of traffic ahead of you, if your car begins to move before the light turns red, you'll make it through the light on the next cycle. *William T. Mandeville, engineer, Liverpool, New York*

ROMANCE

1234 ... THE NUMBER OF DATES BEFORE SEX RULE   Have 12 dates with a man before you have sex. *Scott Parker, data specialist, Beaumont, Texas*

INSECTS

1235 ... CATCHING A SWARM OF BEES   A swarm of bees in May is worth a load of hay; a swarm of bees in June is worth a silver spoon; a swarm of bees in July is hardly worth a fly. *Otis Hassler, shovel operator*

BUILDING

1236 ... SELLING CONSTRUCTION EQUIPMENT   Construction equipment dealers make 75 percent of their profits repairing and servicing equipment already in the field. *Scott Parker, data specialist, Beaumont, Texas*

1237 ... **THE PROFESSIONAL TOOLS RULE** Engineers and computer programmers need equipment equal to one year's earnings to work at top speed. Anything less slows them down. *William Blake, engineering manager, New Haven, Connecticut*

1238 ... **THE REWRITING RULE** If you're bothered, however slightly, by the way you've written something—fix it. *Robert Kanigel, writer and editor, Baltimore, Maryland*

1239 ... **GIVING GIFTS TO KIDS** When giving presents to siblings of the same sex, always give the same gift unless one is a baby or a teenager. *Steven M. Keisman, New York City high school resource coordinator*

1240 ... **MANAGING PEOPLE** All new employees do well for two to six weeks. *Captain Haggerty, animal trainer, actor, author, and philosopher, New York, New York*

1241 ... **READING POETRY** The Iliad can be recited in ancient Greek at 10 lines per minute. At this pace, the entire poem takes about 40 hours to recite. *Norman Brenner, Fleetwood, New York*

1242 ... **STUNT FLYING** To avoid hitting the ground if your engine quits while performing a roll on takeoff, accelerate the aircraft to twice the rotation speed of a normal takeoff before beginning the roll. *Steve Poleskie, artist and stunt pilot*

1243 ... **COMPARING MOVIES TO BOOKS** Comparing a movie to a book is easy when one inspired the other. The one created first will be better. *Mark Alber, Houston, Texas*

1244 ... **ANTICIPATING A FAD** Canadian fads catch on in the United States a year to 18 months later. *Scott Parker, data specialist, Beaumont, Texas*

1245 ... **MAKING WIGS** Dark hair bleaches whiter than blond hair; so as a rule, the best white hair for making wigs comes from the countries that have the best dark hair. *Meg Wallace, counselor*

1246 ... **ESTIMATING YOUR LIFE EXPECTANCY** The life expectancy of a single man who does not smoke is no better than that of a married man who does smoke. *Thomas W. Neumann, anthropological archaeologist, wildlife ecologist, and field crew crisis manager*

1247 ... **LOOKING THROUGH YOUR POCKETS** It takes almost twice as long to find something in your coat pockets when you are not wearing your coat. If you have a flight jacket or parka with more than four pockets, you can usually save time by putting it on just to look through the pockets. *Gerald Gutlipp, mathematician, Chicago, Illinois*

1248 ... **BUYING A HORSE** If its feet are no good, other virtues will be wasted. *Gene Wolfe, Barrington, Illinois*

AS A RULE OF THUMB: WHEN THE MOON IS A CRESCENT, IT'S TIME TO CLIP YOUR TOENAILS. RUDY NFRAT, CHULA VISTA, CALIFORNIA

DESIGN

MANAGEMENT

REAL ESTATE

COOKING

HEARTS

GARDENING

TEMPERATURE

SURVIVAL

DRIVING

ROMANCE

INSECTS

BUILDING

1249 ... **THE FREELANCE TIME RULE** Free lance artists and designers should expect to put in one unbillable hour for every billable hour. *Michael Rider, art director, American Demographics*

1250 ... **CHOOSING BETWEEN TWO THINGS** If you can't decide between two alternatives—let's say between a blue suit and a gray one—toss a coin (heads, it's blue; tails, it's gray). If the coin comes down heads and you have the least inclination to make it two out of three tosses, you know it's the gray suit you want. *Emery Nemethy, Catawissa, Pennsylvania*

1251 ... **BUYING REAL ESTATE** You get the best buys in real estate when you buy out of season. In the South, summer is best; in the North, winter. *Steven M. Keisman, New York City high school resource coordinator*

1252 ... **COOKING RICE** One cup of uncooked rice will feed four people. *Dean Sheridan, electronics technician and deaf actor, Torrance, California*

1253 ... **LOWERING YOUR BLOOD CHOLESTEROL** For every 1 percent drop in your blood cholesterol, you get a 2 percent drop in your risk of a heart attack. *Dr. Stephen S. Scheidt, Professor of Clinical Medicine, Cornell University Medical College, New York City*

1254 ... **GROWING ONIONS** The smaller the onion sets, the larger the onions. *Paul Bauer, West Harrison, Indiana*

1255 ... **THE FROZEN SPIT RULE** When spit freezes before it hits the ground, it's at least 40 degrees below zero Fahrenheit. *Jeanie MacDonough, social scientist*

1256 ... **UNTANGLING YOURSELF** If you are lost in the woods, always travel downstream. If you are lost in the astral plane, always travel toward the light. *Pat Morningstar, anthropologist, Tallahassee, Florida*

1257 ... **THE TOLL BOOTH RULE** The quickest lane is to the right because most cars come from the fast lane on the left. *Pete Romano, Jr., Lewisburg, Pennsylvania*

1258 ... **CHOOSING A SINGLES BAR** The age of the customers at a singles bar is directly proportional to the age of the bar. *Gerry M. Flick, M.D., Ship's Surgeon, S.S. Constitution off Hawaii*

1259 ... **CHECKING A BEEHIVE** One thousand to 1,500 bees die per day under normal summer conditions. All or most are removed from the vicinity of the hive. An accumulation of 3 or 4 dead bees per day in front of the hive entrance is cause for suspicion. *Cornell University*

1260 ... **BUILDING A HOUSE** An odd-angled wall will cost twice as much as a wall built with 90-degree corners. *Rick Eckstrom, plan review officer, Ithaca, New York*

A**S A RULE OF THUMB:**
THE THIRD ITEM
SOMEONE MENTIONS IS
THE MAIN ISSUE.
C**LIFF** M**ARTIN**, E**UGENE**,
O**REGON**

1261 ... **DESIGNING A COMPUTER SYSTEM**   Making a design change when a computer system is nearly complete will cost about ten times as much as making the change before the work has started.   *Clifton Royston, programmer/analyst, Nukualofa, Tonga*

1262 ... **DECIPHERING SCIENTIFIC PAPERS**   The first author of a scientific paper is the scientist who performed most of the experiments. The last author is the director of the lab in which the work was done.   *Dean Sheridan, electronics technician and deaf actor, Torrance, California*

1263 ... **LOOKING AT EYELASHES**   The youngest child has the longest eyelashes.   *Sarah Bynum, Brookline, Massachusetts*

1264 ... **GETTING A JOB**   You have 30 seconds to capture the attention of the person reading your resume.   *Scott Parker, data specialist, Beaumont, Texas*

1265 ... **THE SPELLING RULE**   If an English word is derived from Latin, it ends with "or," as in actor, donor, and doctor. If it is original to English, the proper ending is "er."   *Norman Brenner, Fleetwood, New York*

1266 ... **AVOIDING THUNDERSTORMS WHILE FLYING**   Clear the top of a known or suspected severe thunderstorm by at least 1,000 feet of altitude for each 10 knots of wind speed at the top of the cloud. This will exceed the altitude capability of most airplanes.   *Airman's Information Manual*

1267 ... **ENTERING A CROWDED MOVIE THEATER**   When entering a crowded movie theater, more empty seats will be found on the aisle farthest from the entrance. If all the aisles are essentially straight ahead of the entrance, select the left-most aisle — most people go to the right-hand aisles.   *W. G. Martin, San Diego, California*

1268 ... **USING THE SUBWAY IN NEW YORK CITY**   The average "leafleteer" in a New York City subway station hands out 250 leaflets per hour during morning rush hour.   *Joseph G. Rappaport, coordinator, straphangers campaign, New York, New York*

1269 ... **SHAVING YOUR FACE**   Your face is dry and puffy when you first wake up. Put off shaving two minutes for each hour you slept.   *E.L. Beck, Orlando, Florida*

1270 ... **DECLARING SOMEONE DEAD**   For hypothermia victims, nobody's dead until they're warm and dead.   *Richard Wolkomir, writer*

1271 ... **FINDING A MISSING PERSON**   When looking for missing persons, the elderly usually are found about a mile from the point where they were last seen, hikers within four miles, and suicides within one-quarter mile.   *Marilyn Greene, finder of missing persons, Schenectady, New York*

1272 ... **TAKING CARE OF A HORSE**   Shoe a horse when hoof wear exceeds hoof growth.   *Frank Turley, director, Turley Forge Blacksmithing School, Santa Fe, New Mexico*

DESIGN

1273 ... THE TYPE COLUMN RULE For magazines and similar publications, the columns should be the width required to set one and a half alphabets of lower-case letters in the typeface you are using. *Ray Bruman, Berkeley, California*

MANAGEMENT

1274 ... CONTROLLING YOURSELF If you say, "I'll hate myself in the morning for doing this," you're probably right. *Dr. Angelo Valenti, consulting psychologist, Nashville, Tennessee*

REAL ESTATE

1275 ... APPRAISING PROPERTY WITH TREES Trees contribute 7 percent, on average, to the value of a half-acre home site. They contribute up to 27 percent of the appraised value of a home. *Anonymous*

COOKING

1276 ... STORING CHEESE The harder the cheese, the longer it will keep. *Dean Sheridan, electronics technician and deaf actor, Torrance, California*

HEARTS

1277 ... PUMPING BLOOD Your heart pushes about five tablespoons of blood into your arteries with each beat. *L.M. Boyd, The San Francisco Chronicle*

GARDENING

1278 ... WATERING THE GRASS It's time to water your lawn when the grass has a purplish cast and footprints remain after walking across the lawn, a sign of wilting. *Norman W. Hummel Jr., assistant professor, New York State College of Agriculture and Life Sciences at Cornell University, in The Ithaca Journal*

TEMPERATURE

1279 ... THE DOWN IN THE GROUND RULE The internal temperature of the earth increases with depth. In most places, the temperature increases about 16 degrees Fahrenheit per 1,000 feet. *Steve Parker, aerospace engineer, Princeton, New Jersey*

SURVIVAL

1280 ... CALLING FOR HELP If you are assaulted, scream Fire! People are more likely to come to your aid than if you shout Help! *Boardroom Reports*

DRIVING

1281 ... DRIVING SAFELY If you think your front tire is low, find out by taking your hands off the steering wheel. A low tire will cause the car to drift in the direction of the low tire. *John H. Beauvais, Cambridge, Massachusetts*

ROMANCE

1282 ... THE BAR SEATING RULE In a singles bar, the serious drinkers gather at the near end, the bores at the far end, and the recently divorced in the middle. *Gerry M. Flick, M.D., Ship's Surgeon, S.S. Constitution off Hawaii*

INSECTS

1283 ... HELPING BEES THROUGH THE WINTER It is important to leave enough honey in a hive to feed your bees through the winter. One rule is: Leave ten pounds of honey for each month that winter lasts in your area. *Larry Meyer, beekeeper*

BUILDING

1284 ... THE UNDERWOOD PRETTY CLOSE STUD RULE For standard residential construction with wall studs on 16-inch centers, plan on using one stud per linear foot of wall plus two per opening, and you'll be pretty close. *Jim Underwood, Technology Center for Mountain People, Cherry Grove, West Virginia*

As A RULE OF THUMB: WAIT THREE MONTHS AND SEE WHERE THE PATHS FORM, WHEN PLANNING SIDEWALKS FOR A NEW SCHOOL. MICHAEL HEIMAN, M.D., SONOMA, CALIFORNIA

1285 ... **DESIGNING A COMPUTER SYSTEM**   For every two days spent designing a computer system, figure one day for coding or writing the programs and three days testing them.   *John M. Howe (quoting Edward Brooks), North Quincy, Massachusetts*

1286 ... **WRITING A BOOK**   Someone who can't write three clear sentences in a row will never write a good book.   *Walter Pitkin, literary agent, Weston, Connecticut*

1287 ... **GETTING THROUGH COLLEGE**   Never argue about a grade with a college instructor unless you're pointing out a simple arithmetic error. In the long run, it will cost you more than you gain. If the grading is grossly unfair, drop the course because nothing can save you from disaster.   *Jeff Brown, astronomer, Bloomington, Indiana*

1288 ... **GETTING A JOB**   In the job market, any degree is worth three times any experience.   *Scott Parker, data specialist, Beaumont, Texas*

1289 ... **SPOTTING A BEGINNER**   If signers finish mouthing their names before their hands finish spelling the letters, they've had less than a year's practice at fingerspelling.   *Dean Sheridan, electronics technician and deaf actor, Torrance, California*

1290 ... **FLYING TO HIGHER ALTITUDES**   It is inefficient to climb more than ten minutes per hour of estimated time en route. Climbing to the engine's optimum altitude may not be efficient on a particular trip. Unless there are spectacular tailwinds, high-altitude cruise efficiency will be offset by the fuel burned in the climb.   *Bruce Landsberg, pilot and writer*

1291 ... **PROMOTING A MOVIE**   Marketing and distribution costs for a movie run about 2 1/2 times the film's production budget.   *Scott Parker, data specialist, Beaumont, Texas*

1292 ... **USING THE SUBWAY IN NEW YORK CITY**   On weekends and after 9 p.m. on weekdays, give yourself at least 15 minutes longer to complete your subway trip for every half hour it usually takes.   *Joseph G. Rappaport, coordinator, straphangers campaign, New York, New York*

1293 ... **USING A HOT TUB**   Soaking in a hot tub adds two to three pints of perspiration per hour per person to the water.   *Phil Tomlinson, builder*

1294 ... **SELLING FUNERALS**   The less money people have, the more they spend on a funeral.   *Anonymous*

1295 ... **FINDING A MISSING PERSON**   When looking for a missing person, remember that children usually go to a lower elevation. First-time runaways usually take off with a friend.   *Marilyn Greene, finder of missing persons, Schenectady, New York*

1296 ... **RIDING A HORSE**   If you're trying to get off a horse that kicks, jerk the horse's head towards you as you dismount. This will throw the horse off balance, and you'll keep your teeth longer.   *John H. Beauvais, Cambridge, Massachusetts*

DESIGN

1297 ... *SETTING YOUR RATES* Freelance artists and graphic designers should determine their hourly rate by dividing their annual income requirements by 1,000. *Michael Rider, art director, American Demographics*

MANAGEMENT

1298 ... *MAKING A DEADLINE* When faced with a deadline, if you first tackle what MUST be done, then plan to do what SHOULD be done, saving for last what would be NICE to do, you will seldom get past the first category. However, do those same things in reverse order and somehow they will all get done, often with time to spare. *Isabel T. Coburn, authority at large, Pemaquid Beach, Maine*

REAL ESTATE

1299 ... *APPRAISING PROPERTY WITH TREES* On a half-acre site, 1 to 29 trees add value to an appraisal. But 30 or more trees reduce the value of a property. *Anonymous*

COOKING

1300 ... *MAKING COOKIES* Cookie recipes always make one-quarter fewer cookies than estimated — unless you hate the taste of batter. *Carolyn Lloyd, 15-year-old student, Montreal, Quebec*

HEARTS

1301 ... *CHECKING YOUR EARLOBES* If your earlobes have a diagonal crease, you may have clogged coronary arteries. *Joe Graedon, Medical Self-Care*

GARDENING

1302 ... *REPOTTING AFRICAN VIOLETS* African violets need small pots. As a rule, the pot should be one-third the width of the plant. A 6-inch plant, for instance, needs a 2-inch pot. *Mary Ellen Parker, retired teacher, Cincinnati, Ohio*

TEMPERATURE

1303 ... *TESTING FREEZER TEMPERATURE* A spoon will ring when rapped on a carton of ice cream if your freezer temperature is 0 degrees Fahrenheit or colder. *Cheryl A. Russell, demographer, mother, editor-in-chief, American Demographics*

SURVIVAL

1304 ... *THE SURVIVAL RULE OF THREE* You can live three seconds without blood, three minutes without air, three days without water, and three weeks without food. *Sandy Figuers, geologist, El Paso, Texas*

DRIVING

1305 ... *THE FAMILIAR SIGN RULE* Bridges and overpasses freeze before the rest of the road. *John H. Beauvais, Cambridge, Massachusetts*

ROMANCE

1306 ... *THE LOVE AND SEX RULE* Women give sex to get love. Men give love to get sex. *Anonymous, quoting someone they can't remember*

INSECTS

1307 ... *MANAGING AN APIARY* One skilled person can manage five hundred bee colonies. *Jeff Furman, Ben & Jerry's Ice Cream, business consultant*

BUILDING

1308 ... *BUILDING WITH TUBING* A hollow tube should have a wall thickness that is at least 1/50 of the tube's diameter. If the wall thickness is less, the tube won't work as a structural member. It will crumple like a beer can. *John Schubert, senior editor, Bicycling magazine*

AS A RULE OF THUMB: THE MORE MONEY PEOPLE SPEND ON A WEDDING, THE FEWER YEARS THE MARRIAGE WILL LAST. THE PRESENCE OF ICE SCULPTURES AT THE RECEPTION IS ALMOST ALWAYS FATAL TO THE FUTURE MARRIAGE. *Bruno Colapietro, Matrimonial Lawyer with Over 8,000 Cases, Binghamton, New York*

1309 ... **BUYING A COMPUTER** Every two years, you can buy a computer that performs twice as well for half the price. *Dave McKeown, computer scientist*

COMPUTERS

1310 ... **GETTING AN AGENT** To convince a literary agent to represent you, write him a letter. He deals in the printed word and will trust your well-written letter more than a telephone call. *Walter Pitkin, literary agent, Weston, Connecticut*

WRITING

1311 ... **GETTING A COLLEGE DEGREE** To survive college, do all the homework on the day it is assigned, especially term papers. *Dave Chapman, computer consultant, Forestville, California*

COLLEGE

1312 ... **FINDING A JOB** The interview, not the resume, gets you the job. But a good resume can get you the interview. *Scott Parker, data specialist, Beaumont, Texas*

JOBS

1313 ... **UNDERSTANDING LANGUAGE** Words pertaining to the left usually have fewer letters than their counterparts pertaining to the right. *George H. Amber, p.e., Royal Oak, Michigan*

LANGUAGE

1314 ... **MAXIMIZING YOUR RANGE IN AN AIRPLANE** You will get your maximum range by flying at a speed that equals the airplane's "best-rate-of-climb" speed plus 25 percent. This speed will be close to the 45 percent power setting that is usually the lowest shown on range charts or graphs. In some aircraft, you may only gain a few miles, but they could make a difference. *Bruce Landsberg, pilot and writer*

FLYING

1315 ... **MAKING A DOCUMENTARY** Most documentary film makers plan on shooting ten times the footage that will end up in the finished film. *Sandra A. Kraft, writer*

MOVIES AND FILM

1316 ... **RIDING PUBLIC TRANSPORTATION IN BOSTON** When riding public transportation in Boston, allow one-half hour per transfer plus walking time. For example, a subway to trolley to bus trip would take an hour and a half plus any time spent walking to and from the stations. *Leslie Simpson, Wollaston, Massachusetts*

CERTAIN PLACES

1317 ... **BRUSHING YOUR HAIR** Twenty-five brush strokes per day is considered optimal for best distribution of natural oils. More brushing causes damage. *Dr. Jonathan Zizmor, hair expert*

GROOMING

1318 ... **WORKING TO LIVE LONGER** The self-employed are more likely to live to ripe old age than those who work for others. *Walter Pitkin, literary agent, Weston, Connecticut*

DEATH

1319 ... **KEEPING UP WITH HUGS** Four hugs a day are the minimum needed to meet a person's "skin hunger." *Greg Risberg, clinical social worker, Northwestern University Medical School, Chicago, Illinois*

JOKER

1320 ... **RIDING A HORSE** If your stirrup is the right length, you should be able to look over your knee and see the tip of your toe as you sit in the saddle. *John H. Beauvais, Cambridge, Massachusetts*

HORSES

DESIGN

MANAGEMENT

REAL ESTATE

COOKING

HEARTS

GARDENING

TEMPERATURE

SURVIVAL

DRIVING

JOKER

INSECTS

BUILDING

1321 ... ***THE PARSONS RULE OF DESKTOP DESIGN***   If you are estimating your time for a desktop design job and you think it will take more than one hour, multiply your estimate by two. If you think you can finish the job in less than one hour, multiply your estimate by three.   *John E. Parsons, Production Manager, American Demographics*

1322 ... ***GETTING THINGS DONE***   Make a new "to do" list every day from your larger list of projects, goals, and things to do. If an item gets transferred from one daily list to the next ten times, drop it. There's a reason you're avoiding the item, and your time would be better spent reassessing your motives.   *Andrea Frankel, computer scientist, engineer, holistic health practitioner, San Diego, California*

1323 ... ***INVESTING IN RETIREMENT HOUSING***   If you are building retirement housing, you should plan to spend 20 to 25 percent of the average unit cost for land acquisition and marketing expenditures.   *Anonymous*

1324 ... ***EATING BRAZIL NUTS***   Brazil nuts are 30 times more radioactive than the second most radioactive food.   *Steven M. Keisman, New York City high school resource coordinator*

1325 ... ***CHECKING A BEER BELLY***   Measure the circumferences of your waist and hips. If the waist-to-hips ratio is over 1.0 in men or above 0.8 in women, your risk of heart attack or stroke is five to ten times greater than if the ratio is less.   *US Pharmacist*

1326 ... ***PLANTING A BULB***   If you're not sure how deep to plant a flower bulb, try three times its length.   *Kevin Kelly, Athens, Georgia*

1327 ... ***PREDICTING A FROST***   When the temperature falls below 50 degrees Fahrenheit at sunset, watch out for morning frost.   *Tim Matson, writer and pond maker, Thetford Center, Vermont*

1328 ... ***THE SECOND SURVIVAL RULE OF THREE***   History shows that people repeatedly survive far longer than thought possible. A general rule is to estimate the survival time for a particular person under specific conditions, then multiply by three.   *Tim J. Setnicka, author, Wilderness Search and Rescue*

1329 ... ***FINDING A PARKING SPACE***   Drive to your destination. Then using that as a center, drive in ever-larger circles until you find a spot.   *John H. Beauvais, Cambridge, Massachusetts*

1330 ... ***BETSY'S OVERLOOKED RULE***   Two's company, three's a crowd.   *Betsy Cook, composer, Buckinghamshire, England*

1331 ... ***SWARMING BEES***   Honeybees will start to congregate in a horseshoe-shaped pattern on the front of the hive three days before they swarm.   *Anthony Sykes, orchard worker*

1332 ... ***MIXING FRESH ADOBE***   Good adobe bricks are made from sandy clay or clay loam. If the mixture is too rich in clay, it will stick to your hoe; too rich in sand, your hoe will come up clean. The mixture is just right if it barely slips from your hoe, leaving traces of mud on the blade as you work it.   *Marcia Southwick, writer and builder*

AS A RULE
OF THUMB:
A SMITH AND
WESSON BEATS
FOUR ACES.

CHIC VOLTURNO,
STOREHOUSE
OF WORTHLESS
INFORMATION,
HOLLYWOOD,
FLORIDA

1333 ... *PROGRAMMING A COMPUTER* A computer program in a good high-level language can be written about five to ten times as fast as the same program in assembly language, but it will be longer and run slower. *Clifton Royston, programmer/analyst, Nukualofa, Tonga*

COMPUTERS

1334 ... *GETTING AN AGENT* If you insist on using a telephone to ask an agent to represent you, call and ask the agent how to proceed. Then follow his instructions closely. *Walter Pitkin, literary agent, Weston, Connecticut*

WRITING

1335 ... *SPOTTING A FUTURE SUCCESS* A research director can explain a research project to the layman better than a tenured professor; a tenured professor can do it better than an assistant professor; an assistant professor better than a graduate student. A graduate student who can explain it well is going to be a research director. *Jennifer Evans, writer, Austin, Texas*

COLLEGE

1336 ... *TRAINING FOR A JOB* Only 20 percent of all jobs in the U.S. require more than eight months of training. *Scott Parker, data specialist, Beaumont, Texas*

JOBS

1337 ... *TEACHING SPELLING* When announcing spelling words for average senior-high-school students, pronounce them at the rate of 1 word every 12 seconds. Difficult words can be recalled and written in that period of time if the student knows them. And this interval is short enough that students won't get bored by the easy words. *LeRoy Dagg, English and drama teacher, Topeka, Kansas*

LANGUAGE

1338 ... *STAYING AIRBORNE* Maximum endurance in an airplane is attained at its "best-rate-of-climb" speed, or Vy. Vy, listed in the airplane's manual, approximates the maximum lift-over-drag ratio; it requires the least amount of power to maintain level flight. If you become lost, this speed will stretch the fuel supply and give you more time to spot landmarks or summon help by radio. *Bruce Landsberg, pilot and writer*

FLYING

1339 ... *USING A MOVIE CAMERA* Count at least ten seconds every time you press a movie camera's start button. The biggest single error that novice film makers make is taking many shots in very short spurts. *Flip Schulke, underwater photographer*

MOVIES AND FILM

1340 ... *PLAYING ROCK AND ROLL IN NEW YORK CITY* In New York City, all you need is 45 minutes of original music and your band can play in the bars. *Kid with Mohawk haircut and engineer's boots, overheard in restaurant, Ithaca, New York*

CERTAIN PLACES

1341 ... *THE TOWLE NO HOT WATER RULE* If showers five to seven minutes apart are taken in rapid succession, a 50-gallon natural gas hot-water heater will begin to run out of hot water during the fourth shower. *John Towle, Salinas, California*

GROOMING

1342 ... *LIVING LONGER NEAR HOME* If you live close to the area you grew up in, the chances are you will live longer than most Americans. *Walter Pitkin, literary agent, Weston, Connecticut*

DEATH

1343 ... *FORECASTING THE WEATHER* Green grass at Christmas means brown mounds at Easter. *Joe Gattie, South Buffalo, New York*

HOLIDAYS

1344 ... *FEEDING PACKHORSES AND MULES* When using horses and mules as pack animals in mountains, you'll need to feed each of them three quarts of grain each morning and night and ten pounds of hay per day. *Scott M. Kruse, biogeographer and Martha Betcher, medical technologist, Fresno, California*

HORSES

JOKER

1345 ... *THE RULE OF FIRST IMPRESSIONS* Nothing is ever as good as it first appears. *Jim Riggs, Indio, California*

MANAGEMENT

1346 ... *NOT WAITING TOO LONG* Life will be easier if you go to bed before you get sleepy, eat before you get hungry, and clean your desk before you quit for the day. *V. G. Walkendifer, Churchton, Maryland*

REAL ESTATE

1347 ... *THE RETIREMENT HOME RULE* Target your marketing within a 20-mile radius of the development. *Anonymous*

COOKING

1348 ... *MAKING FROSTING* Although it's tempting to add the last of a box of powdered sugar to frosting, it will make the frosting too goopy — and you'll be out of powdered sugar. *Judith A. Scheinuk, Seattle, Washington*

HEARTS

1349 ... *CHECKING YOUR PULSE* The normal resting pulse rate for humans is about equal to the external temperatures they find most comfortable measured in degrees Fahrenheit - 68 to 72. *J. Eichelberger, Alameda, California*

GARDENING

1350 ... *GROWING YOUR OWN HERBS* If you are setting aside space to grow herbs for your own family, figure two square feet for each variety you plan to grow. *Jean Moses, Lincoln, Nebraska*

TEMPERATURE

1351 ... *THE AIR RISING RULE* Rising air cools about 5.5 degrees Fahrenheit per 1,000 feet. Sinking air warms at the same rate. *Stephen Friends, meteorologist*

SURVIVAL

1352 ... *STORING WATER* A bomb shelter needs a gallon of water per day per person for drinking and washing. *D. Riley, maintenance crew supervisor*

DRIVING

1353 ... *DRIVING SAFELY* If you find yourself driving on ice, deflate your rear tires until they have a double chin (at about 18 pounds). Then slowly drive off the ice and reinflate your tires. *John H. Beauvais, Cambridge, Massachusetts*

MARRIAGE

1354 ... *AGING GRACEFULLY* If you want to know what your girlfriend will look like in 20 years, take a good look at her mother. *Dean Sheridan, electronics technician and deaf actor, Torrance, California*

JOKER

1355 ... *CARING FOR DOGS* Housebreaking a puppy will depreciate the net worth of your home and clothes by 5 to 10 percent. *Al Hassan, veterinarian and doctor, Sacramento, California*

BUILDING

1356 ... *BUILDING WALLS OF ADOBE* The height of an adobe wall should be less than ten times its thickness unless it is stiffened by buttresses or intersecting partitions. *Marcia Southwick, writer and builder*

AS A RULE OF THUMB:
IF THERE'S ANY QUESTION ABOUT WHEN TO DO SOME FINISH WORK ON A WOODWORKING PROJECT, DO IT IMMEDIATELY. CHANCES ARE YOU WON'T DO IT LATER.
PHIL TOMLINSON, BUILDER

1357 ... **DESIGNING A COMPUTER SYSTEM**   When designing and coding a computer system, write as much of the system as possible in the highest level language available. *Clifton Royston, programmer/analyst, Nukualofa, Tonga*

COMPUTERS

1358 ... **WRITING A LETTER**   A letter takes three times as long to write as it does to say. *Glenn Kornblum, St. Louis, Missouri*

WRITING

1359 ... **MAKING IT THROUGH COLLEGE**   Never take a course from the professor who wrote the text book. *Anonymous*

COLLEGE

1360 ... **WEIGHING YOUR SALARY**   If a single career woman is not making her age times $1,000 in annual salary by age 30, she should either change careers or marry a career man making $80,000 or better and become a wife and mother. She can then live comfortably and afford one additional child for each $20,000 per year he makes over $80,000. *Barbara Greenlee, B.S., R.N., Ship's Nurse, Kauai, Hawaii*

JOBS

1361 ... **LEARNING A LANGUAGE**   The more languages you know, the easier it is for you to learn a new one. *Paul A. Delaney, meteorologist, Bellsville, Maryland*

LANGUAGE

1362 ... **LANDING AN AIRPLANE**   Begin your descent 5 miles out for every 1,000 feet of altitude you have to lose. If you are 8,000 feet above the ground, start your descent 40 miles from the airport. *Bruce Landsberg, pilot and writer*

FLYING

1363 ... **ADAPTING A NOVEL FOR A FILM**   As a rule, the more you liked the novel, the less you will like the movie that is made from it. *Rebecca Sawyer, bookkeeper*

MOVIES AND FILM

1364 ... **RENTING A HOUSE IN IOWA**   Don't pay more than one-fourth of your income for rent in Iowa. *Lee Sliger, Burlington, Iowa*

CERTAIN PLACES

1365 ... **FINDING THE RIGHT WIG**   Toupees never look like the real thing. They either look cheap or like a "good one." *Steven M. Keisman, New York City high school resource coordinator*

JOKER

1366 ... **THE SHORT RULE OF LIVING LONGER**   People who are shorter than average are more likely to live to a ripe old age than taller people. *Walter Pitkin, literary agent, Weston, Connecticut*

DEATH

1367 ... **KEEPING A CHRISTMAS TREE**   A fresh Christmas tree should last four weeks without shedding its needles. *The American Christmas Tree Association*

HOLIDAYS

1368 ... **HITCHING UP HORSES**   When you're hitching horses, the double tree or evener should be the same length as the neck yoke. *The Very Rev. Emmet C. Smith, Largo, Florida*

HORSES

MAIL

1369 ... **WEIGHING YOUR MAIL**   Nine pennies weigh one ounce. If you happen to be out of pennies, try two Hershey bars with almonds, unwrapped. *Ron Elkins, Evanston, Illinois*

MANAGEMENT

1370 ... **MEETING YOUR GOALS**   If you always try to do more than you planned to do instead of stopping to congratulate yourself for getting something done, you probably work too hard to be effective and you may be damaging your health.   *Gerald Gutlipp, mathematician, Chicago, Illinois*

REAL ESTATE

1371 ... **INVESTING IN RETIREMENT HOUSING**   Invest in an area that has at least 20 times more elderly households than retirement units. *Anonymous*

COOKING

1372 ... **STUFFING POULTRY**   One baseball-size wad of stuffing per person, and two for the pan. *Dorothy Kirsh, Buffalo, New York*

HEARTS

1373 ... **THE PUBLIC SERVICE RULE OF CHEST PAIN**   Chest pain that lasts more than two minutes could signal a heart attack.   *TV Public Service Announcement "The Manufacturers of Bufferin"*

GARDENING

1374 ... **IDENTIFYING MINTS**   All mints have square stems, but not all square stems are mints. *Scott M. Kruse, Yosemite National Park, California*

TEMPERATURE

1375 ... **THE CALM AIR RULE**   Calm air cools with altitude—about 3.5 degrees Fahrenheit per 1,000 feet. *Scott M. Kruse, biogeographer, Fresno, California*

HEARTS

1376 ... **THE NO-HOLDS-BARRED RULE OF SELF-DEFENSE**   If you are attacked by several people at once, go for the largest and put one or both of his or her eyes out. This will produce sufficient consternation in the others to give you time to flee. *Peter Garrison, writer and pilot*

SURVIVAL

1377 ... **DRIVING SAFELY**   When backing a vehicle with a trailer, turn the bottom of the steering wheel in the direction you want the trailer to go. *Roger Damon, computer game designer, Blairsville, Pennsylvania*

DRIVING

1378 ... **THE LAWYER'S RULE OF DIVORCE**   If someone tells you they want a divorce, ask them first if the sex is still good. Those who say yes won't get a divorce — ask for your fee up front. *Jennifer Evans, writer, Austin, Texas*

DOGS

1379 ... **BETTING ON DOGS**   Don't bet on a dog that urinates just before a race. It's either nervous and will burn out early, or it is too full of water and will be slow. *Bob Horton, consultant and writer, Largo, Florida*

BUILDING

1380 ... **ADDING STRAW TO ADOBE**   Straw is used as a binder to hold adobe bricks together as they dry. You can add up to a handful of very short pieces to a standard 4-by-10-by-14-inch brick. It will take slightly more than one large bale of straw to mix a thousand bricks. *Marcia Southwick, writer and builder*

1381 ... _WRITING COMPUTER SOFTWARE_   A software writer can be expected to generate about ten lines of debugged, high-order language a day. _Anonymous systems engineer_

COMPUTERS

1382 ... _WRITING POETRY_   A poet should write every working day, but for no more than three hours. _Stephen Unsino, poet, Eastchester, New York_

WRITING

1383 ... _VISITING HOME_   When you're at college, go home to visit your parents on the second or third weekend in October, when the football team has an away game. _Phillip Williams, Jr., University of Michigan, Ann Arbor, Michigan_

COLLEGE

As A RULE OF THUMB:
NEVER BUY MORE THAN ONE SLINKY BECAUSE THEY EVENTUALLY WILL BECOME INTERTWINED.
ANDY STEINBERG, LOUISVILLE, KENTUCKY

1384 ... _HOLDING A JOB_   The more you need your job for financial reasons, the worse you will be treated. _J. Johnson, Fort Collins, Colorado_

JOBS

1385 ... _LEARNING A LANGUAGE_   The shorter a word, the more meanings it has. _Paul A. Delaney, meteorologist, Beltsville, Maryland_

LANGUAGE

1386 ... _FLYING IN CROSSWINDS_   Most light planes are capable of taking off or landing in 90-degree crosswinds that are less than 20 percent of the airplane's power-off stall speed. _Gene Miller, engineer_

FLYING

1387 ... _THE SEQUEL RULE_   As a rule, if you didn't care for the original movie, you will like the sequel even less. _A wandering moviegoer, Oklahoma City, Oklahoma_

MOVIES AND FILM

1388 ... _RUNNING A LIGHT IN NEW JERSEY_   New Jersey traffic lights have an amber signal lasting one second for every 10 mph of the posted speed limit. _Steven F. Scharff, cartoonist, Union, New Jersey_

CERTAIN PLACES

1389 ... _AMPLIFYING SOUND_   You need a 250-watt amplifier to produce sound twice as loud as that produced by a 25-watt amplifier. _Steven M. Keisman, New York City high school resource coordinator_

MUSIC

1390 ... _ESTIMATING THE TIME OF DEATH_   To estimate the length of time a person has been dead, take a rectal temperature. If it is above room temperature, subtract from 98. The answer is the number of hours since death. _Thomas O. Marsh, writer and coroner's investigator, Fairfield, Ohio_

DEATH

1391 ... _CHOOSING A FRESH CHRISTMAS TREE_   When you're choosing a Christmas tree, rotate the end of a branch between your forefinger and thumb. If the tree is fresh, you won't end up with a handful of needles. _David and Penny Russell, Dilltown, Pennsylvania_

HOLIDAYS

1392 ... _WATCHING HORSES LOOK_   You can get an idea of what horses are looking at by watching the position of their heads. Horses lower their heads to see objects in the distance. They raise their heads to see objects up close. _George Huebner, Houston Chronicle_

HORSES

MAIL

1393 ... *SPOTTING JUNK MAIL* The more printing on the outside of an envelope, the less important the information inside. *Gerry M. Flick, M.D., Ship's Surgeon, S.S. Constitution off Hawaii*

MANAGEMENT

1394 ... *GETTING SOMETHING DONE* If you want something done, give it to a busy person. *Scott Parker, data specialist, Beaumont, Texas*

REAL ESTATE

1395 ... *BUYING RURAL LAND* Never offer more than two-thirds the asking price for rural land. *Ren Heim, landscaper, Cincinnati, Ohio*

COOKING

1396 ... *HUNTING FOR MUSHROOMS* Mushroom hunting is best when mayapples come up. *Ted, Rock Island, Iowa*

JOKER

1397 ... *PREPARING FOR BAD NEWS* Bad news is never as bad as it sounds at first. *Steven M. Keisman, New York City high school resource coordinator*

GARDENING

1398 ... *WATERING YOUR GARDEN* Don't water your garden unless the soil is dry past the depth of your index finger. *Cally Arthur, managing editor, American Demographics*

TEMPERATURE

1399 ... *THE RATE OF REACTION RULE* The rate of a chemical reaction doubles for every 10 degree Centigrade rise in temperature. *Ken Partymiller, chemist*

SURVIVAL

1400 ... *THE SURVIVAL RULE OF FIFTY* You have a 50 percent chance of surviving for 50 minutes in 50 degree water. *Rick Eckstrom, plan review officer, Ithaca, New York*

DRIVING

1401 ... *DRIVING ON ICE* If the roads in an area ice over only five to ten times a year, half of the season's fender-benders will occur after the first icing. *Walter Pitkin, literary agent, Weston, Connecticut*

MARRIAGE

1402 ... *THE GREEN HUSBAND RULE* Jewish men make the best husbands. *Francine Green, Cherry Hill, New Jersey*

AS A RULE OF THUMB: YOU SHOULD NEVER WEAR A HAT THAT HAS MORE CHARACTER THAN YOU DO. *Bill Spivey, San Francisco, California, quoting Michael Harris, Hat Maker*

DOGS

1403 ... *NAMING A DOG* If you give your dog a fancy name, it's not for your dog but for your pride. You'll end up using a nickname. *Carolyn Lloyd, 15-year-old student, Montreal, Quebec*

BUILDING

1404 ... *PAVING WITH BRICKS* A crew of six bricklayers with one foreman can lay 1,000 square feet of paving brick per day. *R. Pieper, architectural historian*

1405 ... *MANAGING YOUR HARD DRIVE* The hard drive on a personal computer usually stores up to 1,000 K more than advertised. *Steven M. Keisman, New York City high school resource coordinator*

COMPUTERS

1406 ... *WRITING POETRY* If the erasers of your pencils wear out before the graphite, you're too fussy. *Stephen Unsino, poet, Eastchester, New York*

WRITING

1407 ... *GETTING THROUGH GRADUATE SCHOOL* Avoid young professors who are ambitious at the expense of their students. You should also avoid old professors who take out their frustrations on their students. *Stephen M. Lange, graduate student, Hopatcong, New Jersey*

COLLEGE

1408 ... *ASSESSING YOUR JOB TITLE* The longer your job title and job description, the less important you are. *Dean Sheridan, electronics technician and deaf actor, Torrance, California*

JOBS

1409 ... *USING SEMICOLONS* Use semicolons freely; most readers will credit your erudition. *Denis Smith, high school counselor, Camarillo, California*

LANGUAGE

1410 ... *STOPPING AN AIRPLANE* To determine the speed at which an aircraft begins to hydroplane, multiply the square root of the tire pressure by 9. A light twin-engine plane with a tire pressure of 36 pounds will begin hydroplaning about 54 knots, which means that aerodynamic braking will be the major source of stopping power above that speed when there is standing water on the runway. *Bruce Landsberg, pilot and writer*

FLYING

1411 ... *MAKING AN ANIMATED MOVIE* Animated characters are more lifelike if their actions are slightly sped up. *Scott Marsh, photographer*

MOVIES AND FILM

1412 ... *PLANTING IN MASSACHUSETTS* In Massachusetts, plant your peas by Patriot's Day, harvest them by the 4th of July. *Sid Ore (or Sidore), Paris, France*

CERTAIN PLACES

1413 ... *BUYING SPEAKERS* The smaller the speaker, the weaker the bass. *Steven M. Keisman, New York City high school resource coordinator*

MUSIC

1414 ... *DIGGING A GRAVE* The standard size for a human grave is 7'8" long by 3'2" wide by 6' deep, unless there is to be more than one person buried in it. Then add two feet of depth for each body. *Rev. Halsey DeW. Howe, Saint Mark's Church, Springfield, Vermont*

DEATH

1415 ... *SENDING CHRISTMAS CARDS* You should receive at least two Christmas cards for every three you mail out. If you don't, you are sending cards to the wrong people. *Shelley Mosher, Groton, New York*

HOLIDAYS

1416 ... *SHINING UP YOUR HORSE* A horse with a dull coat needs more corn in its diet. *George Huebner, Houston Chronicle*

HORSES

MAIL

MANAGEMENT

REAL ESTATE

COOKING

INJURIES

GARDENING

TEMPERATURE

JOKER

DRIVING

MARRIAGE

DOGS

BUILDING

1417 ... ***WEIGHING A LETTER*** To determine whether a letter needs an extra ounce worth of postage, hold the upper left corner with your left index finger and the lower right corner with your right index finger. If the letter flips off center, you need extra postage. *Jacki B. Kuepker, Coralville, Iowa*

1418 ... ***THE ARTHUR RULE OF ASSIGNING PROJECTS*** Don't give an employee a project after 4:30 unless it can be completed by 5:00. *Cally Arthur, managing editor, American Demographics*

1419 ... ***THE WAYSIDE RULE OF REAL ESTATE*** For every two people who make a good living in real estate, another third falls by the wayside. *Scott Parker, data specialist, Beaumont, Texas*

1420 ... ***COOKING MEAT*** Cook meat for one-half hour at 350 degrees F for each pound. *Anonymous*

1421 ... ***PREPARING FOR PAIN*** Sprains, strains, and sunburn hurt more the second day. *Steven M. Keisman, New York City high school resource coordinator*

1422 ... ***PLANTING TOMATOES*** When set in the field, a young tomato plant should be as wide as it is high. Taller plants are leggy and more prone to wind damage. *Peter van Berkum, Kittery Point, Maine*

1423 ... ***CHECKING THE TEMPERATURE*** One way to check the temperature when you're outdoors is to inhale rapidly. If you feel the moisture in your nostrils begin to freeze, it is 10 degrees Fahrenheit or colder. *Truman Plant, expressman*

1424 ... ***UNDERSTANDING FRENCH PHILOSOPHY*** To understand modern French philosophy, simply assume that everything intangible is real, while everything material is unreal. Thus, disappointment is real, but your Citroen is not. *Gordon Hard, assistant editor, Consumer Reports, Mount Vernon, New York*

1425 ... ***PAYING A TOLL*** Avoid the line with the motorcycle. The biker won't have the money ready. Instead, he'll have to dig into his pocket, and on a cold day he'll have to take off his gloves. *Benjamin Keh, Berkeley, California*

1426 ... ***PATCHING UP AN ARGUMENT*** To stay married, patch up your arguments before you go to bed. *Anonymous*

1427 ... ***JUDGING THE HEALTH OF A DOG'S DIET*** If your dog's stools are hard and well-formed, he's getting the right diet. *Stephen Unsino, poet, Eastchester, New York*

1428 ... ***BUILDING A HOUSE*** It takes four experienced builders about 400 hours to build an average-sized house. *Thomas Peterson, builder*

AS A RULE OF THUMB:
A SON IS ALWAYS TALLER THAN HIS MOTHER.
JANICE M. PROCHASKA, PROFESSOR, UNIVERSITY OF RHODE ISLAND

1429 ... **USING SOFTWARE**   Most people use only one-tenth of the computer software they buy after they get their computer. Of the software they use, most will never use more than 25 percent of the software's capacity.   *Steven M. Keisman, New York City high school resource coordinator*

1430 ... **WRITING POETRY**   To be a professional poet, it takes ten years of steady practice.   *Stephen Unsino, poet, Eastchester, New York*

1431 ... **THE FLICK RULE OF COLLEGE MIXERS**   The most beautiful women at a college mixer are the ones at the entrance taking tickets.   *Gerry M. Flick, M.D., Ship's Surgeon, S.S. Constitution off Hawaii*

1432 ... **HUNTING FOR A JOB**   In your first interview, don't ask about vacations, pay, pensions, or working hours. Doing so will give the impression you are looking for an easy job. First get an offer, then tell the employer what you want.   *John Munschauer, author, Jobs For English Majors and Other Smart People*

1433 ... **MAKING CONVERSATION**   Ninety percent of all conversations use only 1,000 words.   *Scott Parker, data specialist, Beaumont, Texas*

1434 ... **FLYING IN HAZE**   When flying toward a low sun, the visibility will be half what is reported. When flying away from a low sun, the visibility will be twice what is reported.   *Jack Barclay, biologist, pilot, flight instructor, Santa Cruz, California*

1435 ... **MAKING A MOVIE**   Movie credits and subtitles should appear on the screen long enough to be read three times.   *Jim Maas, film maker*

1436 ... **CHASING RATS IN NEW YORK CITY**   There is one rat for every New Yorker—or one New Yorker for every rat.   *Lee Jones, spokesman for Mayor Edward I. Koch, in the Cincinnati Enquirer*

1437 ... **BUYING A STEREO**   Your system will sound like your speakers. The speakers should cost at least as much as the two next-most-expensive components put together.   *Jeff Brown, astronomer, Bloomington, Indiana*

1438 ... **THE DEATH RULE OF TWO**   In a geriatric patient population, twice as many people will die within the two months after their birthday as would be normally expected. One-half as many will die within the two months before their birthday.   *Gerry M. Flick, M.D., Ship's Surgeon, S.S. Constitution off Hawaii*

1439 ... **THE CHRISTMAS TREE RULE OF THREE**   To find out how many lights your Christmas tree needs, multiply the tree height times the tree width times three.   *Michael Spencer, lawyer, San Francisco, California*

1440 ... **BUYING A HORSE**   As far as price is concerned, the best time of year to buy a horse is fall.   *Jeanne K. Posey, horse show judge*

MAIL

1441 ... *TESTING A DIRECT-MAIL CAMPAIGN* For a reliable direct-mail test, you should mail enough pieces to get at least 300 responses. *Cathy Elton, San Francisco, California*

MANAGEMENT

1442 ... *RECOGNIZING THE OBVIOUS* As a rule, clients will recognize the obvious much sooner than professionals. *Dr. Larry R. Hunt, Toronto, Ontario*

REAL ESTATE

1443 ... *THE BEACHFRONT RULE* If you are north of the equator, don't buy property on the south side of a jetty. The drift of the ocean is from south to north, and the beach will erode south of any protrusion that blocks the drift. *Carol Terrizzi, artist and graphic designer, Ithaca, New York*

COOKING

1444 ... *TEARING OFF SOME SARAN WRAP* To tear Saran Wrap smoothly, hold your thumb on the W on the front of the box. *Nancy Heffernan Eckstrom, nutritionist, Barton, New York*

INJURIES

1445 ... *SPOTTING A FRACTURED BONE* If it hurts more when you press your injury with a finger at one spot, it may be a fracture. *Alan R. Brown, New York, New York*

GARDENING

1446 ... *GROWING PLANTS UNDER LIGHTS* You need at least 20 watts of fluorescent light for every square foot of growing area. *Amy Rice, College Park, Maryland*

JOKER

1447 ... *FORECASTING THE WEATHER* If you can hear spiders singing, it will be hot. *Granny Irwin, Kenmore, New York*

TRAVEL

1448 ... *VISITING DISNEY WORLD* At Disney World, the crowd is most likely to turn to the right. Therefore, the rides to the left are less crowded. *Carolyn Lloyd, 15-year-old student, Montreal, Quebec*

DRIVING

1449 ... *HITTING SPEED BUMPS* If the speed bumps are only a few inches in height, you'll feel them less if you speed up rather than slow down. *Jerry Azzaro, San Francisco, California*

MARRIAGE

1450 ... *STAYING MARRIED* The chances of divorce are greatest during the fourth year of marriage. *Anonymous*

DOGS

1451 ... *MEETING A STRANGE DOG* When meeting a strange dog, present him with the back of your closed hand to sniff. Don't show him your fingers — they're threatening. *John H. Beauvais, Cambridge, Massachusetts*

BUILDING

1452 ... *MAKING CONCRETE BY YOURSELF* It takes one person the better part of a day to mix and pour two cubic yards of concrete. *Ken Kern, writer and builder*

AS A RULE OF THUMB: ONE POUND OF DECENT STEAK MAKES TWO DOZEN CHUNKS FOR SHISH KEBABS OR SPIEDIES.
RICK ECKSTROM, PLAN REVIEW OFFICER, ITHACA, NEW YORK

1453 ... *THE RULE OF SOFTWARE SALES* The difference between a used-car salesman and a software salesman is that the car salesman knows when he's lying. *Ben Cota, technology marketing guy, Oakland, California*

1454 ... *WRITING FOR A NEWSPAPER* Instead of submitting newspaper stories one by one, submit a batch of them to reduce the number of questions the editor will ask you about them. *Stephen Unsino, poet, Eastchester, New York*

1455 ... *WATCHING STUDENTS DRINK* A freshman drinks until he feels like he is going to get sick; a senior drinks until he feels like he is going to die. *Phil A. Schrodt, Associate Professor, Northwestern University, Evanston, Illinois*

1456 ... *PLANNING YOUR INTERVIEWS* Interview first for the jobs you care about least—the experience will improve your important interviews. *John Munschauer, author, Jobs For English Majors and Other Smart People*

1457 ... *COMMUNICATING IN A FOREIGN COUNTRY* When traveling in a country whose language you don't know, the words for "Yes," "No," "Beer," "Please," "Thank you," "That," and as many numbers as possible will get you through about 90 percent of the situations you encounter. Memorizing complicated expressions is useless because you will not be able to understand the response. Grammar is irrelevant; correct pronunciation is vital. *Phil A. Schrodt, Associate Professor, Northwestern University, Evanston, Illinois*

1458 ... *FLYING AN ULTRALIGHT AIRCRAFT* For the beginning ultralight aircraft pilot, when the wind is good for kite flying, do that instead. *Tom Hammitt, Flying*

1459 ... *MAKING A MOVIE* The smallest letters in a title should be at least 1/25th the height of the screen. *Scott Marsh, photographer*

1460 ... *TRAVELING IN MASSACHUSETTS* When you are trying to get somewhere in Boston without directions, take a turn at every major intersection — never go straight. When you are trying to do the same on Cape Cod, never turn — always go straight and look for the signs. *David Notkin, Pittsburgh, Pennsylvania*

1461 ... *TRAINING YOUR VOICE* Practice outdoors as often as possible. The open spaces will encourage the production of overtones, which will add health to your voice. *Stephen Unsino, poet, Eastchester, New York*

1462 ... *THE WIDOW RULE* A widow has recovered from the death of her husband when she starts reading Gourmet again. *Robin Masson, attorney and law professor, Ithaca, New York*

1463 ... *DECIDING HOW TO DO UNTO OTHERS* Do unto others as you would have them do unto you. *Norman Brenner, Fleetwood, New York*

1464 ... *THE DIGIOVANI HORSE FACE CAT RULE* Rub a horse's face and ears as gently as you would pet a cat. *Stacey DiGiovani, equestrian*

MAIL

1465 ... WAITING FOR A DIRECT-MAIL RESPONSE The response to a direct-mail campaign peaks one week to ten days after you receive the first reply. *John Pitts, publicist, Boston, Massachusetts*

MANAGEMENT

1466 ... DELEGATING AUTHORITY I make it an absolute rule not to make decisions that somebody else can make. The first rule of leadership is to save yourself for the big decisions. *Richard M. Nixon, former president of the United States, as quoted in TIME magazine*

REAL ESTATE

1467 ... THE MOONEY RULE OF POOLS No more than 10 percent of the people in an apartment complex will try to use the pool at the same time, and about 80 percent will never use it. *Vince Mooney, real estate broker, Tulsa, Oklahoma*

COOKING

1468 ... THE KELLY RULE OF MOLDY FOOD Don't eat mold on food you can mold. *Bill Kelly*

INJURIES

1469 ... RECOGNIZING A FRACTURED BONE If you feel nauseous after injuring an arm or leg, you've probably fractured it. *J. L. McClenahan, Philadelphia, Pennsylvania*

GARDENING

1470 ... PLANTING SEEDS Most seeds should be set as deep as they are wide. *Peter van Berkum, Kittery Point, Maine*

WEATHER

1471 ... FORECASTING THE WEATHER Tough apple skin means a hard winter. *Steven M. Keisman, New York City high school resource coordinator*

TRAVEL

1472 ... EATING ON THE ROAD When traveling, eat what the natives eat. It's cheaper and tastes better than anything else. *Norman Brenner, Fleetwood, New York*

DRIVING

1473 ... AVOIDING A SLOW DRIVER When driving, never get behind a driver wearing a hat. The straighter the hat, the slower the driver. *Sue in San Diego, California*

MARRIAGE

1474 ... SPOTTING A WIFE BEATER If a man hits his wife once, he might not do it again. If he hits his wife twice, he's likely to do it again. *Scott Parker, data specialist, Beaumont, Texas*

DOGS

1475 ... CARING FOR DOGS Owning two dogs is no more work than owning one, but three dogs is hard work. *Captain Haggerty, animal trainer, actor, author, and philosopher, New York, New York*

BUILDING

1476 ... BUILDING A STONE WALL You should plan on ordering (or collecting) two cubic yards of stone for every cubic yard of finished wall. *David Finn, printmaker and stonemason, Boston, Massachusetts*

A**S A RULE OF THUMB:**
YOU SHOULD ALWAYS BUY
ONE MORE BOTTLE OF
CHAMPAGNE THAN YOU
THINK YOU'LL NEED FOR
EVERY FOUR PEOPLE.
D**AVID** N**OWICKI,** W**INE** A**UTHORITY,**
I**NTERLAKEN,** N**EW** Y**ORK**

1477 ... **REPLACING A FLAGPOLE**   A wooden flagpole will need to be replaced every 20 years. *Carolyn Lloyd, 15-year-old student, Montreal, Quebec*

DURABILITY

1478 ... **THE READER FEEDBACK RULE OF THREE**   Don't make changes based on reader feedback until you've heard the same comment from three different people. *Percy Angress, special effects producer, Santa Monica, California*

WRITING

1479 ... **SOLICITING PAPERS FROM STUDENTS**   In a college classroom, roughly 10 percent of the term papers will be handed in late. Increasing the penalty for a late paper has no effect on this statistic unless more than one term paper is required. *Phil A. Schrodt, Associate Professor, Northwestern University, Evanston, Illinois*

COLLEGE

1480 ... **CHECKING A REFERENCE**   If you are checking a reference and you ask someone's former employer, "Would you hire this person again?" any answer but "yes" is a "no." *Edward J. Garrison, nursing home administrator, Watsonville, California*

JOBS

1481 ... **LEARNING A LANGUAGE**   About 150 to 200 hours of instruction and $1,500 worth of tapes and classes should produce credible speaking ability in French, Spanish, or German. For Oriental and Middle Eastern languages, figure 2 or 3 times longer. *Boardroom Reports*

LANGUAGE

1482 ... **OPENING A PARACHUTE**   When cars look as big as ants, it's time to open the parachute. When ants look as big as cars, you've waited too long. *Ernst Luposchainsky, III ("Kahn"), adventurer & nautical enthusiast, inter alia, Hollywood, California*

PARACHUTES

1483 ... **PANNING A SCENE**   You should scan, or "pan," a scene with a moving camera no faster than one frame-width per five seconds. In other words, you need to allow at least five seconds for an object entering one side of the screen to pass out the other side. *Christopher Wordsworth, film maker*

MOVIES AND FILM

1484 ... **WAKING UP IN CALIFORNIA**   When you wake up on a California winter morning and the stars outside your window shine without twinkling, put on your long underwear. *Rob Weinberg, Tassajara Zen Mountain Center, Carmel Valley, California*

CERTAIN PLACES

1485 ... **TAPING OLD RECORDS**   Seven 78-rpm records will fit on one side of a 90-minute audio cassette. *Steven F. Scharff, cartoonist, Union, New Jersey*

MUSIC

1486 ... **THE NURSING HOME RULE**   Patients who are terminally ill are more likely to die after a holiday than before. *Jim Schlobohm, Oak Park, Illinois*

DEATH

1487 ... **RELATING TO A CLERGYMAN**   To profit most from a clergyman, be polite but have other interests in life. *Stephen Unsino, poet, Eastchester, New York*

RELIGION

1488 ... **JUDGING HORSE ADS**   Any mention of horse shows in an advertisement for a horse generally indicates that the horse is pleasing to look at. If training or manners are emphasized and looks are not mentioned, the horse is probably not particularly handsome. A poorly written ad that leaves out vital statistics will generally lead to a mediocre horse. *Jeanne K. Posey, horse show judge*

HORSES

MAIL

MANAGEMENT

REAL ESTATE

COOKING

INJURIES

GARDENING

WEATHER

TRAVEL

DRIVING

MARRIAGE

DOGS

BUILDING

1489 ... **ATTRACTING JUNK MAIL**   For every magazine or newspaper you subscribe to, you will receive at least five pieces of junk mail per month. *John Towle, Salinas, California*

1490 ... **RUNNING A CORPORATION**   A corporation should limit its executive staff to 100 people or less, even though it may have thousands of employees. *Raymond Davies, marketing director*

1491 ... **THE CONDO RULE**   Two out of three people who buy lower priced condos really wanted a house instead. *Vince Mooney, real estate broker, Tulsa, Oklahoma*

1492 ... **MAKING PIE CRUST**   For perfect pie crust, when you're rolling out pie dough and you think it's ready, roll it out one more time. *Jane Adams Stillinger, archaeologist and writer, Watsonville, California*

1493 ... **CHOOSING THE PROPER CRUTCH**   To estimate the proper height of a crutch, the person using it should be able to fit three fingers between the top of the crutch and their armpit. *Sue Baudendistle, administrative supervisor, Cornell University*

1494 ... **ALLEN'S RULE OF PLANTING SEEDS**   Never plant a seed deeper than twice its width. *Jim Allen, Creekside Nursery, Santa Rosa, California*

1495 ... **FORECASTING THE WEATHER**   Clocks and watches tick louder before mild weather. *Dean Sheridan, electronics technician and deaf actor, Torrance, California*

1496 ... **RIDING THE NEW YORK CITY SUBWAY**   To determine where subway doors will open, look at the yellow stripe painted along the edge of the platform. The doors are most likely to open adjacent to the areas where the paint is most worn. *Steven M. Keisman, New York City high school resource coordinator*

1497 ... **TRACING A RATTLE**   A rattle from the underside of your car usually can be traced to the exhaust system. *Paul A. Delaney, meteorologist, Beltsville, Maryland*

1498 ... **MARRYING A DOCTOR**   If a doctor sets up practice in a town with one-fifth or less the population of the town his or her spouse was raised in, they will divorce or move to a larger town within five years. *Gerry M. Flick, M.D., Ship's Surgeon, S.S. Constitution off Hawaii*

1499 ... **CARING FOR DOGS**   The smaller a doghouse is in the winter, the better — as long as the dog can stand up and turn around in it. *Captain Haggerty, animal trainer, actor, author, and philosopher, New York, New York*

1500 ... **THE ARC WELDING RULE**   Welders often need to quickly estimate the amount of welding rod they need to join two pieces of metal along a seam, or bead, as the finished weld is called. As a rule, the length of the rod equals the length of the bead. *Rick Eckstrom, plan review officer, Ithaca, New York*

As a rule of thumb: ON RAINY NIGHTS, 90 PERCENT OF THE WORMS CROSSING A HIGHWAY WILL BE FACING THE SAME DIRECTION. EMERY NEMETHY, CATAWISSA, PENNSYLVANIA

1501 ... TESTING NEW ELECTRONIC EQUIPMENT After you buy some new electronic equipment, use it for 48 hours straight. If it doesn't fail during that period, it probably won't. *Norman Brenner, Fleetwood, New York*

1502 ... EDITING A BOOK When you're collecting literary contributions, throw out all those you get from your most frequent contributor. *Gary D. Stephens, Chino, California*

1503 ... FINDING MONEY FOR COLLEGE Add 5 percent of the value of your assets to your adjusted gross income and divide this figure by the annual costs of the college you are considering. If this yields a result of six or less, you will probably qualify for some sort of loan or financial assistance. *Robert Leider, author, Don't Miss Out*

1504 ... RAISING YOUR SALARY When negotiating salary with a recruiter, make your opening figure at least 30 percent more than your present package (including bonus, perks, and next raise). If the new job will involve moving to a larger city or to the Northeast or West coast, add another 10 percent. *Charles Fleming, author of Executive Pursuit*

1505 ... THE FIRST THREE LETTERS RULE Twenty-five percent of any alphabetical list will be under the first three letters of the alphabet (A-B-C). *Lewy Olfson, contemplative, Stonington, Connecticut*

1506 ... SURVIVING A PARACHUTE MALFUNCTION If your parachute doesn't open at the normal opening altitude (2,500 feet), you've got the rest of your life to solve the problem — all 15 seconds of it. *Ernst Luposchainsky, III ("Kahn"), skydiving pundit and philogynist, inter alia, Hollywood, California*

1507 ... FILMING A SCENE Purely as a guide, ten seconds is quite a long shot and three seconds is quite a short one. *Christopher Wordsworth, film maker*

1508 ... RUNNING A LAUNDRY IN JAPAN Coin laundry machines must run nine times a day to be profitable in Tokyo. In rural Japan, five or six times a day will do. *David A. Lloyd-Jones, Tokyo, Japan*

1509 ... PLAYING ROCK AND ROLL A bass player needs double the power of a guitarist. If your guitarist has a 50-watt combo, you need 100 watts on the bass. *Dean Sheridan, electronics technician and deaf actor, Torrance, California*

1510 ... LOSING A LOVED ONE It takes five years to recover from the death of a beloved spouse. Divorce sometimes takes longer. *Penny Russell, artist, Dilltown, Pennsylvania*

1511 ... BUILDING A CHURCH When a church reaches 80 percent of capacity, it's time to build a new one or expand. *Bill, Muskatene, Iowa*

1512 ... THE PINEO RULE OF NEW BRIDLES The cost of a good silver mounted spade bit for your horse is equal to one month's cowboy wages. *Douglass A. Pineo, biologist and falconer, Spokane, Washington*

MAIL

1513 ... **WEIGHING A LETTER**   If you need to know whether your letter weighs less than an ounce, compare it with the weight of five quarters. For two ounces, use five half dollars.   *Denis Smith, high school counselor, Camarillo, California*

MANAGEMENT

1514 ... **MANAGING SUBORDINATES**   Most managers can effectively handle eight or nine subordinates.   *SMC Hendrick, Inc., management consultants, Framingham, Massachusetts*

REAL ESTATE

1515 ... **SELLING CONDOMINIUMS**   To sell, condominiums should be priced at least 25 percent lower than the starting price of houses in the area. For best success, they should be priced 50 percent below nearby houses. People who buy a $50,000 condo want to live in a $100,000 neighborhood.   *Vince Mooney, real estate broker, Tulsa, Oklahoma*

COOKING

1516 ... **COOKING FISH AND BREWIS**   When cooking fish and brewis, allow one cake of hard bread per person plus one for the pot.   *Stanley G. Laite, St. John's, Newfoundland, Canada*

INJURIES

1517 ... **THE BAND-AID RULE**   Figure on 1 box of 20 Band-Aids per child per month.   *L. Musselman, office manager and mother of young children*

GARDENING

1518 ... **DRYING HERBS**   It takes about four pounds of fresh herbs to make one pound of dry herbs.   *Amy Rice, College Park, Maryland*

WEATHER

1519 ... **FORECASTING THE WEATHER**   If children are unusually wild on the playground, look for bad weather soon.   *Dean Sheridan, electronics technician and deaf actor, Torrance, California*

TRAVEL

1520 ... **RIDING THE SUBWAY IN NEW YORK**   The subway car carrying the conductor is the coolest in the summer and most comfortable in the winter. It is also the safest.   *Steven M. Keisman, New York City high school resource coordinator*

DRIVING

1521 ... **DRIVING SAFELY**   At highway speeds, increasing your speed by 5 miles per hour will save you about 10 minutes for every 100 miles you travel.   *Paul A. Delaney, meteorologist, Beltsville, Maryland*

MARRIAGE

1522 ... **COMPARING MEN AND WOMEN**   For every hour married women spend in paid employment each week, their husbands spend five more minutes working around the home.   *Martha Farnsworth Riche, editor, The Numbers News*

DOGS

1523 ... **HOUSING DOGS**   Pay no more than half the retail price for a used kennel.   *Captain Haggerty, animal trainer, actor, author, and philosopher, New York, New York*

BUILDING

1524 ... **USING A PAINT ROLLER**   The average paint roller will apply two to three square feet of paint per dip.   *Rick Eckstrom, plan review officer, Ithaca, New York*

AS A RULE OF THUMB:
THE BIGGER THE SCREEN, THE OLDER THE MOVIE THEATER.
JIM WILLETT, MUSICIAN, BOSTON, MASSACHUSETTS

1525 ... **BUYING HIGH QUALITY**   With clothing or rugs, the more threads per inch the more durable it will be. *Steven M. Keisman, New York City high school resource coordinator*

DURABILITY

1526 ... **THE VEST RULE OF POEM SIZE**   A poem should be half its original size in finished form. *Steven Vest, librarian and poet, Berea, Ohio*

WRITING

1527 ... **THE MORGAN-FRY SIDEWALK RULE**   To determine where the sidewalks for a new building on campus should be, construct the building without sidewalks and wait for one year. Then put the sidewalks on the paths the students have made. *Larry Morgan and Fred Fry, Kansas City, Missouri*

COLLEGE

1528 ... **RECRUITING AT COLLEGES**   Company recruiters should aim to hire at least one student for every school they visit. Not hiring anyone virtually guarantees a thinner response at the school next year. *William J. McBurney Jr., management consultant, New York City*

JOBS

1529 ... **USING WORDS**   The average American has a vocabulary of about 3,000 words. *Scott Parker, data specialist, Beaumont, Texas*

LANGUAGE

1530 ... **ESTIMATING SKYDIVING FREEFALL TIME**   On the average jump, figure on six or seven seconds of freefall time for every thousand feet of falling. *Ernst Luposchainsky, III ("Kahn"), adventurer & nautical enthusiast, inter alia, Hollywood, California*

PARACHUTES

1531 ... **WRITING A SCREENPLAY**   One page of an average screenplay equals about one minute of screen time. Therefore, the script for a typical feature film should be about a hundred pages long. In fact, many studios and producers won't look at screenplays much longer than a hundred pages. *John Griesemer, writer and actor, New York City*

MOVIES AND FILM

1532 ... **WORKING IN YOSEMITE NATIONAL PARK**   If you are looking for experience, working 1 year as a park ranger in Yosemite is equal to working 12 years in any other national park. *Scott M. Kruse, biogeographer, Fresno, California*

CERTAIN PLACES

1533 ... **BUYING RECORDS**   If you like a new record when you first get it, you'll tire of it in four weeks; if you hate it at first, you'll like it in about six months; if you feel indifferent about it, you'll always feel that way. *Cliff Martin, Eugene, Oregon*

MUSIC

1534 ... **COMMITTING SUICIDE**   How a suicidal person is born influences their choice of suicide method. People who commit suicide by hanging were likely deprived of oxygen at birth. People who shoot themselves in the head were likely delivered with forceps. Mothers of people who overdose were probably anesthetized for the delivery. Caesareans tend to slit their wrists. *Terry Larimore, writer and therapist, Houston, Texas*

DEATH

1535 ... **BUYING PROPERTY FOR A CHURCH**   A church needs 1 acre for every 100 people. *Bill, Muskatene, Iowa*

RELIGION

1536 ... **PROVIDING PASTURE FOR A HORSE**   Provide at least one acre of good pasture per horse. *Clarence Morgan, The Morgan Palomino Ranch*

HORSES

MAIL

MANAGEMENT

REAL ESTATE

COOKING

INJURIES

GARDENING

WEATHER

TRAVEL

DRIVING

MARRIAGE

DOGS

BUILDING

1537 ... **THE STICKING LABELS TO ENVELOPES RULE**   The average person can attach 400 to 450 pressure-sensitive address labels to envelopes per hour. Someone who is very good can do 800.   *David Updike, President, The Mail Box of Ithaca, Ithaca, New York*

1538 ... **THE MANAGER RULE**   No manager or should have responsibility for more than six separate activities.   *Lester R. Bittel, management consultant*

1539 ... **CONVERTING APARTMENTS TO CONDOMINIUMS**   When converting apartments to condominiums, you must be able to sell the condos for twice the price you paid for the apartment building, or you won't make any money.   *Vince Mooney, real estate broker, Tulsa, Oklahoma*

1540 ... **THE ICE CREAM RULE**   If there's frost on the ice cream in your freezer, it's been there too long.   *Kim Murphy, columnist, Portland, Maine*

1541 ... **SAVING SOMEONE'S LIFE**   You have one hour to get trauma patients to a hospital.   *Anonymous doctor*

1542 ... **FERTILIZING TOMATOES**   Fertilize tomatoes for the second time when the first cluster of fruit starts to ripen.   *Peter van Berkum, Kittery Point, Maine*

1543 ... **FORECASTING THE WEATHER**   Raccoons feed heavily 48 hours before the approach of a large winter storm.   *Thomas W. Neumann, anthropological archaeologist, wildlife ecologist, and field crew crisis manager*

1544 ... **SPOTTING A GOOD SHOW**   Follow the worn path in the rug to find the most popular exhibit in a museum.   *Steven M. Keisman, New York City high school resource coordinator*

1545 ... **AVOIDING A SPEEDING TICKET**   If you're speeding on a rural interstate, follow young men in pickups with local plates and CBs. They know where Smokey is.   *Larry Gassan, Jolly Dino Art Direction, Los Angeles, California*

1546 ... **THE INCOME RULE**   The lower a wife's income, the more likely she and her husband will reconcile.   *Lory Peck, social worker, Alpine, New York*

1547 ... **RATIONING DRY DOG FOOD**   Figure on 1 pound of dry food for every 30 pounds of dogs.   *Captain Haggerty, animal trainer, actor, author, and philosopher, New York, New York*

1548 ... **BUILDING A LOG CABIN**   To estimate the cost of a finished log cabin built from a kit, double the cost of the kit and then add some. By the time you are done, it will cost $30,000 to $35,000 to build a log cabin from a $15,000 kit — and that's if you do the work yourself.   *M. Trepkus, builder*

AS A RULE OF THUMB: NEVER BUY A SILVER CAR. THEY RUST SOONER THAN OTHERS.
SKIP EISIMINGER, SHEPHERD, CLEMSON, SOUTH CAROLINA

1549 ... **PEAKING TOO SOON**   The most popular people in high school go downhill from that point. *Thomas W. Neumann, anthropological archaeologist, wildlife ecologist, and field crew crisis manager*

DURABILITY

1550 ... **WRITING SCRIPT**   When writing long-hand, never join two letters if the result seems ugly, awkward, or hard to read.   *Kate Gladstone, Brooklyn, New York*

WRITING

1551 ... **GRABBING GRADES**   Grab as many good grades as possible early in the academic year—they'll come in handy as the year wears on. *Dean Sheridan, electronics technician and deaf actor, Torrance, California*

COLLEGE

1552 ... **THE JOB LEADS FROM RESUMES RULE**   Most job seekers can expect 1 to 5 job leads and/or interviews for every 100 resumes they mail out. *Karen E. O'Neill, career consultant, Englewood, Colorado*

JOBS

1553 ... **SID ORE'S RULE OF UNDERSTANDING FRENCH**   French speakers use twice as many syllables as English speakers. That's why French is so hard to understand. *Sid Ore, Paris, France*

LANGUAGE

1554 ... **SKYDIVING**   The spot that isn't moving is the spot you're approaching. *Ernst Luposchainsky, III ("Kahn"), adventurer & nautical enthusiast, inter alia, Hollywood, California*

PARACHUTES

1555 ... **MAKING A MOVIE**   Some types of scenes are harder to shoot than others. For dialogue scenes, you will need to shoot about four feet of film for every foot you use. For scenes without dialogue, the ratio is more like two or three to one. *Christopher Wordsworth, film maker*

MOVIES AND FILM

1556 ... **COMMUTING IN TOKYO**   In Tokyo, a bicycle is faster than a car for most trips of less than 50 minutes. The same is true against trains, except during rush hours; then the break point is about 30 minutes. A motorcycle, ridden carefully but without regard for the law, is twice as fast as a car. *David A. Lloyd-James, Tokyo, Japan*

CERTAIN PLACES

1557 ... **THE CD RULE**   If you have fewer than 100 record albums, buy a CD player instead of a turntable. *Ed Meenan, sales manager, Harvey Electronics, New York, New York*

MUSIC

1558 ... **WINNING A GUNFIGHT**   If several people are advancing on you in a gunfight, shoot the one furthest away first, the closest one second, and then retreat or repeat the process. *L. Geer, San Diego, California*

JOKER

1559 ... **DEALING WITH GUILT**   Catholics feel guilty for what they weren't supposed to do, and did. Jews feel guilty for what they were supposed to do, and didn't. *Michael Rider, art director, American Demographics*

RELIGION

1560 ... **SADDLING A HORSE**   Check your stirrup length from a mounted, standing position. Stirrups are properly adjusted if you can just fit the palm of your hand between your crotch and the saddle. *Stacey DiGiovani, equestrian*

HORSES

MAIL

MANAGEMENT

REAL ESTATE

COOKING

INJURIES

JOKER

WEATHER

TRAVEL

DRIVING

MARRIAGE

DOGS

BUILDING

1561 ... **MAILING A LETTER**   You can mail five sheets of paper with a 25 cent stamp. *Ron Bean, mechanics of materials student, Madison, Wisconsin*

1562 ... **WORKING OVERTIME**   After working 8 hours per day or 48 hours per week, it takes about 3 overtime hours to produce 2 standard hour's worth of results. For heavy work, count on two hours' time for each hours' worth of output. *Illinois Institute of Technology*

1563 ... **SELLING CONDOMINIUMS**   Any customer who comes to a condominium sales office and asks to see all the models (one-, two-, and three-bedroom units) will never buy anything. *Vince Mooney, real estate broker, Tulsa, Oklahoma*

1564 ... **EATING CHOCOLATE CHIP COOKIES**   Chocolate chip cookies are best four minutes after they come out of the oven. *Marc Pelath, student and programmer, Michigan City, Indiana*

1565 ... **AVOIDING RABIES**   If an animal is alive ten days after it bites someone, it's not rabid. *Scott Parker, data specialist, Beaumont, Texas*

1566 ... **SIZING UP A CALCULUS TEXT**   The longer a calculus textbook, the less it covers. *Bruce Reznick, associate professor of mathematics, Urbana, Illinois*

1567 ... **PREDICTING FOG**   A heavy fog will rise from a body of inland water when the temperature difference between the water and the air is about 40 degrees F. *Thomas W. Neumann, anthropological archaeologist, wildlife ecologist, and field crew crisis manager*

1568 ... **DRIVING IN NEW YORK CITY**   In New York City, the two Fridays before Christmas are the heaviest traffic days of the year. *Steven M. Keisman, New York City high school resource coordinator*

1569 ... **GETTING THROUGH STOP LIGHTS**   You greatly increase your chances of making green lights on a city street if you drive five to seven miles per hour over the posted speed. *L. Geer, San Diego, California*

1570 ... **ANTICIPATING A DIVORCE**   Men who have unstable employment histories are twice as likely to separate from their wives as those who don't. *Lory Peck, social worker, Alpine, New York*

1571 ... **CARING FOR DOGS**   In a suburb of medium density, a dog's bark can be heard in 200 surrounding houses—or by about 800 people. *Scott Parker, data specialist, Beaumont, Texas*

1572 ... **CHOOSING THE PROPER STONES FOR CONCRETE**   The largest stones in a batch of concrete should be one-fourth the thickness of the slab you are going to pour. A driveway six inches thick should have stones no larger than one and a half inches in diameter. *A. D. Elliot, Muncie, Indiana*

AS A RULE OF THUMB: IF YOU WOULDN'T FEEL COMFORTABLE DRIVING HIS CAR AROUND, YOU WON'T FEEL COMFORTABLE WITH HIM AS A STEADY BOYFRIEND. COOKIE OHLSON, BLONDE, UPLAND, PENNSYLVANIA

1573 ... CARING FOR HOSES   A garden hose exposed to the elements will last five years before it leaks. *John Towle, Salinas, California*

DURABILITY

1574 ... MAKING HISTORY   To make a splash as an historian, publish a radically new interpretation of any event from the American Revolution to World War II. Offend as many people as possible, and don't worry about the facts you will need to defend your argument. These will occur to you soon enough. *Walter Pitkin, literary agent, Weston, Connecticut*

WRITING

1575 ... CORRECTING YOUR INSTRUCTOR   When the instructor says, "Please correct me if I made a mistake," do it once and only once. *Dean Sheridan, electronics technician and deaf actor, Torrance, California*

COLLEGE

1576 ... THE INTERVIEW SHORT ANSWER RULE   During a job interview, never spend more than 60 seconds answering a question. *Cheryl A. Russell, demographer, mother, editor-in-chief, American Demographics*

JOBS

1577 ... SETTING TYPE IN SPANISH   Typesetting something in Spanish takes one-third again as much space as doing it in English. *Ellen Klaver, musician, Boulder, Colorado*

LANGUAGE

1578 ... SURVIVING A PARACHUTE MALFUNCTION   If your main parachute malfunctions and you're trying to decide whether to use your emergency chute, spit. If your spit goes up, use your emergency chute. If your spit goes down, your rate of descent is survivable. *Ernst Luposchainsky, III (Khan), skydiving old-timer of 15 years, Hollywood, California*

PARACHUTES

1579 ... FIGURING OUT A MOVIE   In a thriller, you can be certain that any slow-moving camel is crossing the road only to get in the way of a pursuit vehicle. *Paul A. Delaney, meteorologist, Beltsville, Maryland*

JOKER

1580 ... FORECASTING SNOW IN FLORIDA   It snows significantly in north Florida about once every seven winters. *Dennis Palaganas, Gainesville, Florida*

CERTAIN PLACES

1581 ... BUYING A MUSICAL INSTRUMENT   If you're buying a musical instrument for a beginner, spend twice as much as you think you should. The instrument will be better built, easier to play, and it will sound better. And it will have a better resale value. *Jim Willett, musician, Boston, Massachusetts*

MUSIC

1582 ... DESIGNING A SLING   The length of the sling depends on your height. Hold the sling by your side with both cords, as if you're ready to use it. The pouch should reach to the middle of your calf. *Scott Parker, data specialist, Beaumont, Texas*

WEAPONS

1583 ... ADDRESSING THE CLERGY   Always call a Roman Catholic priest "Father" unless he is wearing some purple. Then call him "Bishop" or "Your Excellency." *Rev. Halsey DeW. Howe, Saint Mark's Church, Springfield, Vermont*

RELIGION

1584 ... BETTING ON A HORSE   If you don't have much information before a race, bet on a horse that is swishing his tail straight up and down. *Donald Mycrantz, Tulsa, Oklahoma*

HORSES

MAIL

MANAGEMENT

REAL ESTATE

COOKING

INJURIES

MATHEMATICS

WEATHER

TRAVEL

DRIVING

MARRIAGE

DOGS

BUILDING

1585 ... **THE JUNK MAIL RULE** You can figure that three out of four pieces of advertising mail are opened and glanced at. About one in four is opened and read thoroughly. *Carol Williams, Washington, D.C.*

1586 ... **CRITICIZING AN EMPLOYEE'S PERFORMANCE** In a performance review, don't offer more than three criticisms. That's all an employee can digest. *Nancy Humphries, personnel consultant, Ithaca, New York*

1587 ... **RENTING APARTMENTS** Unless you get a name and phone number, half the people who make appointments to see rental property won't show up. *Vince Mooney, real estate broker, Tulsa, Oklahoma*

1588 ... **THE BREAD RULE** Two out of three people order white bread. *Anonymous*

1589 ... **CARING FOR AN INSECT STING** Ammonia for a bee sting; vinegar for a wasp sting. *Dr. Bill Grierson, professor emeritus, University of Florida*

1590 ... **CHECKING YOUR FIGURES** Always check the magnitude and first digit of a result in your head. *Norman Brenner, Fleetwood, New York*

1591 ... **FORECASTING THE WEATHER** The prevailing weather is most likely to change three days before the new moon and three days before the full moon. *Cynthya Rackerby, medical office manager, Rio Linda, California*

1592 ... **FINDING AIR FOR YOUR TIRES** In New York State, any gas station with four or more pumps has an air hose. *Steven M. Keisman, New York City high school resource coordinator*

1593 ... **FOLLOWING ANOTHER CAR** Leave a three second interval between you and the car in front of you. This provides enough room to stop at any speed. *Dirck Z. Meengs, management consultant, Canoga Park, California*

1594 ... **LOWERING THE CHANCES OF A DIVORCE** For each year in a person's life that marriage is delayed, the chances of separating fall by 1 percent. *Lory Peck, social worker, Alpine, New York*

1595 ... **DEALING WITH DOGS** Anything over 45 minutes seems like forever to your dog. You will be greeted as enthusiastically coming back from a two-hour shopping trip as you will coming back from a two-day vacation. *Andrea Frankel, computer scientist, engineer, holistic health practitioner, San Diego, California*

1596 ... **HIRING CONSTRUCTION WORKERS** Two workers can do three times as much work as one. Three workers can do four times as much work as one. Four workers can do four times as much work as one. *Rick Lazarus, residential contractor, Spencer, New York*

AS A RULE OF THUMB:
IF YOU CHANGE ONE THING,
YOU SCREW UP TWO.
BILL WENDT, DENTON, TEXAS

1597 ... **BUYING AN ORIENTAL CARPET**   A good carpet should last at least two generations. *Scott Parker, data specialist, Beaumont, Texas*

DURABILITY

1598 ... **WRITING A POEM**   When you're writing a poem, eliminate nine out of ten adjectives and adverbs in the first draft and cut everything you've heard before. *Jennifer Welch, poet and editor, Columbus, Ohio*

WRITING

1599 ... **WORKING WITH SCIENCE PROFESSORS**   Science professors are notorious misspellers. Correct them whenever your G.P.A. is low. *Dean Sheridan, electronics technician and deaf actor, Torrance, California*

COLLEGE

1600 ... **THE PHONE CALL INTERVIEW RULE**   Most job seekers can expect 1 to 4 job leads and/or interviews for every 40 telephone calls they make. *Karen E. O'Neill, career consultant, Englewood, Colorado*

JOBS

1601 ... **COMMUNICATING IN A FOREIGN COUNTRY**   In foreign countries, talk to people who speak a second language that you know too. Two people who both know a little of the same language will communicate better than one who is fluent and one who is not. *Peter Reimuller, Point Arena, California*

LANGUAGE

1602 ... **BLOWING BUBBLES**   One cup of Dawn detergent per gallon of water makes spectacular soap bubbles. *Denis Smith, high school counselor, Camarillo, California*

JOKER

1603 ... **DIVIDING A TANGERINE**   The average tangerine has nine parts. *Carolyn Lloyd, 15-year-old student, Montreal, Quebec*

FRUIT

1604 ... **THE WEDNESDAY RULE OF DRIVING IN MANHATTAN**   Avoid driving in mid-town Manhattan on Wednesdays — the Broadway theater matinees make for heavy traffic. Especially avoid Wednesdays before Thanksgiving and Christmas. *Steven M. Keisman, New York City high school resource coordinator*

CERTAIN PLACES

1605 ... **CHOOSING A CONCERT**   To determine how much you will enjoy an orchestra concert, remember, the only good composer is a dead composer. *Cynthia P. Beukema, season ticket holder, Minneapolis, Minnesota*

MUSIC

1606 ... **THROWING A KNIFE**   If your knife balances more than one inch from the tang on the handle side, it is handle heavy and should be thrown from the blade. Likewise, if it balances more than one inch from the tang on the blade side, it is blade heavy and should be thrown from the handle. *Survivalist at a gun show, Lansing, New York*

WEAPONS

1607 ... **ADDRESSING THE CLERGY**   When in doubt, call a Protestant minister or a rabbi, "Doctor." Even if the person isn't a doctor, he (or she) will be flattered. *Rev. Halsey DeW. Howe, Saint Mark's Church, Springfield, Vermont*

RELIGION

1608 ... **THE CAVALRY RULE**   Up the hill gallop me not. Down the hill trot me not. On the plain spare me not. In the stable forget me not. *The Very Rev. Emmet C. Smith, Largo, Florida*

HORSES

MAIL

MANAGEMENT

REAL ESTATE

COOKING

INJURIES

MATHEMATICS

WEATHER

TRAVEL

DRIVING

MARRIAGE

DOGS

JOKER

1609 ... **DETERMINING THE PROPER POSTAGE**   Use one stamp for every six sheets of paper. Envelopes count as one sheet of paper if you must fold the contents, two otherwise.   *Michael & Virginia Thompson, engineer and accountant, Charlotte, North Carolina*

1610 ... **ATTENDING A MEETING**   A meeting is not worth the trip if it will take you longer to get there than the meeting itself will last.   *David Liddle, pastor, Columbus, Indiana*

1611 ... **HEATING A RENTAL UNIT**   You can expect a 40 percent reduction in energy consumption when a tenant assumes responsibility for the energy bills.   *Larry Beck, joiner, Ludlowville, New York*

1612 ... **EATING CHILI PEPPERS**   In general, the smaller the chili pepper, the hotter.   *L. M. Boyd, The San Francisco Chronicle*

1613 ... **MASSAGING AN INJURED AREA**   Don't heat or massage an injury if, when you hold your hand 1/2" from the skin, you can feel more heat in the injured area than the surrounding area.   *Andrea Frankel, computer scientist, engineer, holistic health practitioner, San Diego, California*

1614 ... **JUDGING THE QUALITY OF A SURVEY**   A random sample of 1,000 is sufficient for most purposes. A random sample of 100 or less is too small for most purposes.   *John Allen Paulos, mathematician*

1615 ... **ANTICIPATING AN ACORN CROP**   A wet spring and a dry summer encourage acorn production.   *Stephen Unsino, poet, Eastchester, New York*

1616 ... **PREDICTING SPICINESS**   The closer to the Tropic of Cancer, the spicier the food.   *Thomas W. Neumann, anthropological archaeologist, wildlife ecologist, and field crew crisis manager*

1617 ... **PASSING A CAR**   You can safely cut in front of the car you are passing when you see its headlights in your inside rearview mirror.   *Leslie Simpson, Wollaston, Massachusetts*

1618 ... **CHOOSING A SPOUSE**   If your fiance does something that bothers you before you're married, it will bother you ten times more after you're married.   *Bruno Colapietro, matrimonial lawyer with over 8,000 cases, Binghamton, New York*

1619 ... **DEALING WITH FRIGHTENED DOGS**   A stray dog who is afraid of people will trust the people associated with the dogs it plays with.   *Andrea Frankel, computer scientist, engineer, holistic health practitioner, San Diego, California*

1620 ... **THE DECK RULE**   The space between the boards of a deck should be slightly less than the width of your wife's narrowest heel.   *Jerry Turem, bureaucrat*

DURABILITY

WRITING

COLLEGE

JOBS

LANGUAGE

SCUBA DIVING

FRUIT

JOKER

MUSIC

WEAPONS

RELIGION

HORSES

A**S A RULE OF THUMB:**
YOU CAN DETERMINE
WHETHER A GHOST IS
REAL, BY CROSSING
YOUR EYES. IF THE
IMAGE DOUBLES, THE
GHOST IS THERE. IF NOT,
IT'S ALL IN YOUR MIND.
SCOTT PARKER, DATA SPECIALIST,
BEAUMONT, TEXAS

1621 ... **SAVING YOUR PLUMBING**   If you turn off your tap too hard, it will damage the rubber washer — which you can replace easily. If you let the tap drip, it will erode the metal valve seat — which means a new tap and a plumber to install it.   *Dr. Bill Grierson, professor emeritus, University of Florida*

1622 ... **USING A WORD PROCESSOR**   Using a word processor will not save time; it will only increase quality. The time you save in retyping is canceled out by the time you spend making tiny revisions.   *Phil A. Schrodt, Associate Professor, Northwestern University, Evanston, Illinois*

1623 ... **WATCHING A CLASSMATE**   The more a classmate jots down during a lecture, the less he understands the lecture.   *Dean Sheridan, electronics technician and deaf actor, Torrance, California*

1624 ... **GETTING A CONSULTING JOB**   Personal contacts are best for getting consulting jobs. Twenty leads should produce one assignment.   *Dr. Jeffrey L. Lant, Jeffrey Lant Associates, Inc., Cambridge, Massachusetts*

1625 ... **COMPARING FRENCH PRINT TO GERMAN**   A text printed in German will take up a third more space than the same one in French.   *Dick Brenton, record producer*

1626 ... **FOLLOWING UNDERWATER BUBBLES**   When scuba diving, don't rise to the surface any faster than the smallest bubbles you exhale.   *Alex Stewart, Atlanta, Georgia*

1627 ... **THE APPEALING FRUIT RULE**   In the tropics, don't eat fruit you can't peel   *Francine Green, Cherry Hill, New Jersey*

1628 ... **BUYING A BICYCLE LOCK**   The lighter the bicycle, the heavier the lock should be.   *Karen Missavage, Birmingham, Michigan*

1629 ... **STORING MUSICAL INSTRUMENTS**   The higher the humidity, the duller and thicker a wooden instrument will sound.   *Alan T. Whittemore, YMCA Physical Director, South Deerfield, Massachusetts*

1630 ... **WINNING A DUEL**   When dueling with firearms, always aim lower than your opponent's vital area—to pierce the heart, aim at the knees.   *Jim Barber, historian, Springfield, Missouri*

1631 ... **SIZING UP AN EVANGELIST**   A Christian evangelist will almost always quote to you from the Book of Romans, a sure sign of a Fundamentalist Christian.   *Steven F. Scharff, cartoonist, Union, New Jersey*

1632 ... **KEEPING A HORSE**   If you can't afford better fencing than barbed wire, you can't afford a horse.   *Clarence Morgan, The Morgan Palomino Ranch*

MAIL

MANAGEMENT

REAL ESTATE

COOKING

INJURIES

MATHEMATICS

WEATHER

TRAVEL

DRIVING

MARRIAGE

DOGS

CARPENTRY

1633 ... ***ACCUMULATING JUNK MAIL*** Junk mail lies around the house a week before it gets thrown out. *Mark McMullen, accountant, Alexandria, Virginia*

1634 ... ***TRAINING VOLUNTEERS*** You generally need three volunteers to make training them worthwhile. If you have to train one volunteer, you will save time if you skip the training and do the work yourself. *Terry Larimore, writer and therapist, Houston, Texas*

1635 ... ***RAISING THE RENT*** A 1 percent increase in interest rates requires a 5 percent increase in rents. *Tony Gaenslen, amateur landlord, somewhere in New Hampshire*

1636 ... ***CHARCOALING CHICKEN*** If you're going to barbecue chickens for a large group of people, you'll need one pound of charcoal per whole chicken. *John Van Der Mark, city fireman, Ithaca, New York*

1637 ... ***NED FREDERICK'S INJURY RULE OF SIX*** It takes six weeks to completely recover from a musculoskeletal injury, though you feel better in three weeks. *Ned Frederick, writer, Exeter, New Hampshire*

1638 ... ***ROUNDING NUMBERS*** When adding a list of fractional numbers with a calculator, your answers will be more accurate if you begin with the numbers closest to 0. *Dean Sheridan, electronics technician and deaf actor, Torrance, California*

1639 ... ***FORECASTING THE WEATHER*** Whatever the weather on the first of the month, you'll have the opposite weather for the rest of the month. *Phyllis Johns, Snyder, New York*

1640 ... ***SPOTTING GERMANS*** If you see someone drinking a bottle of orange juice, replacing the cap on the bottle, and putting the bottle down after each sip, the person is probably German. *Jeff Brown, astronomer, Bloomington, Indiana*

1641 ... ***THE ROTARY RULE*** When entering a traffic rotary, stay on the outside if you're taking the first exit, otherwise get on the inside lane. *Leslie Simpson, Wollaston, Massachusetts*

1642 ... ***ACCEPTING AN ENGAGEMENT RING*** The cost of an engagement ring was once considered to be an important gauge of a gentleman's character. A smart young lady would look for a suitor who spent one month's wages on a ring. Any young man who spent less than a month's salary on a ring was most likely cheap; one who spent more was a show-off. *Adam Perl, antique dealer*

1643 ... ***PIERCE BUTLER'S NEW DOG'S AGE TO HUMAN'S RULE*** The old rule—multiplying a dog's age by 7 to find the equivalent human age—is fallacious. A dog is able to reproduce at 1 year and has reached full growth by 2 years. To calculate a dog's age in human terms, count the first year as 15, the second year as 10, and each year after that as 5. *Pierce Butler, Natchez, Mississippi*

1644 ... ***SETTING NAILS*** When setting a nail with a nail-setter, drive it down as deep as it is wide at its head. *Dean Sheridan, electronics technician and deaf actor, Torrance, California*

1645 ... PRESERVING YOUR SHOES Shoes last half again as long if you keep them in a shoe box when you aren't wearing them. *Kirstin Hark, 7th grade student, Conroe, Texas*

DURABILITY

1646 ... USING SEMICOLONS When in doubt, use the semicolon; the average reader won't understand its use and will give you credit for erudition. *Denis Smith, high school counselor, Camarillo, California*

WRITING

1647 ... RAISING MONEY University fund raisers plan on getting one-third of their money from 10 big contributors, one-third from 100 medium contributors and one-third from everyone else. *Anonymous university fund raiser*

COLLEGE

1648 ... THE JOB OFFER RULE You should expect 1 job offer per 15 interviews. *Paul Shaker*

JOBS

1649 ... SPEAKING FRENCH IN ENGLISH One in 20 words and phrases spoken in everyday French is actually English. *"The Story of English," hosted by Robert MacNeil, PBS*

LANGUAGE

1650 ... SCUBA DIVING IN SHALLOW WATER You don't need to worry about decompression stops if you scuba dive at depths of 30 feet or less. *Alex Stewart, Atlanta, Georgia*

SCUBA DIVING

1651 ... BUYING THE BEST FRUIT Always pick fruit from the back of the shelf. Most people are too lazy to reach. *Leonard Morgenstern, pathologist, Moraga, California*

FRUIT

1652 ... ACCEPTING YOUR MISTAKES If you aren't making mistakes, you aren't trying hard enough. *Steven M. Keisman, New York City high school resource coordinator*

QUALITY

1653 ... APPRECIATING CLASSICAL MUSIC If a piece of classical music was written after you were born, you are not obliged to appreciate it. *Francis Cooke, composer (born 1910)*

MUSIC

1654 ... KNOCKING AWAY A GUN If an assailant is actually touching you with a handgun, you can knock it out of line before he or she can fire it. *Leslie Simpson, Wollaston, Massachusetts*

WEAPONS

1655 ... DEALING WITH A NEW AGE EVANGELIST If a person has experienced only one kind of transformational experience, take everything he or she says with a lot of salt. *Andrea Frankel, computer scientist, engineer, holistic health practitioner, San Diego, California*

RELIGION

1656 ... PACKING HORSES Plan on using one pack horse for every 150 pounds of supplies you need to carry. *Jim Stevens, outfitter*

HORSES

MAIL

1657 ... THE McMULLEN RULE OF JUNK MAIL You receive four pieces of junk mail for every bill. Seven pieces for every letter. *Mark McMullen, accountant, Alexandria, Virginia*

JOKER

1658 ... MANAGING PARKING METERS Most cities can expect the annual income from parking meter fines to be twice the income from parking meter deposits. *Marie E. Witmer, director of technical services, Institutional and Municipal Parking Congress, Fredericksburg, Virginia*

REAL ESTATE

1659 ... APPRAISING A RENTAL PROPERTY The market value of a rental property is six times the gross rent. *Larry Beck, joiner, Ludlowville, New York*

COOKING

1660 ... CHECKING YOUR FOOD Foods that are normally hard are bad if they've turned soft. Foods that are normally soft are bad when they've turned hard. *Herman N. Cohen, personnel manager, New York City*

INJURIES

1661 ... CHECKING FOR SUNBURN You can check for sunburn by pressing an exposed part of your body with your finger. If your skin is burned, it will turn white when you lift your finger. *Elsbeth Cates, writer, Rising Star, North Dakota, in New Age Journal*

MATHEMATICS

1662 ... MEASURING AN ANGLE For a small angle x measured in radians, $\sin x = x$. *R.A. Heindl, design engineer, Euclid, Ohio*

WEATHER

1663 ... FORECASTING THE WEATHER If the snow looks like meal, it will snow a great deal. *Betty Winklowski, Hamburg, New York*

TRAVEL

1664 ... BEATING THE CROWDS AT A PARK Ninety percent of visitors see only 10 percent of a national park. *Cheryl A. Russell, demographer, mother, editor-in-chief, American Demographics*

DRIVING

1665 ... DRIVING DEFENSIVELY Drive like you are playing a video game with your last quarter. After ten minutes of this, you will have a better idea what defensive driving is all about. *Gerald Gutlipp, mathematician, Chicago, Illinois*

MARRIAGE

1666 ... CHOOSING A SPOUSE When women marry, they think their husbands will change. When men marry, they think their wives will never change. Both are wrong. *Bruno Colapietro, matrimonial lawyer with over 8,000 cases, Binghamton, New York*

DOGS

1667 ... SHOWING A DOG The more nervous you are while showing your dog, the more nervous your dog will be. *Kari Casher, breeder of Australian terriers, Oakland, California*

CARPENTRY

1668 ... THE CARPENTRY RULE Customers give carpenters the hardest time on the smallest jobs. *Antonio V. Farulla, carpenter, Sherman Oaks, California*

AS A RULE OF THUMB: THE NUMBER OF MINUTES YOU WILL WAIT IN LINE AT THE BANK IS EQUAL TO THE NUMBER OF PEOPLE AHEAD OF YOU DIVIDED BY THE NUMBER OF TELLERS TIMES 2.75.

CHUCK DAVIS, WRITER AND BROADCASTER, SURREY, BRITISH COLUMBIA

1669 ... **BUYING A TYPEWRITER**   Portable typewriters cost four times more to operate than office models and last only one-fourth as long. *Scott Parker, data specialist, Beaumont, Texas*

DURABILITY

1670 ... **WRITING A MAGAZINE ARTICLE**   After your notes are prepared and your outline is written, count on one hour of writing time for every double-spaced typewritten page. *Brad Edmondson, editor, American Demographics*

WRITING

1671 ... **THE EXAM RULE**   Before you sign up for a college class, find out what time of day the final exam will be given. Choosing a time that suits you could mean a letter difference in your grade. *Andy Steinberg, Louisville, Kentucky*

COLLEGE

1672 ... **RELATING SALARY TO HEIGHT**   A person's annual income rises by $600 for each additional inch of height. *N. R. Kleinfield, The New York Times*

JOBS

1673 ... **TALKING TO FOREIGNERS**   When you are conversing in your native language with people who don't speak it fluently, assume that they understand about half as much as they look like they understand. *Stephen Cudhea, English-language instructor, Ishikawa, Japan*

LANGUAGE

1674 ... **CHOOSING A FACE MASK**   A face mask for skin diving fits properly if you can hold it on your face, out of the water, with nothing but the suction from your nose. *Dorothy Hooker, Hollywood, Florida*

SCUBA DIVING

1675 ... **CHOOSING A PLANTAIN**   The darker the peel the better. *Anonymous*

FRUIT

1676 ... **BUYING A HAND TOOL**   Never buy a hand tool that does not have the manufacturer's name permanently inscribed on it. The absence of a name indicates poor quality. *Dirck Z. Meengs, management consultant, Canoga Park, California*

QUALITY

1677 ... **LISTENING TO JIGS AND REELS**   The way to tell the difference between a jig and a reel is to sing along with it. With a jig you will be able to sing, "jiggity jig, jiggity jig." If the tune is a reel you can sing, "I think I can, I think I can." *Wild Asparagus*

MUSIC

1678 ... **LOADING A MUSKET**   In a pinch, the proper powder charge for a muzzle-loading rifle or musket is the amount that will just cover the ball when you hold it in the hollow of your palm. *Bob Chaney, Carlsbad, California*

WEAPONS

1679 ... **WINNING THE HEARTS OF YOUR PARISH**   The first year the parish loves you, the second year they hate you, the third year they understand you. *The Very Rev. Emmet C. Smith, Largo, Florida*

RELIGION

1680 ... **FEEDING HORSES**   Grass alone won't feed a hard-working horse. As a rule, a horse needs at least five pounds of grain for every half-day of work. *Kevin Reede, Burlington, Vermont*

HORSES

JOKER

1681 ...**MAILING FILM**   You can send 110 and 126 cartridge film through the mail using only one first-class stamp without incurring postage due, although nearly all developers recommend using two stamps. *Rusty Cartmill, Athens, Georgia*

MONEY

1682 ...**CALCULATING PAY**   If your hourly pay rate includes dollars and cents, and the cents are evenly divisible by 5, then your gross pay for an 80-hour pay period will be an even number of dollars with no cents. *Ernst Luposchainsky, III ("Kahn"), penniless polyhistor, inter alia, Hollywood, California*

REAL ESTATE

1683 ...**SIZING-UP THE REAL ESTATE MARKET**   To size up an area's real estate market, compare the difference between the original asking price and the final selling price on recent home sales. A difference of 1 to 4 percent means it's a seller's market. A difference greater than 5 percent means it's a buyer's market. *Susan Bondy, financial columnist, News America Syndicte (or Syracuse Post-Standard)*

COOKING

1684 ...**MAKING HOT FUDGE**   Your hot fudge is ready when you can write your name in the surface with a spoon without the letters disappearing before you finish writing. *Robin Masson, attorney and law professor, Ithaca, New York*

INJURIES

1685 ...**CHECKING FOR NERVE DAMAGE**   Skin with damaged nerves doesn't wrinkle in warm water. *Scott Parker, data specialist, Beaumont, Texas*

MATHEMATICS

1686 ...**THE MATH PAPER RULE**   For mathematics professors, each published math paper is worth $10,000 in salary. *Scott Parker, data specialist, Beaumont, Texas*

WEATHER

1687 ...**THE CURDLY RULE**   A curdly sky never leaves the ground dry. *Anonymous*

TRAVEL

1688 ...**THE TRAVEL RULE**   Go the way you know; it is always faster. *Anonymous*

1689 ...**NOSING YOUR CAR TO A WALL**   When you are parking a car head on to a wall, turn on your high beams and look at the reflection on the wall as you slowly move closer. When the brightest part, the umbra, falls out of view, you are close enough. *Jon Roppolo, student, Flushing, New York*

DRIVING

1690 ...**CHOOSING A MATE**   When choosing a mate, consider not only what kind of spouse he or she will make, but also what kind of ex-spouse he or she will be. *Robin Masson, attorney and law professor, Ithaca, New York*

MARRIAGE

1691 ...**CHOOSING A PUPPY**   If a dog tolerates gentle handling between its toes, it probably is suited for children. *The Pets Are Wonderful Council*

DOGS

1692 ...**SELECTING A NAIL**   Choose a nail that's 2 1/2 to 3 times longer than the thickness of the piece of wood you want to nail. *Alan H. Haeberle, Ithaca, New York, quoting Blair & Ketchum's Country Journal*

CARPENTRY

AS A RULE OF THUMB: WALKING IS FASTER THAN WAITING FOR A BUS IF YOU'RE GOING LESS THAN 20 BLOCKS.
T*ANYA* K*UCAK*, P*ALO* A*LTO*, C*ALIFORNIA*

1693 ... SAVING YOUR SHOES   If you switch back and forth between three pairs of shoes, they will last as long as five pairs worn out one pair at a time. *Joe Cosentini, shoe store owner, Ithaca, New York*

DURABILITY

1694 ... WRITING A TECHNICAL MANUAL   A technical manual takes about one hour to write and three hours to edit per page, after the basic research is done. *Bruce Nevin, editor and technical writer, Gloucester, Massachusetts*

WRITING

1695 ... OUTFITTING A COLLEGE STUDENT   Three pairs of jeans and three pairs of sweatpants are all that a college student needs 90 percent of the time. *Dennis Palaganas, Gainesville, Florida*

COLLEGE

1696 ... SETTING YOUR HOURS   If a person's job ends at 5, it's a job. If it goes beyond that time, it's a career. *Steven M. Keisman, New York City high school resource coordinator*

JOBS

1697 ... THE CRYPTIC RULE OF SECRET CODES   If the high-frequency letters ETOANIRSH occur very often, in this order, you can assume that you are dealing with a transposition cipher in which the letters remain the same but are rearranged in a new pattern. On the other hand, the repeated appearance of low-frequency letters indicates that a message has been written in a substitution code. *John Laffin, cryptologist*

LANGUAGE

1698 ... SCUBA DIVING   A scuba diver should never ascend faster than 60 feet per minute. *Jack T. Marshall, professional diving instructor, Trumansburg, New York*

SCUBA DIVING

1699 ... BUYING A PINEAPPLE   To choose a ripe pineapple, tap it with your finger. If the sound is the same as when you tap the inside of your wrist, it's ripe. *Jack Fleming, formerly from Maui, Hawaii, Aliquippa, Pennsylvania*

FRUIT

1700 ... JUDGING FIREWORKS   To judge the quality of a fireworks display, watch for color, especially blue. If you see good blues, you are watching a topnotch fireworks display. *Dr. John A. Conkling, Executive Director, American Pyrotechnics Association*

QUALITY

1701 ... THE ALBUM RULE OF SINGLES   On a pop or rock music album, the first and second songs on side A, the first song on side B, and the title track (if there is one and it doesn't fit into any of the other three categories) will be released as singles. *Chris Carter, East Lansing, Michigan*

MUSIC

1702 ... GROUPING YOUR BULLETS   A gun shooting at its best usually produces round, uniform bullet patterns on a target. If your bullet groups are generally uniform but with an occasional random flyer, the problem is probably ammo. But if the flyers tend to go in the same direction, the problem is more likely caused by the rifle. *Jim Carmichel, Shooting Times*

WEAPONS

1703 ... ANTICIPATING A PASTORATE   As a general rule, a long pastorate is followed by a short one. *The Very Rev. Emmet C. Smith, Largo, Florida*

RELIGION

1704 ... CARING FOR A HORSE   You should allow at least one hour per day to feed and groom a horse. *Mary Flinn, Starlane Farms, Lansing, New York*

HORSES

MAIL ORDER

1705 ... **CHARTING MAIL-ORDER RETURNS**   If you're not getting 1 percent of your mail-order shipments returned, your product is underpriced. *Peter Reimuller, Point Arena, California*

MONEY

1706 ... **THE INFLATION RATE RULE** Each 10 percent drop in the dollar's value adds 1.5 percent to the inflation rate. Each 10 percent drop in oil's value subtracts 1 percent from the inflation rate. *Norman Brenner, Fleetwood, New York*

REAL ESTATE

1707 ... **MANAGING AN UNFURNISHED APARTMENT** For unfurnished apartments, expect a tenant turnover of about 45 percent per year. *Scott Parker, data specialist, Beaumont, Texas*

COOKING

1708 ... **THE SHAPIRO RULE OF TOFU**   One pound of soybeans yields 2 1/2 pounds of tofu. *Rob Shapiro, flight instructor, Ithaca, New York*

INJURIES

1709 ... **THE BLOSSOM INTUBATION RULE**   Sometimes a tube down the throat is used to restore free breathing. For an emergency guess, the diameter of a child's smallest finger is about the diameter of the largest endotracheal tube that he or she can be intubated with. *The Blossoms, Fresno, California*

MATHEMATICS

1710 ... **EXPLAINING A MATHEMATICAL THEOREM**   If you can't explain a mathematical theorem to a ten-year-old, you don't understand it yourself. *G.S. Tahim, mathematician, Bloomington, Indiana*

WEATHER

1711 ... **FORECASTING THE WEATHER**   The last spring frost comes after the daffodils bloom, plus three sugar snows. *Anonymous*

TRAVEL

1712 ... **FINDING YOUR WAY**   The more often you make turns, the closer you are to your destination. *James Parker, civil engineer, Medford, Massachusetts*

DRIVING

1713 ... **THE CHIEF HASTINGS DRIVING RULE OF 50**   If you're traveling a long distance by car and you need to tell someone when you expect to arrive, use the Rule of 50. Divide the distance by 50 to obtain the number of hours your drive will take. This usually will allow for a leisurely drive without causing undue anxiety for those awaiting your arrival. *Robert Hastings, Master Chief Petty Officer, United States Coast Guard*

JOKER

1714 ... **SPOTTING A REAL FRIEND**   If you want to discover your true friends, ask them to help you move. *Russell T. Johnson, Temple City, California*

DOGS

1715 ... **WATCHING A DOG FIGHT**   If two dogs are headed for a fight and they appear about evenly matched, the dog on his home turf will win easily. *Walter Pitkin, literary agent, Weston, Connecticut*

CARPENTRY

1716 ... **PLANNING A FLIGHT OF STAIRS**   A flight of stairs in a home should have 13 rises. *Alex Fraser, Washington, D.C.*

AS A RULE OF THUMB:
THE HEART OF THE MATURE ELEPHANT WILL FILL A BUSHEL BASKET.
JIM RIGGS, INDIO, CALIFORNIA

1717 ... **GETTING THINGS FIXED**   Items that originally cost less than $50 are rarely worth repairing. It's usually cheaper to buy new ones. *Glamour, quoted in Bottom Line Personal*

DURABILITY

1718 ... **WRITING A MAGAZINE ARTICLE**   When writing a magazine article, begin with a snappy lead sentence, then write the piece to match the tone of the lead. Before submitting the article, delete the lead sentence. *Gordon Hard, assistant editor, Consumer Reports, Mount Vernon, New York*

WRITING

1719 ... **SMITH'S RULE OF LEARNING MANNERS**   We learn half our manners from those who have good manners and half from those who have no manners. *The Very Rev. Emmet C. Smith, Largo, Florida*

JOKER

1720 ... **BELIEVING YOUR RESUME**   Once you begin to believe your own resume, you will not be happy with your current job or salary. *Steven M. Keisman, New York City high school resource coordinator*

JOBS

1721 ... **LEARNING A FOREIGN LANGUAGE**   Half a semester of foreign-language instruction at the college level is equal to one year of language instruction at the high school level. *David S. Russell, Minneapolis, Minnesota*

LANGUAGE

1722 ... **SCUBA DIVING**   For practical reasons and safety, 100 feet is usually considered to be the maximum depth for sport diving. *Jack T. Marshall, professional diving instructor, Trumansburg, New York*

SCUBA DIVING

1723 ... **PICKING RASPBERRIES**   When you start to find garden spiders in your raspberries, you have one week left to pick. *Carol Ayer, raspberry grower, West Bend, Wisconsin*

FRUIT

1724 ... **BUYING A FUR**   Buy the best fur in a breed that you can afford. If your limit is $3,000, buy a fine beaver rather than a so-so mink. *Eloise Salholz, Savvy*

QUALITY

1725 ... **AMASSING A RECORD COLLECTION**   You will not tire of your record collection if you have 200 or more albums. *Rusty Cartmill, Athens, Georgia*

MUSIC

1726 ... **ADJUSTING THE SIGHTS ON A RIFLE**   If your rifle has more zip than a .30-30 and you sight it to hit a couple of inches above the point of aim at 100 yards, it will put most bullets close to the bull's-eye at 200 yards. *Shannon Tompkins, columnist, The Beaumont Enterprise, Beaumont, Texas*

WEAPONS

1727 ... **THE PARKER CHURCH PARKING RULE**   A church needs 2 acres of parking for every 300 members. *Mary Ellen Parker, retired teacher, Cincinnati, Ohio*

RELIGION

1728 ... **GUESSING THE AGE OF A HORSE**   A horse develops folds in its eyelids at the age of seven, and it adds one fold a year after that. *Paul Glover, writer, artist, activist, revolutionary, Ithaca, New York*

HORSES

MAIL ORDER

MONEY

REAL ESTATE

COOKING

INJURIES

MATHEMATICS

WEATHER

TRAVEL

DRIVING

RELATIONSHIPS

DOGS

CARPENTRY

1729 ... ***SELLING THINGS BY MAIL*** Most people selling things by mail need at least a 200 percent markup to make money. You shouldn't pay more than $10 for something you sell for $30. *Jim Kobs, Kobs and Brady Advertising, Chicago, Illinois*

1730 ... ***MAKING SAFE PREDICTIONS*** In economics, predict what or when, but never both. *Norman Brenner, Fleetwood, New York*

1731 ... ***REFINANCING YOUR HOME*** It makes sense to refinance a home mortgage if the money you save with lower interest pays for the cost of refinancing within three years. *John T. Reed's Real Estate Investor's Monthly*

1732 ... ***HOWARD'S RULE OF COOKING*** Anything can be improved by adding garlic. But if that doesn't work, add chocolate chips. *Howard Wainer, statistician, Princeton, New Jersey*

1733 ... ***TREATING SERIOUS BURNS*** Add a burn victim's age to the percent of the body covered with second- or third-degree burns. If the sum is less than, the patient is apt to survive. *Gerald Myers, Redway, California*

1734 ... ***MAKING A NAME IN MATHEMATICS*** In the field of mathematics, if you haven't made an important discovery by the time you're 22, you probably never will. *Gerald Gutlipp, mathematician, Chicago, Illinois*

1735 ... ***FORECASTING THE WEATHER*** If you see cirrus clouds in the sky, the weather will change. *Joseph Liberkowski, ex-ocean lifeguard, Medford Lakes, New Jersey*

1736 ... ***STAYING ON COURSE*** A 1 degree error in course will take you about 1 mile off track for every 60 miles you travel. *Dr. Bill Grierson, professor emeritus, University of Florida*

1737 ... ***SPEEDING ON THE FREEWAY*** If you must speed on a freeway, speed in the slow lane. Your chances of getting a ticket are one-fourth that of speeding in the fast lane. *Vince Mooney, real estate broker, Tulsa, Oklahoma*

1738 ... ***FINDING SOMEONE YOU CAN TRUST*** Never trust a woman who smiles at you. *Jimmy, Mrs. Cohen's 4th grade class, Placerville, California*

1739 ... ***MAKING FRIENDS WITH A DOG*** If you want to be friends with somebody else's dog, let the dog make the first move, and don't be too quick to respond. *Walter Pitkin, literary agent, Weston, Connecticut*

1740 ... ***LOCATING A STUD*** If you need to locate a stud in a stick-framed wall, remember that most electricians are right handed. Find an outlet, and tap the wall directly to its left. The odds are in your favor that the stud will be there, and you can measure away from it in 16-inch increments to find other studs. *Art McAfee, Edmonton, Alberta, in Fine Homebuilding*

As A RULE OF THUMB: A RESTAURANT MUST HAVE GOOD FOOD AND PARKING. NOTHING ELSE MATTERS. Gene Wolfe, Barrington, Illinois

1741 ... **BUYING A DURABLE CAMERA**   If you want a durable camera, you should buy the simplest camera in the highest price range you can justify. *Robert B. Yepson, Jr., editor, The Durability Factor*

1742 ... **WRITING SENTENCES**   Limit yourself to one thought per sentence. The sentences will end up with different lengths, because some thoughts will be long and some short. The result will be a conversational tone.   *Albert Joseph, president, International Writing Institute Inc., Industry Week*

1743 ... **SPOTTING A GOOD TEACHER**   If you can walk into a lecture ten minutes late and catch up on most of the material you missed, the lecturer is a good teacher. *Norman Brenner, Fleetwood, New York*

1744 ... **SPOTTING AN IMPORTANT PERSON**   The most important perk on any job is a private bathroom. This is one way of determining those with the greatest authority in an organization. *Steven M. Keisman, New York City high school resource coordinator*

1745 ... **TRANSLATING GREEK**   If you can't identify a word in a Greek sentence, it is a verb with a prefix. To figure it out, go through the lexicon chopping off one letter from the front at a time.   *Gene Wolfe, Barrington, Illinois*

1746 ... **THE LEAD SINKER RULE OF SCUBA DIVING**   Scuba divers use a belt with lead weights to adjust their buoyancy in the water. The average diver will need 10 percent of his or her body weight in extra lead. *Jack T. Marshall, professional diving instructor, Trumansburg, New York*

1747 ... **CHOOSING A WATERMELON**   A watermelon is ripe when you hear "punk" rather than "pank" or "pink" when you tap it with your finger. *Paul Kastner, Nagano, Japan*

1748 ... **FINDING DECENT DIAMONDS**   Only one in five diamonds is of gem quality. *Scott Parker, data specialist, Beaumont, Texas*

1749 ... **PACKING UP A ROCK BAND**   If you are in a four-piece rock band, it takes about eight hours to pack up your equipment, travel to your local gig, unload, set up, play one set, break down, load up, and return home. Add one-half hour for each additional piece, and add one hour for each additional set played. *Mark McMullen, accountant, Alexandria, Virginia*

1750 ... **CHOOSING A GUN STOCK**   You can quickly check the fit of a shotgun stock by holding it with your trigger arm. The butt of the stock should fit snugly in the crotch of your elbow, with your hand on the grip and your finger on the trigger. *Wayne Jennings, maintenance mechanic, Cayutaville, New York*

1751 ... **THE CHURCH HEALTH RULE**   The amount of participation required of the congregation is a good indicator of a church's health. If you have 55 jobs per 100 members, you have a growing church. If you have 26 jobs, your church is holding even. Fewer jobs indicate a church in decline.   *Steve Parker, aerospace engineer, Princeton, New Jersey*

1752 ... **PREDICTING THE ADULT SIZE OF A HORSE**   To estimate the adult size of a young horse, first measure the distance from the nostrils over the ears and down the neck. Then measure from the withers to the hoof. The amount by which the first exceeds the second is the amount the horse will grow. *Mark S. Patterson, scored 100 on his last civil service test, Lyons, New York*

MAIL ORDER

MONEY

REAL ESTATE

COOKING

INJURIES

MATHEMATICS

WEATHER

TRAVEL

DRIVING

RELATIONSHIPS

DOGS

CARPENTRY

1753 ... **MAIL-ORDER ADVERTISING**   Ten to 15 percent of the people who accept a trial offer will decide for one reason or another to return the merchandise. But a trial offer will normally produce about twice as many orders as a money-back guarantee.   *Jim Kobs, Kobs and Brady Advertising, Chicago, Illinois*

1754 ... **CALCULATING INVESTMENT VALUE**   Divide 116 by the annual simple interest rate to determine the number of years it will take an investment to triple if interest is compounded yearly.   *Jud Town, author, St. Albert, Canada*

1755 ... **MANAGING YOUR PERSONAL DEBT**   Your monthly mortgage payments (principal, interest, taxes, and insurance) should not exceed 28 percent of your gross monthly salary. The payments for your mortgage and consumer loans combined should not exceed 35 percent of your gross salary.   *Jane Bryant Quinn, in Woman's Day, cited in Bottom Line/Personal*

1756 ... **THE RHUBARB RULE**   Three pounds of rhubarb makes two pies or one imperial gallon of homemade wine.   *Richard Patching, acoustician, Calgary, Alberta*

1757 ... **ELLIOT'S RULE OF PULLED MUSCLES**   For pulled muscles, twisted joints, and other musculoskeletal injuries, use ice on new injuries, heat on old ones.   *George Elliot, physical education teacher*

1758 ... **EXPERIMENTING WITH PEOPLE**   If you're using people as subjects of experiments, use at least 30 to be statistically significant.   *Dean Sheridan, electronics technician and deaf actor, Torrance, California*

1759 ... **FORECASTING THE WEATHER**   A storm from the northeast lasts three days.   *Joseph Liberkowski, ex-ocean lifeguard, Medford Lakes, New Jersey*

1760 ... **CHOOSING A LUXURY SHIP**   The longer and more expensive the cruise, the older the average age of the passengers.   *Gerry M. Flick, M.D., Ship's Surgeon, S.S. Constitution off Hawaii*

1761 ... **FOLLOWING ANOTHER CAR**   Regardless of your speed, you should stay at least two full seconds behind the car ahead in good weather. When the weather is bad, increase the time to three seconds or more.   *Chris Carter, East Lansing, Michigan*

1762 ... **GAINING RESPECT**   Men despise those who court them and respect those who do not give way.   *Walter Pitkin, literary agent, Weston, Connecticut*

1763 ... **KEEPING A SLED DOG**   It costs $1.50 a day to feed and care for a sled dog.   *Robert Lieberman, novelist and filmmaker, Ithaca, New York*

1764 ... **CURING LUMBER**   Air-dry lumber for one year per inch of thickness.   *John Kelsey, editor, Fine Woodworking magazine*

AS A RULE OF THUMB: A DEEP-DRAFT SHIP MAKES A 180 DEGREE TURN OR COURSE REVERSAL IN ABOUT THE SAME LENGTH OF TIME IT TAKES TO COMPLETELY SMOKE A KING-SIZE CIGARETTE.
JOHN TOWLE, SALINAS, CALIFORNIA

1765 ... **WEARING OUT TREADS**   A pair of shoes is good for 1,000 miles. A pair of bicycle tires is good for 4,000 miles. *Kevin Kelly, Athens, Georgia*

1766 ... **THE MASSIVE WRITING RULE**   Writers overuse the word "massive." If you grunt and turn blue when you try to pick it up — it's massive. If you don't — it isn't. *Ben Hansen, editor, The Beaumont Texas Enterprise, Beaumont, Texas*

WRITING

1767 ... **NOT WASTING YOUR TIME**   If you learn nothing new from a lecture after ten minutes, leave. *Norman Brenner, Fleetwood, New York*

EDUCATION

1768 ... **HELPING A CUSTOMER LOAD LUMBER**   If there is an odd number of items, let the customer load the first one. If there is an even number of items, let the customer load the first two. *Anonymous lumber yard worker*

JOKER

1769 ... **LEARNING A FOREIGN LANGUAGE**   You've become comfortable with a foreign language when you dream in that language. *Dennis Palaganas, Gainesville, Florida*

LANGUAGE

1770 ... **LOOKING AT THINGS UNDER WATER**   Because of refraction, underwater objects viewed through a flat face mask or camera port appear about 25 percent larger and closer. *Jack T. Marshall, professional diving instructor, Trumansburg, New York*

SCUBA DIVING

1771 ... **SELECTING A HONEYDEW MELON**   A honeydew melon is ripe if the end opposite the stem gives easily when you press it with your thumb. Also, when you rub the skin with your finger, it should feel slightly sticky. *Cindy Watanabe, Honolulu, Hawaii*

FRUIT

1772 ... **CHOOSING THE RIGHT BOOT**   Generally, the fewer seams a boot has, the better it is. The best boots have only one seam running up the back. *Alwyn T. Perrin, editor, Explorers Ltd. Source Book*

QUALITY

1773 ... **TIMING A GIG**   If your musical engagement is less than two hours long, you will spend as much time setting up and taking down equipment as you will playing music. *Ellen Klaver, musician, Boulder, Colorado*

MUSIC

1774 ... **SELECTING THE RIGHT ARROW** To quickly estimate the arrow length best for you, hold the end of a yardstick against your breast bone with your hands together stretched in front of you. Read the arrow length where your fingertips touch the yardstick. *Dana Burdick, electronic technician*

WEAPONS

1775 ... **FIGURING THINGS OUT**   Simple things are more complicated than they seem, but most complicated things are actually very simple. *Cliff Martin, Eugene, Oregon*

JOKER

1776 ... **PREDICTING THE ADULT SIZE OF A HORSE**   Measure a young horse from the knee to the withers, then from the knee to the coronet. When the ratio of the first to the second is two to one, the horse is fully grown. *Mark S. Patterson, scored 100 on his last civil service test, Lyons, New York*

HORSES

MAIL ORDER

1777 ... SELLING THINGS BY MAIL   Past customers will respond three to six times as well as good prospects who are not past customers.   *Jim Kobs, Kobs and Brady Advertising, Chicago, Illinois*

MONEY

1778 ... CALCULATING INVESTMENT VALUE   Divide 150 by the annual simple interest rate to determine the time it will take an investment to quadruple if interest is compounded yearly.   *Jud Town, author, St. Albert, Canada*

REAL ESTATE

1779 ... RENOVATING A LARGE BUILDING   Renovation generally saves only 10 to 15 percent of the cost of new construction.   *James Colby, civil engineer*

COOKING

1780 ... FRYING DONUTS   When a film of smoke begins to rise from the hot fat, it is the right temperature for frying donuts.   *Helen Ward, Cincinnati, Ohio*

INJURIES

1781 ... CHOKING ON FOOD   If a choking person can verbally request the Heimlich maneuver, he or she doesn't need it.   *James Macmillan, M.D.*

JOKER

1782 ... OCCAM'S RAZOR   The simplest explanation is the one most likely to be true.   *Dean Sheridan, electronics technician and deaf actor, Torrance, California*

WEATHER

1783 ... BARAK'S WEATHER MEGARULE   Plan for stormy weather if there is a red sun at morn, no dew or frost at night, a rainbow in the morning, a ring around the moon, or if insects are bothersome, swallows fly low, campfire smoke heads straight up and then beats downward, breezes expose the underside of leaves, distant sounds carry farther, ax heads tighten up, or frogs croak loudly.   *Barak Rosenshine, professor of education, Urbana, Illinois*

TRAVEL

1784 ... GETTING SICK ON A SHIP   The more expensive your cabin on a cruise, the greater the possibility that you will get seasick. This is because the expensive cabins are found forward, high, and with outside bulkhead exposure. This subjects them to more rolling and pitching than the less expensive cabins located near the ship's center of gravity.   *Gerry M. Flick, M.D., Ship's Surgeon, S.S. Constitution off Hawaii*

DRIVING

1785 ... SORTING OUT INTERSTATES   Three-digit interstate highways typically go around cities when the first digit is even and through cities when the first digit is odd.   *Bob Horton, consultant and writer, St. Petersburg, Florida*

RELATIONSHIPS

1786 ... GETTING SOMEONE TO TRUST YOU   A man trusts his ears less than his eyes.   *Walter Pitkin, literary agent, Weston, Connecticut*

DOGS

1787 ... BUILDING A DOG KENNEL   A kennel should be two times the length of the dog you are building it for. Measure the dog from its nose to the tip of its tail.   *Charles Stoehr, robotics technician, Cincinnati, Ohio*

CARPENTRY

1788 ... USING SCREWS   When using lag screws in soft wood, drill a pilot hole that is one-half the diameter of the screw thread.   *Joseph Smith, carpenter*

1789 ... **NORMAN'S RULE OF BATHTUB TOYS**   Bathtub toys from Singapore generally last longer than those from Taiwan. *Norman Bloom, Calois, Vermont*

DURABILITY

1790 ... **USING A BIG WORD**   If you're writing something and you have to look up the definition of a word, you probably shouldn't use it. *Scott Parker, data specialist, Beaumont, Texas*

WRITING

1791 ... **TEACHING**   Teach by alternating theory with examples, starting with examples. Even better, start with a paradox. *Norman Brenner, Fleetwood, New York*

EDUCATION

1792 ... **CUTTING FIREWOOD**   It takes 24 man-hours for a nonprofessional logger to bring a cord of wood from the stump to the stove. *Michael Blyskal, state real estate appraiser, Albany, New York, in The New York State Conservationist*

LOGGING

1793 ... **THE RULE OF SQUEAKY CLEAN**   If it doesn't squeak, it isn't clean. *Marie Broyles, Pataskala, Ohio*

JOKER

1794 ... **SUFFERING FROM NITROGEN NARCOSIS**   The deeper a scuba diver descends, the more nitrogen he absorbs from the air he is breathing. Increased levels of nitrogen in the blood cause an intoxicating condition known as nitrogen narcosis or "rapture of the deep." Divers will often use martinis as a rough measure of narcosis: each 50 feet of depth makes you feel as disoriented as one martini on an empty stomach. *W. Suter, Arlington, Virginia*

SCUBA DIVING

1795 ... **MAKING APPLE CIDER**   A bushel of apples will make slightly more than three gallons of cider. *Martin Stillwell, farmer*

FRUIT

1796 ... **BUYING A HOUSE**   The first thing to check in a house is the doors and door hardware. If the doors don't fit well or the hardware is cheap and flimsy, the house will be full of problems. *Walter Pitkin, literary agent, Weston, Connecticut*

QUALITY

1797 ... **PERFORMING TASTELESS BLUEGRASS**   In bluegrass music, the most tasteless licks, especially on the banjo, get the best response. *Ellen Klaver, musician, Boulder, Colorado*

MUSIC

1798 ... **CHOOSING AN ARROW**   To quickly estimate the arrow length best for you, take 38 percent of the distance between your fingertips with your arms extended sideways. *Cliff Burns, bow hunter*

WEAPONS

1799 ... **GETTING A GOOD NIGHT'S SLEEP**   Give yourself one week to get used to a new mattress and one night to get used to a new pillow. *Steven M. Keisman, New York City high school resource coordinator*

SLEEP

1800 ... **MAKING HORSESHOES**   To size a piece of steel for a horseshoe, measure the hoof side-to-side at its widest point, double that measurement and add two inches. *Frank Turley, director, Turley Forge Blacksmithing School, Santa Fe, New Mexico*

HORSES

AS A RULE OF THUMB:
WHEN THE WORD "VOLUNTARY" IS USED IN TRADE AGREEMENTS, AS IN "VOLUNTARY RESTRAINT AGREEMENT," IT MEANS JUST THE OPPOSITE.
JONATHAN GELL, TRENTON, NEW JERSEY

MAIL ORDER

1801 ... **MAIL-ORDER SALES**   The best months to sell something by mail are September, November, and January. Of those, September and January are best.   *L. Perry Wilbur, mail-order expert, Money in Your Mailbox*

MONEY

1802 ... **THE KORNBLUM RULE OF COIN COLLECTOR**   The more coins people have in their desk drawer, the more likely they will be to save the ones in their pocket.   *Glenn Kornblum, St. Louis, Missouri*

REAL ESTATE

1803 ... **SELLING REAL ESTATE**   Rental property should sell for about 100 times its monthly rental income.   *Tom Wolfe, writer*

1804 ... **COOKING FISH**   Cook fish ten minutes per inch of thickness.   *Michael Rider, art director, American Demographics*

COOKING

1805 ... **DECIDING WHETHER OR NOT YOU'RE FAT**   A man's waist measurement should not exceed his hip measurement, and a woman's waist measurement should not be greater than 80 percent of her hip measurement. In addition, any rear end with a row of lights and a sign saying "Your Message Goes Here" could also use some slimming.   *Jim Knippenberg, columnist*

JOKER

FARMING

1806 ... **PLANTING CORN**   When tulips bloom, the ground is warm enough to sow sweet corn outdoors.   *Vivian Brubaker, Bettendorf, Iowa*

WEATHER

1807 ... **BARAK'S WEATHER MEGARULE**   Expect fair weather for at least 12 more hours if you see a red sky at night, bees swarming, a gray morning sky, very high clouds, a late-afternoon rainbow, steadily rising camp smoke, morning mist rising from mountain ravines, a sky full of stars, a sea that appears darker than the sky at dawn, or a large number of bats flying in the early evening.   *Barak Rosenshine, professor of education, Urbana, Illinois*

TRAVEL

1808 ... **RIDING A BUS**   On a Greyhound bus, the side with the bathroom has more leg-room than the side with the driver.   *Neil Hess, ski instructor, Syracuse, New York*

DRIVING

1809 ... **DRIVING IN THE MOUNTAINS**   When driving in the mountains, brake before the curve, accelerate into the curve, and always be able to stop in the distance you can see.   *Alex Stewart, Atlanta, Georgia*

RELATIONSHIPS

1810 ... **BRENNER'S MALE SEX RULE**   It takes seminal vesicles three days to fill, and they empty by one-third at each ejaculation.   *Norman Brenner, Fleetwood, New York*

DOGS

1811 ... **USING DOGS TO CARRY PACKS**   A dog can comfortably carry half his weight in a backpack. Working dogs can carry up to twice their body weight for short periods.   *Alwyn T. Perrin, editor, Explorers Ltd. Source Book*

CARPENTRY

1812 ... **BUILDING STAIRS**   A staircase will be pleasant to use if the height of one step (the riser) multiplied by the width of one tread equals 70 to 75 inches.   *Stephen Gibian, architect and stonemason, Ithaca, New York*

1813 ...REMOVING BUTTONS Twist buttons only in one direction and they'll come off much faster. *Kate Gladstone, Brooklyn, New York*

WRITING

1814 ...WRITING PROFESSIONAL SENTENCES Professional writers average about 20 words per sentence. *Scott Parker, data specialist, Beaumont, Texas*

EDUCATION

1815 ...TEACHING TEACHERS In any introductory-level college course, the poorest students are the elementary education majors. *Jeff Brown, astronomer, Bloomington, Indiana*

LOGGING

1816 ...CUTTING FIREWOOD It takes ten eight-inch maple trees to make a cord of wood. *Michael Blyskal, state real estate appraiser, Albany, New York, in The New York State Conservationist*

LISTENING

1817 ...MAKING CONVERSATION If a person talks out of one side of his mouth, his hearing in the opposite ear probably is impaired. *Jeff Brown, astronomer, Bloomington, Indiana*

JOKER

1818 ...SPOTTING A WINNING BASEBALL TEAM Never root for a team whose uniforms have elastic waistbands. It is why the Cubs never make it. *Susan Sarandon, actress*

FRUIT

1819 ...MAKING APPLE CIDER It takes three apples to make a glass of apple cider. *States Cider Mill, Odessa, New York*

QUALITY

1820 ...FUR TRAPPING You can tell the condition of an animal pelt by looking at the fleshy side. Pelts that are blue when skinned or turn blue as they dry on a stretcher have not reached their prime. *J. E. Wertenbach, trapper*

MUSIC

1821 ...KEEPING YOURSELF IN STRINGS The first string that breaks on a guitar is usually the high E (1st string); next likely to break are the D and G strings (3rd and 4th). *Ellen Klaver, musician, Boulder, Colorado*

WEAPONS

1822 ...CHOOSING A SHOTGUN STOCK When you snap your shotgun to your shoulder and sight along the barrel, you should see only the bead at the end. If you have to jam your cheek against the stock to do this, something has to be altered. *Nelson Bryant, The New York Times*

SLEEP

1823 ...REMEMBERING YOUR DREAMS Before going to sleep, drink half a glass of water and leave the other half by your bed. When you wake up, drink the other half. Then you'll remember your dreams. *Valerie D'Acquisto, secretary, Brooklyn, New York*

JOKER

1824 ...THE CULTURE RULE To find out what's really going on in a culture, look for the places where language is being created and where lawyers are congregating. *Brad Edmondson, editor, American Demographics, quoting Stewart Brand*

AS A RULE OF THUMB: RIGHT-HANDED PEOPLE PUT THEIR RIGHT LEG IN THEIR PANTS FIRST.

Rob Shapiro, Pilot and Flight Instructor, Ithaca, New York

MAIL ORDER

1825 ... _SELLING THINGS BY MAIL_   If you get more than two replies for every hundred pieces of mail you send out, you're doing great.   *Peter K. Francese, President, American Demographics*

MONEY

1826 ... _SAVING MONEY WITH COUPONS_   If a coupon is worth less than 23 cents, it's not worth clipping, sorting, and storing.   *Lempert Media Information Service*

REAL ESTATE

1827 ... _SELLING A BUSINESS_   If you can't think of a reasonable price to sell a retail business for, a good starting point is one year's gross income. But you probably will have to settle for less.   *John Pitkin, photographer*

COOKING

1828 ... _MICROWAVING VEGETABLES_   When microwaving solid vegetables, figure seven minutes per pound.   *Andrea Frankel, computer scientist, engineer, holistic health practitioner, San Diego, California*

DIETING

1829 ... _SPOTTING DIET RIP-OFFS_   A total fast burns off 1/2 to 3/4 pound of body fat a day. No diet can cause a more rapid weight loss than this.   *Norman Brenner, Fleetwood, New York*

FARMING

1830 ... _GROWING FOOD_   It takes 0.4 hectare to grow enough food to feed one person.   *R.A. Heindl, design engineer, Euclid, Ohio*

WEATHER

1831 ... _FORECASTING THE WEATHER_   Eighteen hours elapse from the first snowflake to the last in a northeaster.   *Anonymous*

TRAVEL

1832 ... _SUFFERING CULTURE SHOCK_   Culture shock occurs only in the first three foreign countries you visit; after that you subconsciously focus on similarities rather than differences.   *Gary Gaile, geographer*

DRIVING

1833 ... _THE INTERSECTION RULE_   It takes about as long for the car in front of you to start moving as it does for the traffic coming the other way to reach you.   *Bruce Nevin, editor and technical writer, Gloucester, Massachusetts*

RELATIONSHIPS

1834 ... _THE COST OF COURTING RULE_   It costs a man 50 percent of his after-tax income to court a woman.   *Thomas W. Neumann, anthropological archaeologist, wildlife ecologist, and field crew crisis manager*

DOGS

1835 ... _HITCHING YOUR DOG TO A SLED_   One medium-sized dog in good condition, but a bit out of shape (like most pets), can easily pull a fair-sized child on a sled; two dogs can pull a child and an adult.   *Alwyn T. Perrin, editor, Explorers Ltd. Source Book*

CARPENTRY

1836 ... _BUILDING STAIRS_   A set of steps will be comfortable to use if two times the height of one riser, plus the width of one tread is equal to 26 inches.   *Alice Lukens Bachelder, gardener, San Anselmo, California*

As A RULE OF THUMB:
THE AMOUNT OF CORRUPTION IN A SOCIETY IS DIRECTLY PROPORTIONAL TO THE NUMBER OF LAWS THAT THE SOCIETY HAS.
JIM BUTLER, KEALA KEKUA, HAWAII

1837 ... **BUYING A LAWNMOWER** The higher the ratio between horsepower and blade diameter, the longer the motor will last. *Steven M. Keisman, New York City high school resource coordinator*

DURABILITY

1838 ... **WRITING IN ENGLISH** About half the elements used in writing are chosen by the writer. The rest are required by the structure of the language. *Scott Parker, data specialist, Beaumont, Texas*

WRITING

1839 ... **GETTING GOOD GRADES** The grade decreases as distance from the blackboard increases. *R. L. Liming, Indianapolis, Indiana*

EDUCATION

1840 ... **INVESTING IN TIMBER** To be a worthwhile investment, a timberland should be at least 300 acres, be accessible by a paved road, and have good soil. *George Baker, manager of Merrill Lynch's timber division, in The Wall Street Journal*

LOGGING

1841 ... **LISTENING TO YOUR TEAKETTLE** The teakettle sings before a storm. *Anonymous*

LISTENING

1842 ... **SPOTTING NEWCOMERS AT THE BALLPARK** Anyone who takes a photograph at a Major League baseball game is a first-timer. *Carolyn Lloyd, 15-year-old student, Montreal, Quebec*

SPORTS

1843 ... **EATING A PEAR** A pear is ripe when the flesh near the stem yields lightly to thumb pressure. *Gladys Sherwood, Memphis, Tennessee*

FRUIT

1844 ... **BUYING CLOTHES** A garment is probably well made if stripes or plaids are matched at the seams. The more seams that match the better the garment. *Stephanie Judy, writer, British Columbia, Canada*

QUALITY

1845 ... **ADDING ECHO** When adding echo to a vocal track, add half-again as much as you think you should. *Dick Brenton, record producer*

MUSIC

1846 ... **CHOOSING A BOW** A beginner archer should be able to hold a bow fully drawn for 10 seconds without his or her arm shaking. An experienced archer should be able to hold a bow at full draw for 15 or 20 seconds before starting to shake. *Cliff Burns, bow hunter*

WEAPONS

1847 ... **THE NAP RULE** An hour's nap in the middle of the day equals three hours of sleep at night. *Paul A. Delaney, meteorologist, Beltsville, Maryland*

SLEEP

1848 ... **FINDING A GOOD LAWYER** The best lawyer is the one who teaches about your problem. Call the dean's office of a nearby law school to locate the person who teaches a course in the specialty you need. Then call the teacher and ask if he practices privately. *Steven M. Keisman, New York City high school resource coordinator*

LAWYERS

MAIL ORDER

MONEY

REAL ESTATE

COOKING

DIETING

FARMING

WEATHER

TRAVEL

DRIVING

RELATIONSHIPS

DOGS

CARPENTRY

1849 ... **MAIL-ORDER CATALOGS**   You're not ready to publish your own mail-order catalog until you have at least 10,000 customers.   *L. Perry Wilbur, mail-order expert, Money in Your Mailbox*

1850 ... **SPOTTING A FAKE**   Offer to buy a panhandler a meal on the spot. If he says he's not hungry but needs the money for his cat, smile and go on your way.   *John H. Beauvais, Cambridge, Massachusetts*

1851 ... **PLANNING A POND**   The value of a finished pond is roughly three times the cost of constructing it.   *Tim Matson, writer and pond maker, Thetford Center, Vermont*

1852 ... **TESTING BREAD DOUGH**   To test your bread dough, poke two holes into it the depth of the first joint of your thumb. If the holes are still there after 30 seconds, it has risen enough.   *Andrea Frankel, computer scientist, engineer, holistic health practitioner, San Diego, California*

1853 ... **BURNING CALORIES**   Seventy calories are burned per mile, regardless of speed.   *Norman Brenner, Fleetwood, New York*

1854 ... **EATING WILD PLANTS**   When harvesting wild plants, bigger means bitter.   *Mary Ellen Parker, retired teacher, Cincinnati, Ohio*

1855 ... **WATCHING DEER**   If you see deer out feeding in the early afternoon, expect a change in the weather in 24 to 48 hours.   *Glen Fritz, Burlington, Iowa*

1856 ... **CHOOSING THE RIGHT CAMEL**   Don't choose a camel that trembles while sitting. This means its front legs are bad.   *Lauren Stockbower, photo-journalist, in Empire/Pan Am Clipper magazine*

1857 ... **DODGING DRUNK DRIVERS**   On Friday and Saturday nights, one in ten cars coming toward you has a drunk driver behind the wheel.   *Scott Parker, data specialist, Beaumont, Texas, quoting Parade magazine*

1858 ... **THE RULE OF THREE**   For every dollar a woman spends on a courtship, she will receive $3 worth of gifts and entertainment.   *Thomas W. Neumann, anthropological archaeologist, wildlife ecologist, and field crew crisis manager*

1859 ... **WEANING A PUPPY**   The best time for taking a puppy from its litter—psychologically and physically—is when it is 49 days old.   *Steven M. Keisman, New York City high school resource coordinator*

1860 ... **BUILDING STAIRS**   A set of steps will be comfortable to use if two times the height of one riser, plus the width of one tread is equal to 25 inches.   *Ken Vineberg, architect*

AS A RULE OF THUMB: THE BICYCLE IS THE PERFECT MACHINE FOR COMMUTING LESS THAN SIX MILES IN LOS ANGELES. CARRY A CHANGE OF SHIRTS.

LARRY GASSAN, JOLLY DINO ART DIRECTION, LOS ANGELES, CALIFORNIA

1861 ... **THE KICK IT RULE OF LOW TECH**   If you kick it and it works better, that's low tech.   *Debbie McLaughlin, somewhere in Washington*

JOKER

1862 ... **INDEXING**   An average index has three to five entries for each page of text. A light index has one to two entries per page. A scholarly or technical index has ten entries per page.   *Bill Kaupe, consultant, Philadelphia, Pennsylvania*

WRITING

1863 ... **TEACHING CHILDREN**   The biggest child in your class will be your most cooperative student. The shortest child will be the class bully.   *Carol Martindale, teacher, New York, New York*

EDUCATION

1864 ... **THE LOGGING RULE OF EIGHT**   For some reason, most serious sawing accidents happen to beginners or to professionals in their eighth year of logging.   *Ned Bounds, sawyer, Salmon, Idaho*

LOGGING

1865 ... **SPOTTING THE GUILTY DRIVER**   The person doing the talking after a fender-bender is usually the person who caused the accident.   *Steve Carver, illustrator, Ithaca, New York*

LISTENING

1866 ... **WINNING TENNIS**   You can break your tennis opponent's concentration by smiling while you serve.   *Carolyn Lloyd, 15-year-old student, Montreal, Quebec*

SPORTS

1867 ... **EATING A CANTALOUPE**   A cantaloupe is ripe when it has a musky smell at the end opposite the stem.   *Brad Edmondson, editor, American Demographics*

FRUIT

1868 ... **THE CAFETERIA RULE**   Cafeterias serve institution-grade foods. Never imagine anything else.   *Dean Sheridan, electronics technician and deaf actor, Torrance, California*

JOKER

1869 ... **TUNING A MUSICAL INSTRUMENT**   A stringed instrument is less apt to slip out of pitch if the strings are tuned up from flat than it is if the strings are tuned down from sharp.   *Robbie Aceto, musician*

MUSIC

1870 ... **DESIGNING A GUN THAT DOESN'T KICK**   A safe rule, if you want to design a gun with recoil that is not too unpleasant, is to make the gun weigh at least 96 times the load of shot it is built to fire.   *W. W. Greener, arms maker, from The Gun and Its Development (written in the 1800s)*

WEAPONS

1871 ... **CHOOSING A MATTRESS**   The amount you move during sleep is directly proportional to the hardness of your mattress. Generally then, the greater the back problem the harder your mattress should be. The unforgiving surface forces you to move often, and your muscles won't become stiff from lack of movement.   *Alan T. Whittemore, YMCA Physical Director, South Deerfield, Massachusetts*

SLEEP

1872 ... **WINNING AN APPEAL**   If you're defending the judgment of the trial court, it is good strategy to make the proceedings and judgment seem boring and obvious.   *Stephen Unsino, poet, Eastchester, New York*

LAWYERS

MAIL ORDER

1873 ... SELLING THINGS BY MAIL   Using direct-mail ads, or what is commonly called "junk mail," it is almost impossible to make money selling something that costs less than $10.   *J. Persiponco, Centerville, Indiana*

MONEY

1874 ... KEEPING A FRIEND   Never loan a friend more than you can afford to give away.   *Reed Alvord, Hamilton, New York*

REAL ESTATE

1875 ... BUYING A HOUSE   Don't pay more than twice your average annual income for a house.   *Scott Parker, data specialist, Beaumont, Texas*

COOKING

1876 ... THE 17TH CENTURY RULE   The best oil is on the top; the best wine is in the middle; and the best honey is on the bottom.   *Tom Robinson, computer programmer, Berkeley, California*

DIETING

1877 ... ESTIMATING ENERGY USE   Different species consume the same energy per body weight for similar movements. A step for a human is equivalent to a wing flap for a bird or a tail flip for a fish.   *Norman Brenner, Fleetwood, New York*

FARMING

1878 ... ESTIMATING THE NEED FOR CHEMICALS   Sixty to 90 percent of the chemicals sprayed on crops are used only to make produce look better.   *Paul A. Delaney, meteorologist, Beltsville, Maryland*

WEATHER

1879 ... THE BIRD CHATTER RULE   When the birds — especially the bluejays — seem to chatter more than usual, expect a storm within 24 hours.   *Virginia Williams, Burlington, Iowa*

TRAVEL

1880 ... TRAVELING BY CAMEL   A good camel should be able to travel 80 to 100 kilometers per day easily.   *Lauren Stockbower, photo-journalist, in Empire/ Pan Am Clipper magazine*

DRIVING

1881 ... AVOIDING A CRASH IN A CAR RACE   At high speed, nothing stays in the same place for long. Aim your car at the spot where you see an accident start. Chances are the accident will have moved by the time you get there.   *Joie Chitwood, former Indy driver and owner of the Joie Chitwood Thrill Show*

RELATIONSHIPS

1882 ... THE FIRST IN FIRST OUT RULE   Women are last in and first out of romantic relationships; men are first in and last out.   *Thomas W. Neumann, anthropological archaeologist, wildlife ecologist, and field crew crisis manager*

DOGS

1883 ... WINNING THE IDITAROD   The first musher to reach the town of Iditarod — the halfway point — in the Alaska Iditarod sled dog race will not win the race.   *Russ Wilmot, Iditarod race volunteer, Eagle River, Alaska*

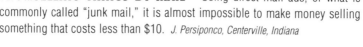
CARPENTRY

1884 ... BUILDING STAIRS   Build steps that are seven inches high and ten inches wide.   *Harry Pate, builder, Camden, New Jersey*

As a rule of thumb: IF A WOMAN CAN TALK ON THE TELEPHONE DURING A CONTRACTION, THE BIRTH IS A LONG WAY OFF. IF THE WOMAN CAN'T SPEAK DURING A CONTRACTION, THE BIRTH IS NEAR.

Dr. K. Emmott, Vancouver, British Columbia

1885 ... *SPOTTING A CONSERVATIVE*   Conservatives prefer strawberry ice cream.
Dean Sheridan, electronics technician and deaf actor, Torrance, California

1886 ... *REPRESENTING AN AUTHOR*   A prospective client for a literary agency who begins his letter of application with the words "My name is..." should not be seriously considered. *Walter Pitkin, literary agent, Weston, Connecticut*

1887 ... *TEACHING CHILDREN*   The more rules you have in the classroom, the more time you'll spend enforcing them. *Cookie Ohlson, teacher, Prospect Park Middle School, Pennsylvania*

1888 ... *MANAGING A WOOD LOT*   A properly managed wood lot in a good location will produce about two-thirds of a cord of hardwood per acre per year. A 10- to 12-acre wood lot can easily meet the heating needs of the average, well-insulated house. *Gary Goff, extension forester*

1889 ... *THE CONCERT RULE OF HEARING*   If you have to shout to your date at a concert, then the noise is destroying your hearing. *Gerry M. Flick, M.D., Ship's Surgeon, S.S. Constitution off Hawaii*

1890 ... *WINNING HORSESHOES*   In a game of horseshoes, avoid opponents sporting either a glove or a tattoo. Especially avoid those with both. *John S. Haydon, certified public accountant, Hollister, California*

1891 ... *SQUEEZING AN ORANGE*   One orange will make half a cup of juice. *The Lansing Methodist Church Women's Society*

1892 ... *FINDING A GOOD RESTAURANT*   If a restaurant displays favorable newspaper reviews in the window, then it is neither really bad (no reviews available) nor really exclusive (too snobby to display reviews). *Norman Brenner, Fleetwood, New York*

1893 ... *PLAYING A MUSICAL INSTRUMENT*   Music played on a high-quality musical instrument sounds better no matter who's playing. *Mark McMullen, accountant, Alexandria, Virginia*

1894 ... *SHOOTING AN AUTOMATIC PISTOL*   When an automatic pistol malfunctions, try a new brand of ammunition and a new magazine before taking it to a gunsmith. *Gene Wolfe, Barrington, Illinois*

1895 ... *FALLING ASLEEP TO MUSIC*   If you want to fall asleep with the stereo on, turn the volume down to a level that would be too quiet when you are awake. In less than five minutes, that level will feel comfortable, but if you're still awake in 15 minutes you may have to turn it down again. *Rusty Cartmill, Athens, Georgia*

1896 ... *TAKING SOMEONE TO COURT*   Pain and suffering awards start at three times the cost of the therapy. Rib injuries—though agonizing—do not offer a good return because tape and pain-killers cost little. Back injuries are better because they cost so much money to treat. *Brad Lowry, freelance producer of international video, Philadelphia, Pennsylvania*

MAIL ORDER

1897 ... **ORDERING FROM A CATALOG**   If it doesn't say it, it doesn't have it.   *Cheryl A. Russell, demographer, mother, editor-in-chief, American Demographics*

MONEY

1898 ... **SELLING PERFUME**   When the dollar is weak, perfume sales soar.   *Scott Parker, data specialist, Beaumont, Texas*

REAL ESTATE

1899 ... **SELLING REAL ESTATE**   In a good real estate market, listings should be sold within 30 days.   *Steven M. Keisman, New York City high school resource coordinator*

COOKING

1900 ... **POPPING CORN**   To get popping-corn oil hot enough, place three kernels in the oil as it heats; when all three pop, the oil is hot enough.   *Richard L. Holloway, Associate Professor, University of Minnesota*

DIETING

1901 ... **THE AMOUNT OF FAT RULE**   Fat should account for no more than 30 percent of your daily calories.   *Anonymous*

FARMING

1902 ... **PLANTING BARLEY**   How much do you lose per acre by planting your barley late? A bushel a day after the first of May.   *Marty Schlabach, co-owner, "Shelter Goods," Rochester, New York*

WEATHER

1903 ... **WATCHING YOUR COWS**   Expect a storm when your cows become agitated, start to bawl, and head for the barn.   *Anonymous talk-show respondent, Burlington, Iowa*

TRAVEL

1904 ... **CHOOSING A FOREIGN RESTAURANT**   When traveling in a foreign country, avoid restaurants with menus printed in more than two languages—they are for tourists.   *Michael Rider, art director, American Demographics*

DRIVING

1905 ... **PAINTING A HIGHWAY**   A road must carry traffic of at least 400 cars per day for a reflective centerline to be a cost-effective improvement.   *John Schubert, senior editor, Bicycling magazine*

RELATIONSHIPS

1906 ... **ESTIMATING POPULATION SIZE**   The number of adult married women in a population is equal to the number of hearths. While women might share a husband, they will not share a hearth.   *Thomas W. Neumann, anthropological archaeologist, wildlife ecologist, and field crew crisis manager*

JOKER

1907 ... **THE NUMBER OF PERSONS PER PYTHON RULE**   For capturing pythons, anacondas, boas and other large constrictors, it is wise to have one person for every 4 or 5 feet of snake.   *Donald R. Gentner, Cardiff by the Sea, California*

CARPENTRY

1908 ... **FINISHING A CABINET**   Finishing work such as sanding, scraping, oiling, rubbing, and varnishing is 30 percent of any cabinet-making job.   *Dennis Pollack, builder, Danby, New York*

As a rule of thumb: IT'S TIME TO OPEN YOUR PARACHUTE WHEN CARS LOOK AS BIG AS ANTS. WHEN ANTS LOOK AS BIG AS CARS, YOU'VE WAITED TOO LONG.

Ernst Luposchainsky, III ("Kahn") Skydiving Pundit and Philogynist, Inter Alia, Hollywood, California

1909 ... JUDGING POLITICAL SYSTEMS Capitalism is the exploitation of man by man; socialism is the exact opposite. *Norman Brenner, Fleetwood, New York*

1910 ... TYPING PAGES Two handwritten pages equals one typed page. *Carl Mitcham, philosophy teacher, Brooklyn, New York*

1911 ... TEACHING CHILDREN The rule for getting along with seventh and eighth graders is: don't do anything that annoys them. And they know what annoys them better than you do. *Cookie Ohlson, teacher, Prospect Park Middle School, Pennsylvania*

1912 ... MANAGING A WOOD LOT A wood lot managed primarily for saw timber will produce about four times as much money as a wood lot managed for firewood. *Gary Goff, extension forester*

1913 ... THE TENNIS SHOT SOUND RULE Your tennis shot will improve if you try to make it sound good. *Tom Robinson, computer programmer, Berkeley, California*

1914 ... THE SPORTS BAND RULE The better the band, the worse the football team. *Tom Lucas, software artist, Berkeley, California*

1915 ... SQUEEZING LIMES An average lime contains about three tablespoons of lime juice (and no lemon juice). *Dave and Moddi McKeown, Pittsburgh, Pennsylvania*

1916 ... FINDING A GOOD RESTAURANT Steak restaurants serve good seafood, but seafood restaurants serve terrible steak. *Glenn Kornblum, St. Louis, Missouri*

1917 ... ARRANGING SPEAKERS The closer speakers are to eye level, the better the stereo separation. *Steven M. Keisman, New York City high school resource coordinator*

1918 ... PACKING A PISTOL The handle of your holstered revolver should hang midway between your wrist and your elbow with your arms at your side. *Alan Ladd, in the movie Shane, 1953*

1919 ... GETTING TO SLEEP BEFORE MIDNIGHT Each hour of sleep before midnight is equal to two hours of sleep after midnight. *Nick O'Conner, San Francisco, California*

1920 ... AVOIDING JURY DUTY To avoid being picked for jury duty, read a book. Lawyers avoid jurors who are reading books because they might be too independent. *Scott Parker, data specialist, Beaumont, Texas*

JOKER

1921 ... *BUYING SODA FROM A MACHINE* If your money falls right through a soft-drink machine and lands in the coin return, forget about feeding it coins and try pulling a bottle out of the machine. The chances are about one in five that you will get a free soda. Someone else put money in the machine, but the relay didn't release the bottles until after they gave up and left. *Eric Kimple, motorcycle racer, Columbus, Ohio*

MONEY

1922 ... *DEALING WITH LARGE SUMS OF MONEY* Large sums of money engender both stinginess and personal extravagance. *D. Branner, New York City*

JOKER

1923 ... *INVESTING IN THE STOCK MARKET* The stock market moves in the same direction as the hemlines on women's skirts. *R.A. Heindl, design engineer, Euclid, Ohio*

COOKING

1924 ... *COOKING VEGETABLES* Cook vegetables the way they grow: Cook roots, covered, starting them in cold water. Cook greens uncovered in boiling water. *Kelly Yeaton, quoting "The Mystery Chef," a 1930s radio cooking guide*

DIETING

1925 ... *OVEREATING* The first time it occurs to you that you have eaten enough, you have. *Andrea Frankel, computer scientist, engineer, holistic health practitioner, San Diego, California*

FARMING

1926 ... *BLOCKING THE WIND* A semipermeable row of plants will shelter the ground behind it for a distance 20 times the height of the plants — whether they are 10 inches or 200 feet tall. For example, a shelterbelt of 60-foot poplars with a shrubbery understory will protect the soil downwind for 1,200 feet — regardless of windspeed. *Pierce Butler, Natchez, Mississippi*

WEATHER

1927 ... *THE FAMOUS RULE OF SUNSET* Red sun at night, sailor's delight; red sun in the morning, sailor take warning. *Isabel T. Coburn, authority at large, Pemaquid Beach, Maine*

TRAVEL

1928 ... *SCHEDULING A CRUISE* Change the date of your cruise if over 5 percent of the other passengers have won the trip instead of paying for it out of their own pockets. *Gerry M. Flick, M.D., Ship's Surgeon, S.S. Constitution off Hawaii*

DRIVING

1929 ... *PASSING A CAR* If you are passing another car on a two-lane road and are confronted with an oncoming car, there are two things you can do: accelerate or brake. You should brake; in all cars, the brakes are a lot more powerful than the engine. The only time you shouldn't brake is if another car is right behind you also passing. In that case, your luck has run out anyway. *J. Baldwin, designer and writer*

RELATIONSHIPS

1930 ... *THE FIRST DATE RULE* On a first date, watch how your date treats the waiter, the bartender, and so on. That's how she'll be treating you after three months. *Jeff Brown, astronomer, Bloomington, Indiana*

FISH

1931 ... *TROLLING FOR BLUEFISH* Troll your lure at five times the length of your boat. *Bill Berger, Cincinnati, Ohio*

CARPENTRY

1932 ... *CARING FOR NEW WOODWORK* Rub linseed oil into new woodwork once a day for a week, once a week for a month, once a month for a year, and once a year from then on. *Marilyn Rider, Body & Soul, Ithaca, New York*

1933 ... **WINNING VOTES**   Physical appearance wins 40 percent of the votes. A personable manner accounts for almost as much. Competence plays a small role and experience even less. Being recognized as a hero can overcome all of the above.   *Martin M. Bruce, Ph.D., psychologist, Larchmont, New York*

POLITICS

1934 ... **WRITING A FINAL SENTENCE**   When writing, if you're searching for a final sentence, you've probably already written it.   *Cheryl A. Russell, demographer, mother, editor-in-chief, American Demographics*

WRITING

1935 ... **PREDICTING A STUDENT'S BEHAVIOR**   A student's classroom behavior is inversely proportional to his or her classroom participation.   *Marc Pelath, student and programmer, Michigan City, Indiana*

EDUCATION

1936 ... **THE CHAINSAW RULE**   When breaking in a new chainsaw, adjust the chain tension twice during the first tank of fuel, once during the second tank, and once every tank for the rest of the day.   *Ned Bounds, sawyer, Salmon, Idaho*

LOGGING

1937 ... **COUNTING GUNSHOTS**   If you hear shots while hunting: One shot equals game bagged. Two shots equals game possibly bagged. Three shots means there's a chance game was bagged. Four shots means you're listening to a frustrated hunter.   *Thomas Lack, somewhere on the east shore of Lake Michigan*

LISTENING

1938 ... **WINNING SOFTBALL**   If you can keep the other team from scoring more than nine runs, you will probably win.   *Glenn Boyce, Oakland, California*

SPORTS

1939 ... **DRYING FRUIT**   Only high-quality fruit should be dried. If it is not good enough to eat fresh, it is not good enough to dry.   *D. Antoni, Scottsdale, Arizona*

FRUIT

1940 ... **RUNNING A RESTAURANT**   When they're unhappy at a restaurant, the French call the headwaiter and abuse him in front of everyone. The English call the manager and abuse him quietly and with dignity. The Americans don't say a thing. They just never come back, nor do their friends.   *Richard Malone, Vancouver, Washington*

RESTAURANTS

1941 ... **PLAYING A FRENCH HORN**   The deeper you put your hand into the bell, the poorer the sound.   *John J. Chiment, student of horns, Perry City, New York*

MUSIC

1942 ... **FOLLOWING FOSSILS**   Northern fossils generally are larger than southern fossils.   *John J. Chiment, paleobiologist and editor, Perry City, New York*

SCIENCE

1943 ... **DECIDING WHAT YOU WANT**   If you don't know what you want, it's probably sleep.   *Timothy Wenk, magician, West Stockbridge, Massachusetts*

SLEEP

1944 ... **THE VERDICT RULE**   The sooner a jury returns with a verdict, the more likely it decided for the defense.   *Scott Parker, data specialist, Beaumont, Texas*

LAWYERS

AS A RULE OF THUMB:
THE REPLACEMENT PART
WHOSE PACKAGE SAYS,
"FITS MOST MODELS,"
WILL NOT FIT THE MODEL
YOU OWN.
DENNIS HENDRIX, TERRE HAUTE,
INDIANA

SALES

1945 ... *NEGOTIATING A SALE* Customers who produce a written quote from a competitor early in a sales negotiation won't buy from you. They're using you as leverage against their quote. *Bob Horton, consultant and writer, Largo, Florida*

MONEY

1946 ... *HODGE'S RULE OF AUDITS* If you don't receive an invitation for an IRS audit, you probably forgot to deduct something. If you don't receive an invitation for an IRS audit within a year of filing your return, chances are that you won't be audited for that year. *Ronald R. Hodge, investment executive and commercial pilot, Long Beach, California*

STOCK

1947 ... *KEISMAN'S FOOTBALL RULE OF ECONOMICS* The Dow Jones Industrial Average always rises in years when an original National Football League team wins the Super Bowl. If a team from the original American Football League wins, buy shorts or long-term put options. *Steven M. Keisman, New York City high school resource coordinator*

COOKING

1948 ... *CHECKING YOUR MUSSELS* Squeeze a mussel. If it doesn't stay shut, it's dead. *Margaret Wagner, Brooklyn, New York*

DIETING

1949 ... *DECIDING WHAT TO EAT* If you can't figure out what you want to eat, you're not hungry. *Andrea Frankel, computer scientist, engineer, holistic health practitioner, San Diego, California*

FARMING

1950 ... *DETERMINING THE HEALTH OF A FARM* If a farm has a debt-to-asset ratio of more than 70 percent, it is in severe trouble. If the debt-to-asset ratio is between 40 and 70 percent, the farm is facing serious problems. And if the debt-to-asset ratio is less than 30 percent, the operator is safe. *Rex R. Campbell, professor of rural sociology, U. of Missouri-Columbia, in American Demographics*

WEATHER

1951 ... *LISTENING TO CHICKADEES* The warm weather of spring has finally arrived when the chickadees change their cry from "chick a dee dee dee" to "dee dee." *Ronald and Christine Newberry, Cayutaville, New York*

TRAVEL

1952 ... *GETTING SOMEWHERE ON TIME* To make sure you get somewhere on time, double the estimated travel time for a trip of 10 minutes or less; add 15 minutes to a trip of 30 minutes or less; add 50 percent to a trip of 30 minutes to 2 hours; and add 25 to 30 percent to a trip of more than 2 hours. *Gail Smith, parts unknown*

DRIVING

1953 ... *ADJUSTING YOUR CAR SEAT* You should check your seat adjustment with your hands at the ten and two o'clock positions on the steering wheel. You should be close enough so that you can make almost a full half-turn of the wheel without having to lean forward or having your elbows touch your body. *Alan Johnson, SCCA national driving champion*

RELATIONSHIPS

1954 ... *THE RAMAGE RULE OF MARRIAGE* A young man marries for a mistress, a middle-aged man for a companion, and an old man for a nurse. *R. W. Ramage, Cheshire, Great Britain*

FISH

1955 ... *CARING FOR FISH* In a new aquarium, feed the fish half as much food as you want to and change the water twice as often. *Steven Vest, librarian and poet, Berea, Ohio*

CARPENTRY

1956 ... *THE SANDING RULE* Sanding is 10 percent of all cabinet making. *Joel Warren, cabinet maker*

AS A RULE OF THUMB:
IT TAKES TWO FUTONS TO
MAKE A COMFORTABLE BED.

STEVE KEAST, HAZARD
INVESTIGATOR, SLATERVILLE
SPRINGS, NEW YORK

1957 ... **THE FATIGUE RULE**   Never trust a politician who wears military fatigues to breakfast. *Scott Parker, data specialist, Beaumont, Texas*

POLITICS

1958 ... **REVISING YOUR WORK**   The greater the sense of exultation and accomplishment upon completing the first draft of a work of fiction, the greater the need for revision. *James McConkey, writer, Trumansburg, New York*

WRITING

1959 ... **SIZING UP A SCHOOL PROGRAM**   The more trivial a school program, the more pretentious the jargon used to justify it. *Emery Nemethy, Catawissa, Pennsylvania*

EDUCATION

1960 ... **CHOPPING WOOD**   Most people who try chopping a tree with an axe soon discover that the axe will wedge in the wood if the cut is not wide enough. In most cases, the width of the chop area should be as wide as the tree is thick. *Peter van Berkum, Kittery Point, Maine*

LOGGING

1961 ... **LISTENING TO PEEPERS**   When the spring peepers start, the maple sugaring stops. *Cheryl A. Russell, demographer, mother, editor-in-chief, American Demographics*

LISTENING

1962 ... **WINNING A GAME**   If you do exceptionally well in a game of bowling or a round of golf, your next game or your next round will be exceptionally bad. *George Mackie, Nokomis, Florida*

SPORTS

1963 ... **BUYING FRUIT**   An orange is ripe when its surface is smooth rather than bumpy because its pustules are swollen with juice. *Brad Edmondson, editor, American Demographics*

FRUIT

1964 ... **THE WAITER RULE**   After he first greets you, the waiter in a high-class restaurant will not speak unless spoken to. *Frank Turley, director, Turley Forge Blacksmithing School, Santa Fe, New Mexico*

RESTAURANTS

1965 ... **REWINDING AN AUDIOCASSETTE**   It takes five seconds to fast forward or rewind one minute of audiocassette tape. *Dennis Palaganas, Gainesville, Florida*

MUSIC

1966 ... **MAKING PARTICLES**   The shorter the life of the particle, the more it costs to make. *Scott Parker, data specialist, Beaumont, Texas*

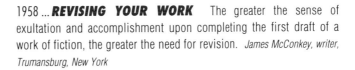

SCIENCE

1967 ... **BUYING JUST THE MATTRESS**   If you want to buy just a mattress, take the price of the set (box spring and mattress), divide by two, and add $25. *James Parker, civil engineer, Medford, Massachusetts*

SLEEP

1968 ... **WINNING A CASE**   When you don't have much of a case, argue the law. *Scott Parker, data specialist, Beaumont, Texas*

LAWYERS

SALES

1969 ... SPOTTING THE BEST SALESPERSON   The best salespeople have the most reorders. *Steven M. Keisman, New York City high school resource coordinator*

MONEY

1970 ... THE VENTURE CAPITALIST RULE   Venture capitalists expect to get back five to ten times the amount of money they invested within three to five years. *Scott Parker, data specialist, Beaumont, Texas*

STOCK

1971 ... NICHOLSON'S CUT AND RUN RULE   Cut your losses quickly. Let your profits run. *Isadore Nicholson, San Diego, California*

COOKING

1972 ... WHIPPING UP A CASSEROLE OR STEW   To make a casserole or stew without a recipe, use approximately equal volumes of all the main ingredients, and double that volume of the main starch — rice, potatoes, noodles, etc. *Gail Smith, parts unknown*

DIETING

1973 ... BURNING CALORIES   For every kilometer (6/10ths of a mile) you run, you burn one calorie per kilogram of your body weight. Swimming a kilometer requires about four calories per kilogram of body weight. Cycling a kilometer requires about one-third calorie per kilogram. *Ned Frederick, writer, Exeter, New Hampshire*

FARMING

1974 ... MAKING MONEY WITH PIGS   It takes the profit from four pigs to pay the cost of keeping a sow. The fifth pig is the first one that makes you money. *Julius E. Nordby, author, Swine*

WEATHER

1975 ... WAITING FOR THE FIRST FROST   The first frost will come six weeks after you hear the first cricket. *Fred Brehm, vegetable grower, Dilltown, Pennsylvania*

TRAVEL

1976 ... ADJUSTING TO TIME NEW ZONES   It takes your body one day to adjust for each time zone you cross. If you travel across three time zones, plan on spending three days adjusting to it. *Cheryl A. Russell, demographer, mother, editor-in-chief, American Demographics*

DRIVING

1977 ... FOLLOWING ANOTHER CAR   You should keep at least one car length between your car and the car ahead for every ten miles per hour of speed. *Carla Corin, biologist, Eagle River, Alaska*

RELATIONSHIPS

1978 ... THE EVANS HEFTY SWEETHEART RULE   If you want to know how fat your sweetheart will be in 20 years, look at your sweetheart's parents. *Jennifer Evans, writer, Austin, Texas*

FISH

1979 ... EXAMINING A TROUT   Native trout have whole fins. Hatchery trout have ragged fins. *Russell T. Johnson, Temple City, California*

JOKER

1980 ... UNTANGLING SOMETHING   To untangle anything stringlike, keep pulling the mess outward, making it larger and looser until the loops untangle themselves. This is your only hope of success. *Kevin Kelly, Athens, Georgia*

1981 ... **ESTIMATING PUBLIC OPINION** Each sincere letter or phone call a politician receives from a constituent represents another 1,000 voters with the same opinion. *Scott Parker, data specialist, Beaumont, Texas*

POLITICS

1982 ... **THE THESAURUS RULE** If you feel that you need a thesaurus to write something, you are probably trying too hard. *John Shed, language instructor*

WRITING

1983 ... **SIZING UP A TEACHER** A teacher who complains that his or her students are all stupid is probably a poor teacher. *Bruce Reznick, associate professor of mathematics, Urbana, Illinois*

EDUCATION

1984 ... **USING A CHAINSAW** Plan on spending half an hour of maintenance for each two hours of chainsaw use. *Rob Weinberg, Tassajara Zen Mountain Center, Carmel Valley, California*

LOGGING

1985 ... **DESIGNING AN ELEVATOR** Traveling faster than ten miles per hour in an elevator will make your ears pop. *Scott Parker, data specialist, Beaumont, Texas*

LISTENING

AS A RULE OF THUMB: YOU SHOULD ALLOW ONE WEEK TO HITCHHIKE A THOUSAND KILOMETERS IN AFRICA. *Henning Pape-Santos, Linguist, Ithaca, New York*

1986 ... **PUTTING NEAR WATER** All putts break toward the water because the slope of greens are contoured for drainage. *Donald B. Lilley, water tester, Leco Laboratory, Trenton, New Jersey*

SPORTS

1987 ... **ANTICIPATING A COST OVERRUN** The final cost of a government program, including overruns, divided by the original cost will closely approximate pi. *Warren Harris, Sacramento, California*

JOKER

1988 ... **SPOTTING A GOOD RESTAURANT** The flashier the sign, the worse the food. *John H. Beauvais, Cambridge, Massachusetts*

RESTAURANTS

1989 ... **BUYING A RECORD ALBUM** You'll like an album if you like at least one-fourth of the songs on it. *Dennis Palaganas, Gainesville, Florida*

MUSIC

1990 ... **LOOKING FOR ENGINEERING CORRELATIONS** If you are trying to describe a phenomenon rigorously, correlate aggregate parameters in such a way that all the units cancel out. For example, don't study the effect of changing pipe diameter, which has units of distance. Study changes of pipe diameter divided by pipe length, which has units of distance divided by distance. The result is dimensionless. These correlations are more resilient to changes in materials and scale. *David R. Throop, chemical engineer, Austin, Texas*

SCIENCE

1991 ... **TAKING A SHOWER** A ten minute shower is worth an hour and a half of sleep. *Laurie Baldwin, student, Oregon State University*

SLEEP

1992 ... **SPOTTING A DEFENSE LAWYER** The more luxurious the law office, the more likely it serves defendants rather than plaintiffs. *Gerry M. Flick, M.D., Ship's Surgeon, S.S. Constitution off Hawaii*

LAWYERS

SALES

MONEY

STOCK

COOKING

DIETING

FARMING

WEATHER

TRAVEL

DRIVING

RELATIONSHIPS

FISH

CRAFTS

1993 ... **SELLING CARS**   A customer who arrives in a car with a full tank of gas won't make any deals. *Jim, disc jockey, Seattle, Washington*

1994 ... **GETTING A MORTGAGE**   When interest rates are high, banks will allow you to spend up to 33 percent of your total income on the principal, interest, and insurance on a home mortgage. When interest rates are low, 25 percent of your total income. *Scott Parker, data specialist, Beaumont, Texas*

1995 ... **INVESTING WISELY**   Take your losses when your investment value has dropped by 12 to 15 percent. *Isadore Nicholson, San Diego, California*

1996 ... **PLANNING POTATO SALAD**   When making potato salad, figure 1 1/2 medium potatoes and 1 egg per person. *Scott M. Kruse, biogeographer, Fresno, California*

1997 ... **DETERMINING YOUR BASAL METABOLIC RATE**
Your basal metabolic rate is equal to your weight in kilograms. For example, a 60 kg (132 lb.) person burns about 60 calories per hour at rest. *Ned Frederick, writer, Exeter, New Hampshire*

1998 ... **FOLLOWING FARMERS**   Every six farmers that go broke take a rural business with them. *Cally Arthur, managing editor, American Demographics*

1999 ... **FOLLOWING FALL**   On the east coast of the United States, the fall foliage change moves south by 50 miles a day. *Margaret Wagner, Brooklyn, New York*

2000 ... **TALKING TO CAB DRIVERS**   If a taxi driver talks a lot, let him; if he doesn't talk, don't ask him to; and if he laughs all the time, never ask him why. *Mark McMullen, accountant, Alexandria, Virginia*

2001 ... **STOPPING A CAR**   If you can't see the rear tires of the car in front of you at a stoplight, you're too close. *Anonymous British driving student*

2002 ... **THE FIDELITY AND SUCCESS RULE**   People's capacity for fidelity is inversely proportional to their success in life. *Stephen Unsino, poet, Eastchester, New York*

2003 ... **FISHING WITH COWS**   If cows remain lying in a group on a rainy day, then fish will not bite. *Anna L. Curtis, Cedar Falls, Iowa*

2004 ... **SEWING**   Never use a knot in hand sewing. *Anonymous*

AS A RULE OF THUMB: ON A SAFETY-CONSCIOUS ROCK-CLIMBING EXPEDITION, THE MOST LIKELY INJURIES WILL BE SELF-INFLICTED WITH POCKET KNIVES AT LUNCH. BRET PETTICHORD, COMPUTER PROGRAMMER, MEDFORD, MASSACHUSETTS

2005 ... PREDICTING VOTER TURNOUT   You need a black population of 65 percent in an area to get a 50 percent black voter turnout. You lose 5 percentage points because of the younger age structure of the black population, 5 percentage points for under-registration of blacks compared to whites, and 5 percentage points because blacks are less likely to vote than whites, even if they are registered. *Bill O'Hare, Joint Center for Political Studies, Washington, D.C.*

2006 ... WRITING FOR THE GENERAL PUBLIC   If you're writing directions, write at a seventh-grade English level. *Dean Sheridan, electronics technician and deaf actor, Torrance, California*

2007 ... THE STUDENT IS READY RULE   When you're ready to do something about a problem, almost anything can help. When you're not ready, no amount of workshops, counseling, or programs will effect a lasting change. The rule is: when the student is ready, the teacher appears. *Andrea Frankel, computer scientist, engineer, holistic health practitioner, San Diego, California*

2008 ... CUTTING FIREWOOD BY YOURSELF   One person, working alone, can cut, haul, and stack about a cord of firewood a day. *John Fay, apple grower*

2009 ... LISTENING TO ARC WELDERS   The length of your arc determines the quality of your weld. A good arc sounds like frying bacon. An arc that's too long starts to hiss and sound hollow; an arc that's too short stops arcing. *Smokey Olsen, Lawrenceburg, Indiana*

2010 ... SURVIVING A SKI   If you can't see it, you can't ski it. *Paul A. Delaney, meteorologist, Beltsville, Maryland*

2011 ... RUNNING A SUCCESSFUL CALL-IN SHOW   A successful call-in show will attract 10 to 15 calls an hour. *Dan Leonard, disc jockey, Buffalo, New York*

2012 ... SPOTTING A CLEAN RESTAURANT   A restaurant is safe to eat in if its bathrooms are clean. *Gary Heilig, Lansing, Michigan*

2013 ... TYING SHOELACES   If one shoelace is loose, you need to retie both. *James McConkey, writer, Trumansburg, New York*

2014 ... CHEMICAL REACTIONS   Plan on a 10 percent loss of material for each step in a sequential chemical reaction. *David Finn, printmaker, New York City*

2015 ... SLEEPING WITH A BABY   Most babies will sleep through the night after reaching a weight of 11 pounds or an age of 6 weeks, whichever comes first. *Linda McCandless, shepherd*

2016 ... SUING FOR MEDICAL EXPENSES   Three times the medical expenses is a reasonable amount to sue for in a court of law. *Judge Wapner, People's Court*

SALES

2017 ... **SELLING DOOR-TO-DOOR**   If no one stops the dog from barking within 15 seconds, no one will answer the door.   *Elaine Brooks, former Avon sales lady, Charlotte, Michigan*

MONEY

2018 ... **ATTRACTING A VENTURE CAPITALIST**   Venture capitalists invest in only about 3 percent of the deals that come across their desks each year.   *Scott Parker, data specialist, Beaumont, Texas*

STOCK

2019 ... **INVESTING YOUR MONEY**   The stocks that decline the most during a down cycle will gain the most during the next up cycle.   *John B. Armesto, Buffalo, New York*

COOKING

2020 ... **MEASURING RICE**   When using rice in casseroles, use one handful per person.   *J. Michaelson, asset manager, Phoenix, Arizona*

DIETING

2021 ... **LOSING WEIGHT**   You lose a pound of fat for every 3,500 calories you burn or don't eat.   *Ned Frederick, writer, Exeter, New Hampshire*

FARMING

2022 ... **BLOWING STUMPS OUT OF THE GROUND**   You can blow most tree stumps out of the ground if you use one stick of dynamite for every four inches of stump diameter. Trees with tap roots take less.   *Joe Kaiser, Covington, Kentucky*

WEATHER

2023 ... **THE NEW HAMPSHIRE RULE OF DROUGHT**   If the ash buds before the oak, look for fire and smoke. If the oak buds before the ash, look for a summer splash!   *Mr. and Mrs. Strearns Smalley, Wonalancet, New Hampshire*

TRAVEL

2024 ... **TIPPING THE PORTER**   Tip the porter a buck a bag.   *Jon Reis, photographer, Ithaca, New York*

DRIVING

2025 ... **STOPPING A CAR**   If you can't see the license plate of the car in front of you at a stoplight, you're too close.   *James Vincent, driver education instructor*

RELATIONSHIPS

2026 ... **DEALING WITH EMERGENCIES**   When suddenly stricken, men fall forward while women fall backward, because their centers of gravity differ.   *Scott Parker, data specialist, Beaumont, Texas*

FISH

2027 ... **FEEDING A PIKE**   Given a choice, Northern Pike prefer prey that is about a third of their own length.   *Phil Johnson, State University of New York, Albany, in The New York State Conservationist*

CRAFTS

2028 ... **WORKING WITH HANDSPINNERS**   It takes seven handspinners to keep one weaver busy.   *Jon Reis, photographer, overheard at a craft show, Ithaca, New York*

AS A RULE OF THUMB: YOUR TIRE PRESSURE IS TOO HIGH IF SMALL STONES POP OUT FROM UNDER YOUR BICYCLE TIRES AS YOU RIDE OVER GRAVEL.

RAMBLIN' JACK BARCLAY, BIOLOGIST, BUSH PILOT, FLIGHT INSTRUCTOR, SANTA CRUZ, CALIFORNIA

2029 ... *MAKING A POLITICAL PROMISE* A politician should never promise anything, however simple, to a constituent. Instead, use the phrase "I'll see what I can do..." *Milton Rakove, political scientist, as related by Phil A. Schrodt*

2030 ... *WRITING AN ARTICLE* For general feature writing, figure on interviewing 5 to 8 sources per 1,000 words of final manuscript. For a trend story, use up to double that number of sources. *Scott Baltic, editor, Chicago, Illinois*

WRITING

2031 ... *SENDING CHILDREN TO SCHOOL* When universal education was introduced in the Philippine Islands, there were no birth records and sorting children by age was a problem. The teachers found that a child is old enough to send to school when he can cross his arms over his head and grasp his ears with his opposite hands. *Arma L. Curtis, Cedar Falls, Iowa*

EDUCATION

2032 ... *FIGHTING A FOREST FIRE* One trained firefighter with a sharp tool can dig 6 chains (about 400 feet) of finished fireline, 2 feet wide and down to mineral soil, every day for 2 weeks. *Ned Bounds, sawyer, Salmon, Idaho*

LOGGING

2033 ... *CHOOSING A FRESH ARTICHOKE* Fresh artichokes squeak when rubbed together. *Sunny Lenz, New Canton, Virginia*

LISTENING

2034 ... *FIRING THE FOOTBALL* A quarterback has three seconds to fire the ball; after that he'll get sacked. *Bob O'Halloran, talkshow host, WHBY Radio, Appleton, Wisconsin*

SPORTS

2035 ... *LISTENING TO THE RADIO* If a radio station is playing "Stairway to Heaven," the disc jockey is in the bathroom. *Archer, Q-105 FM, Portland, Oregon*

RADIO

2036 ... *SPOTTING A BAD RESTAURANT* If your entree is neat and square, it was frozen. If the marks on a grilled entree are even and clearly marked, they were made on the frozen entree with food coloring. *Eleanor Benelisha, library and information services, Richmond, California*

RESTAURANTS

2037 ... *RUNNING FAST* Don't move your head from side to side when you run. *Carolyn Lloyd, 15-year-old student, Montreal, Quebec*

RUNNING

2038 ... *REPEATING AN EXPERIMENT* If you can't repeat your own experiment, you are probably not doing science. If no one else can repeat your experiment, you are probably lying. *Gary Marlow, scientist, Ithaca, New York*

SCIENCE

2039 ... *SLEEPING WITH A BABY* Most babies will sleep through the night at eight weeks of age, or three months of age, one or the other. *Louise Mudrak, ecologist*

SLEEP

2040 ... *THE TRIAL RULE* Anytime a district attorney brings a defendant to trial, he or she is convinced that the defendant is guilty, even though proving it may be impossible. *Anonymous lawyer, Chicago, Illinois*

LAWYERS

SALES

2041 ... ***SPOTTING A BAD DEAL***   If someone says, "buy now," don't buy at all. *Russell T. Johnson, Temple City, California*

MONEY

2042 ... ***BILLING A GOVERNMENT AGENCY***   When doing business with a government agency, expect to wait a minimum of 45 days to get paid, and don't get excited if it takes 90 to 120 days. *Scott M. Kruse, biogeographer, Fresno, California*

STOCK

2043 ... ***INVESTING IN THE STOCK MARKET***   Watch out if the portfolio manager leaves the mutual fund in which you're invested. One manager is often responsible for a stellar track record. *Dean Sheridan, electronics technician and deaf actor, Torrance, California*

COOKING

2044 ... ***KNEADING BREAD***   Knead bread dough until your arm is tired and then do 25 more punches. *J. Michaelson, asset manager, Phoenix, Arizona*

DIETING

2045 ... ***LOSING WEIGHT***   Never try to lose more than two pounds per week. *Ned Frederick, writer, Exeter, New Hampshire*

FARMING

2046 ... ***SHEARING A SHEEP***   You can make one sweater for every two pounds of wool you shear from a sheep. *Mary Catherine, preschool teacher*

WEATHER

2047 ... ***WATCHING HORSES YAWN***   When a horse yawns, the weather's going to change. *Rita Pitkin, Albany, Vermont*

TRAVEL

2048 ... ***CHECKING YOUR BAGGAGE***   If you have more than ten bags, immediately tip the porter $20. More times than not, he will check your baggage through without extra baggage charges. *David Gluck, cinematographer, Photosynthesis Productions, Ithaca, New York*

DRIVING

2049 ... ***THE RULE OF 22***   Unless someone screws up, heavy traffic tends to keep itself at a speed of about 22 miles per hour, the speed that allows the most cars to use a road at once. *John Schubert, senior editor, Bicycling magazine*

RELATIONSHIPS

2050 ... ***WOODHEAD'S RULE OF SEXUALITY***   Highly intelligent women seem more masculine than average. Highly intelligent men seem more feminine than average. *Jeffrey K. Woodhead, Davis, California*

FISH

2051 ... ***WEIGHING A PIKE***   You can estimate the weight, in pounds, of a Northern Pike by cubing its length, in inches, and dividing by 3,500. *Phil Johnson, State University of New York, Albany, in The New York State Conservationist*

CRAFTS

2052 ... ***CHOOSING A SHOW FOR YOUR CRAFTS***   Craft show attendance figures are exaggerated. Cut the advertised attendance figures in half and expect even less. *Bob Van Streader, Wood 'n Indian, Rochester, New York*

2053 ... *DEFINING WILDERNESS* In the western United States, any area that has more than 1 mile of road per 1,000 acres will have a tough time gaining Congressional protection as a wilderness area. *Henning Pape-Santos, linguist, Ithaca, New York*

2054 ... *LARIMORE'S RULE OF STARTING TO WRITE SOMETHING* Never put pen to paper until you know what you want to accomplish. If you don't know what success looks like for a particular project, you are too unclear to even begin. *Terry Larimore, writer and therapist, Houston, Texas*

2055 ... *TALKING TO HIGH SCHOOL STUDENTS* When giving instructions to a high school class, you should assume that three students will follow them incorrectly. *David T. Russell, retired high school teacher, Dilltown, Pennsylvania*

2056 ... *THINNING TREES FOR LUMBER* A trained thinner will use about three-quarters of a gallon of fuel and one-third of a gallon of bar oil per day, regardless of the number of acres covered. *Ned Bounds, sawyer, Salmon, Idaho*

2057 ... *FOOLING YOUR EARS* The sense of hearing is the easiest to trick. *Steven M. Keisman, New York City high school resource coordinator*

2058 ... *SIZING A DOWNHILL SKI* Standing vertically in front of you, the top of the ski should curve directly over your head. *Neil Hess, ski instructor, Syracuse, New York*

2059 ... *THE NEWS CONFERENCE RULE* If you're holding a news conference, start your presentation ten minutes after the scheduled start. Reporters are always late. *Trudie Mason, assignment editor/reporter, CJAD Radio News, Montreal, Quebec*

2060 ... *EATING IN A RESTAURANT* If the price of the veal is equal to or only slightly above the price of the chicken, order the chicken. *Len Coloccia, Clifton, New Jersey*

2061 ... *RUNNING TIPS* A full-time runner wears out a pair of running shoes every four months. *Christa Childsen, Bellevue, Washington*

2062 ... *UNDERSTANDING EVOLUTION* Individuals in evolving lineages tend to become larger as time goes on. *John J. Chiment, paleobiologist and editor, Perry City, New York*

2063 ... *CHANGING YOUR SLEEP SCHEDULE* It is easier to shift your regular bedtime to a later hour than an earlier hour. It's hard to go to sleep 30 to 60 minutes earlier per night, while you can easily stay up 60 to 90 minutes later. *Dennis Palaganas, Gainesville, Florida*

2064 ... *DECIDING TO TELL A LIE* If you're trying to decide whether to tell the truth so you won't get punished or pull a Reagan and say you can't remember, root for the Gipper. If you tell the truth, they'll punish you anyway. *Dean Sheridan, electronics technician and deaf actor, Torrance, California*

SALES

2065 ... ***BUYING AN ORIENTAL CARPET*** Most carpet sellers price a carpet at twice what they expect to get for it after the bargaining process. *Scott Parker, data specialist, Beaumont, Texas*

MONEY

2066 ... ***FOLLOWING INTEREST RATES*** On a 15-year adjustable-rate mortgage, every percentage-point rise in interest will boost your monthly payment by about 5 percent. *William C. Banks, writer, Money*

STOCK

2067 ... ***INVESTING IN THE STOCK MARKET*** Never buy more of a stock when its price goes down. You only compound your losses. *Brendan Boyd, columnist*

COOKING

2068 ... ***CHOOSING A STICK FOR HUNTING MUSHROOMS*** Resting on the top of your boot, a morel hunting stick should extend to your chest. *Malfred Ferndock, authority on Morels, Dennison, Minnesota*

DIETING

2069 ... ***LOSING WEIGHT WHILE GAINING AGE*** You should lose 1 pound of body weight every 3 years after age 30 to offset the increase in body fat that accompanies aging. *Ned Frederick, writer, Exeter, New Hampshire*

FARMING

2070 ... ***GROWING A TOWEL*** A 20-by-30-foot patch of ground, sown with two pounds of flax seed, should provide enough fiber to weave a small tablecloth or towel. *Jean Heavrin, weaver*

WEATHER

2071 ... ***WATCHING BIRDS*** If you see birds rotating way up — turning small, tight circles and not clapping their wings — you're going to get a blow. *Alec Wilkinson, The New Yorker, quoting Raymond Duarte, Provincetown, Massachusets*

TRAVEL

2072 ... ***LOWERING YOUR TRAVEL RISKS*** Pick a hotel room between the third and sixth floors. Three floors puts you above street attacks and random shootings, while six floors will keep you in range of a cherry picker or fireman's ladder if the place goes up in flames. *Stephen Kindel, quoting Eugene Mastrangelo and Jerry Hoffman, security analysts, in Savvy*

DRIVING

2073 ... ***MAINTAINING YOUR TIRE PRESSURE*** For every 10-degree drop in temperature, tire pressure goes down one pound. *Peter van Berkum, Kittery Point, Maine*

RELATIONSHIPS

2074 ... ***FRANKEL'S RULE OF ASKING FOR PERMISSION*** It's generally easier to ask forgiveness than permission. *Andrea Frankel, computer scientist, quoting Grace Hopper, mother of Cobol, San Diego, California*

FISH

2075 ... ***HEATING AN AQUARIUM*** You need three watts worth of aquarium heater per gallon in a room of normal temperature. Use four watts per gallon for rooms that are cooler than normal. *Mary Ellen Parker, retired teacher, Cincinnati, Ohio*

CRAFTS

2076 ... ***GLAZING A POT*** In order to properly coat a pot, a glaze should be the consistency of heavy whipping cream. *M. N., Enterprise, Oregon*

2077 ... **PLACING YOUR NAME ON A BALLOT**   In a political race where none of the candidates is well-known, the name listed first on the ballot (typically they are in alphabetical order) has a major advantage.   *Pierce Butler, Natchez, Mississippi*

POLITICS

2078 ... **THE TYPEWRITER RULE**   A full, double-spaced typewritten page will have about 250 words on it if typed with a pica typewriter, 330 words if typed with an elite typewriter.   *Michael Armstrong, writer, Anchorage, Alaska*

WRITING

2079 ... **TEACHING EFFECTIVELY**   To teach effectively, a teacher should limit a class to 25 students. A class of 25 to 32 students should have a teacher's aide. A group with more than 32 students should be split into two classes.   *Leslie Warren, music teacher, Kittery Point, Maine*

EDUCATION

2080 ... **NOTCHING TREES WITH A CHAIN SAW**   A logger can control the path of a falling tree by notching the trunk in the direction of fall. For safety's sake, a notch or front cut should be used to fell any tree over 6 inches in diameter.   *Ned Bounds, sawyer, Salmon, Idaho*

LOGGING

2081 ... **PREDICTING SUCCESSFUL INVASIONS**   The worse the national cooking, the less likely a country will be successfully invaded.   *Thomas W. Neumann, anthropological archaeologist, wildlife ecologist, and field crew crisis manager*

JOKER

2082 ... **SELECTING A SKI POLE**   Turn the ski pole upside down, stand it next to you, and grasp the shaft directly below the basket. If your elbow makes a right angle, your pole is the right length.   *Neil Hess, ski instructor, Syracuse, New York*

SPORTS

2083 ... **THE RADIO CONTEST RULE**   The listener response to a radio call-in contest depends on the size of the prize. You can expect ten call-in contestants for every dollar you are giving away.   *Don Burley, radio talk-show host, Kansas City, Kansas*

RADIO

2084 ... **SPOTTING A GOOD CHINESE RESTAURANT**   The best ones don't do take-out.   *Ling Ling & Dave, Binghamton, New York*

RESTAURANTS

2085 ... **PROTECTING YOUR FEET**   The foot hits three times harder when running than when walking.   *Scott Parker, data specialist, Beaumont, Texas*

RUNNING

2086 ... **UNDERSTANDING EVOLUTION**   Repeated similar structures in individual organisms tend to become less numerous and functionally more differentiated.   *John J. Chiment, paleobiologist and editor, Perry City, New York*

SCIENCE

2087 ... **FILING THINGS**   Three-quarters of the things filed in a typical office should have been placed in the wastebasket.   *Edwin C. Bliss, time management expert*

JOKER

2088 ... **CARING FOR DOGS**   You've added enough water to dry dog food when it is the texture of wet cement.   *Captain Haggerty, animal trainer, actor, author, and philosopher, New York, New York*

TEXTURE

SALES

2089 ... *SELLING A NEW CAR* Your customer has decided to buy the car when he or she asks what colors are available. Stop selling and close the deal. *Dirck Z. Meengs, management consultant, Canoga Park, California*

MONEY

2090 ... *ACCEPTING A CHECK* Be wary when accepting a check with a check number lower than 250. *Sue Viders, The Artist's Magazine*

STOCK

2091 ... *INVESTING IN THE STOCK MARKET* It's tempting to sell out when a stock rises in price by 25 to 50 percent. But if you're speculating on low-priced stock, look for a bigger return. *Brendan Boyd, columnist*

COOKING

2092 ... *BUYING AN EGGPLANT* To avoid a seedy eggplant, choose one that has a round scar at the end opposite the stem. An oval scar means a female plant—it will have more seeds. *Cindy Watanabe, Honolulu, Hawaii*

DIETING

2093 ... *SWAPPING MUSCLE FOR FAT* About 40 percent of your body weight is muscle. If you swap nine pounds of muscle for nine pounds of fat, you'll shrink by about 1 percent because muscle is denser. *Ned Frederick, writer, Exeter, New Hampshire*

FARMING

2094 ... *BUILDING A POND* An earthen dam should never slope more than one foot in three. *J. P. Hunter, retired engineer*

WEATHER

2095 ... *AVERAGING THE WEATHER* The average of the average temperatures across North America is usually fairly even. When it's cold in the west, it's warm in the east, and vice versa. *Walter Pitkin, literary agent, Weston, Connecticut*

TRAVEL

2096 ... *ENJOYING YOUR VACATION* You will have more fun on your vacation if you maintain a mental age of 18 or less. Act just old enough to make your travel connections and stay out of trouble. *Joe Schwartz, editor, Danby, New York*

DRIVING

2097 ... *DRIVING IN A FOREIGN COUNTRY* Slow down for donkeys, speed up for goats, and stop for cows. Donkeys will get out of your way, it's almost impossible to hit a goat, and it's almost impossible to avoid hitting a cow. *P. J. O'Rourke*

RELATIONSHIPS

2098 ... *THE BULLY RULE* The more a person tries to come across in a certain way, the less likely that he feels that way about himself. In other words, the bigger the bully, the more insecure he feels. *Drs. Kim and Jack Arthur, child psychotherapists, Baltimore, Maryland*

FISH

2099 ... *ESTIMATING THE WEIGHT OF A BROWN TROUT* You can estimate the weight of a brown trout if you remember that a 20-inch fish weighs 3 pounds and a 25-inch fish weighs 5 pounds. For every inch over 25 inches, add 1 pound to the weight of the fish. For example, a 27-inch brown trout weighs 7 pounds. *Thomas Lack, somewhere on the east shore of Lake Michigan*

CRAFTS

2100 ... *GLAZING A POT* Hold a pot in the glaze for the time it takes your heart to beat four times. *Kathy Edmondson, Ithaca, New York*

AS A RULE OF THUMB: IF YOU NEED TO TOUCH THE BRAKES AS YOU RETURN TO YOUR LANE AFTER PASSING ANOTHER CAR, YOU SHOULD NOT HAVE PASSED AT ALL.

Dr. Bill Grierson, Professor Emeritus, University of Florida

2101 ... *MEASURING SOCIAL STABILITY* To measure the social stability of a country, compare the income of the top tenth of the population with that of the bottom tenth. If the top tenth is getting more than 15 times the income of the bottom tenth, you've got a problem. *Daniel Shively, Indiana, Pennsylvania, quoting futurist Marvin Cetron*

POLITICS

2102 ... *BUYING REAL ESTATE* Smart rich people buy expensive houses, not expensive cars. Houses appreciate, cars don't. *Steven M. Keisman, New York City high school resource coordinator*

JOKER

2103 ... *THE GRADE SCHOOL RULE OF FIVE* Subtract five from the age of a child to determine his or her grade in school. Conversely, add five to the grade of a child to determine his or her age. A fourth grader, for instance, is usually nine years old. *Pat Howard, teacher*

EDUCATION

2104 ... *THE LANDSLIDE RULE* A bank is subject to landslides and rockslides until enough mud or rock has fallen against it to form a pile of debris, or talus, with a 37-degree slope. *Rob Weinberg, Tassajara Zen Mountain Center, Carmel Valley, California*

JOKER

2105 ... *STAFFING AN ARMY* In the armed forces, the ratio of enlisted men to officers is ten to one — the optimum ratio of workers to bosses. *Dean Sheridan, electronics technician and deaf actor, Torrance, California*

MILITARY

2106 ... *CHOOSING SHOES FOR SPORTS* For sports requiring quick lateral movements, the older you get, the higher your shoes should extend up your ankle. *Alan T. Whittemore, YMCA Physical Director, South Deerfield, Massachusetts*

SPORTS

2107 ... *HOSTING A RADIO TALK SHOW* During a radio talk show, at least 1 percent of the callers will phone in with nothing more to say than how hard it is to call the show. *Rob Kersting, WVLK AM/FM, Lexington, Kentucky*

RADIO

2108 ... *SPOTTING A GOOD CHINESE RESTAURANT* The good ones hire only Chinese. *Ling Ling & Dave, Binghamton, New York*

RESTAURANTS

2109 ... *PLANNING A LONG RUN* Plan to do your longest training runs on an empty stomach, beginning before 8 a.m. For each hour after 8 that you begin, cut the distance by 10 percent. Add 10 percent if you have one to two cups of coffee before starting. *Tom Ferguson, M.D., Editor, Medical Self-Care, Inverness, California*

RUNNING

2110 ... *UNDERSTANDING EVOLUTION* Organisms do not return to any ancestral condition or completely lose the effects of any ancestral condition. *John J. Chiment, paleobiologist and editor, Perry City, New York*

SCIENCE

2111 ... *DESIGNING A CLOSET* When calculating the closet space needed for shoes, allow 8 inches for each pair of women's shoes and 9.5 inches for each pair of men's shoes. *Bob Horton, consultant and writer, Largo, Florida*

STORAGE

2112 ... *CHECKING A PEARL* To tell if a pearl is genuine, rub it against your teeth. A fake pearl will feel smooth; the real thing will grate. *Quinith Janssen, pearl expert, USAir magazine*

TEXTURE

SALES

2113 ... ***MOONEY'S RULE OF SALESPEOPLE***   You could fire half of all the salespeople in the country and never notice a drop in sales.   *Vince Mooney, real estate broker, Tulsa, Oklahoma*

MONEY

2114 ... ***THE PAPER MONEY RULE***   You are close to poverty when paper towels are a luxury item.   *Sharon K. Yntema, writer, Ithaca, New York*

STOCK

2115 ... ***INVESTING IN STOCKS***   An average stock portfolio will out-perform an average bond portfolio over time.   *Phil Smith, Alameda, California*

COOKING

2116 ... ***PREPARING FROZEN FOODS***   When cooking a frozen meal, ALWAYS increase the maximum recommended cooking time by 10 to 15 percent. When warming a frozen pizza, add oregano. With all other foods, add butter.   *Markus Mueller, student, Pepper Pike, Ohio*

DIETING

2117 ... ***ESTIMATING THE CALORIE CONTENT OF FOODS***   Solid foods high in carbohydrates and protein contain about 100 calories per ounce. Fatty foods contain about 200 calories per ounce.   *Ned Frederick, writer, Exeter, New Hampshire*

FARMING

2118 ... ***GROWING CITRUS FRUITS***   A freeze will destroy a citrus crop. If the temperature in a citrus grove drops to 28 degrees Fahrenheit or less before 10 p.m., fire up the smudgepots.   *Darryl Payne, orange grower*

WEATHER

2119 ... ***THE DEW RULE OF SPIDERWEBS***   If in the evening you can find beads of dew on spiderwebs, the next day will bring good, dry haying weather.   *Retired dairy farmer in Albany, Vermont*

TRAVEL

2120 ... ***TRAVELING IN EUROPE***   Count each kilometer as a mile when planning a trip by car. It will take as long to drive 300 kilometers in Europe as it takes to drive 300 miles in the United States.   *Robert Cumberford, Austin, Texas*

JOKER

2121 ... ***AVOIDING ANIMALS WITH YOUR CAR***   To avoid an animal that leaps in front of your car, aim for it. By the time you get there, it will be gone.   *Paul R. Bowlby, Pompton Lakes, New Jersey*

RELATIONSHIPS

2122 ... ***CHANGING YOUR SEX***   A male who changes his sex to female will look like a woman who is five years older because men's faces look more rugged than women's. On the other hand, female to male sex-change patients will look 10 to 12 years younger. A 30-year-old woman will look and sound like a boy of 18 or 20. We call it the "Peter Pan" effect.   *Marge Willes, counselor, Gateway Gender Alliance*

FISH

2123 ... ***CHECKING A FLY ROD***   A fly rod with reel should balance somewhere within six inches of the handle.   *Sheridan Anderson, author, The Curtis Creek Manifesto*

CRAFTS

2124 ... ***MAKING CANDLES***   One pound of wax will make eight 8-inch candles.   *Nancy Heffernan Eckstrom, nutritionist, Barton, New York*

Aᔕ A RULE OF THUMB:
THE MORE COMFORTABLE YOU
MAKE YOUR SUBJECT, THE
BETTER THE PORTRAIT WILL BE.
GREG HENSHALL,
INDUSTRIAL PHOTOGRAPHER,
NITRO, WEST VIRGINIA

2125 ... **POLITICAL PLANNING**   People moving into a new tract development are politically inert for five years. *Gary Evans, city planner*

POLITICS

2126 ... **CHECKING A HARD-BOILED EGG**   A hard-boiled egg will spin like a top; a fresh egg won't. *Ernst Luposchainsky, III ("Kahn"), polymathic layabout, inter alia, Hollywood, California*

EGGS

2127 ... **READING TO KIDS**   After 15 minutes, even well-behaved children in kindergarten or first grade get fidgety. *John Towle, Salinas, California*

EDUCATION

2128 ... **MAKING MAPLE SYRUP**   The more ice you pick out of sap buckets on cold spring days, the sweeter the sap and the less boiling it will need. *Walter Pitkin, literary agent, Weston, Connecticut*

MAPLE SYRUP

2129 ... **WINNING A WAR**   In attacking an entrenched position, the attackers should outnumber the defenders by three to one. *Walter Pitkin, literary agent, Weston, Connecticut*

MILITARY

2130 ... **RACING A BOBSLED**   In bobsled competition, every second lost at the start costs three seconds at the finish. On a luge run, the time lost at the start is multiplied by four times at the finish. *ABC TV Winter Olympics commentator, 1984 Winter Olympics*

SPORTS

2131 ... **THE RULE OF HISTORY**   History repeats itself. The first time is tragedy, the second farce. *Norman Brenner, Fleetwood, New York*

JOKER

2132 ... **SPOTTING A GOOD RESTAURANT**   If you're visiting a small town and must choose between a restaurant at street level and another one flight up, go to the one upstairs. The food will be better and the prices 15 to 20 percent less. *Gerry M. Flick, M.D., Ship's Surgeon, S.S. Constitution off Hawaii*

RESTAURANTS

2133 ... **PREDICTING YOUR MARATHON TIME**   You can predict your marathon time by multiplying your best 10 kilometer time by 4.65. *Ned Frederick, writer, quoting physiologist Jack Daniels, Exeter, New Hampshire*

RUNNING

2134 ... **THE RULE OF ISLAND EVOLUTION**   On islands, small species will evolve toward larger size, and large species will evolve toward smaller size. *John J. Chiment, paleobiologist and editor, Perry City, New York*

SCIENCE

2135 ... **DESIGNING CLOSETS**   Women have three times as many clothes as men, but they need only twice as much hanging space. Men's clothes take up more space per hanger. *Bob Horton, consultant and writer, Largo, Florida*

STORAGE

2136 ... **FEELING YOUR OIL**   Rub a little of your motor oil between your thumb and forefinger. If you can feel any grit, it's time to change your oil. *Donny Bates, gas station attendant, Cincinnati, Ohio*

TEXTURE

SALES

2137 ...**DEALING WITH CUSTOMERS**   Customers are most difficult to deal with during the full moon. The next most trying phase is the new moon. *Georgia Chapman, pharmacist, Bedford, Virginia*

MONEY

2138 ...**SAVING MONEY**   You should budget your money so that you can put 10 to 15 percent of your earnings into savings. *Merrie Spaeth, USA Weekend*

STOCK

2139 ...**INVESTING IN MUTUAL FUNDS**   In most cases, mutual fund managers and their funds will out-perform your own portfolio. *Phil Smith, Alameda, California*

COOKING

2140 ...**COOKING YOUR DINNER**   Things cooking in the oven are almost done when you can smell them in the living room. *Gordon Hard, assistant editor, Consumer Reports, Mount Vernon, New York*

DIETING

2141 ...**LOSING WEIGHT**   The best way to lose weight is to leave food on the plate. *Mrs. Eileen Lightfoot, Burlington, Iowa*

FARMING

2142 ...**WEBB'S NOTCHED NAIL RULE OF PIGS**   When a sow conceives, make a notch just above the moon on your fingernail. When this mark grows off the end of the nail, the sow is about to give birth. *Doug Webb, Brooktondale, New York*

WEATHER

2143 ...**CHECKING FOR DEW**   Brush your hand over the grass well after sunset. If it is dry, the next day will be too wet for haying. *Retired dairy farmer in Albany, Vermont*

TRAVEL

2144 ...**THE TRAVELING RULE OF TWO**   When traveling, take twice the money and half the clothes you think you will need. *Betsy Wackernagel, Ithaca, New York*

HITCHHIKING

2145 ...**HITCHING A RIDE**   If you hitchhike on the near side of a red light at an intersection, you double your chances of getting a ride. *Gerry M. Flick, M.D., Ship's Surgeon, S.S. Constitution off Hawaii*

RELATIONSHIPS

2146 ...**CHER'S RULE OF GREAT KISSERS**   If a man's a good kisser, he's a great f—." *Cher, quoted in People*

FISH

2147 ...**FEEDING A BASS**   A largemouth bass can eat a fish one-half its length. *Walter Booth, outboard engine repairman*

CRAFTS

2148 ...**THROWING A POT**   One pound of clay thrown with reasonable competence on a potter's wheel will make a vessel large enough to hold one average serving of most kinds of food. *Jim Dunn, potter, Belews Creek, North Carolina*

AS A RULE OF THUMB:
THE HARDER YOU HAVE TO BRAKE TO AVOID HITTING SOMEONE WHO PULLS OUT IN FRONT YOU, THE SOONER YOU'LL HAVE TO BRAKE FOR THEM TO TURN OFF.
TANIA WERBIZKY, HISTORIC PRESERVATIONIST, ITHACA, NEW YORK

2149 ... **WILBUR'S RULE OF POSITIVE FEEDBACK** If you are personally canvassing door-to-door within two weeks of an election and three of ten voters both recognize you and give you positive feedback, you will probably win. *Tom Wilbur, county commissioner, East Lansing, Michigan*

POLITICS

2150 ... **RAISING OSTRICHES** When raising ostriches, expect to hatch 60 percent of the eggs. *Anonymous*

EGGS

2151 ... **ASKING STUDENTS QUESTIONS** A teacher should wait three seconds, no more and no less, before saying anything after a question. *Steven M. Keisman, New York City high school resource coordinator*

EDUCATION

2152 ... **TAPPING MAPLE TREES FOR SAP** To keep from girdling a maple tree when tapping it for sap, figure that an area the size of your hand dies around each tap and avoid that area in following years. *Debby Hart, carpenter, Ithaca, New York*

MAPLE SYRUP

2153 ... **UNDERSTANDING THE MILITARY BUDGET** New military projects cost at least $30 billion so that every Congressional district can get a significant piece of the action. That works out to about 2,000 jobs per district. *Norman Brenner, Fleetwood, New York*

MILITARY

2154 ... **WATCHING WILD PITCHES** For someone scoring a baseball game from the press box: If a pitch is in the dirt, it'll be scored as a wild pitch. *Red Barber, commentator and sports announcer, National Public Radio*

SPORTS

2155 ... **SPOTTING THE MURDERER** In a mystery play on your local stage, the murderer will be the best actor among the suspects. In a mystery TV show, the murderer will be the best-known actor. *Jennifer Evans, writer, Austin, Texas*

THEATER

2156 ... **SPOTTING A GOOD RESTAURANT** A restaurant is never better than its bread. *Agustin R. Anitart, Metairie, Louisiana*

RESTAURANTS

2157 ... **PREPARING TO RUN A MARATHON** You need to run at least 40 miles a week for at least 6 weeks to prepare for a marathon. *L.M. Boyd, The San Francisco Chronicle*

RUNNING

2158 ... **THE RULE OF COLD** Among related species of mammals, the larger species will occur closer to the poles, and the smaller species will occur closer to the equator. *John J. Chiment, paleobiologist and editor, Perry City, New York*

SCIENCE

2159 ... **THE SHOE RULE** As family income rises, the ratio of women's shoes to men's shoes increases accordingly. *Bob Horton, consultant and writer, Largo, Florida*

STORAGE

2160 ... **JOHN'S RULE OF FOREIGN TRAVEL** The softer the currency, the harder the toilet paper. *John Fountain, Riverside, Connecticut*

TEXTURE

SALES

MONEY

STOCK

COOKING

DIETING

FARMING

WEATHER

TRAVEL

HITCHHIKING

RELATIONSHIPS

FISH

CRAFTS

2161 ... **MAKING A SALE**   A manufacturer's representative should expect to make three calls per sale. *Jerry Hay, manufacturer's rep, Burlington, Iowa*

2162 ... **DEFINING WEALTH**   Wealth is any income that is $100 more a year than the income of your wife's sister's husband. *H. L. Mencken*

2163 ... **SELECTING INVESTMENTS**   When selecting investments, unwarranted conservatism, sloth, and inertia will outweigh logic and careful study about 50 percent of the time. Avarice, ignorance, and greed will outweigh logic and careful study about 15 percent of the time. *Phil Smith, Alameda, California*

2164 ... **LOOKING AT FROZEN FOOD**   On a package of frozen food, if it takes longer to read the ingredients than to cook it in a microwave, choose another product. *Susanna Levin, assistant editor, New Age Journal*

2165 ... **EATING LIKE A THIN PERSON**   Before you eat, ask yourself how hungry you are on a scale from 1 to 10 — 1 representing a growling stomach and 10 representing the stuffed, bloated, I-think-I'm-going-to-die-feeling often experienced after Thanksgiving dinner. Eat only when you rate your hunger a 1 or 2. Then stop when you reach 5. *Evette M. Hackman, RD, PhD, consulting nutritionist, BHIHRI*

2166 ... **THE FLUE AREA FIREPLACE RULE**   The flue area of a fireplace should be equal to or slightly greater than one-tenth of the area of the fireplace opening. *Stephen Gibian, architect and stonemason, Ithaca, New York*

2167 ... **FOLLOWING SPRING NORTH**   Spring moves north about 13 miles a day. *Jon Reis, photographer, Ithaca, New York*

2168 ... **MAKING A NEW AIRLINE RESERVATION**   If your flight is canceled, you'll get a new reservation twice as fast if you phone the airline rather than wait in line. *Alex Fraser, Washington, D.C.*

2169 ... **HITCHING A RIDE**   If you're hitchhiking a great distance, don't use a sign announcing your destination. Instead, use signs giving the direction you're going, such as "North," South," "East," or "West." *Gerry M. Flick, M.D., Ship's Surgeon, S.S. Constitution off Hawaii*

2170 ... **TESTING YOUR SEX DRIVE**   Your sex drive is inversely proportional to the sensitivity of your funny-bone. *Bob Cornett, photographer, New York City*

2171 ... **STREAM FISHING FOR TROUT**   Trout do most of their surface feeding in the upstream third of a pool. *Sheridan Anderson, author, The Curtis Creek Manifesto*

2172 ... **MAKING A SERVING DISH**   To make a ceramic serving dish, casserole, or bean pot, use one pound of clay for each person you want the pot to serve. For example, five pounds of clay will make a dish that will serve five people, with second helpings for some. *Jim Dunn, potter, Belews Creek, North Carolina*

2173 ... ***THE CAMPAIGN RULE*** If more than 40 percent of the likely voters have a favorable impression of an incumbent six months before an election, then he or she is probably unbeatable. *Tom Wilbur, county commissioner, East Lansing, Michigan*

2174 ... ***DR. BLOOR'S FRESH EGG PROPORTIONS RULE*** As an egg ages, the central part of the white lowers and the outer part of the white broadens. *John H. Bloor, M.D., Ph.D., Buffalo, New York*

2175 ... ***CONTROLLING STUDENTS*** Students tend to be most unruly on Fridays with a full moon. *Steven M. Keisman, New York City high school resource coordinator*

2176 ... ***TAPPING MAPLE TREES FOR SAP*** Wind north to west, the flow is best; wind south to east, the flow is least. *Karen Spaulding, Concord, New Hampshire*

2177 ... ***THE RICE RULE*** Peasants carrying supplies for a Chinese army will eat one-third of the rice, regardless of the distance. *Norman Brenner, Fleetwood, New York*

2178 ... ***THE HAT BILL FLY BALL RULE*** If you play center field, wear a billed cap and keep your head level. Go in on any ball that is hit so that it never disappears over the top of the bill; go out on any ball that disappears over the bill. If the ball is hit high and shallow, you will have time to recover. *Henning Pape-Santos, linguist, Ithaca, New York*

2179 ... ***DIRECTING A PLAY*** Once you decide to direct a play, everything you see will relate to it. *Suzy Willhoft, drama teacher, Arlington, Virginia*

2180 ... ***AVOIDING FOOD POISONING*** Beware of food kept warm for more than two hours, because most steam tables and chafing dishes aren't hot enough to prevent food poisoning. *Anonymous*

2181 ... ***RUNNING A RACE*** Three times the average distance you run every day is close to the maximum distance you should run in a race. *Jeff Furman, Ben & Jerry's Ice Cream, business consultant*

2182 ... ***COUNTING FOSSILS*** In a faunal list based on fossil evidence, large animals will be greatly overrepresented. In contrast, a floral list based on fossil evidence will overrepresent smaller plants. *John J. Chiment, paleobiologist and editor, Perry City, New York*

2183 ... ***GETTING ORGANIZED*** Don't store anything in the way of retrieving something else. *Nils Oliver, cellist, Los Angeles, California*

2184 ... ***COOKING A STEAK*** If you want a medium-rare steak, it should be as firm as the puffy area between your thumb and your index finger. If you want your steak rarer, it should be softer; more done, harder. *J. Harb, sous-chef, Restaurant La Residence, Chapel Hill, North Carolina*

SALES

2185 ... *THE SALE COST RULE* Regardless of the business, about one in three sales calls is to a new customer, and considering all costs — salaries, commissions, benefits, travels, advertising, and follow-up calls — it costs about $1,500 to close a sale. *Elisabeth Colford, Cahners Publishing Company, Des Plaines, Illinois*

MONEY

2186 ... *REFINANCING A HOME* Homeowners should explore refinancing their homes if market rates drop two or three percentage points below their mortgage rate. *David Lane, Lincoln, Nebraska*

STOCK

2187 ... *THE RULE OF CONTRARY INVESTING* In the stock market, whatever the crowd does, do the opposite. *Lou Aleksich Jr., Billings, Montana*

COOKING

2188 ... *MARTIN'S RULE OF MOVING FOOD* Transportation costs are 60 percent of the price of food. *Edward Martin, Davenport, Iowa*

DIETING

2189 ... *CHECKING YOUR WEIGHT* A man who is 5 feet tall should weigh 106 pounds. If taller, add 6 pounds for every inch of height. For example, a man who's 5 feet 10 inches tall should weigh 166 pounds. A woman who's 5 feet tall should weigh 105 pounds. If taller, add 5 pounds for every inch of height. *Dr. Richard Freeman, vice chairman of medicine, University of Wisconsin in Madison, in USA Today*

FARMING

2190 ... *GRINDING WHEAT* One pound of wheat will make about three cups of flour. *Ronald MacInerney, Duluth, Minnesota*

WEATHER

2191 ... *FINDING A LOW-PRESSURE SYSTEM* To determine the approximate direction of the center of a low-pressure system, stand with your back to the wind and your arm extended sideways. If you move your arm forward about 45 degrees, you will be pointing to the center of the low. If a low-pressure system is to the west of you, it often means you are in for poor weather. *Stephen Friends, meteorologist*

TRAVEL

2192 ... *STAYING IN A HOTEL* A hotel that cares about its customers will have a red message light on the telephones. *Bob Greene, author*

HITCHHIKING

2193 ... *PICKING UP HITCHHIKERS* If a second person emerges from behind a tree or sign as you stop, keep going. And always have a hitchhiker sit in the front seat, never behind you. *John H. Beauvais, Cambridge, Massachusetts*

RELATIONSHIPS

2194 ... *DOING THERAPY WITH FRIENDS* Let your friend be a client and you'll end up with neither. *Jeffrey A. Schaler, gestalt therapist, Silver Spring, Maryland*

FISH

2195 ... *STOCKING A TROUT POND* A healthy trout pond should be stocked with 300 fingerling trout per acre per year. *Cornell University*

CRAFTS

2196 ... *DESIGNING A POTTERY KILN* For every foot of horizontal flue in a kiln, you need two extra feet of chimney to maintain a proper draft. *Daniel Rhodes, professor of ceramic art, Alfred University*

2197 ... **DETERMINING THE ORIGIN OF A MAP** You can tell where a map of the world was made by seeing which country is smack dab in the middle. *Adham Loutfi, Oakland, California*

2198 ... **THE BROWN TROUT RULE OF 50** At a constant water temperature of 50 degree F, brown trout eggs will hatch in 50 days. *Larry Beck, fisherman, Ludlowville, New York*

2199 ... **TIMING YOUR LESSONS** The most successful teaching lessons last 22 minutes, the exact length of the average TV sit-com. *Steven M. Keisman, New York City high school resource coordinator*

2200 ... **MAKING MAPLE SYRUP** It takes about 100 maple trees to make 25 gallons of syrup. *Stephen Pitkin, maple syrup maker*

2201 ... **MAKING AN ATOMIC BOMB** You need 15 pounds of plutonium to make one atomic bomb. *William Hill, soda vendor, Riverfront Stadium, Cincinnati*

2202 ... **CHIPPING THE BALL** In golf, to make your chipping iron shots rise, hit down on the ball. *Tom Robinson, computer programmer, Berkeley, California*

2203 ... **STARTING A SHOW** The opening curtain of a play will rise seven to ten minutes after the announced time—later in bad weather. Movies, on the other hand, start precisely on time. *Kelly Yeaton, teacher and stage manager, State College, Pennsylvania*

2204 ... **RUNNING A RESTAURANT** For fast-food restaurants, the drive-through accounts for 50 percent of sales. *Anonymous*

2205 ... **RUNNING A RACE** You won't have endurance for a race longer than one-third of your average weekly training mileage. *Tom Werner, management consultant, Athens, Georgia*

2206 ... **RESPONDING TO STIMULI** Law of Stimulus: The perception of stimulus intensity increases linearly when the actual stimulus increases logarithmically. *John J. Chiment, paleobiologist and editor, Perry City, New York*

2207 ... **ESTIMATING HOW MANY FILING CABINETS YOU NEED** To estimate the number of filing cabinets you need, consider that 1 file drawer holds 2,500 pages. The average document has 2.5 pages. That means you need 1 file drawer for every 1,000 documents. *Anonymous*

2208 ... **TESTING THE TEXTURE OF DIRT** You can decide whether to disk harrow a field or not by balling up some dirt, holding it with both hands at arm's length, and dropping it. If the dirtball doesn't break, it is too wet to disk. *Peter van Berkum, Kittery Point, Maine*

AS A RULE OF THUMB:
YOU HAVE ENOUGH MILK IN THE BOWL WHEN THE EDGE OF YOUR PILE OF CHEERIOS FIRST STARTS TO MOVE.
MIKE RAMBO, PHOTOGRAPHER, ITHACA, NEW YORK

SALES

2209 ... *SELLING AND TALKING* The sale is made while the customer is talking. *David Lyon, writer and advertising authority, Westport, Connecticut*

MONEY

2210 ... *THE TELLER RULE* The average bank teller loses about $240 a year. *Scott Parker, data specialist, Beaumont, Texas, quoting The Wall Street Journal*

STOCK

2211 ... *HOLDING AN ODD INVESTMENT* You should be willing to hold an odd investment like stamps or coins for three to five years. *Michael Weinstein, The Gold and Silver Galleries, Ithaca, New York*

COOKING

2212 ... *POPPING CORN* You should get 34 cups of popcorn from a cup of kernels. Top-quality kernels will give you an extra 10 cups. *John O'Rourke, contributing editor, Let's Live*

DIETING

2213 ... *MANAGING YOUR WEIGHT AND YOUR WARDROBE* Your weight should vary to the extent that your wardrobe can handle it. *sunny bat-or, star of Fit, Fat, & Fabulous, Ithaca, New York*

FARMING

2214 ... *SNAKEHOLING A BOULDER* You can blow up a boulder by digging underneath it and putting dynamite in the hole, a practice known as snakeholing. Use two sticks of dynamite for every foot of rock thickness. *Joe Kaiser, Covington, Kentucky*

WEATHER

2215 ... *FORECASTING THE WEATHER* When first-graders get disruptive as a class, there's going to be a major change in weather. *Lin Spaeth, first-grade teacher*

TRAVEL

2216 ... *STAYING IN A HOTEL* The most important part of your hotel room is the bathroom. No matter how nice your bedroom, if the bathroom is bad, it can ruin your trip. *Bob Greene, author*

HITCHHIKING

2217 ... *HITCHHIKING IN MISSISSIPPI* In Mississippi, a man hitchhiking alone will be passed by about 200 cars before 1 will stop. Having a woman companion or wearing a military uniform will cut the wait by more than half; being accompanied by another man or a dog will double or triple it. *Pierce Butler, Natchez, Mississippi*

RELATIONSHIPS

2218 ... *THE SEX IN THE CLASSROOM RULE* A computer science class will be about one-third female. A math class will be about one-tenth female. *Janet Blumer, math grad student, Denver, Colorado*

FISH

2219 ... *FISHING WITH A BAROMETER* The lower the barometer, the better the fishing. *Charles Vanderpool, Chattanooga, Tennessee*

CRAFTS

2220 ... *UPHOLSTERING A SOFA* It takes between 10 and 12 yards of fabric to reupholster a full-size sofa. *Phil Tomlinson, builder*

AS A RULE OF THUMB: YOU NEED ONE ROBOTICS TECHNICIAN FOR EVERY FOUR INDUSTRIAL ROBOTS. *C*HARLES *S*TOEHR, *R*OBOTICS *T*ECHNICIAN, *C*INCINNATI, *O*HIO

2221 ... **THE CANVASS RULE**   When you are canvassing door-to-door, you can optimize your "time per voter" by spending no more than 20 to 30 seconds with each person you meet. Most people will decide whether they like you within that time, and most will want to get back to whatever they were doing when you interrupted them. You should, however, take time to discuss issues with the interested persons.   *Tom Wilbur, county commissioner, East Lansing, Michigan*

2222 ... **PAINTING YOUR CHICKEN COOP**   If you paint the inside of your chicken coop orange, your chickens will lay more eggs.   *Diana Souza, illustrator, Ithaca, New York*

2223 ... **UNDERSTANDING AN UNRULY STUDENT**   The first thing to check about a disruptive elementary student is his or her eyesight.   *Steven M. Keisman, New York City high school resource coordinator*

2224 ... **BOILING DOWN MAPLE SAP**   It takes a cord of wood to boil down 1,000 gallons of maple syrup.   *Stephen Pitkin, maple syrup maker*

2225 ... **NORMAN'S RULE OF MILITARY MORALE**   Morale is to material as 3 is to 1.
Norman Brenner, Fleetwood, New York

2226 ... **GETTING TO THE GREEN**   To hit a ball to the green, first decide which club will hit it to the green with your best swing, then swallow your pride and use the next longest club and a more relaxed swing (instead of a 5-iron use a 4-iron). You'll be on the green far more often than you'll be over it. The ball will fly straighter too.   *Michael D. Miles, Aloha, Oregon*

2227 ... **TIMING A SCRIPT**   It takes 1 1/2 to 2 minutes to perform the average page of script. A 70-page script is about right for most plays.   *Kelly Yeaton, teacher and stage manager, State College, Pennsylvania*

2228 ... **EATING AT A VEGETARIAN RESTAURANT**   Don't order anything at a vegetarian restaurant that would have meat in it if served elsewhere.   *Steve Carver, illustrator, Ithaca, New York*

2229 ... **RUNNING A RACE**   Watch your pace closely for the first half of a race and try not to cut more than five seconds per mile off the pace you hope to run. Every second more than five you cut from your mile pace in the first half of a race will cost you one to two seconds per mile in the second half of the race.   *Jim Crissman, veterinary pathologist, Midland, Michigan*

2230 ... **USING SOMEONE'S PHONE**   If you know someone well enough to use their toilet without asking, then you can also use their phone for a local call.   *Peter Thudgill, author*

2231 ... **PLANNING A PARKING LOT**   If you are designing a parking lot, plan on 300 square feet per vehicle.   *Dirck Z. Meengs, management consultant, Canoga Park, California*

2232 ... **TESTING FOUNDRY SAND**   You can test a sample of foundry sand for casting by scooping up a handful and squeezing it in the palm of your hand. The sample should make a good clean impression of your fingers and be firm enough to break without crumbling.   *Howard Spencer, Elmira, New York*

SALES

2233 ...RUNNING A BOOTH AT A TRADE SHOW An industrious salesperson working a booth at a trade show should be able to chat briefly with about 100 people per day. Ten percent of those people are likely to be good leads. *Allen Konopacki, president of Incomm International, in Business Week*

MONEY

2234 ...TRACKING A PAYROLL Every dollar of a paycheck turns over seven times in the local economy. *Scott Parker, data specialist, Beaumont, Texas*

STOCK

2235 ...THE VENTURE CAPITAL INVESTMENT RULE Only one out of ten enterprises that a venture capitalist invests in will pay off — and it must pay for the losses on the other nine. *Walter Pitkin, literary agent, Weston, Connecticut, quoting Adam Smith, investment counselor*

COOKING

2236 ...WATCHING YOUR HOTDOGS Discard hotdogs when the liquid in the package becomes cloudy. *Zak Mettgar, writer and vegetarian, Washington, D.C.*

DIETING

2237 ...DIETING FOR DOLLARS Fat corporate executives earn less money. Each pound you are overweight costs you about $1,000 a year in salary. *Dr. Albert Stunkard, psychiatrist and obesity expert, quoted in The Syracuse Post Standard*

FARMING

2238 ...RAISING CORN You can expect to produce about 18 tons of corn silage per acre per year. *George Shepard, farm help, Rochester, New York*

WEATHER

2239 ...FOLLOWING AIR MASSES Air masses travel about 750 miles per day (slower in summer, faster in winter). *Eric Sloane, artist and writer*

TRAVEL

2240 ...THE FOOD TRAVEL RULE Never travel for food. *Bob Greene, author*

2241 ...THE HITCHHIKING WITH BOOKS RULE Each textbook you carry while hitchhiking reduces your wait by five minutes. *Tim Hoff, 20th century bureaucrat, APO New York*

HITCHHIKING

2242 ...GETTING EMOTIONALLY INVOLVED Wait at least a year after a divorce before becoming emotionally committed to someone else. Some psychologists say that a person needs one year to resolve a divorce for every five years of marriage. *Corinne Abbott, Manitou Springs, Colorado*

RELATIONSHIPS

2243 ...TAKING FISH FROM YOUR POND Bluegills will overrun your bass if you don't keep the population in balance. Take out 15 times as many bluegills as bass. By weight, take out 2 or 3 pounds of bluegill for every pound of bass. *Cornell University*

FISH

2244 ...LYNN FELLOWS' PENCIL TEST Before throwing a pot on a potter's wheel, test your clay for plasticity. Wrap a pencil-sized stick of clay around your index finger. If the sample breaks or cracks in a number of places, it will not throw well. *Lynn Fellows, potter*

CRAFTS

AS A RULE OF THUMB: AN EXPERT IS SOMEONE WHO TELLS YOU THAT SOMETHING THAT LOOKS EASY IS IMPOSSIBLE AND SOMETHING THAT LOOKS IMPOSSIBLE IS EASY.
LEONARD MORGENSTERN, PATHOLOGIST, MORAGA, CALIFORNIA

2245 ... **POLITICAL CAMPAIGNS**   Candidates with strong, aggressive personalities and "programs" to sell get elected half as often and last half as long as accommodating, compromising candidates who are interesting persons and want to provide "constituent services." *Tom Wilbur, county commissioner, East Lansing, Michigan*

POLITICS

2246 ... **CHECKING AN EGG**   When placed in a bowl of water, a fresh egg will sink and lie on its side. An egg that's not fresh but still edible will sink and stand partially erect on its tapered end. A rotten egg will float. *David Hechler, writer, Rockport, Texas*

EGGS

2247 ... **TEACHING IN THE U.S.A.**   The farther a teacher's homeland is from the U.S.A., the more likely he will teach calculus. *Dean Sheridan, electronics technician and deaf actor, Torrance, California*

JOKER

2248 ... **BOILING DOWN MAPLE SAP**   It takes about 40 gallons of maple sap to make a gallon of maple syrup. *Rick Eckstrom, plan review officer, Ithaca, New York*

MAPLE SYRUP

2249 ... **SPOTTING AN ENEMY**   The first time is happenstance, the second time coincidence, the third time is enemy action. *Norman Brenner, Fleetwood, New York*

MILITARY

2250 ... **FINDING YOUR IDEAL WEIGHT**   An ideal weight for an endurance athlete, in pounds, is twice his height in inches. *Ned Frederick, writer, Exeter, New Hampshire*

SPORTS

2251 ... **UPSTAGING SOMEONE**   The more another performer is upstaging you, the fewer moves you should make. The audience is more fascinated with the leaning palm tree than the hurricane. *Dean Sheridan, electronics technician and deaf actor, Torrance, California*

THEATER

2252 ... **THE POLYNESIAN COCKTAIL RULE**   A Chinese restaurant that features Polynesian cocktails is unlikely to use authentic seasonings. *Bruce Reznick, associate professor of mathematics, Urbana, Illinois*

RESTAURANTS

2253 ... **JOGGING**   Jogging is difficult and painful the first six weeks, hard work for the next six weeks, and as easy as walking from then on. *Dr. Larry R. Hunt, Toronto, Ontario*

RUNNING

2254 ... **GETTING PUT ON HOLD**   If you get put on hold for more than 90 seconds, hang up and call back, saying you think you were disconnected. Your second call usually will go right through. *Steven M. Keisman, New York City high school resource coordinator*

TELEPHONES

2255 ... **SHOPPING FOR PARKING**   A shopping mall should have 5.5 parking spaces for every 1,000 square feet of gross leasable area. *Darryl Thomas, Rochester, New York*

STORAGE

2256 ... **TESTING WET SAND FOR CEMENT**   You can test the water content of sand by squeezing it into a ball with your fist. If it feels wet but won't form a ball, it contains about one-quarter of a gallon of water per cubic foot. If it will form a ball without soaking your hands, it has about half a gallon of water per cubic foot. Very wet sand is dripping wet and holds about three-quarters of a gallon of water per cubic foot. *Bob Syvanen, concrete expert*

TEXTURE

SALES

2257 ...**WORKING WITH PURCHASING AGENTS**   Most firms change 20 percent to 25 percent of their suppliers every year. *Scott Parker, data specialist, Beaumont, Texas*

MONEY

2258 ...**KAHN'S BANKING RULE FOR SMALL BUSINESSES**   Consider a new bank if the one you now use changes your loan officer and the new officer doesn't visit you within 30 days. You should also consider a switch if they change your loan officer twice in one year.   *Robert Kahn, editor, Retailing Today*

STOCK

2259 ...**DECIDING IF IT'S INSIDER TRADING**   If an investor even suspects that a stock tip is based on insider information and that the stock price would be affected if the public knew about it, it probably is illegal for him to trade in the stock.   *Gary Lynch, director of enforcement at the Securities and Exchange Commission, in The New York Times*

COOKING

2260 ...**MAINTAINING YOUR WEIGHT**   To calculate the calories you need to maintain your weight, multiply your weight by ten. *Dr. Robin Kanarek, in Tufts University Diet & Nutrition Letter*

DIETING

2261 ...**THE COOK HAMMER RULE**   Properly dried peas and corn should shatter when hit with a hammer. *Betsy Cook, composer, Buckinhamshire, England*

FARMING

2262 ...**CHECKING YOUR FIELDS FOR DRAINAGE**   Watch your fields as the snow melts in the spring. Poorly drained areas will green up first. *Martin Stillwell, farmer*

WEATHER

2263 ...**THE PEEPER RULE OF THREE**   Don't count on spring until you've heard the peepers in full voice for three consecutive nights. *James McConkey, writer, Trumansburg, New York*

TRAVEL

2264 ...**AVOIDING A FOREIGN JAIL**   If the water and food in a country are suspect, take similar precautions with the law. *Anonymous, quoting an article in Insight*

HITCHHIKING

2265 ...**HITCHHIKING NEAR SIGNS**   The more graffiti on the back of a road sign, the harder it will be to hitch a ride standing next to it. *John Gize, reprobate, Calgary, Alberta*

RELATIONSHIPS

2266 ...**CHANGING YOUR SEX**   A sex change operation will age you five years. *A. A. Kennerly, New York City*

FISH

2267 ...**CATCHING FISH**   Wind from the west, fishing is best; wind from the east, fishing is least. *J. J. Everhart, retired, Spartanburg, South Carolina*

CRAFTS

2268 ...**MAKING CLOTHES**   Always sew the seams on a garment from the hem up. *Madeleine Yardley, art teacher, Worcester, Massachusetts*

AS A RULE OF THUMB: THE VALUE OF THE GIFTS YOU RECEIVE AT A WEDDING WILL BE NO MORE THAN ONE-THIRD THE COST OF STAGING THE EVENT.
WARREN HARRIS, SACRAMENTO, CALIFORNIA

2269 ... THE CAMPAIGN INVOLVEMENT RULE For every person who gets involved in your campaign by contributing money, putting up a lawn sign, distributing literature, or signing an endorsement letter, expect 10 to 15 votes on election day. *Tom Wilbur, county commissioner, East Lansing, Michigan*

2270 ... THE DISGUSTING RULE OF HEN CHECKING You can tell whether a hen is laying eggs or not by sizing her cloaca with your fingers. If one finger fits in her cloaca, she's not laying; if two fingers fit, she might be; if three fingers fit, she's laying for sure. *Peter van Berkum, Kittery Point, Maine*

2271 ... THE HANDWRITING RULE OF AFFECTION A woman who makes large long loops in her y's and g's is highly affectionate and responsive. *L.M. Boyd, The San Francisco Chronicle*

2272 ... MAKING MAPLE SYRUP Obviously, the amount of syrup you get depends on the number of taps you put into trees. You can plan on one quart of finished syrup per tap per season. *Cally Arthur, managing editor, American Demographics*

2273 ... WINNING A WAR To carry out an amphibious assault, you need a five to one superiority. *Dave Chapman, computer consultant, Forestville, California*

2274 ... BRINGING IN THE INFIELD Here's an old baseball rule: When you bring in the infield, you make a .400 hitter out of a .200 hitter. *Henning Pape-Santos, linguist, Ithaca, New York*

2275 ... DESIGNING A STAGE SET Check your design for a stage set by squinting your eyes If any prop or color pops out, tone it down. *Dean Sheridan, electronics technician and deaf actor, Torrance, California*

2276 ... THE DINING-OUT RULE The total meal will cost about two times the price of the entrees. *Richard Patching, acoustician, Calgary, Alberta*

2277 ... RUNNING A RACE Five percent of your total training mileage in the last eight weeks before a race equals your personal breaking point in a race. *Jeff Furman, Ben & Jerry's Ice Cream, business consultant*

2278 ... GETTING SOMEONE TO CALL BACK If you call someone and they aren't available, always leave a time limit for them to get back to you. Even if they don't know you, they will feel obligated to call by that time. *Steven M. Keisman, New York City high school resource coordinator*

2279 ... THE PERDUE CHICKEN RULE You need to provide 3/4 of a square foot of space per chicken. *Henning Pape-Santos, linguist, Ithaca, New York*

2280 ... TESTING A BONE FOR FOSSILIZATION It's a fossil only if it's heavy and solid. *Scott Parker, data specialist, Beaumont, Texas*

SALES

2281 ... _BOYD'S RULE OF STRAWBERRY SHORTCAKE_ Rectangular servings of strawberry shortcake sell better than round servings. *L. M. Boyd, The San Francisco Chronicle*

MONEY

2282 ... _TICHNOR'S RULE FOR ESTIMATING YOUR SALARY_ To estimate a yearly salary from an hourly wage, double the wage and change the decimal point to a comma. Thus, $3 per hour becomes $6,000 per year. This figure is about 4 percent low, but with taxes the way they are, it doesn't make much difference. *Don Tichnor, farmer*

STOCK

2283 ... _MAKING A SPECULATIVE INVESTMENT_ Speculative investments, such as silver, should never exceed 10 percent of your investment portfolio. *Merrie Spaeth, USA Weekend*

COOKING

2284 ... _THE NED BOUNDS MASHED POTATO FACTOR_ People will eat one and a half to two times the number of potatoes mashed that they would eat baked. *Ned Bounds, sawyer, Salmon, Idaho*

DIETING

2285 ... _CHARBONEAU'S WEIGHT MAINTENANCE RULE_ You can estimate the approximate number of calories it takes to maintain your weight by multiplying your current weight by 15. To lose or gain weight, alter your calorie intake by 20 percent in the desired direction. *F. Jill Charboneau, publisher, American Demographics*

FARMING

2286 ... _PLANNING A POND_ In most of the eastern United States, you'll need a five-acre watershed to supply a one-acre pond fed entirely by run-off water. *G. Hickey, heavy equipment operator*

WEATHER

2287 ... _FORECASTING THE WEATHER_ If birds and bats are flying close to the ground, a storm is approaching. *Dennis Palaganas, Gainesville, Florida*

TRAVEL

2288 ... _PLANNING A SUBWAY TRIP_ You can plan how long most subway trips will take by multiplying the total number of stops by two minutes and adding five minutes for every time you change trains. *Adam Meyers, Manhattan*

HITCHHIKING

2289 ... _HITCHHIKING_ When you're hitchhiking, look like who you want to pick you up. *Stewart Brand, publisher, The CoEvolution Quarterly*

RELATIONSHIPS

2290 ... _MEETING WOMEN_ Under ideal circumstances, a man will seek a woman half his age plus seven years. *Elaine Renner, Ithaca, New York*

FISH

2291 ... _CATCHING FISH_ A wind from the south blows a hook in the mouth. *Chet Meyers and Al Lindner, fishing experts*

CRAFTS

2292 ... _KNITTING_ Allow one inch of yarn for every stitch you want to cast on your needle. *M. N., Enterprise, Oregon*

2293 ... **THE WALLACE RULE OF POLITICAL LOSS** While money doesn't guarantee a victory, the lack of money guarantees a loss. *Neil Wallace, unsuccessful congressional campaigner*

POLITICS

2294 ... **BUYING EGGS** If the difference in price between medium and large eggs is less than eight cents per dozen, the large eggs are a better deal. *Janet Salmons, home economist*

EGGS

2295 ... **LOOKING AT HANDWRITING** Handwriting that contains a haphazard mix of capital and lower-case letters was most likely written by a man. *Sarah Padula, teacher and pilot, Freeville, New York*

HANDWRITING

2296 ... **USING DYNAMITE** Wait at least an hour before investigating a charge of dynamite that didn't go off. *Joe Kaiser, Covington, Kentucky*

JOKER

2297 ... **DODGING BULLETS** If you hear the shot, it won't kill you. *Gene Wolfe, Barrington, Illinois*

MILITARY

2298 ... **PUTTING A SHOT** When you're throwing a shot put, release it at an angle of 40 to 43 degrees to get maximum distance. As the distance you throw increases, so should the angle. *David Dawson, student, University of Texas, Austin, Texas*

SPORTS

2299 ... **WATCHING PISTOLS IN PLAYS** If there is a pistol on the wall in the first act, it will be fired by the third act. *Bob Larson, Stuttgart, Germany, quoting Anton Chekov*

THEATER

2300 ... **LEAVING A TIP** Tip the waiter 20 percent of the bill minus 2 percent for each instance of poor service (minus 5 percent for anything spilled on you). *Paul Egert, South Plainfield, New Jersey*

RESTAURANTS

2301 ... **RUNNING A MARATHON** You should be able to run 50 miles per week on a regular basis before you try running a marathon. *Jeff Furman, Ben & Jerry's Ice Cream, business consultant*

RUNNING

2302 ... **SPOTTING A SALES PITCH** Any telephone call that starts with, "How are you this evening, Ms.—" is from a telemarketer. You should hang up immediately. *Jeff Brown, astronomer, Bloomington, Indiana*

TELEPHONES

2303 ... **COUNTING SHOES** Most people will have twice the number of pairs of shoes in their closets that they will guess they have. *Gail Smith, parts unknown*

STORAGE

2304 ... **ESTIMATING THE VOLUME OF GARBAGE** On average, each person throws away one automobile tire a year. *Anonymous*

WASTES

SALES

2305 ... **SELLING THINGS DOOR-TO-DOOR**   After knocking, stand at least four feet back from the door. *Benjamin Snyder, Bible salesman*

MONEY

2306 ... **SAVING MONEY**   You should have six months' salary in savings for emergencies. *Bob Horton, statistics consultant, West Lafayette, Indiana*

STOCK

2307 ... **PERUSING A STOCK OFFERING**   For a young company going public that hasn't produced much in the way of earnings, look at the ratio of its total offering price to its annual sales. This market-capitalization-to-sales ratio generally exceeds 2.7. *Francine Schwadel, staff reporter, quoting various experts in The Wall Street Journal*

COOKING

2308 ... **THE CHEESE THICKNESS FLAVOR RULE**   The quality of the flavor of cheese is inversely proportional to the thickness of the slice. *Jas. C. O'Neill, Baraboo, Wisconsin*

DIETING

2309 ... **LOSING WEIGHT**   A woman should not diet below an intake of 1,200 calories a day; a man, below 1,600 calories. *Jean Mayer, nutritionist, and Jean Goldberg, journalist*

FARMING

2310 ... **GROWING HEAT**   One-eighth of an acre, an area about 50 by 100 feet, will grow enough wheat for an average homesteading family. For this, you will need to plant about 15 pounds of seed. *Richard Bacon, writer and historian*

JOKER

2311 ... **SAILING IN HEAVY SEAS**   On a cruising sailboat in wind conditions that are increasing, canvas should be reduced the first time it seems like a good idea. *Michael Spencer, lawyer, San Francisco, California*

TRAVEL

2312 ... **CHOOSING A TRAIN ON WEEKENDS**   Take the local, not the express, on weekends if it is in the station and you're headed for a local station. If you wait for the express, you'll end up on the same local you skipped earlier. *Jim and Marilyn Ranish, Manhattan*

JOKER

2313 ... **JEAN'S WHITE CAR RULE**   The drivers of white cars are jerks. This could be a California problem. *Jean Lee Mahakian, Novato, California*

RELATIONSHIPS

2314 ... **THE THINGS THAT BITE RULE**   As a matter of biology rather than sexism, if something bites you, it is probably female. *Scott M. Kruse, biogeographer, Fresno, California*

FISH

2315 ... **FISHING FOR TROUT**   If you can see the fish, the fish can see you. *Grant Wootton, fly-fishing pundit*

CRAFTS

2316 ... **GLAZING POTTERY**   Dividing a pot in half with a glaze makes it weaker visually. *Corinne Abbott, Manitou Springs, Colorado*

AS A RULE OF THUMB:
YOU SHOULD NEVER
ORDER A BAKED POTATO
NEAR CLOSING TIME.
CHERYL A. BAUDENDISTLE,
ADMINISTRATOR, CORNELL
UNIVERSITY, ITHACA, NEW YORK

2317 ... *POLITICAL ELECTIONS* The better the weather on election day, the better it is for Democrats. *Michael Rider, art director, American Demographics*

POLITICS

2318 ... *THE HAYWARD SMALL EGG RULE* Seven quail eggs equal one chicken egg. *Terry Hayward, medical technician*

EGGS

2319 ... *SPOTTING A LEFT-HANDER* If you can spot even one right-to-left stroke in a handwriting sample, it was almost certainly written with the left hand. This does not apply to writing that reads right-to-left, such as Hebrew. *Kate Gladstone, Brooklyn, New York*

HANDWRITING

2320 ... *LOOKING AT LEAVES* Leaves appear light if you face them with the wind at your back, and dark if you face them from downwind. *Walter Pitkin, literary agent, Weston, Connecticut*

TREES

2321 ... *ESTIMATING DISTANCE TO GUNFIRE* As soon as you see the flash of a gunshot, count rapidly from one to ten — repeating the count if necessary — until you hear the report. Each number you count represents 100 yards. *Frank Turley, director, Turley Forge Blacksmithing School, Santa Fe, New Mexico*

MILITARY

2322 ... *DRESSING FOR A SKI* When cross-country skiing, if you are warm when you first walk outside, you're wearing too much. *Jeremy Bishop, windsurfing expert, Hood River, Oregon*

SPORTS

2323 ... *THE MEMORY RULE* Snapshots encourage memories, videos replace them. After watching a video of your vacation, your memory of the vacation will be the video. *Cheryl A. Russell, demographer, mother, editor-in-chief, American Demographics*

JOKER

2324 ... *PRICING A NIGHT CLUB* In a bar or night club, when the lights go down, the prices go up. *Lori Edwards, Frederick, Maryland*

RESTAURANTS

2325 ... *BUYING RUNNING SHOES* To decide how many dollars you should spend on a pair of running shoes, take the number of miles you run each week and multiply it by two. *Diane Gerhart, accountant*

RUNNING

2326 ... *USING THE TELEPHONE* When ordering something over the phone, ask for the order-taker's full name. Then he or she won't make a mistake with your order. *Jennifer Evans, writer, Austin, Texas*

TELEPHONES

2327 ... *STORING DOCUMENTS* Every ten degrees you lower the temperature of stored documents will double their life. *Jan Rich, journalist, Austin, Texas*

STORAGE

2328 ... *CLEANING UP ROADSIDE LITTER* When a state passes a bottle bill, paper and plastic litter disappears from roadsides and parks in the same proportion that beverage bottles and cans do — which is almost totally. *Isabel T. Coburn, authority at large, Pemaquid Beach, Maine*

WASTES

SALES

2329 ... **THE SALES RULE OF 80-20**   Salespeople should talk only 20 percent of the time during their first visit with a potential customer and listen the other 80 percent. During later visits, the salespeople should do most of the talking to sell the benefits of their products. *Andrew Keaton, national sales manager, The Dietzgen Corporation*

MONEY

2330 ... **THE INDICATORS RULE**   Anytime the index of leading economic indicators moves in the same direction two months in a row, it means the economy will move that way in a few months. *Philip Greer, "When Do Indicators Stop Indicating?"*

STOCK

2331 ... **PERUSING A STOCK OFFERING**   Established companies generally go public for $10 a share or more. An offering price of less than $1 a share signals an extraordinary amount of risk, while a price of $1 to $5 a share means the issue is very speculative. *Francine Schwadel, staff reporter, quoting various experts in The Wall Street Journal*

COOKING

2332 ... **LOOKING FOR MUSHROOMS**   Look for morel mushrooms when the apple trees are blooming. *John Schubert, senior editor, Bicycling magazine*

DIETING

2333 ... **EATING MEALS**   Don't eat your largest meal at supper when your body needs it least. As a rule, you should eat breakfast like a king, lunch like a prince, and supper like a pauper. *Jane Brody, nutrition columnist, The New York Times*

FARMING

2334 ... **PLANTING CORN**   You need five pounds of corn seed to plan an acre of corn. *Peter van Berkum, Kittery Point, Maine*

WIND

2335 ... **STAYING DRY**   Most of the time, it's too windy to use an umbrella for more than five city blocks. Wear a hat to keep the rain off your head. *Steven M. Keisman, New York City high school resource coordinator*

TRAVEL

2336 ... **CHOOSING A SUBWAY TRAIN**   If there are two trains in a station, take the one that was moving most recently. *Alan Breznick, reporter, Manhattan*

PERSONALITIES

2337 ... **BRUCE'S SUBWAY RULE**   In any full subway car in any major city, there will be one ambulatory schizophrenic. *Martin M. Bruce, Ph.D., psychologist, Larchmont, New York*

JOKER

2338 ... **MAKING DECISIONS**   Never make a decision with a full bladder. *Mark Staneart, bureaucrat, Grass Valley, California*

FISH

2339 ... **THE CAST RULE**   The first cast is critical; your chances of catching a fish diminish with each cast. *Sheridan Anderson, author, The Curtis Creek Manifesto*

CRAFTS

2340 ... **MEASURING MACRAME'**   To estimate the length of each strand of cord in a piece of macramé, multiply the length of the finished piece by eight. *Ned Bounds, sawyer, Salmon, Idaho*

AS A RULE OF THUMB: THE OTHER LANE WILL ALWAYS LOOK SMOOTHER, WHEN DRIVING ON A TWO-LANE DIRT ROAD. THIS WILL TEMPT YOU TO CHANGE LANES. DON'T. IT ISN'T.
JOHN C. HICKS, MAKATI, PHILIPPINES

2341 ... *THE NO INFO VOTING RULE* About 5 to 15 percent of the voters in a local race will cast a vote with no information at all (more if they are nearing the end of a long ballot). You can plan on getting a random half of these votes. *Tom Wilbur, county commissioner, East Lansing, Michigan*

POLITICS

2342 ... *THE BIG EGG RULE* One ostrich egg will serve 24 people for brunch. *The Joy of Cooking*

EGGS

2343 ... *SPOTTING A FORGERY* The most legible handwriting is the least forgeable. A complicated style is easy to forge, even when legible. Calligraphy is nearly impossible to forge. *Kate Gladstone, Brooklyn, New York*

HANDWRITING

2344 ... *ESTIMATING THE AGE OF A TREE* A tree is as old in years as its diameter is in centimeters, measured at 1.2 meters above the ground. For high water-table trees, like willows, cottonwoods, or sycamores, their age is generally half their diameter in centimeters. *Thomas W. Neumann, anthropological archaeologist, wildlife ecologist, and field crew crisis manager*

TREES

2345 ... *BUILDING WAR MACHINES* It costs five to seven times more to design and build a new piece of war machinery than it costs to outfit an existing machine with new weapons. *Charles R. Morris, author*

MILITARY

2346 ... *CHOOSING A TENNIS RACQUET* To choose the right grip for a tennis racquet, measure the distance from the tip of your middle finger to the crease in the middle of your palm. That equals the right size handle. *Dr. David Bachman, Tribune Media Services*

SPORTS

2347 ... *RENTING VIDEO EQUIPMENT* Video equipment rents for 5 percent per day. If you're planning to rent equipment for more than two months, you might as well buy it. *Brad Lowry, freelance producer of international video, Philadelphia, Pennsylvania*

VIDEO

2348 ... *THE RULE OF PEPPER* The quality of food at a restaurant is inversely proportional to the size of the pepper grinders. *Morris J. Markovitz, A.C. Israel Enterprises, White Plains, New York*

RESTAURANTS

2349 ... *JOGGING LONG DISTANCES* If you can run 1 1/2 miles in 12 minutes, 6 days a week, you can run any distance you like. *Dr. Larry R. Hunt, Toronto, Ontario*

RUNNING

2350 ... *ANSWERING THE TELEPHONE* If you say, "Mr Jones speaking," the caller will think you're a stuffed shirt. If you say, "Frank speaking," the caller will think you're a blue-collar worker. If you say, "Frank Jones speaking," the caller's impression of you will be neutral, which is what you want on the first contact. *Richard Malone, Vancouver, Washington*

TELEPHONES

2351 ... *PLANNING A KITCHEN* Plan about 12 square feet of cupboard space for glassware and china and an additional 6 square feet per family member for general storage. *Marcia Southwick, writer and builder*

STORAGE

2352 ... *JUDGING THE SIZE OF CLEAN-UP OPERATION* You can determine how big the clean-up operation is at the site of an environmental disaster by counting the number of telephones and portable johns the crew has on hand. A job with 16 phones and 4 portable johns is a big job. *Tom Massey, on-the-scene EPA coordinator at a burning tire dump, Winchester, Virginia*

WASTES

SALES

MONEY

STOCK

COOKING

DIETING

FARMING

WIND

JOKER

PERSONALITIES

NEGOTIATING

FISH

CRAFTS

2353 ... **SELLING APPLIANCES**   When greeting a customer, make sure your first remark refers directly to the product you hope to sell. *Mike Hart, appliance dealer*

2354 ... **USING YOUR MONEY**   A dollar bill is about six inches long. *Jeffrey Bald, piano tuner and guitar maker, San Jose, California*

2355 ... **WAITING FOR THE MARKET TO PLUNGE**   A stock market low occurs every four years. *Scott Parker, data specialist, Beaumont, Texas*

2356 ... **COOKING SPAGHETTI**   When spaghetti is done, it will stick to the wall. *Numerous students*

2357 ... **RESTING AND CALORIES**   The average person, resting comfortably for 24 hours, will burn about 1,700 calories. *Steve Hinshaw, Farmland, Indiana*

2358 ... **DIGGING A WELL BY HAND**   It is difficult and dangerous to hand-dig a narrow hole with vertical sides. If you are digging a surface well by hand, make the top of your hole three times the width you hope to have at the bottom. *Harlan Cooke, cattle hauler*

2359 ... **SURFING**   A west wind means good surf. *Joseph Liberkowski, ex-ocean lifeguard, Medford Lakes, New Jersey*

2360 ... **BOILING AN EGG**   The hymn "Onward, Christian Soldiers" sung in a not-too-brisk tempo makes a good egg-timer. If you put the egg into boiling water and sing all five verses, with the chorus, the egg will be just right when you come to Amen. *Mrs. G.H. Moore, London, England, quoted in The New Yorker*

2361 ... **DRIVING SAFELY**   Maintain a safe distance from cars with bumper stickers that say their owners are going straight to hell — or straight to heaven. *Bill Bickel, Hillside, New Jersey*

2362 ... **GETTING A GOOD DEAL**   No deal is so good that you can't walk away from it. It will always be better the next time you sit down at the table. *Steven M. Keisman, New York City high school resource coordinator*

2363 ... **RAISING CATFISH**   If at their first daily feeding, catfish rapidly swim to the surface, stick their heads out of the water, and gulp for food, everything is O.K. If they are sluggish or don't come to the surface, promptly change the water. *John Todd, The New Alchemy Institute, Woods Hole, Massachusetts*

2364 ... **PRICING YOUR WORK**   To price a quilt, sweater, or similar piece of handiwork, multiply the cost of your materials by three. The resulting figure should represent a reasonable hourly wage, while keeping the price in what most people consider the affordable bracket. *Carol Terrizzi, artist and graphic designer, Ithaca, New York*

AS A RULE OF THUMB: PICK "D" ON A MULTIPLE CHOICE TEST, IF YOU DON'T HAVE A BETTER ANSWER. CINDY WATANABE, HONOLULU, HAWAII

2365 ... **THE TALL CANDIDATE NAME RULE** Tall candidates with short names get elected twice as often as short candidates with long names. *Tom Wilbur, county commissioner, East Lansing, Michigan*

2366 ... **COOKING AN EGG** Never boil an egg. They need not go above 160 degrees F. *Kelly Yeaton, teacher and stage manager, State College, Pennsylvania*

2367 ... **ANALYZING HANDWRITING** If handwriting consists of all capitals, the chances are greater than 50 percent that it is a man's. If the capitals are slanted or joined, the odds are 75 percent that it is a man's. If the capitals are both slanted and joined, 85 percent of the time it was written by a man. *Kate Gladstone, Brooklyn, New York*

2368 ... **THE ROOT SYSTEM RULE** The larger the seed produced by a tree, the deeper its root system and the more likely it is to have a massive taproot. *Thomas W. Neumann, anthropological archaeologist, wildlife ecologist, and field crew crisis manager*

2369 ... **UNDERSTANDING THE MILITARY** When the press announces a new military concept, the military has already invested 10 to 15 years in its research and development. *Dean Sheridan, electronics technician and deaf actor, Torrance, California*

2370 ... **CHOOSING A TENNIS RACQUET** If your tennis racquet twists in your hand, the grip is probably too small. If your arm tires from hanging on tightly, the grip is too big. *Diversion, quoted in Bottom Line/Personal*

2371 ... **EDITING A VIDEOTAPE** Figure on 12 edits per hour, or 1 finished minute per hour. Commercials take longer. *Brad Lowry, freelance producer of international video, Philadelphia, Pennsylvania*

2372 ... **CHOOSING A RESTAURANT** Pick the restaurant with the most cars in front of it. *Mr. and Mrs. Edward Hughes, Arlington, Virginia*

2373 ... **BUYING RUNNING SHOES** Never buy a running shoe that doesn't feel great in the store. *Steven M. Keisman, New York City high school resource coordinator*

2374 ... **MAKING A PERSON-TO-PERSON PHONE CALL** Don't call person-to-person unless you know that the person you're calling is rarely home and that his or her phone is likely to be answered by someone else. *Richard Malone, Vancouver, Washington*

2375 ... **THE CAR PARKING RULE** One acre will park a hundred cars. *E. Mankin, journalist, Venice, California*

2376 ... **USING A HOMEMADE COMPOSTING OUTHOUSE** When using a 55-gallon drum as a receptacle in a composting outhouse where you add a good scoop of hay or woodshavings after each use, six people will fill one drum in about six weeks. *Pierce Butler, Natchez, Mississippi*

SALES

2377 ... **HANGING UP A TELEPHONE**   Telephone salespeople should always let the customer hang up first. Jumping the gun can cut off a last minute add-on order. *Januz Direct Marketing Letter, Lake Forest, Illinois*

MONEY

2378 ... **THE CONSULTING RULE**   A consultant should charge at least three times the rate he or she would expect to receive for comparable full-time work with fringe benefits. *John Schubert, senior editor, Bicycling magazine*

STOCK

2379 ... **RESEARCHING A BUSINESS VENTURE**   When you are researching a venture capital project, speak to at least 25 people, 20 of whom were not suggested by the entrepreneur. *Scott Parker, Beaumont, Texas, quoting George Weller, attorney and venture capital consultant*

COOKING

2380 ... **USING HERBS AND SPICES**   When using a recipe, double the amount of herbs and spices called for, and quadruple the onions and garlic. *Stephanie Mills, writer*

DIETING

2381 ... **THE CALORIES AND JOGGING RULE**   Jogging burns about 100 calories per mile. *J. Benze, plumber's apprentice*

FARMING

2382 ... **PLANTING CORN**   Plant corn when the oak leaves are the size of squirrels' ears. *Penelope Wickham, marketing director, American Demographics*

WIND

2383 ... **AVOIDING FLIES ON THE BEACH**   A west wind means flies. *Joseph Liberkowski, ex-ocean lifeguard, Medford Lakes, New Jersey*

TIME

2384 ... **CROWDING A DEADLINE**   The more time you have to finish a project, the later you will start it. *Dean Sheridan, electronics technician and deaf actor, Torrance, California*

PERSONALITIES

2385 ... **GUESSING A PERSON'S OCCUPATION**   It's a safe bet that someone taking karate lessons works in a technical field. *Paul A. Delaney, meteorologist, Beltsville, Maryland*

NEGOTIATING

2386 ... **TEMPORARILY WINNING AN ARGUMENT**   When you're arguing with a man, you've gotten to him if he shuts up. If he also turns away from you, he is either going to be violent or hold a grudge. *Jeff Brown, astronomer, Bloomington, Indiana*

FISH

2387 ... **FISHING FOR TROUT**   If you don't catch anything after 7 casts, move on to the next likely spot on the stream. Three casts should be enough for pockets and holes that are less than 8 feet in diameter. *Sheridan Anderson, author, The Curtis Creek Manifesto*

JOKER

2388 ... **THE BUSTED FRISBEE RULE**   A Frisbee will crack and break when you can see your breath. *Grady Wells, editor*

AS A RULE OF THUMB:
CULTS DEPEND ON THE RULE
"THOU SHALT NOT DISAGREE."
BREAK THE RULE
AND YOU BREAK THE SPELL.
JEFFREY A. SCHALER, GESTALT
THERAPIST, SILVER SPRING,
MARYLAND

2389 ... SPOTTING A SPY   One out of every three Soviet or Soviet-bloc diplomats in this country is a spy or has some sort of intelligence-gathering responsibility. *William Webster, FBI Director*

POLITICS

2390 ... FEEDING A PARKING METER   Always feed a parking meter with the smallest denomination coins you have. You will almost always get more time for your money if you use pennies instead of dimes. And if the meter jams, you win big. *Gerald Gutlipp, mathematician, Chicago, Illinois*

JOKER

2391 ... ANALYZING HANDWRITING   If a person's handwriting is a haphazard mix of print and script, but capital letters are properly placed, the author was educated in the U.S. or Canada. If the handwriting also slants backward and/or has eccentric letters for "a," "i," and "s," the writer is a young woman. *Kate Gladstone, Brooklyn, New York*

HANDWRITING

2392 ... MANAGING A WOOD LOT   You need a minimum of ten acres to grow timber for commercial production. *Scott Parker, data specialist, Beaumont, Texas*

TREES

2393 ... PLAYING WITH NUCLEAR WEAPONS   Exploded on the ground, a nuclear bomb will vaporize its yield. A 100-kiloton bomb will vaporize 100,000 tons of rock or soil. *Dave the Nuclear Terrorist*

MILITARY

2394 ... CHOOSING A CROSS-COUNTRY SKI POLE   You can size a ski pole by standing with one arm held straight out from your side at shoulder height. A cross-country ski pole is the right length for you if it fits comfortably between the floor and your armpit. *Donald Page, chemist*

SPORTS

2395 ... THE RULE OF TELEVISION JINGLES   You're watching too much television if you can sing the jingles from the commercials word for word. *Paul A. Delaney, meteorologist, Beltsville, Maryland*

VIDEO

2396 ... KEEPING YOUR CUSTOMERS HAPPY   If a customer likes your restaurant, he'll tell two other people. If a customer hates your restaurant, he'll tell seven other people. *Jeff Hamilton, ex-waiter*

RESTAURANTS

2397 ... THE JUDGEMENT RULE   Good judgment comes from experience, and experience comes from bad judgment. *Fred Brooks, University of North Carolina, Communications of the ACM*

JOKER

2398 ... USING THE TELEPHONE   If you hear three series of clicks when your call is placed on hold or transferred, you have been disconnected. *Warren Harris, Sacramento, California*

TELEPHONES

2399 ... CUTTING A DIAMOND   A cut and polished diamond will weigh half what it did in the rough. *Darryl T. Mix, Phoenix, Arizona*

JOKER

2400 ... FINDING BOTTLES IN GEORGIA   Only one in ten bottles tossed on the roadside in Georgia will be returnable, and six of the remaining nine will be beer bottles. *Rusty Cartmill, Athens, Georgia*

WASTES

SALES

2401 ... *ORDERING FRENCH FRIES* The counter help in fast-food restaurants will usually try to sell you some French fries if you don't include any in your order. As a rule, one out of five customers will accept their offer. The score for hot cherry pies is somewhat lower. *Nancy, McDonald's restaurant counter help*

MONEY

2402 ... *QUADRUPLING YOUR MONEY* To determine the number of years it takes money to quadruple at a compound rate, divide the simple annual rate into 145. *Jud Town, author, St. Albert, Canada*

STOCK

2403 ... *BUYING AND SELLING STOCK* You're trading too much if you turn over an average of more than one-third of your portfolio each year. *Gerald W. Perritt, editor, Investment Horizons*

COOKING

2404 ... *CHECKING A BRINE SOLUTION* A 10 percent brine solution will float a two-ounce egg so the shell just breaks the surface of the liquid. *The Joy of Cooking*

DIETING

2405 ... *DIETING* Most overeating happens at night. If you can't diet all the time, diet after dark. *Arthur Phillips, Fort Myers*

FARMING

2406 ... *PLANTING CORN IN INDIANA* Getting your corn in late is costly. You lose a bushel an acre a day for every day you wait after May 10. *Steve Bruns, farmer*

WIND

2407 ... *FORECASTING THE WEATHER* If the day is even slightly windy and the wind suddenly dies, expect a wind shift. *Kim Murphy, columnist, Portland, Maine*

TIME

2408 ... *PASSING TIME* The days will seem shorter if you have lunch early. *Glenn Kornblum, St. Louis, Missouri*

PERSONALITIES

2409 ... *PREDICTING BEHAVIOR* The best predictor of future behavior is past behavior. *Dr. Angelo Valenti, consulting psychologist, Nashville, Tennessee*

NEGOTIATING

2410 ... *NEGOTIATING WITH HONOR* If a man talks about his honor, make him pay cash. *Jeff Brown, astronomer, Bloomington, Indiana*

FISH

2411 ... *SETTING UP AN AQUARIUM* Provide at least one gallon of water for each inch of fish. *Jeff Furman, Ben & Jerry's Ice Cream, business consultant*

MECHANICS

2412 ... *BUYING AN ALL-TERRAIN VEHICLE* When buying a used four-wheel all-terrain vehicle, put one hand over the end of the exhaust pipe and open the throttle. If the hand on the exhaust pipe gives way, it's a sign of good compression. *Dean Sheridan, electronics technician and deaf actor, Torrance, California*

AS A RULE OF THUMB: ANYONE WHO SAYS MORE THAN TWO OR THREE SENTENCES ABOUT THEIR CURRENT MOTORCYCLE RESTORATION PROJECT IS NEVER GOING TO FINISH IT. MAKE THEM A DECENT OFFER IN A YEAR FOR THE HALF-ASSEMBLED WRECK. JAKE WILLIAMS, ABERDEENSHIRE, SCOTLAND

2413 ... _EXTENDING CREDIT_   Republicans always pay their bills. Democrats don't. _Anonymous landlord, Albany, New York_

JOKER

2414 ... _SPOTTING AN INFLUENTIAL NEIGHBORHOOD_   In a city, the degree of ecological incongruence is directly proportional to the amount of cultural influence. _Thomas W. Neumann, anthropological archaeologist, wildlife ecologist, and field crew crisis manager_

NEIGHBORHOODS

2415 ... _ANALYZING HANDWRITING_   If a person's handwriting is printed just as printing is taught in elementary school, the writer is either an elementary-school teacher, an able 6- or 7-year-old, or mentally retarded. _Kate Gladstone, Brooklyn, New York_

HANDWRITING

2416 ... _GROWING CHRISTMAS TREES_   You can plan on eventually harvesting 400 to 500 Christmas trees for every 1,000 seedlings you plant. _Jay Waring, tree grower and plant specialist_

TREES

2417 ... _DESIGNING NUCLEAR WEAPONS_   A properly designed fission bomb will yield 1 kiloton of plutonium per kilogram. _Dave the Nuclear Terrorist_

MILITARY

2418 ... _DIVING RULE OF TWO_   The height of a cliff usually looks much greater than it really is when you are about to dive off it. To estimate the actual distance to the water, divide the apparent height by two. _John Lilly, mechanical engineer and cliff diver_

SPORTS

2419 ... _ADDING CANNED LAUGHTER_   A TV sitcom needs at least a slight chuckle from the audience every 30 seconds. If not, you need to add a laugh track. _Rick Mitz, author, The Great TV Sitcom Book_

VIDEO

2420 ... _WORKING FOR TIPS_   The best tippers are men dining with their dates...not their wives. _Johnnie Putnam, WIND radio, Chicago, Illinois_

RESTAURANTS

2421 ... _PROTECTING YOUR HEARING_   If you need to raise your voice to talk to people only three feet away, you should be wearing ear protectors. _Ann M. Barker, M.A., audiologist, Davenport, Iowa_

SAFETY

2422 ... _SPOTTING A HUCKSTER_   A person who calls himself "mister" on the phone or in a letter is either under 28 years of age or is doing something he does not believe in. In either case, he is not worth listening to. _Fred B. Scobey, business and retirement planning consultant, Campbell, California_

TELEPHONES

2423 ... _USING A WRENCH_   One good pull on a nut with a socket wrench is equal to about 20 foot-pounds of torque. _John Towle, Salinas, California_

TOOLS

2424 ... _MAKING GARBAGE_   The average person generates one ton of garbage per year. _Ellen Marsh, conference manager, American Demographics_

WASTES

JOKER

MONEY

STOCK

COOKING

DIETING

FARMING

WIND

TIME

PERSONALITIES

NEGOTIATING

FISH

MECHANICS

2425 ... **RUNNING A GROCERY**   If you're even thinking about smelling it to determine whether it's fresh, throw it out. *Anonymous*

2426 ... **USING AN AUTOMATIC TELLER MACHINE**   To cut down on your trips to the automatic teller machine, estimate how much money you need to withdraw, round up to the next $10, and add $20. *Dennis Palaganas, Gainesville, Florida*

2427 ... **TAKING A LOSS**   Whenever you've lost 10 percent on an investment, take your losses and get out. *Paul Lisseck, health food broker, North Hampton, Massachusetts*

2428 ... **CRACKING NUTS**   A pound of nuts in the shell yields about half a pound shelled. *The Joy of Cooking*

2429 ... **ESTIMATING CALORIES**   To estimate the calories in a wedge of rich dessert, make a fist and place it next to the base of the wedge. Count each knuckle that spans the base of the wedge. Each knuckle represents 100 calories. *Ronald Arturi, teacher, Santa Barbara, California*

2430 ... **HERDING SHEEP**   Indian shepherds plan on using three and a half acres of desert land for each sheep they graze. *Roger Peterson, Phoenix, Arizona*

2431 ... **FORECASTING THE WEATHER**   If the wind shifts to the north or northeast behind a cold front, the front is becoming stationary and is likely to return as a warm front. If the wind is a strong northwesterly, it means the front is moving out. If the wind is more southerly than forecast, the weather will be worse than forecast. *Anonymous*

2432 ... **MAKING PEACE WITH THE ENVIRONMENT**   When you try to improve on Mother Nature, you see the real cost in 20 years. *William Cooper, zoologist, Michigan*

2433 ... **SQUARE DANCING**   The fact that someone is a square or contra dancer greatly increases the chance that he or she is also a computer programmer or scientist (At least in Colorado, Vermont, and Washington). *Ellen Klaver, musician, Boulder, Colorado*

2434 ... **WINNING AN ARGUMENT**   When two people argue, the one who responds the most wins. *Jennifer Evans, writer, Austin, Texas*

2435 ... **TRANSPORTING FISH**   Iced fish keeps better than fish refrigerated at 32 degrees Fahrenheit. You will need about one pound of crushed ice for every two pounds of fish. *Kenn and Pat Oberrecht, commercial fishers*

2436 ... **ESTIMATING THE VALUE OF A MACHINE**   The value of a machine is directly proportional to the amount of cast iron it contains. The more cast iron, the greater the value. *William A. Lowe, William A. Lowe Custom Millwork, Ensley, Alabama*

AS A RULE OF THUMB: REPEATING ALGEBRA 1 RARELY RAISES THE GRADE BY MORE THAN ONE LETTER (C TO B, D TO C, ETC.) R. C. WOODS, TEACHER, MIRANDA, CALIFORNIA

2437 ... **GIVING A SPEECH**   When giving a public science lecture to a general audience, there will always be one weirdo who asks questions that have nothing to do with your lecture. There will also be one smart-aleck who asks questions to show how smart he is. The faster you silence both of them, the happier your audience will be. *Jeff Brown, astronomer, Bloomington, Indiana*

SPEAKING

2438 ... **SPOTTING A BAD NEIGHBORHOOD**   If you're in a fast-food restaurant that's part of a national chain and the premises are dirty, you're in a very dangerous neighborhood. *Jeff Brown, astronomer, Bloomington, Indiana*

NEIGHBORHOODS

2439 ... **RAISING YOUR HAND**   When a teacher needs someone to volunteer an answer, raise your hand at the same time as the class genius. If you time it right, neither of you will be picked. *Dean Sheridan, electronics technician and deaf actor, Torrance, California*

JOKER

2440 ... **FIGHTING FIRES**   Forest fires move twice as fast up a 10 degree slope than on level ground. *L. M. Boyd, The San Francisco Chronicle*

TREES

2441 ... **THE CIVIL WAR RULE**   Plan on using a man's weight in lead to kill one in battle. *Bob O'Halloran, talkshow host, WHBY Radio, Appleton, Wisconsin*

MILITARY

2442 ... **FIELDING A BASEBALL**   A ball hit to left field by a left-handed hitter, will slice toward the left-field line. It works exactly the opposite way with a right-handed hitter. *Pete Rose, first baseman, Pete Rose's Winning Baseball*

SPORTS

2443 ... **WATCHING WEIGHT AND TELEVISION**   Obesity in 12-to-17-year-olds increases 2 percent for each hour of television watched per day. *William Dietz and Steven Gortaker, Boston researchers, quoted in New Age Journal*

VIDEO

2444 ... **SCHEDULING BARTENDERS**   When you're scheduling bartenders for a college town bar, figure that 25 hard-drinking townies equal 75 college students. *Cheryl Plumb, Ithaca, New York*

RESTAURANTS

2445 ... **PROTECTING YOUR HEARING**   If you notice ringing in your ears after you've been exposed to noise, you should have worn ear protection. *Ann M. Barker, M.A., audiologist, Davenport, Iowa*

SAFETY

2446 ... **USING A TELEPHONE**   Don't wait for a pay phone someone else is using. It will be faster to find another phone than to wait. *Kim Wennerberg, truck driver, Point Richmond, California*

TELEPHONES

2447 ... **CHECKING A BLADE**   Sharp saws and chainsaws produce large chips when they cut wood; fine dust means a dull blade. *Pierce Butler, Natchez, Mississippi*

TOOLS

2448 ... **LOOKING AT TRASH**   The average ten-ton pile of municipal trash will contain six or seven tons of paper. *Scott Parker, data specialist, Beaumont, Texas*

WASTES

SHOPPING

2449 ... GETTING GOOD SERVICE   If you address salespeople by the name you see on their name tags, you'll get good service.   *Eleanor Benelisha, library and information services, Richmond, California*

JOKER

2450 ... BORROWING THINGS   Never loan a possession unless you borrow an item of equal importance at the same time.   *Steven Kropper, telecommunications consultant, Watertown, Massachusetts*

STOCK

2451 ... FOLLOWING THE STOCK MARKET   The stock market rarely advances more than 10 or 12 days in a row without a minor setback. On a longer-term basis, it rarely rises more than six or seven weeks without a setback or "correction" that lasts two to four weeks.   *Boardroom Reports*

COOKING

2452 ... THE FAMOUS PINT RULE   A pint's a pound, the world around.   *Jeffrey Bald, San Jose, California, and countless other people*

DIETING

2453 ... ESTIMATING YOUR IDEAL BODY WEIGHT   To estimate your ideal body weight, figure on 110 pounds for the first 5 feet of height if you're a man, then 5 pounds for every inch of height over 5 feet. If you're a woman, figure on 100 pounds for the first 5 feet, and 5 pounds for every inch above that.   *David Kumaki, physician, Shelburne, New Hampshire*

FARMING

2454 ... FEEDING PIGS VINEY PLANTS   Never feed pigs viney plants; it gives them the itch.   *Clayton Mitstifer, machinist, Cayutaville, New York*

WIND

2455 ... FORECASTING THE WEATHER   A strong southwesterly flow means bad things might come true.   *Anonymous*

TIME

2456 ... BUYING GASOLINE   To get gassed up fast, ask for $5 worth, because the attendant won't have time to leave your pump.   *Ed, in Greshen, Oregon*

PERSONALITIES

2457 ... OFFENDING PEOPLE   The people who offend others most easily are often the most easily offended themselves.   *Joel R. Stegall, dean, Ithaca College School of Music, Ithaca, New York*

NEGOTIATING

2458 ... UNDERSTANDING YOURSELF   The more vehemently you defend yourself, the more likely it is that you're trying to convince yourself.   *Janet Wallace, Fair Oaks, California*

FISH

2459 ... CHOOSING A FISHING POLE   Your fishing pole should be twice the length of your arm.   *Hillary Schaefer, age 10, essay contest winner, "Advice to Pres. Bush," Wausau, Wisconsin*

MECHANICS

2460 ... THE DOUBLING YOUR SPEED RULE   Doubling the speed requires four times the force and eight times the power.   *R.A. Heindl, design engineer, Euclid, Ohio*

AS A RULE OF THUMB:
IF YOU'RE DEBATING
ABOUT WHETHER IT'S
COLD ENOUGH TO WEAR A
HAT — WEAR ONE.
ROBERT RITER, ANN ARBOR,
MICHIGAN

2461 ... **TALKING TECH WITH REPORTERS**   When explaining a technical point to a reporter, talk as if you're addressing an attentive seven-year-old and avoid analogies. *Jeff Brown, astronomer, Bloomington, Indiana*

2462 ... **FINDING THE BEST NEIGHBORHOODS**   The better neighborhoods are upwind of a city's industrial district. *George Smith, architect, designer, reader, Fairburn, Georgia*

2463 ... **PASSING A TEST**   If you're taking a multiple choice test and you don't know the right answer to a question: 1) Choose the longest answer; 2) Eliminate the answer that includes the words "always" or "never;" 3) Choose B or C because test makers avoid A and D. *Dean Sheridan, electronics technician and deaf actor, Torrance, California*

2464 ... **DETERMINING THE AGE OF A SPRUCE TREE**   You can determine the approximate age of a spruce tree by counting the layers of limbs on its trunk. A tree that has ten layers of limbs is roughly ten years old. *Thomas O. Marsh, writer and amateur naturalist, Fairfield, Ohio*

2465 ... **MAINTAINING FIGHTER AIRCRAFT**   Northrop Corporation estimates that a unit of 24 F-20s can be kept flying by 164 people; a unit of F-16s requires 323 people, and a unit of F-15s, 476. *Gregg Easterbrook, staff writer, The Atlantic Monthly*

2466 ... **CHOOSING A CROSS-COUNTRY SKI**   You can size a cross-country ski by standing with one arm held straight in the air. A ski is the right length for you if it reaches from the floor to the palm of your hand. *Donald Page, chemist*

2467 ... **REDUCING YOUR SAMPLING ERROR**   Sampling error is an important factor in the interpretation of television audience ratings. To cut the sampling error by half, quadruple your sample size. *Hugh Malcolm Beville Jr., author, Audience Ratings: Radio, Television, Cable*

2468 ... **LEAVING A TIP**   You should always leave at least 25 cents per plate for breakfast, 50 cents per plate for lunch, $1.00 per plate for dinner, or 15 percent of the bill, whichever is higher. *Bernice Duda, grandmother and part-time waitress, Chicago, Illinois*

2469 ... **LAUNCHING FIREWORKS**   When you're launching fireworks, make sure the audience stands five steps back for every ounce of propellant in the missile. *Alan R. Reno, Watertown, New York*

2470 ... **USING THE TELEPHONE**   If you want to get off the phone and the other person shows no sign of hanging up, say "I appreciate your calling." The caller usually gets the message. *Kim Murphy, columnist, Portland, Maine*

2471 ... **LEANING A LADDER**   When you use an extension ladder, you should put the bottom of the ladder one foot away from the wall for every four feet of vertical height. *Scott M. Kruse, biogeographer, Fresno, California*

2472 ... **TREATING MUNICIPAL SEWAGE**   You can plan on one-fifth of a pound (dry weight) of body waste per person. Anaerobic digestion of a pound of this material produces 18 cubic feet of gas with a heat value of 650 BTUs per cubic foot. *Dan Cortinovis, sanitary engineer, Lafayette, California*

SHOPPING

SHELLFISH

STOCK

COOKING

JOKER

FARMING

WIND

TIME

PERSONALITIES

NEGOTIATING

FISH

MECHANICS

2473 ... **MINING THE SHELVES FOR PRICES** In a supermarket, don't pick the item at the front of the shelf because it will have the higher price. Instead, mine the shelf—the items at the back will have the lower prices. *Ann German, East Islip, New York*

2474 ... **ESTIMATING THE AGE OF A LOBSTER** Estimate the age of a large lobster by multiplying its weight, in pounds, by seven. *Scott Parker, data specialist, Beaumont, Texas*

2475 ... **PLAYING THE GOLD MARKET** In the gold market, if the public is selling, buy. If the public is buying, sell. *J. Snyder, credit manager*

2476 ... **THE PRICE RULE** A 1 percent shortage of a particular food will cause a 4 percent increase in price. *Richard Elliot, Warwick, Rhode Island*

2477 ... **THINKING ABOUT CALIFORNIA** The more someone dislikes Californians, the more likely he or she is from an eastern state. The more extreme the dislike, the more likely he or she is from Ohio. *Edward J. Garrison, nursing home administrator, Watsonville, California*

2478 ... **FENCING LIVESTOCK** An electric fence should be three-quarters of the shoulder height of the animals it is to enclose. *Carla Corin, biologist, Eagle River, Alaska*

2479 ... **THE RIDGWAY WINDCHILL FACTOR** To estimate the windchill factor, subtract the wind velocity from the temperature. *Becky Ridgway, Wichita, Kansas*

2480 ... **ESTIMATING THE AGE OF A RIVER** The more curves in a river, the older it is. *Paul A. Delaney, meteorologist, Beltsville, Maryland*

2481 ... **SIZING UP A PATIENT** Therapy clients who make their first contact by mail have difficulty with intimacy. Those who make their first contact in person have few problems with intimacy. Phone contacts are somewhere in between. *Terry Larimore, writer and therapist, Houston, Texas*

2482 ... **WINNING AN ARGUMENT** To win an argument, make sure your opponent is sitting down. *Anonymous*

2483 ... **BUYING FISH** Cold-water fish have more flavor than warm-water fish because cold-water fish have more fat. River fish taste better than lake fish because they get more exercise. *Dennis Palaganas, Gainesville, Florida*

2484 ... **ADJUSTING WHEEL BEARINGS** Tighten the wheel bearing nut until there is no slop, then back it up 1/8 turn. *Garry Harned, authority on frog communication, Ithaca, New York*

A**S A RULE OF THUMB:**
THE BEST OPENING LINE IS "HI."
D**EAN** S**HERIDAN,** E**LECTRONICS** T**ECHNICIAN AND** D**EAF** A**CTOR,** T**ORRANCE,** C**ALIFORNIA**

2485 ... *GIVING A SPEECH* When you're giving a speech, target the modal level of intelligence of your audience (the intelligence level of the greatest number of listeners). *R. W. Ramage, Cheshire, Great Britain*

SPEAKING

2486 ... *ESTIMATING A NEIGHBORHOOD'S INCOME* The more mail a neighborhood receives, the higher the income. *R. Gingery, Berwyn, Illinois*

NEIGHBORHOODS

2487 ... *TAKING A TEST* On a multiple-choice test, the longest answer is usually the right one — especially if it's the next-to-the-last answer. *Steven M. Keisman, New York City high school resource coordinator*

TESTS

2488 ... *PLANTING A TREE* When you're planting a tree, make the hole twice as wide and twice as deep as the root ball. Then refill the hole one-fourth of the way with good soil before putting in the tree. *Andrea Frankel, computer scientist, engineer, holistic health practitioner, San Diego, California*

TREES

2489 ... *THE BALLISTIC MISSILE TARGET RULE* Submarine-launched ballistic missiles lack the accuracy of ground-launched weapons. At best, you can expect one to land within 1,500 feet of a target. *Drew Middleton, military analyst, The New York Times, 1983*

MILITARY

2490 ... *WATCHING A BOXING MATCH* A boxer has delivered an effective blow to the body if his opponent lifts one foot clear of the ground. *Angelo Dundee, boxing authority*

SPORTS

2491 ... *LOOKING GOOD ON TV* You always look 15 percent more serious on TV than you do in real life, so try to look 15 percent less serious when you are on camera. *Sharon K. Yntema, writer, Ithaca, New York*

VIDEO

2492 ... *READING A MENU* The more adjectives on a menu, the worse the food. *Larry Tuttle, Elmira, New York*

RESTAURANTS

2493 ... *AVOIDING POISON IVY* Leaflets three, let it be. *Stephen Unsino, poet, Eastchester, New York*

SAFETY

2494 ... *CALLING A COLLEGE DORM* Most dormitory phones are answered just after the second ring. If a call hasn't been answered by the fourth ring, chances are it won't be. *Chris Carter, East Lansing, Michigan*

TELEPHONES

2495 ... *DIPPING A BRUSH* Don't dip your paint brush into the paint more than one-third to one-half of the length of its exposed bristles. *Joseph R. Provey, editor, Home Mechanix*

TOOLS

2496 ... *SLOPING SEWER PIPES* Sewage flows best in a pipe that is sloped 1/4 inch per foot. If the pitch is too steep, the liquid runs off and leaves the solids behind; too shallow, and nothing runs at all. *Raleigh Fillings, plumber*

WASTES

SHOPPING

2497 ... *BUYING FOOD*   To get out of the grocery store faster, go to the check-out lines on the ends. Most grocery shoppers choose the lines in the middle. *Scott Parker, data specialist, Beaumont, Texas*

SHELLFISH

2498 ... *CATCHING CRABS IN TEXAS*   Crabbing season in Texas consists of all the months with the letter r in them. You can catch crabs during the other months, but they aren't good to eat. *David Hechler, writer, Rockport, Texas*

STOCK

2499 ... *DOUBLING YOUR MONEY*   You can quickly calculate the number of years it will take to double your money by dividing the number 72 by your interest rate. For example, if your money is invested at 6 percent interest, it will take 72 divided by 6 or 12, years to double. *Steve Parker, aerospace engineer, Princeton, New Jersey*

COOKING

2500 ... *COOKING RICE*   To cook rice, rest the tip of your index finger on top of the rice and add enough water to reach the first joint. This works for any size pot. *E. Mankin, journalist, Venice, California*

BEACHES

2501 ... *BUILDING A SAND CASTLE*   To build a sand castle, the sand should be firm. Your footprints should barely show when you stand on it. *Dean Sheridan, electronics technician and deaf actor, Torrance, California*

FARMING

2502 ... *USING YOUR BRAINS*   In a pinch, you can tan a skin with the brain of the animal that provides the skin. The brains are mashed and rubbed into the hide with a smooth rock. Conveniently, one deer brain is enough to tan one deer skin, and one mouse brain is enough to tan one mouse skin. *Larry Dean Olsen, survival instructor, Outdoor Survival Skills*

WIND

2503 ... *WATCHING THE WIND*   Wind from the west, sailors like best. Wind from the north, sailors go forth. Wind from the east, sailors like least. Wind from the south, you shutta your mouth. *W. R. C. Shedenhelm, wind salesman, Encino California*

TIME

2504 ... *USING A TOILET*   Total flush and fill time on a standard toilet should be 60 to 75 seconds. *John Towle, Salinas, California*

JOKER

2505 ... *THE RULE OF THUMB RULE*   A rule of thumb works four out of five times (including this one). *Paul Delaney, engineer, Golden, Colorado*

NEGOTIATING

2506 ... *THE ARGUMENT RULE*   Never argue with someone whose job depends upon not being convinced. *Barak Rosenshine, professor of education, Urbana, Illinois*

JOKER

2507 ... *LIMING A LAKE*   It takes about 2 1/2 tons of limestone per acre of lake to neutralize the effects of acid rain. *K. Hammond, Wilmington, Delaware*

MECHANICS

2508 ... *FOLLOWING BACKFIRES*   If a gasoline engine backfires through the carburetor, the mixture is too lean. If it backfires through the tailpipe, it is too rich. *Scott Parker, data specialist, Beaumont, Texas*

As a rule of thumb:
AVOID EYE-CONTACT WHEN YOU ARE APPROACHING SOMEONE ON A SIDEWALK AND YOU SENSE THAT YOU'RE HEADED FOR ONE OF THOSE AWKWARD HEAD-ON DEADLOCKS. INSTEAD, WATCH A SPOT JUST IN FRONT OF THE PERSON'S APPROACHING FEET WHILE CONTINUING TO WALK STRAIGHT AHEAD. IN A MOMENT, THE PERSON WILL VEER TO THE LEFT OR RIGHT, AND YOU'LL SEE HIS FEET GO AROUND YOU.
MICHELLE KRELL, SAN FRANCISCO, CALIFORNIA

2509 ... **PREPARING A SPEECH**   A good 5-minute speech requires one month's advance notice. A 15-minute speech requires a week's notice. A 1-hour speech requires no advance notice.   *Dirck Z. Meengs, management consultant, Canoga Park, California*

SPEAKING

2510 ... **THE OBVIOUS INCOME RULE**   The better the cars parked at the curb, the better the neighborhood.   *R. Gingery, Berwyn, Illinois*

NEIGHBORHOODS

2511 ... **PASSING A TEST**   To get an A on an essay test when you only vaguely know the answer, write the answer as a sonnet.   *Suzette Haden Elgin*

TESTS

2512 ... **THE HAT HANGER PRUNING RULE**   When pruning a branch from a tree, never leave a stub you can hang your hat on.   *Ronald Newberry, retired, Cayutaville, New York*

TREES

2513 ... **FIGHTING GUERRILLA SOLDIERS**   To fight a guerrilla army, a national army needs ten soldiers for every one guerrilla.   *Dr. Constantine Menges, Special Assistant to the President for National Security Affairs, on National Public Radio*

MILITARY

2514 ... **BUYING SKI BOOTS**   Properly fitted cross-country ski boots should feel like bedroom slippers.   *Gordon Burt, ski instructor*

SPORTS

2515 ... **LOOKING GOOD ON TV**   You will look more alert on TV if you lean forward. You will look even more alert if you cross your legs.   *Sharon K. Yntema, writer, Ithaca, New York*

VIDEO

2516 ... **THE CHINESE LEFTOVER RULE**   When you order Chinese food, order one entree less than the number of people in the group to avoid unwanted leftovers.   *Claire Forchheimer, Flushing, New York*

RESTAURANTS

2517 ... **CHECKING CANNED FOOD**   When you open a can or bottle, keep a thumb on the top. If the top pops up when you break the seal, it's fine; if it pops down, throw it out.   *Leslie Simpson, Wollaston, Massachusetts*

SAFETY

2518 ... **SIZING UP A CALLER**   Usually a telephone caller makes three points. The third one is the real reason for the call.   *Peter A. Lake, Marina Del Rey, California*

TELEPHONES

2519 ... **ADJUSTING AN ANVIL**   Adjust the height of your anvil to match the bottom of your natural hammer stroke.   *Dennis Williams, blacksmith*

TOOLS

2520 ... **THE TRAILHEAD LITTER RULE**   The number of people and the amount of litter decrease with the cube of the vertical distance and the square of the horizontal distance to the trailhead.   *Scott M. Kruse, biogeographer, Fresno, California*

WASTES

SHOPPING

SHELLFISH

STOCK

COOKING

BEACHES

FARMING

WIND

TIME

PROPORTIONS

NEGOTIATING

CONTAINERS

MECHANICS

2521 ... **SHOPPING AT LIQUIDATION SALES**   Items at liquidation sales should sell for about one-tenth their normal cost. *J. Michael Kanouff, writer, Home Mechanix*

2522 ... **SERVING SHRIMP**   For three servings, you need one pound of shrimp in the shell or half a pound of cooked shrimp without the shell. *The Joy of Cooking*

2523 ... **BUYING STOCK**   Don't move a substantial portion of your wealth into or out of the market at one time. Ease in, ease out. *The American Association of Individual Investors*

2524 ... **COOKING RICE**   Old Japanese/Hawaiian rule: one knuckle rice, two knuckles water. *Nani Paape, textile designer, Seattle, Washington*

2525 ... **AVOIDING SHARKS**   If you see a school of porpoise, the water is free from sharks. *Joseph Liberkowski, ex-ocean lifeguard, Medford Lakes, New Jersey*

2526 ... **RAISING PORK**   A hog, dressed and hung in the meat locker, will weigh one-third of its live weight. *Harry Pound, butcher*

2527 ... **COUNTING WHITE CAPS**   If there are more white caps than you can count, it is probably blowing over 15 knots. *Jeremy Bishop, windsurfing expert, Hood River, Oregon*

2528 ... **CLEANING A BATHROOM**   It takes one hour to thoroughly clean a bathroom. *John Towle, Salinas, California*

2529 ... **JUDGING BEAUTY**   The larger the eyes, the smaller the nose, the smaller the chin, the bigger the cheekbones, and the larger the smile, the more attractive the woman's face. *Scott Parker, data specialist, Beaumont, Texas*

2530 ... **CURBING SQUABBLES**   If a supervisor spends more than 10 percent of her time dealing with the squabbles of subordinates, the organization is overstaffed and the subordinates do not have enough work. *Dirck Z. Meengs, management consultant, Canoga Park, California*

2531 ... **ESTIMATING NUMBERS OF PENNIES**   It takes 4,500 pennies to fill a one-gallon container. *A.R. Wadum, St. Louis, Missouri*

2532 ... **BREAKING OFF BOLTS AND STUDS**   If a bolt breaks while you are screwing it in, you will be able to remove the broken piece, but if it breaks while you are unscrewing it, forget trying to remove the broken piece. Drill it out and retap the threads. *Chris Packard, The Packard Company, Newton Centre, Massachusetts*

AS A RULE OF THUMB:
THOSE WHO TALK LOUDLY
DURING THE PREVIEWS
WILL TALK LOUDLY DURING
THE FEATURE.
SUZY WILLHOFT, DRAMA TEACHER,
ARLINGTON, VIRGINIA

2533 ... **GIVING A SPEECH**   A good speech will present one idea per 5-minute period, and no more than 2 or 3 ideas in a 20-minute talk. *Roberta Prescott, writer, USAir*

2534 ... **CHOOSING A NEIGHBORHOOD**   You will usually find the more affluent, attractive neighborhoods on the north and west sides of a city; the poorer and more crime-prone neighborhoods will be on the south and east sides. *David Chapple, electrical contractor, Palo Alto, California*

2535 ... **TAKING THE SAT TEST**   For the easy questions, the obvious answer is correct. For the hard questions, narrow the possible answers down to two, then pick the one that seems least likely. *Scott Parker, data specialist, Beaumont, Texas*

2536 ... **COOLING WITH TREES**   One large tree has the cooling power of 5 average air conditioners running 20 hours a day. *Debra Prybyla, writer, The New York State Conservationist*

2537 ... **FEEDING SOLDIERS WITH SNAILS**   Napoleon's troops carried canned snails as emergency rations. Their rule was: 1,000 snails per soldier per week. *Michael McRae, Harrowsmith*

2538 ... **FLYING A KITE**   A kite automatically assumes its own zenith. It is difficult, if not impossible, to alter this position. Should you continue to let out string, the kite will move longitudinally away from you. In this case, due to the added weight of the string, the kite will be pulled slightly lower. *Tal Streeter, kite builder*

2539 ... **THE TV TONGUE RULE**   For TV appearances, match the color of your make-up to the color of the tip of your tongue. *Sharon K. Yntema, writer, Ithaca, New York*

2540 ... **THE FURMAN RESTAURANT RULE OF THREE**   The third restaurant to go into a space is generally the one that succeeds. *Jeff Furman, Ben & Jerry's Ice Cream, business consultant*

2541 ... **RIDING A MOTORCYCLE**   New motorcyclists get cocky and reckless when they've put 3,000 miles—or the equivalent of one trip across the United States—on their bikes. *Wolfman, Hell's Angel, Natchez, Mississippi*

2542 ... **BEAN'S DEPTH RULE OF PHONE POLES**   One-fifth of the length of a telephone pole should be planted in the ground. *Ron Bean, mechanics of materials student, Madison, Wisconsin*

2543 ... **ADJUSTING AN ANVIL**   Stand with your arms at your side. The height of your anvil should be the height of your knuckles. *Charles McRaven, blacksmith*

2544 ... **SPOTTING A GOOD RULE OF THUMB**   The usefulness of a rule of thumb is inversely proportional to its accuracy. *A.R. Wadum, St. Louis, Missouri*

SHOPPING

2545 ... TIMING A SHOPPING TRIP It will take 20 to 30 minutes to shop for 1 item if you know exactly what you want and where to go. Thus, if you go out at lunch to buy 3 different things, plan on being gone for 1 to 1 1/2 hours. *Jim Kauffold, Belmont, California*

SHELLFISH

2546 ... EATING SHRIMP One pound of unpeeled shrimp is usually more than one person can eat. *Pamela Monell, computer programmer*

STOCK

2547 ... BUYING STOCK Don't buy common stock with money you feel that you will need in less than four years. *The American Association of Individual Investors*

COOKING

2548 ... MAKING COTTAGE CHEESE A gallon of milk will make about a pound of cottage cheese. *Mary Ellen Parker, retired teacher, Cincinnati, Ohio*

BEACHES

2549 ... ANCHORING A BEACH UMBRELLA To keep your beach umbrella from blowing away, bury one-third of its handle in the sand. *Joseph Liberkowski, ex-ocean lifeguard, Medford Lakes, New Jersey*

FARMING

2550 ... PANNING FOR GOLD A good miner, doing a careful job of panning, can handle about 6 pans per hour, or 60 in ten hours — about one-third of a cubic yard of gravel. An expert working in sandy gravel without much clay or hardpan might double this, panning two-thirds of a cubic yard in a day. Under the most favorable conditions, a yard a day is just about the top limit for panning. *William F. Boericke, gold miner*

WIND

2551 ... ESTIMATING THE WIND SPEED ABOVE The wind velocity at 2,000 feet is 2 to 3 times the speed at the surface. *Richard L. Collins, aviation writer*

TIME

2552 ... EMMON'S RULE OF BREATHING When you're relaxed, 12 breaths is approximately equal to 1 minute. *Emmon Bodfish, Oakland, California*

PROPORTIONS

2553 ... MAKING A PLEASING RECTANGLE The closer the proportions of a rectangle are to 3 by 5, the more pleasing it is to the eye. *Don Naish, Dryden, Michigan*

NEGOTIATING

2554 ... REACHING A COMPROMISE You know you've reached a good compromise if both sides are dissatisfied. *Thomas O. Marsh, writer and former charter commission chairman, Fairfield, Ohio*

CONTAINERS

2555 ... THE CAN RULE It takes 150 aluminum cans to fill a 32-gallon trash can. At 2 cents per can, that's $3 per trash can. *John Towle, Salinas, California*

MECHANICS

2556 ... LISTENING TO YOUR ENGINE KNOCK If your engine knocks during acceleration, it's probably the connecting rod. If the engine knocks during deceleration, it's probably the piston wrist pin. If you have piston slap (too much room between the piston and cylinder wall), the knock will be loudest when the engine is cold and idling. *Ray Hill, car-care columnist*

AS A RULE OF THUMB: IF YOU DON'T KNOW THE ANSWER TO A MULTIPLE CHOICE QUESTION ON A CIVIL SERVICE TEST, PICK THE LONGEST ANSWER.

MARK S. PATTERSON, SCORED 100 ON HIS LAST CIVIL SERVICE TEST, LYONS, NEW YORK

2557 ... *EDITING SLIDES FOR A PRESENTATION* When you're choosing slides for a presentation, spread them on a light table and toss out any that have type too small to read with the unaided eye. *Tim McGrath, engineer, Boston, Massachusetts*

SPEAKING

2558 ... *CHOOSING A SUBWAY TRAIN* Never get on a train with a chalk outline on the floor. *Russ Haven, lawyer, Brooklyn, New York*

JOKER

2559 ... *TAKING A MULTIPLE CHOICE TEST* 1. Think long—think wrong. 2. Nine out of ten times, your first answer was the correct answer. 3. When in doubt, pick answer "C." *Robert Hastings, Master Chief Petty Officer, United States Coast Guard*

TESTS

2560 ... *MOVING A TREE* A truck-mounted tree spade should cut a root ball 10 times the diameter of the tree trunk. A tree with a 5-inch trunk, for example, should have a root ball 50 inches in diameter. *Dr. George E. Fitzpatrick, Fort Lauderdale, Florida*

TREES

2561 ... *RUNNING GUNS* On average, it takes $125,000 to buy enough military weapons to kill one person. *Scott Parker, data specialist, Beaumont, Texas*

MILITARY

2562 ... *THE STREETER STRAIGHT UP KITE RULE* Generally, a kite that does not fly straight does not fly up. *Tal Streeter, kite builder*

SPORTS

2563 ... *RENTING A VIDEOTAPE* Never rent a videotape from a store to which it will be inconvenient to return it. *Chris Packard, The Packard Company, Newton Centre, Massachusetts*

VIDEO

2564 ... *CHOOSING A RESTAURANT* There is one almost infallible way to find honest food at just prices: count the wall calendars in a cafe. No calendar: same as an interstate pit stop. One calendar: preprocessed food assembled in New Jersey. Two calendars: only if fish trophies present. Three calendars: can't miss on the farm-boy breakfasts. Four calendars: try the homemade pie, too. Five calendars: keep it under your hat, or they'll franchise. *William Least Heat Moon, author of Blue Highways*

RESTAURANTS

2565 ... *WATCHING YOUR WOODSTOVE* When your woodstove is going full bore, you should be able to hold your hand firmly pressed on any nearby combustible surface. If you can't, you need to increase the clearance between the surface and the stove, or install a heat shield. *Peter R. Lammert, Thomaston, Maine, in Country Journal*

SAFETY

2566 ... *USING A TELEPHONE* If a phone rings more than six times, it probably won't be answered. *Cheryl A. Russell, demographer, mother, editor-in-chief, American Demographics*

TELEPHONES

2567 ... *ADJUSTING A WORKBENCH* If you stand at attention, your wrist is at the right height for a woodworking bench and your elbow is at the right height for the top of a metal-working vice. *W. Oakley, shop expert*

TOOLS

2568 ... *ESTIMATING WATER PRESSURE* Water pressure increases at 1 atmosphere per 34 feet of descent in fresh water. *Ernst Luposchainsky, III ("Kahn"), adventurer & nautical enthusiast, inter alia, Hollywood, California*

WATER

SHOPPING

2569 ... **PAYING FOR GROCERIES**   Figure $1.50 per item to estimate the cost of your groceries at the check-out counter. Inflation is not a factor; as prices rise, packages shrink. *Penny Russell, artist, Dilltown, Pennsylvania*

SHELLFISH

2570 ... **FEEDING LOBSTERS**   Freshly caught lobsters can be kept alive in tanks if properly fed. Plan on using 1 bushel of fish scraps per week per 100 pounds of lobster. *T. M. Prudden, lobster expert*

STOCK

2571 ... **BUYING STOCK**   Don't buy stock that is included in the Fortune 500 or Standard & Poor's 500. The chances of such stocks being undervalued are virtually nil. *The American Association of Individual Investors*

COOKING

2572 ... **FIXING A LEEK**   It takes 15 seconds for the average geek to harvest and wash off the average leek. *James Macmillan, M.D.*

BEACHES

2573 ... **ESCAPING THE UNDERTOW**   If you're caught in an undertow, go with it. You'll be free of it when it dissipates, usually before you run out of oxygen. *Joseph Liberkowski, ex-ocean lifeguard, Medford Lakes, New Jersey*

FARMING

2574 ... **GROWING CORN**   Your corn should be knee-high by the Fourth of July. *Nancy Dunn, production manager, Sausalito, California, and countless other people*

WIND

2575 ... **WATCHING THE WIND AND THE TIDE**   On the seashore, the wind rises when the tide changes. *David Lyon, writer and advertising authority, Westport, Connecticut*

TIME

2576 ... **FIRING A SALUTE**   Repeating, "If I wasn't a gunner, I wouldn't be here," will give you the two-second interval between rifle salutes. *John Fountain, Riverside, Connecticut*

PROPORTIONS

2577 ... **DESIGNING MAPS**   A relief map needs to have its vertical proportions exaggerated by a factor of two. *Peter Reimuller, Point Arena, California*

NEGOTIATING

2578 ... **BAILEY'S RULE OF CITY SLICKERS**   Never trust a man who parts his hair in the middle or his name on the side. *John Bailey, Deer Lick Farm, Interlaken, New York*

CONTAINERS

2579 ... **DESIGNING OFFICE SPACE**   To determine the number of square feet of office space a company needs, figure on 250 square feet per employee. *Mike Senna, president, Matrix Consultants, Boston, Massachusetts*

MECHANICS

2580 ... **BUYING AN ENGINE**   If you are checking out a used engine that doesn't run, ignore the cleanliness of the outside and look into the carburetor throat. If it is stained reddish brown, chances are good that the engine has been well cared for. A black stain below the choke butterfly is an indication of a tired engine. *LeRoi Smith, writer and car builder*

2581 ... **WRITING A SPEECH**   Professional speech writers budget an hour and a half of research, thinking, and writing for every minute of speech. *Canadian Business*

SPEAKING

2582 ... **ESTIMATING THE SPEED OF A TRAIN**   To estimate the speed of a train in miles per hour, count the number of clicks in 29 seconds. *Don Dalley, Buffalo, New York*

TRAINS

2583 ... **TAKING A MULTIPLE CHOICE TEST**   Don't change your first guess on a multiple choice question when checking over your answers. The first guess is always the best. *William H. Smith, Cincinnati, Ohio*

TESTS

2584 ... **PLANTING CONIFER SEEDLINGS**   Two people equipped with mattocks or dibble bars can plant 800 to 1,000 conifer seedlings in a day, if no beer is served before noon. *Joe Schwartz, editor, Danby, New York*

TREES

2585 ... **BUDGETING SOLDIERS**   In ground warfare, one man behind a fortification is equal to five in the open field. *Scott Parker, data specialist, Beaumont, Texas*

MILITARY

2586 ... **PLAYING SOCCER**   If it moves, kick it. If it doesn't move, kick it until it does. *Phil Woosnam, commissioner, North American Soccer League*

SPORTS

2587 ... **SYNDICATING A TV SERIES**   A television series needs to have been produced for 3 years or 80 episodes before it is an attractive candidate for daily syndication. *John Efroymson, media analyst*

VIDEO

2588 ... **CHECKING A PLATE**   If a dinner plate looks clean, it probably is. *Mark McMullen, accountant, Alexandria, Virginia*

RESTAURANTS

2589 ... **THE ICE SKATING RULE**   You need to have three consecutive days of sub-20-degree weather before a pond will be safe for skating. *Holley Bailey, editor, Deer Lick Farm, Interlaken, New York*

SAFETY

2590 ... **RECOGNIZING A BUREAUCRAT**   You can be fairly sure you are dealing with a bureaucrat if he or she has to dial 9 to get an outside line. *Burnham Kelly, Ithaca, New York*

TELEPHONES

2591 ... **TESTING AN EDGE**   You can test the edge of a blade by shaving the hairs on your forearm. A knife is as sharp as it can possibly be if the hairs seem to actually pop at the touch of the blade. *D. Petzel, editor, Mechanix Illustrated magazine*

TOOLS

2592 ... **FINDING A WATER FOUNTAIN**   In a public building, the water fountains are near the restrooms. *Norman Brenner, Fleetwood, New York*

WATER

SHOPPING

SHELLFISH

STOCK

COOKING

BEACHES

FARMING

WIND

TIME

PROPORTIONS

NEGOTIATING

CONTAINERS

MECHANICS

2593 ... **BUYING GROCERIES**   Groceries cost about $10 to $12 per bag. *Rick Eckstrom, plan review officer, Ithaca, New York*

2594 ... **TRAPPING LOBSTERS**   Plan on losing about 33 percent of your lobster pots each year to storms and heavy seas. *T. M. Prudden, lobster expert*

2595 ... **BUYING STOCK**   Don't buy stock that is getting a lot of play in the press. *The American Association of Individual Investors*

2596 ... **BUTTERING BREAD**   One pound of butter will spread three to four pounds of sandwich bread. *The Joy of Cooking*

2597 ... **THE OCEAN LIFEGUARD RULE**   If bathers are chest high, you have a safe beach. *Joseph Liberkowski, ex-ocean lifeguard, Medford Lakes, New Jersey*

2598 ... **THE THOMAS STALKING TO WALKING RULE**   When you are stalking deer (or "still-hunting" as the experts call it), patience and an extremely slow pace are essential. If you travel more than a quarter of a mile in an hour, you are traveling too fast. *J. P. Thomas, still-hunter*

2599 ... **THE COW FACING WIND RULE**   If you can't find any waving flags or smoke plumes to indicate the wind direction, check the way the cows are facing. Cows prefer to face away from the wind when they're grazing and when they're lying on the ground chewing their cuds. *Sigmund Sameth, Irvington, New Jersey*

2600 ... **GETTING QUICK ANSWERS AT WORK**   You'll spend less time getting answers from people if you go to their offices to ask them questions. That way, you control when the conversation ends. *Dean Sheridan, electronics technician and deaf actor, Torrance, California*

2601 ... **ARRANGING FLOWERS**   A flower arrangement should usually be about one and a half times the height or width of the container. *Pamela Reeger, florist*

2602 ... **NEGOTIATING AN AGREEMENT**   When negotiating, use a deadline. Ninety percent of the agreement will come in the last 10 percent of the time allotted. *Lory Peck, social worker, Alpine, New York*

2603 ... **ESTIMATING THE VOLUME OF A TANK**   A cylindrical tank 15 inches in diameter holds about 1 gallon for each inch of height. A 30-inch diameter tank holds 4 gallons per inch. *Millard Zeisberg, Elkton, Maryland*

2604 ... **TIMING YOUR IGNITION**   You can set your ignition timing very nicely by testing it on the road. Slowly advance the distributor until a slight ping can be heard when the throttle is suddenly opened at 30 miles per hour in high gear. Then retard the distributor just a bit until the ping disappears. This setting will be close to perfect. *LeRoi Smith, writer and car builder*

AS A RULE OF THUMB:
A CUBIC FOOT OF STEEL
WEIGHS ABOUT 500 POUNDS.
MIKE TRIPLETT, MILLWRIGHT,
YELLOW SPRINGS, OHIO

2605 ... **THE AUDIENCE IQ RULE**   Address your lecture to the median intelligence of your audience.   *Carla van Berkum, Russian studies teacher, Baltimore, Maryland*

2606 ... **ESTIMATING THE SPEED OF A TRAIN**   To estimate the speed of an Amtrak train in miles per hour, count the number of telegraph poles it passes in 30 seconds and multiply by three.   *Don Bennett, Pittsburgh, Pennsylvania*

2607 ... **CHANGING YOUR ANSWERS**   The closer you are to running out of time, the less you should mess with your essay answers. When you change a sentence on an essay test, other sentences need to be changed as well.   *Dean Sheridan, electronics technician and deaf actor, Torrance, California*

2608 ... **THE TREE ROOT RULE**   You can assume that the roots of normally shaped trees extend at least to the drip line of the branches.   *Shelly Wade, tree specialist*

2609 ... **SHOOTING AT HELICOPTERS**   North Vietnamese ground troops used their thumbs to determine whether they could reach enemy aircraft with hand-held weapons. If an airplane or helicopter was bigger than a thumb held at arm's length, they could bring it down with ground fire.   *D. Tanner, Fort Wayne, Indiana*

2610 ... **MAKING THE COVER OF SPORTS ILLUSTRATED**   Two to ten weeks after athletes appear on the cover of Sports Illustrated their career begins to decline.   *Steven M. Keisman, New York City high school resource coordinator*

2611 ... **PLANNING A TELEVISION NEWSCAST**   For a 30-minute local newscast, plan on 13 minutes of news, 5 minutes of weather, and 6 minutes of sports.   *Jim Scauten, KBMT TV, Beaumont, Texas*

2612 ... **SPOTTING A GOOD RESTAURANT**   Cute names for restaurants suggest that the owners aren't serious about food.   *Andy Rooney, television commentator*

2613 ... **WALKING ON SNOW-COVERED ICE**   On snow-covered ice, stay away from areas without snow. This could be a sign of thin ice that has only recently frozen.   *Jim Keneely, professional guide*

2614 ... **SELLING SOMETHING OVER THE PHONE**   If you use someone's first name seven times in a phone conversation, you can sell them anything.   *Sharon K. Yntema, writer, Ithaca, New York*

2615 ... **TESTING AN EDGE**   You can test the edge of a blade by running it lightly across the flat of your thumbnail. If the blade slides easily, it is dull. A sharp edge catches and digs in.   *Lester McCann, Chicago, Illinois*

2616 ... **THE HOSE RULE**   When fighting a fire with a 1.5 inch line, bring the pressure up to 100 psi — then add 15 pounds of pressure for each additional 100 feet of line to overcome friction loss in your nozzle.   *John Fischer, volunteer fireman, Joliet, Montana*

SHOPPING

2617 ... *BUYING MILK* If you notice a lot of ads for milk on TV, you can bet the price is going up soon. *R. C. Woods, teacher, Miranda, California*

SHELLFISH

2618 ... *THE DEAD LOBSTER RULE* A lobster tail should always curl. If it does not, the lobster is dead or dying. If the tail does not curl on a boiled lobster, the lobster was dead before it was boiled. *T. M. Prudden, lobster expert*

STOCK

2619 ... *BUYING GROWTH STOCKS* Don't buy safe, low-risk stocks. Instead, buy growth stocks with some of your money and, for balance, put the rest into bonds or other minimum-risk securities. *The American Association of Individual Investors*

COOKING

2620 ... *THE McMULLEN CHILE RULE* Chile is best on the third day. *Mark McMullen, accountant, Alexandria, Virginia*

BEACHES

2621 ... *ESCAPING A RIP TIDE* If you're caught in a rip tide, never swim against it. Instead, swim at a 90 degree angle at an easy pace until you're well clear of it. Then head back to shore. *Jack Fleming, formerly from Maui, Hawaii, Aliquippa, Pennsylvania*

FARMING

2622 ... *MAKING A SNOWSHOE* You can tailor-make a snowshoe by having the intended user hold his or her arms in a circle, just touching at the fingertips. The size of the loop formed by the arms is the size of the snowshoe frame. *Anonymous American Indian snowshoe-maker*

WIND

2623 ... *SAILING INTO PORT* If the wind is strong, the tide can be wrong; if the wind is light, the tide must be right. *Gary Closter, sailor with a broken engine*

TIME

2624 ... *USING THE DRIVE-UP WINDOW* If there are more than three cars in line ahead of you at a bank or fast-food drive-up window, you'll save time if you get out of the car and go inside. *Bill Lowe, Birmingham, Alabama*

PROPORTIONS

2625 ... *TEACHING* For student-paced teaching, you need 1 teacher for every 10 students. For teacher-paced teaching, 1 teacher for every 30 students will do. *Tom Werner, management consultant, Athens, Georgia*

NEGOTIATING

2626 ... *LOSING AN ARGUMENT IN JAPAN* In Japan, the first person to raise his voice loses the argument. *Cally Arthur, managing editor, American Demographics*

CONTAINERS

2627 ... *MEASURING CRICKETS* A quart jar will hold 1,000 crickets. *Jack Armstrong, president, American Cricket Growers Association, West Monroe, Louisiana*

2628 ... *DESIGNING A RACE CAR* Race-car builders substitute light-weight aluminum for steel whenever possible. When working with aluminum, figure one-third the weight and three times the cost of steel. *Joe Ottati, car builder*

MECHANICS

2629 ... **GIVING A SPEECH**   You should expect the actual speech to take one-third more time than it took you during practice. *Bert Decker, Decker Communications, San Francisco, California*

SPEAKING

2630 ... **RIDING A TRAIN**   To hop a moving freight train, use the ladder at the front of the car. The speed of the train will throw you against the car. If you use the ladder at the end of the car, you could be thrown between cars. *John H. Beauvais, Cambridge, Massachusetts*

TRAINS

2631 ... **SHERIDAN'S ESSAY QUESTION ANSWER RULE**   Answer an essay question as if you were talking to your parents. *Dean Sheridan, electronics technician and deaf actor, Torrance, California*

TESTS

2632 ... **THE SCHAEFER TREE ROOT RULE**   The diameter of a tree trunk in inches is the radius of the root system in feet. *J. T. Schaefer, pilot*

TREES

2633 ... **HINCKLE'S RULE OF RATIONS**   If a can of C-rations has a B in the serial number, it probably contains fruit cocktail. *Dave Hinckle, musician, Neon Baptist*

MILITARY

2634 ... **PLAYING GOLF**   If you're hitting an approach shot with an iron to the green and you don't know which iron to use, always use the longer one. *Andy Cruickshank, Aiea, Hawaii*

SPORTS

2635 ... **ANNOUNCING THE NEWS**   It takes about 1 minute to read 15 double-spaced typewritten lines on the air, or about 4 seconds per line. *Charles Osgood, CBS, news commentator*

VIDEO

2636 ... **SPOTTING A GOOD RESTAURANT**   Food and entertainment are best kept apart. *Andy Rooney, television commentator*

RESTAURANTS

2637 ... **PUTTING OUT A FIRE**   Direct your fire extinguisher at the base of the flames from a distance of less than ten feet. If you can't get any closer than ten feet, the fire is probably too large for a hand-held fire extinguisher. Concentrate your efforts on leaving the vicinity of the fire. *Norman Lewis, volunteer fireman*

SAFETY

2638 ... **WATCHING COMPANY CALLS**   For every 1,000 telephone calls made by a large corporation, 100 are outside local, 10 are long distance, and 1 is international. *Steven Kropper, telecommunications consultant, Watertown, Massachusetts*

TELEPHONES

2639 ... **TESTING AN EDGE**   Any cutting edge that reflects light, from a razor blade to a chainsaw tooth, is in need of sharpening. *Michael Mangan, stained-glass designer, Carrollton, Ohio*

TOOLS

2640 ... **PROVIDING WATER FOR FAMILIES**   A family of four uses roughly one acre-foot of water per year — that's the amount of water it takes to cover one acre of land with a foot of water. *William R. Doerner, writer*

WATER

SHOPPING

2641 ... *SITING A SHOPPING CENTER* People are willing to drive for 30 minutes to get to a regional shopping center. *Terry Moloney, applied geographer, Tydac Technologies Corporation, Arlington, Virginia*

SHELLFISH

2642 ... *THE LOBSTER TANK RULE* Provide at least two gallons of refrigerated water per pound of lobster. *T. M. Prudden, lobster expert*

STOCK

2643 ... *BUYING STOCK* Don't buy stocks for a year after a presidential inauguration. For some reason, the market almost always goes down in that period. *The American Association of Individual Investors*

COOKING

2644 ... *MAKING TEA* When steeping tea, allow one spoonful per person and one for the pot. *Stanley G. Laite, St. John's, Newfoundland, Canada*

BEACHES

2645 ... *THE RISING WATER BEACH RULE* Along the eastern coast of the U.S., a one-foot rise in sea level moves beach erosion 100 feet inland. *Dr. Stephen P. Leatherman, Associate Professor of Geomorphology, University of Maryland, in the New York Times*

FARMING

2646 ... *GROWING MARIJUANA* One skilled California marijuana grower can properly maintain 33 plants. Two growers can maintain 100 plants. *J. K., Harvest Moon Growers, Mendocino and Humboldt, California*

WIND

2647 ... *WATCHING SUNSETS* A red sky at sunset means that wind is on the way. *Rose Bowen, seamstress*

TIME

2648 ... *SUFFERING A STROKE OR HEART ATTACK* You are most likely to suffer a stroke or heart attack between 8 and 9 in the morning. *Scott Parker, data specialist, Beaumont, Texas*

PROPORTIONS

2649 ... *SELLING INVENTIONS* Less than one patented invention in a hundred makes any money for the inventor. *Scott Parker, data specialist, Beaumont, Texas*

NEGOTIATING

2650 ... *CARRYING CLOUT* In any group, the person doing the least talking is the one with the most power. *David Lyon, writer and advertising authority, Westport, Connecticut*

CONTAINERS

2651 ... *HAULING BOOKS* You can fit 2,000 mass-market paperbacks in a Datsun pickup. *Dave Ewan, Wind Chimes Book Exchange, Millville, New Jersey*

MECHANICS

2652 ... *ADJUSTING THE POINTS ON YOUR CAR* In an emergency, you can set the gap on your ignition points by using an ordinary paper match as a feeler gauge. Most matches are about .015 inch thick. *Dave Sellers, engineer*

Photo by Clemens Kalischer

AS A RULE OF THUMB: YOU SHOULD ALWAYS DRESS ONE STEP BETTER THAN THE BEST DRESSED PERSON IN YOUR AUDIENCE. IF HE OR SHE IS WEARING JEANS, FOR EXAMPLE, YOU SHOULD WEAR A SUIT; IF A SUIT, THEN A TUX. TIMOTHY WENK, MAGICIAN, WEST STOCKBRIDGE, MASSACHUSETTS

2653 ... *LECTURING IN BULGARIA* If you are speaking English to Bulgarians, write 20 minutes of material for a 60-minute speech to allow time for translation. *Robert Horvitz, artist*

SPEAKING

2654 ... *ESTIMATING ENGINE SPEED* The top speed of a steam engine is one mile per hour per inch of drive-wheel diameter, plus 10 percent. *Raymond Spears, Santa Clara, California*

TRAINS

2655 ... *TAKING A FEDERAL EXAM* On any government multiple-choice test, the longest answer is usually the correct one. *Michael F. Brown, patent attorney*

TESTS

2656 ... *FERTILIZING TREES* Most trees need about half a pound of nitrogen per inch of trunk diameter. *Shelly Wade, tree specialist*

TREES

2657 ... *MAINTAINING AN AIR FORCE* American, West German, and British air forces expect to have 40 percent of their aircraft under repair at any given time. *Brent Wiggans, artist, computer scientist, and military buff*

MILITARY

2658 ... *BOB'S RULE OF WINNING FOOTBALL* If the receiving team gets the opening kickoff in a football game and scores a three-point field goal, and the second team takes its kickoff and scores a touchdown after a series of plays, not a runback, the second team will win. This rule holds true only if there are no punts or turnovers during either of the first two series, and it applies only to these series. *Greg Henshall, industrial photographer, Nitro, West Virginia*

SPORTS

2659 ... *PLANNING A NEWS BROADCAST* A half-hour network news broadcast reduced to type will fill about half the front page of a newspaper. *Roger Carpenter, news buff*

VIDEO

2660 ... *SPOTTING A GOOD RESTAURANT* Don't go to a restaurant that has a sign in the window advertising for waiters. It's hard enough to get waited on in a restaurant that thinks it has plenty of help. *Andy Rooney, television commentator*

RESTAURANTS

2661 ... *CHECKING THE ICE FOR SKATING* One inch, keep away; two inches, one may; three inches, small groups; four inches, O.K. *Holley Bailey, editor*

SAFETY

2662 ... *KROPPER'S TELEPHONE REVENUE RULE* Telephone companies earn 80 percent of their revenues from 20 percent of their customers. *Steven Kropper, telecommunications consultant, Watertown, Massachusetts*

TELEPHONES

2663 ... *CHECKING A LADDER* To check a fire ladder for proper lean, stand perfectly erect with the toes against the ladder beam and the arms straight out. If your hands fall on the rung in a comfortable grasping position, the ladder is set properly for climbing. If only the fingertips touch the rung, the base of the ladder is too far from the building. If the heel of the hand touches the rung, the base of the ladder is too close to the building. *The National Fire Protection Association*

TOOLS

2664 ... *CHECKING YOUR WATER FOR HARDNESS* You can tell if your water is hard or soft by looking at your ice cubes. Hard-water cubes have a white spot in the center where minerals congregate; soft-water cubes are uniformly cloudy. *Lou J. Smith, executive director, Canadian Water Quality Association, in The Houston Chronicle*

WATER

SHOPPING

2665 ... **THE SALE RULE** Discontinued stock often carries a price that ends in a 7, such as $1.97. *Steven F. Scharff, cartoonist, Union, New Jersey*

SHELLFISH

2666 ... **KEEPING LOBSTERS** Lobsters are very susceptible to chemicals and aerosol sprays used in the vicinity of tanks. As a rule, anything that will kill a fly will kill a lobster more quickly. *T. M. Prudden, lobster expert*

STOCK

2667 ... **SELLING OUT** When a technology stock loses 5 percent of its value in one week, sell it. *Steven M. Keisman, New York City high school resource coordinator*

COOKING

2668 ... **CHOOSING RHUBARB** With rhubarb, the redder the stalk, the sweeter the pie. *Kelly Yeaton, teacher and stage manager, State College, Pennsylvania*

BEACHES

2669 ... **ANNETTE'S RULE OF WAVE WATCHING** Every seventh wave is a big one. *Annette Arthur, wave watcher*

FARMING

2670 ... **THE UNIVERSAL RANCHER'S RULE** Always leave a gate the way you found it. *Merritt Holloway, Deep Springs Ranch, California*

WIND

2671 ... **FLYING A KITE** A wind that rustles leaves and that you can barely feel on your face is blowing from 4 to 7 miles an hour. A wind moving about 12 miles an hour will keep tree leaves in constant motion. This is the upper limit for most kite flying. If the wind is lifting loose paper off the ground and raising dust, it is too strong for the average kite. *Tal Streeter, kite builder*

TIME

2672 ... **THE DIFFERENCE IS NIGHT AND DAY RULE** During Ramadan, the sacred ninth month of the Moslem year, fasting is practiced daily from sunrise to sunset. For people lacking better indicators, the point when day becomes night is the point when you can't tell a black thread from a white one. *George Sheldon, artist and traveler*

PROPORTIONS

2673 ... **ARRANGING FLOWERS** Some color schemes are less risky than others. Three strong colors to a quiet one is usually a pleasing proportion. *Christine Newberry, retired teacher*

2674 ... **NEGOTIATING** If you are negotiating for money, pay careful attention to the increments of change in your opponent's demands. When the increments begin to decrease in size, your opponent is reaching his or her bargaining limit. *Jeff Furman, Ben & Jerry's Ice Cream, business consultant*

CONTAINERS

2675 ... **MEASURING MICE** There are approximately 250 mice to the gallon. *Lecki Ord, Melbourne, Australia*

MECHANICS

2676 ... **USING PULLEYS** Two pulleys connected by a belt should be separated by at least the difference between their individual diameters. *John H. Parker, mechanical engineer*

2677 ... LEADING A SEMINAR   If you are leading a seminar, allow six seconds for a response to your questions. If someone is going to respond, they'll do it within six seconds. *Tom Werner, management consultant, Athens, Georgia*

SPEAKING

2678 ... HEINDL'S TRAIN RULE   The typical freight train has 1 engine for every 25 cars. *R. A. Heindl, design engineer, Euclid, Ohio*

TRAINS

2679 ... PASSING A PHYSICS TEST   If you're taking a multiple-choice physics test and don't know how to calculate a certain value to solve a problem, manipulate the data mathematically until you get a value with the same units as the one you're trying to calculate. *Dennis Palaganas, Gainesville, Florida*

TESTS

2680 ... PRUNING TREES   After pruning a tree, paint all wounds that are larger than your thumbnail. *Shelly Wade, tree specialist*

TREES

2681 ... RIDING A HORSE INTO BATTLE   A trooper should march on foot, leading his horse, every third hour. *The Very Rev. Emmet C. Smith, Largo, Florida*

MILITARY

2682 ... PLAYING TENNIS   If you're nervous, the first thing that goes is your footwork. *Dennis Palaganas, Gainesville, Florida*

SPORTS

2683 ... BEING QUOTED ON THE EVENING NEWS   If you can't say it in less than 30 seconds, it won't make the evening news. *Terry Larimore, writer and therapist, Houston, Texas*

VIDEO

2684 ... READING A MENU   The more flaps on a menu, the better the food. *Jugglers & Thieves, touring rock band*

RESTAURANTS

2685 ... AVOIDING HAZARDOUS MATERIALS   Hold your arm straight with your thumb pointing up. Center your thumb over the area of hazardous materials. If you can still see the area, you are too close. *John Fischer, volunteer fireman, Joliet, Montana*

SAFETY

2686 ... ANSWERING THE TELEPHONE   Expect telemarketers to call right after dinner, early in the week. *Mark McMullen, accountant, Alexandria, Virginia*

TELEPHONES

2687 ... RAISING A LADDER   The base of a ladder should be 30 percent of its height from the base of the wall it is leaning against. *Rick Eckstrom, plan review officer, Ithaca, New York*

TOOLS

2688 ... DRINKING WATER   Any time your lips feel dry, you need water. *Michael Rozek, reporting on the Air Force Survival School in National Wildlife*

WATER

A

Arc welding 1500, 2009

Archaeological sites 32, 56

Architectural projects 852

Arms 1469

Arrows 1774, 1798

Art auctions 540

Artichokes 2033

Ash 2023

Astronomical Units 67

Atmospheric pressure 354

Atomic bomb 1219, 2201

Attics 60

ATVs 1227

Audiocassettes 1965

Auto racing 249

Automatic pistols 1894

Automobile colors 321, 417, 465, 841, 854, 937, 1150, 2089, 2313

Automobile noises 1497

Avalanches 896

Axe 1960

B

Baby pictures 183

Baby talk 951

Baccarat 339

Back injuries 1896

Back pain 5, 101

Backpacking 584, 1811

Bacteria 731

Bacterial infections 677

Bad checks 670, 2090

Baggage 612

Baldness 15

Band-Aids 1517

Banjos 1797

Banks 2624

Barbed wire 1632

Barley 1902

Barometers 2219

Bartenders 473, 593, 1930, 2444

Basal metabolism 1997

Baseball 411, 1818, 2274

Baseball caps 99

Bass 2147, 2243

Bass players 1509

Bathrooms 60

Baths 271, 1053

Bathtub toys 1789

Bats 1807

Batteries 648

Beaches 179, 2645

Beams 732, 876

Beans 785

Bear grease 1204

Bears 1019

Beauty salons 146

Beaver 1724

Bedrooms 60

Beds 156

Bedtime 2063

Bee stings 1589

Beef 246, 270, 558, 606, 654, 822

Beef carcasses 606

Beer 244, 281, 592, 664, 1224, 1457, 2400, 2584

Beer bellies 1325

Bees 1091, 1235, 1259, 1283, 1307, 1331, 1807

Bicycle accidents 90, 114

Bicycle parts 18, 42, 138, 186, 282, 1628, 1765

Bids 554

Billboards 361, 505

Bills 155

Biology 2314

Bird books 11

Bird collisions 570

Bishops 142

Black bears 1204

Black furniture 61

Blackjack 3, 339

Bladders 2338

Blasting 2022

C

D

L

L.L. Bean 1220

Labels 1033

Labor 89, 113, 137, 161

Ladders 2687

Landscaping 799

Landslides 2104

Languages 1361

Las Vegas 595

Latin 1265

Laundromats 284

Laundry 380

Lawns 237, 556, 820, 1278, 1837

Lawsuits 2016

Lawyers 1824

Layoffs 805

Layouts 878, 902, 1273

Lead sentences 1718

Leadership 1466

Lear Jets 954

Leaves 2320

Leaving home 63

Lecturers 1743

Lectures 1767

Legs 23, 186, 258, 1469

Lettuce 918

Lexicons 1745

Liars 730

Libraries 38, 62

Library of Congress 302

License plates 849

Lie detectors 814

Lies 2064

Life insurance 843, 939

Lifeguarding 2597

Light bulbs 307

Light-years 67

Lightning 403

Limes 1915

Linseed oil 1932

Lions 707

Litter 2328

Loan officers 2258

Loans 153

Lobster pots 2594

Lobster tails 2618

Lobsters 2594, 2642, 2666

Log cabins 1548

Logging 1864

Lost people 464

Lottery tickets 99

Low tech 1861

Low-pressure 2191

LSD 976

Luge 2130

Lumber 996, 1764, 2056

Lunchboxes 1081

Lungs 186, 629

Macramé 2340

Make-up 1173

Malta 1148

Mammals 635, 953

Managing 1514

Manhattan 1604

Manners 1719

Manufacturing 1010

Manure 750

Manuscripts 686

Maps 2197

Maple sugaring 1961, 2128, 2152, 2176, 2200, 2224, 2248

Maple trees 1816

Marathons 2133, 2157, 2301

Margarine 797

Marijuana 2646

Markers 673

Market-capitalization 2307

Masai 407

Mass Transit 650

Massachusetts 1460

Massages 725, 1613

Q

R

S

Sage grouse 35

Sailboards 154, 178, 226, 250

Sailing 58

Sails 178

Salary 1174, 1360, 1504, 1642, 1672, 1682, 1686, 1720, 1755, 2237, 2282, 2306

Salespeople 1969

Scalps 911

Scarf joints 370

Schizophrenics 844, 2337

Science fiction 566

Scrabble 723

Screenplays 1531

Screws 148, 1788

Scrimshaw 325

Scripts 1550

Scuba diving 1746

Sea level 2645

Seafood 1916

Seagulls 34, 391

Seasonings 2252

Seat adjustments 1953

Seattle 1196

Secretaries 1178

Sedges 1014

Seeds 1038, 1062, 1470, 1494, 2310, 2368

Self-employed 1318

Seller's markets 1683

Selling a business 98, 146, 194, 218, 242, 266, 290, 314, 338, 362

Semicolons 1646

Seminal vesicles 1810

Seminars 2677

Sequels 1387

Serum calcium 964

Serum albumin 964

Serum creatinine 988

Serum sodium 940

Serves 1866

78-rpm records 1485

Sewing 2004

Sex drive 2170

Sex 35

Sex-changes 2122, 2266

Sexism 2314

Shadows 80

Shaving 1269

Sheepshearing 2046

Shelterbelts 1926

Sherpas 992

Ships 274

Shirts 260, 428, 668

Shivering 895

Shocks 273

Shoe sizes 311

Shoe soles 68

Shoelaces 2013

Shoes 644, 735, 855, 1645, 1693, 1765, 2106, 2111, 2303

Shoplifting 934, 1078

Shopping centers 2641

Shot puts 2298

Shotgun stocks 1750, 1822

Shoulders 95

Showers 1053, 1991

Showing your dog 1667

Shrimp 821, 2546

Sidewalks 1527

Silage 2238

Silicon Valley 829, 1093

Silicone 383

Silk 1115

Simians 883

Sincerity 95

Singapore 1789

Singles 1701

Skating 2589, 2661

Skiing 2010, 2058, 2082, 2322

Skin 431, 605, 1685